West on One

The Stories Behind The Scenery

Kathryn Manry

West on One

The Stories Behind The Scenery

Kathryn Manry

Fascinating Stories, Facts and Pictures

along the Trans-Canada Highway

from Calgary to Lake Louise

Pipestone Press
110 Dalgleish Bay NW
Calgary, Alberta T3A 1K8
www.pipestonepress.ca

14 13 12 11 10   4 3 2 1
First Edition

LIBRARY AND ARCHIVES CANADA CATALOGUING IN PUBLICATION DATA

Manry, Kathryn, 1958 –
       West on One: The Stories Behind the Scenery / by Kathryn Manry

Includes biographical references and index.
ISBN 978-0-9865384-0

1. Rocky Mountains, Canadian (Alberta) – Historical geography 2. Landscape – Rocky Mountains, Canadian (Alberta) 3. Rocky Mounatins, Canadian (Alberta) – Description and Travel. I. Title

Editor: McElgunn Editing & Writing
All photographs and illustrations are by K. Manry unless otherwise noted.

This book was written and published with the assistance of the Alberta Historical Resources Foundation.

Printed and bound in Canada by Friesens Printers, Manitoba.

- -

Table of Contents

Mount Rundle

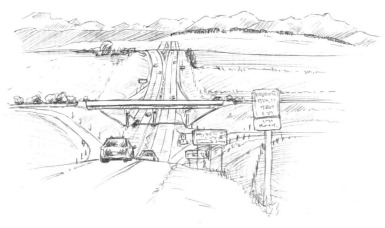

The concept for this book was born while I was researching an earlier book, mooching around in archives, and talking to interesting people for that project. I kept bumping into interesting tidbits of information that diverged from my focus at the time. The stories were interesting but distracting from my work! I had to set these other stories aside and promise myself that I would come back to them at a later date. This book is where these "other" stories have found a home.

Many of us travel the highway from Calgary to Banff and Lake Louise on a regular basis. Over the years I have explored the body of literature that has grown up around the history and highlights of that area. But there has always seemed to be a gap. Most of the published information addresses only the area within the mountains, and particularly within Banff Park itself. But there is so much more! The stories don't start 80 kilometres west of Calgary – they start right from Calgary and grow westward. There is so much of interest right from the city limits!

I quickly realized that I would need to set some clearly defined boundaries. I decided to stick to things I could see from that vital artery, that very historical and symbolic ribbon that crosses the country, the Trans-Canada Highway. Also known as Highway One, this road has an interesting history in itself, but it also provides the parameters to direct what is included in this book. I admit that I ended up stretching this rule a bit in places to include some interesting items – I claim author's prerogative on this.

Once I started writing, the question became: Where do I stop? How far west to go? As it turned out, in order to link many of the stories together, I needed to pursue them well into the mountains. Lake Louise serves as an end point with a sense of completion that a more easterly terminus could not have done. It is also the western destination for many visitors to the area – and a comfortable day's excursion from Calgary.

Travelling west, if you want to stop and have a better look at the sites along Highway One, please be aware that many of the places discussed on these pages are on private property. This cautionary comment applies particularly to the Stoney Nakoda Reserve – it is not public land to be accessed freely. Visitors are certainly welcome to go across Morley Road to the Morley townsite and McDougall Church, and to visit the facilities at Chiniki Village, but please do not explore further around the lands held by the reserve unless you get permission. The Stoney Nakoda people are very welcoming, but they are also understandably protective of their privacy.

In other locations mentioned in these pages, such as the Jumping Pound Community Hall, for example, be aware that these buildings are on private land and should be respected as such. You are welcome to drive by and have a look, but please do not wander in to check it out more closely without permission from the land owner.

I want to add a quick comment about terminology. One of the things I struggled with was the appropriate name for the indigenous people of the area. Should I call them Natives, Aboriginals, First Nations People, Indians…? First Nations

People is probably the most politically correct, but being a relatively contemporary phrase it does not fit in to historical discussions well – and it is a pretty cumbersome mouthful when used frequently. Natives and Aboriginals are both seen as somewhat negative terms by these people, so I tried to limit their use. Finally, I settled on Indians. This is also not a popular term, but it is used consistently in the historical references, and I hope that it is understood that I use it with the utmost respect. Some other terms need clarification. "Tribe" refers to a group of people who have been histori-cally associated as sharing the same geographical area and the same language roots. The Stoney Nakoda are a tribe, as are the Siksika (Blackfoot) and Tsuu T'ina (Sarcee). "Bands" are groups that have historically been recognized within the tribe – thus the Bearspaw is a band of the Stoney Nakoda and the Peigan are a band of the Blackfoot tribe. "Nation" is a more contemporary term, sometimes used in the same context as tribe, sometimes used as an umbrella term for all tribal people.

On a related topic – where names are given in the languages of the various tribes, I have tried my best to find the correct spelling. Circumflex accents are frequently used in Stoney Nakoda words, indicating that the indicated letter is spoken with a nasalized sound.

Regarding units of measure, in deference to common usage they are given in kilometres, pounds, acres and Celsius. This is inconsistent, I realize, but is probably the most functional approach.

Some navigational notes for the text will be useful. A great cast of characters is mentioned in the course of the book and they frequently make repeat appearances in the test. To help clear up the muddle of "who's who", there is a Dramatis Personae at the back of the book. I have also included a timeline to help clarify the order of events. This is particularly useful for comparing when things occurred in relation to other events.

Some of the test has been set in colour to highlight recurring themes. Wildlife Spotting items are in brown, Tree ID items are in green. I have given the geology theme a grey colour. Other general items of interest are set in blue.

Finally, I would like to make a comment about safety. It seems obvious that stopping at any point along a busy highway like the Trans-Canada involves a level of risk, and I encourage travellers to restrict themselves to safe pullouts or side roads to make any stops. I would especially like to encourage drivers to be aware of cyclists on the highway – the Trans-Canada is a popular route for people on bikes. Avoid driving on the shoulder, especially where you cannot see far ahead, just in case two-wheeled travellers are using that space. Be aware of other traffic on the highway and think carefully before you stop. Please be very, very safe, and enjoy gaining a greater understanding of all that you see along the Trans-Canada highway west of Calgary.

And watch out for wildlife along the road!

Map Notes

You may want more than a standard road map to follow along the route, which would provide more detail at a larger scale. The maps made by Gem Trek are a good choice – and will be useful for hikes if you are heading away from the Trans-Canada to explore on foot. Gem Trek's "Trail maps" series provides more information about what you are seeing than the "Driving maps" series. The most useful one for the Banff National Park section is the "Banff and Mount Assiniboine" trail map. To cover the area between The Gap and Banff, pick up their "Canmore and Kananaskis" map.

Alternatively, from the Backroad Mapbook series, the volume on Southwestern Alberta covers the entire route (and much more!) and provides good detail about the sights along the highway.

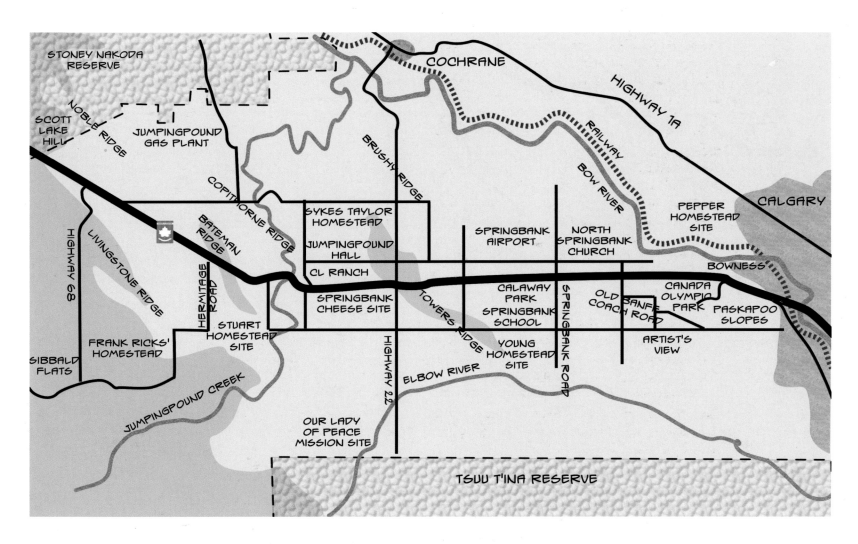

Map 1 - Calgary to Scott Lake Hill

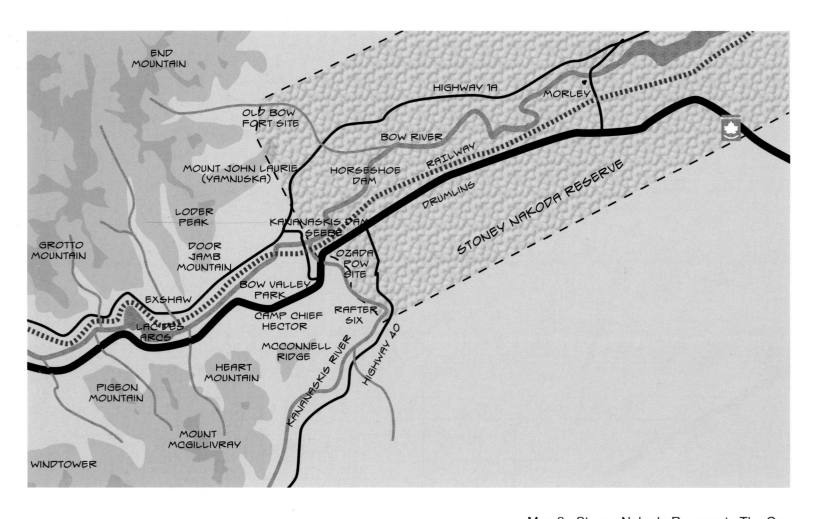

Map 2 - Stoney Nakoda Reserve to The Gap

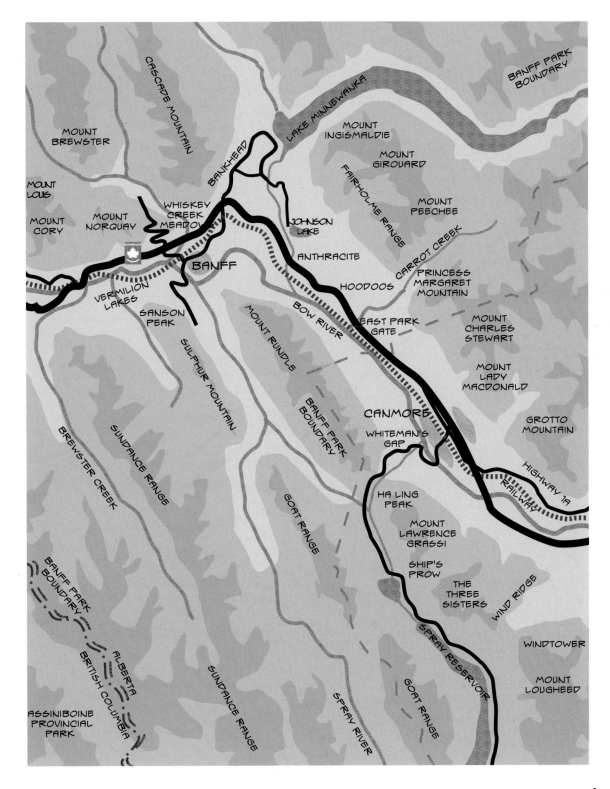

Map 3 - Mount
Lougheed to
Sunshine Turnoff

Map 4 - Healy
Creek to Lipalian
Mountain

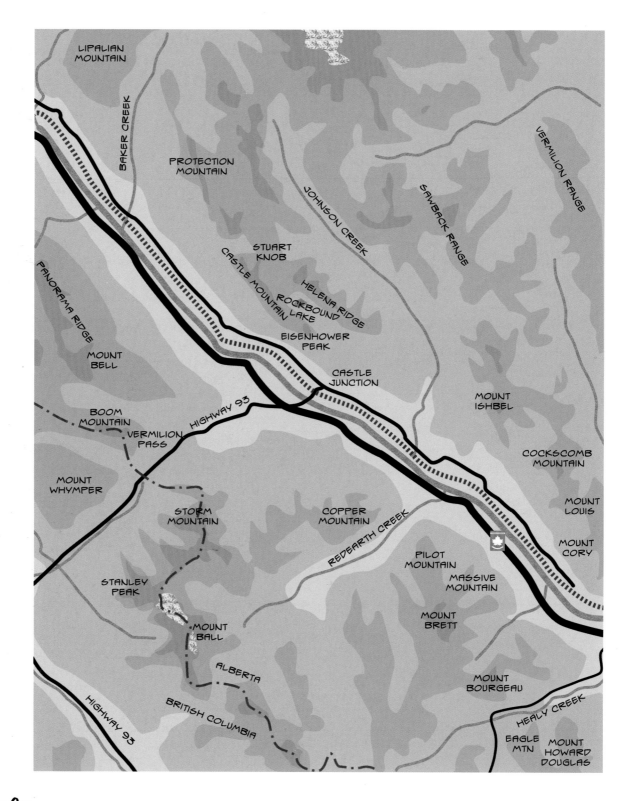

West on One

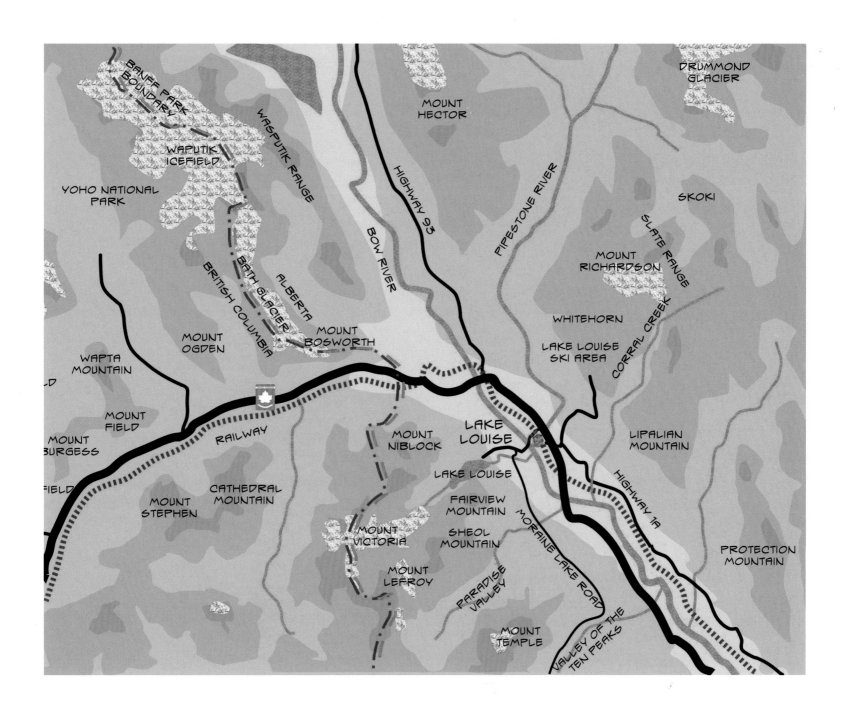

Map 5 - Protection Mountain to... The Road Ahead

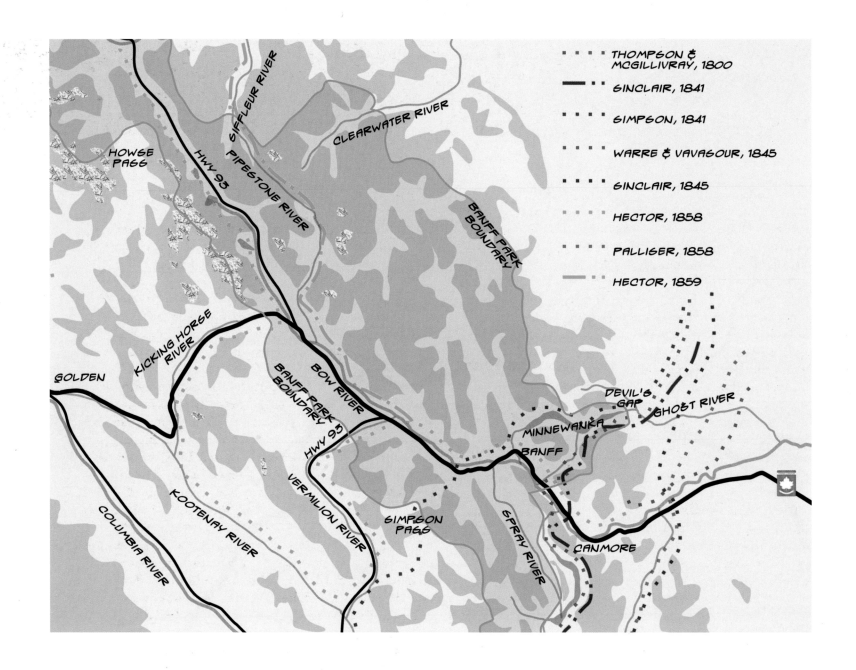

The Routes of the Explorers

For Canadians, the existence of the Trans-Canada Highway is simply a fact of life. It functions as an essential link across the wide expanse of our huge country, the third-longest national highway in the world, spanning 7,821 kilometres and six time zones. The highway has immense economic, social, and political implications for the people of Canada. But the story of how the highway came into being covers a rather rocky road, metaphorically speaking.

It would be nice to say that the Trans-Canada Highway had been a visionary project, efficiently constructed in a cross-country exercise of common intent. But in truth, the birth of the highway was fraught with the problems that are typical of so many Canadian initiatives of a national scope – squabbling between the federal and provincial governments and disagreements among various provinces, which obstructed progress.

To start at the beginning, in 1903 Henry Ford introduced the first mass-produced automobile to the world. From that point, the car practically exploded into general use as its potential for transportation, moving goods, and auto tourism was realized. By the 1920s, Canadians were the second-largest owners of cars per capita in the world.[1] Demand for suitable roads grew quickly. Among the many groups that began actively promoting the development of a network of roads were the farm organizations, automobile clubs (a formidable force during this period), and promoters of the budding auto-tourism sector. In Western Canada, a rudimentary road network began to be developed, but initially most of the attention went into constructing north-south routes to provide access to the United States. This was exactly counter to the idea of an east-west connecting route,

"Carefree highway, let me slip away on you"

Gordon Lightfoot, "Carefree Highway"

and directed planning and financial resources away from a potential Trans-Canada concept.

During the 1920s, governments began to look toward methods of extracting revenue from the automobile boom, and many provinces enacted a program of licensing both vehicles and drivers, as well as a gasoline tax, to allow them to cover road-development costs. By the early 1930s, revenue associated with motor vehicles represented about 30% of many provinces' general net revenue.[2] However, this was still far short of what was needed to keep up with the heavy demand for roads.

In 1919, the *Canada Highways Act* was passed as a post-war reconstruction and employment effort. This was not yet the Trans-Canada concept, but it *was* an effort toward a more inter-connected network. However, this initiative immediately became problematic. According to the *British North America Act* of 1867, roads and highways were entirely under provincial jurisdiction. So, although the government could offer money to the provinces, it was in no position to tell them how to spend it. Conflicts developed immediately, while demand for road construction grew. As the *Canada Highways Act* expired in 1929, little progress had been made.

It is hard to pin down an exact date when the specific concept of the Trans-Canada Highway per se was born. The first mention of it is in the *Unemployment Relief Act* of 1930. According to this document, the provinces were directed to collectively come up with a proposal for a linked cross-country route, to be approved by the feds. That really led to problems. How the money would be administered was

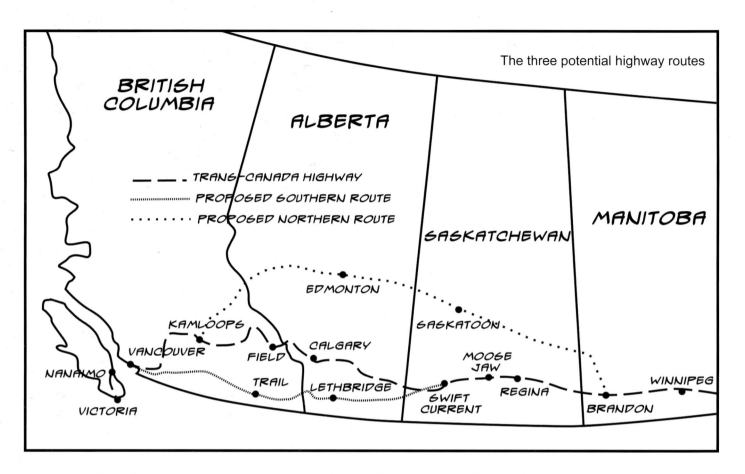

The three potential highway routes

contentious from the start. Route options were argued over endlessly. Progress was slow.

The outbreak of war in 1939 meant that any money that had been dedicated to road construction was redirected to the war effort. Post-war, the situation became even more urgent as the private use of motor vehicles skyrocketed, access to resources became paramount, transportation of goods shifted from railways to roads, and tourism boomed. The need for development outweighed most of the qualms that the provinces may have still felt about federal participation, and so work resumed – but slowly…

By October 1942, one could finally drive from Halifax to Vancouver – all 6,380 kilometres – continuously. But only about half of that was on a hard-surfaced road, and in places you were far better off to slip across the border into the United States. In 1944, a Special Parliamentary Committee on Reconstruction and Re-establishment recommended that

"as soon as possible after the war, a first-class, permanent, all-season highway be constructed right across Canada." [3] The committee also advised that it should be connected to all national parks, with access points to U.S. highways along the way – a recognition of the growing importance of tourism to Canada's economy. By the summer of 1945, each province had provided a detailed plan for road construction and was demanding federal assistance. However, Ottawa held back. Lacking of a single federal body to in charge of planning and administering the project, the government stalled.

In 1949, 20 years after it had first been suggested, the *Trans-Canada Highway Act* was finally tabled by the federal government. Predictions of low employment and the referendum in Newfoundland about joining Confederation may have added motivation. Money was committed to cover a portion of the costs, with the budget to wind up in 1956.

Of course, the squabbling between the feds and the provinces did not stop. Now the issue of route selection became contentious. Many provinces pointed out that the "most direct route" requirement would not be consistent with their local traffic flow, B.C. argued that the federal government should cover the full cost of the highway, and Quebec claimed that the Trans-Canada was a ploy by the feds to gain control over all aspects of transportation. The inequality of what the provinces faced in terms of wealth and topography also caused friction. But finally all four western provinces signed on, and they got down to the work of making the highway happen.

There were three route options under consideration in the West. One possibility went north through Saskatoon, Edmonton, and the Yellowhead Pass. Another went south through Regina, Lethbridge, and on to connect with Nelson and Trail in Southern B.C. A central option went through Regina, Calgary, Banff, and Field. The federal government had a strong aversion to influencing routing, standards or anything that would require Ottawa to deal with the provinces individually and so it left the bickering to the provinces. Finally a decision was made for the central option. A bit more progress was made.

The "On to Nelson" campaign for the southern route of the Trans-Canada, 1948, Glenbow NA-5327-748

The Official Opening

"This highway, may it serve to bring Canadians closer together, may it bring to all Canadians a renewed determination to individually do their part to make this nation greater and greater still, worthy of the destiny that the Fathers of Confederation had expected when through their act of faith they made it possible. Above all, I express the hope and the prayer that this highway will always serve the cause of peace, that it will never hear the marching tramp of warlike feet."

Prime Minister John Diefenbaker, at the official opening of the Trans-Canada Highway on September 3, 1962

In 1950, the federal government finally created the Trans-Canada Highway Division within the Department of Resources and Development which set some standards for the project. But this was immediately problematic. B.C. could not fit the required dimensions through tight mountain passes, safety concerns from increased traffic called for straighter and flatter roads than the initial standards required, and road-surface quality did not keep pace with the weight and speed capacities of newer vehicles.

By 1956, when the *Trans-Canada Highway Act* was to end, none of the provinces had yet completed its section of the highway and the project had already exceeded the assigned budget. However, an election was approaching, so the potential for an embarrassing situation worried the federal government. The required standards were softened, funding was restructured, and the Act was extended to 1960. A growing sense of national pride in the highway also gave an incentive for the government to give the Trans-Canada more attention, and the National Film Board even made a film about it, called "Canada's New Main Street."

Finally, in desperation to show some closure on the project, the Trans-Canada was officially opened (although still not fully completed) in September 1962 – five years before the country's centennial in 1967. W.A.C. "Wacky" Bennett, the premier of B.C., had jumped the gun and held an opening of his own at Revelstoke a month earlier. He did not attend the

highway. The federal - provincial agreement on the Trans-Canada ended in 1970, and the two levels of government then started squabbling over who was responsible for maintenance costs.

Signage along the Trans-Canada was changed to metric in 1975, with a period in which both kilometres and miles were posted. This was a somewhat controversial move, but Canadians adapted fairly quickly.

More recently, in 2006, a report was prepared by the Canadian Automobile Association (motoring clubs are still lobbying on behalf of the highway) that stated that, "Canadians face an estimated $22 billion deficit in our National Highway System" and that, "If we are to retain our competitive position with the U.S., our federal government needs to spend at least $4.8 billion per year on our highways, highway safety and transit."[4] A plea was made for the federal government to develop a National Highway Policy in conjunction with the provinces, and for it to show some leadership and accountability regarding highways.

September opening. The event was marked by a cavalcade of 11 cars – one for each province, plus one to represent the feds – which drove the highway from St. John's, Newfoundland, to Victoria, B.C. Yet parts of the drive were still on gravel roads, and the route was not fully completed until 1971 – more than four decades since the idea had been proposed. Confusingly, in another sign of the lack of agreement, it is marked as "mile 0" (kilometre 0 now?) at both ends. After a birthing process at the pace of a mollusc, the Trans-Canada was finally a paved route from sea to sea.

But in places, the road was already encountering new problems. Some sections had become woefully inadequate for the level of traffic they received, and upgrading and twinning were becoming a necessity for several parts of the

The enlargement of the highway through the parks has become a very touchy subject, as the environmental impacts of busy roads have become better understood. Upgrading and expanding the Trans-Canada continues on a piecemeal basis, without an overall plan or financial program. And so the situation continues…

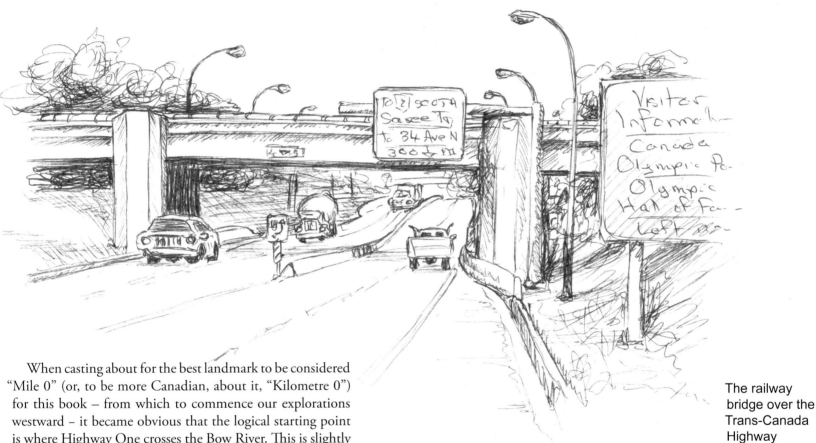

The railway bridge over the Trans-Canada Highway

When casting about for the best landmark to be considered "Mile 0" (or, to be more Canadian, about it, "Kilometre 0") for this book – from which to commence our explorations westward – it became obvious that the logical starting point is where Highway One crosses the Bow River. This is slightly east of the Sarcee Trail interchange with 16th Avenue NW as it heads west from Calgary. This is the only point in Calgary where the Trans-Canada crosses the Bow River, and thus, HERE, where two dominant geographical features of this book intersect, Highway One and the Bow River, we will establish our starting starting point.

The Bow River accompanies the Trans-Canada through the valley along the entire route covered in this book. Downstream, to the east of Calgary, the river joins the Oldman River just west of Medicine Hat and becomes the South Saskatchewan, 623 km from its source in the mountains. The South Saskatchewan then joins the North Saskatchewan near Saskatoon, and collectively they form the Nelson Watershed System that drains most of the prairies and dumps the water into Hudson Bay. Looking in the other direction, the Bow River is born in the Bow Glacier, which is part of the great Wapta Icefield to the southwest of the Icefields Parkway toward Jasper.

The name "Bow" is a translation of the Cree name for the river: *Manachaban sipi*, or "bow wood river." The native people considered the wood growing along the riverbanks to be particularly suitable for making their hunting bows, which needed to be supple yet strong and resilient. The Stoney Indian name for the Bow is *Mînî Thnî Wapta*, meaning "cold water river" – a concise description of this river.

For many long-time Calgarians, the intersection with the Bow is the beginning of the stretch of road that signifies that you are "leavin' town, headin' west, goin' to the mountains…" This is where 16th Avenue feels like it is turning into The Highway, and the urban speed restriction of 50 kph is lifted so the driver may press the pedal down to climb out of the Bow River Valley and cruise up to highway speed of 110 and leave the city behind.

But before we leave Calgary in the rear-view mirror, there are a number of interesting sites to consider within the city limits.

Bowness

This area was first surveyed by the Dominion Land Surveyors in 1881, and marked out in the township and range system that would be the legal land description for all rural land in Alberta.

In 1872, the *Dominion Lands Act* was passed in Canada, which was modeled on the American *Homestead Act* of a decade earlier. This Act provided a tract of one quarter section (160 acres) to individuals on the condition that they would within three years prove that they had undertaken productive cultivation of that land and built a dwelling on it. But in 1881 the Act was amended to instead allow a 21-year grazing lease, at a rate of one cent per acre, for up to 100,000 acres. (More details on grazing leases are in Chapter Three.) This opened the door for large cattle companies to occupy enormous tracts of land and conduct the business of ranching on a corporate scale. One of the first to take advantage of this opportunity was the Cochrane Ranche Company, which leased 109,000 acres of land in a swath about five miles wide, west from the city of Calgary toward the present town of Cochrane. The community of Bowness is the eastern portion

of what was once this huge ranch. The history of this ranch will be told in greater detail in Chapter Six, but suffice to say here that, as conflicts developed between these huge leases and settlers wanting to purchase land, the Cochrane Ranche moved further west and portions of land along the Bow River were put up for sale. The Bowness Ranche was established in 1890, the first appearance of this name in the area. One of its owners had loved to spend time in Bowness-on-Windermere in Westmorland, England, and the name was probably a bit of nostalgia for the home country.

This piece of land then passed through a number of other owners, and eventually ended up in the hands of John Hexall, an English solicitor, who ranched on it for a number of years before he entered into the crazy world of real-estate speculation in Western Canada in the early 20th century. In 1910, Calgary was experiencing a boom, and ventures in real estate were in a frenzied state. But transportation problems presented an obstacle to putting Hexall's riverside lots from the old ranch on the market – there was only one road linking the location to Calgary at the time, and that rough track took a circuitous route that made it an impractical connection to town. So Hexall made a deal with the city to extend the new streetcar system out to Bowness in return for his donation of 100 acres on two islands in the Bow River that would be made into a park. Hexall also built a bridge to accommodate the new streetcar line, which is still in use as a pedestrian bridge and is known as the Hexall Bridge.

Hexall was then able to start promoting lots, and he even built houses on a number of them in preparation for the grand community expected to spring up along the Bow. However, sales did not exactly take off. Hexall had the problem of his lots being a substantial distance from the city centre, and this was further complicated by aggressive counter-marketing by other developers and some quite negative press in a local paper, which wrote: "How and why this single trolley line was laid between Calgary and the wilderness known as Bowness, is hard to conceive."[1] Then, in 1913, there was a slump in the economy. And in 1914, the start of World War I finished off the idea as the real-estate market collapsed completely. Hexall died in April of that year.

The 100 acres that Hexall donated for a park lay largely undeveloped during the war years. The city had great dreams for the area and compared its plans for this land to Vancouver's Stanley Park. The islands in the Bow had been linked to the riverbank by weirs in the 1890s as part of an enterprise to divert irrigation water. This created an attractive lagoon and complex of small watercourses that provided places for picnicking and boating, and for skating in the winter. Once development of the area finally got under way after the war, the park included a dance pavilion, outdoor swimming pool, rides (including a merry-go-round, now at Heritage Park) and later miniature golf and a children's train ride. It became a popular weekend destination for Calgarians, who wobbled out on the streetcar at between 5 and 20 miles per hour, spent the day frolicking in the park, and caught a late train home. If it rained, there was great consternation as the picnickers

tried to get a spot on the train to escape the rain and return to the city. On fair days, as the final run of the day drew near, the conductor of the streetcar would count the canoes still out on the lagoon and estimate the number of streetcars that would be needed, then send the rest of the cars back to the barn – hoping that he had got the number right! As for the reverse direction, Bowness old-timers relate how they had to make sure they caught the last run out from downtown Calgary to get home, which was frustrating because the last trip departed about 15 minutes before most of the theatres let out.

After World War I, the town of Bowness began to grow, and it experienced a population boom in post-war immigrants, mostly of Dutch and German origin. Valerie

---

The Dominion Land Survey and Land Descriptions in Alberta

In 1871, the enormous task of surveying and describing the western lands of the country was initiated, starting from Manitoba's eastern border and working its way west. The method used to demarcate the land into an organized grid that could be legally named and located remains in use to this day, known as the township and range system.

The township and range system functions to establish a location with an east-west division within the western province in relation to meridians (grid lines on the globe running north and south). These imaginary lines are designated the 1st, 2nd, 3rd, 4th and 5th meridians, commencing in Manitoba, east of Winnipeg. The 5th Meridian runs roughly north-south along Barlow Trail where it intersects the Trans-Canada Highway in Calgary (in fact, there is an adjacent road called Meridian Road), and thus the land covered in this book is all described as "west of the 5th Meridian." The area between these meridian divisions is then further broken down to six-mile measures, which are called ranges, numbered from east to west. Thus, you can situate the east-west location of a place according to its range within the 5th Meridian.

The township part of the designation is also for six-mile divisions, in this case running south to north. These are numbered consecutively, starting with 1 on the Montana border up to 126 where the province meets the Northwest Territories. You now have an imaginary grid laid over the land, created by township and range lines. But to locate a specific parcel, this needs to be refined even further.

Confusingly, each six-by-six mile township and range block formed where the range and township divisions intersect is also termed a "township." Every township block is then further divided into 36 sections, each being one square mile (six miles times six miles equals 36 square miles). Township blocks are further broken down into quarters, and these are designated by their location as NE, NW, SE or SW. A section encompasses 640 acres, and a quarter is thus 160 acres. As the meridians become closer together in Northern Alberta, accommodation is made by dropping the sections along the west edge of the block, thus keeping the sections the same size, but resulting in fewer of them.

Got that? With this information, you can now decipher a legal rural land description. So NW 34-24-2-W5 (which is the portion of the Cochrane Ranche that would later become the town of Bowness) indicates that it comprises the Northwest Quarter of Section 34, found in Township 24 and Range 2, located west of the 5th Meridian. Whew…

the end of 1949, the streetcar had made its last run and the service was replaced by buses. In the early 1950s, Bowness had a population of about 900, and achieved town status. In 1964, after a contentious plebiscite in the community regarding annexation, Bowness was amalgamated into the City of Calgary.

Aviation in Bowness

One of the popular spectacles to enjoy on a trip to Bowness was the air show, and joy rides were offered by local flyers for a modest fee. Bowness is closely connected to early aviation history in the Bow Corridor, and many early developments in local aviation took place here.

It is possible that the very first flight to happen in the area took off from Bowness. In 1914, Frank Ellis and Tom Blakely repaired a damaged Curtis biplane that they had salvaged for $200 from an American barnstormer who had crashed it in Moose Jaw, Saskatchewan. It was built of wood and wire, with tricycle-wheel landing gear and a 45 hp motor that would keep it in the air for 15 minutes. They refurbished the little plane, named it the West Wind, and spent a few months in Bowness practising flying – mostly just hops off and back to the ground. Their little experiment in aviation ended in 1915 when their contraption crashed on landing. The intrepid pair repaired the wreck, but other damage from UV exposure caused the right wing to give way. This was followed by a big windstorm, and despite the plane being well pegged down it broke loose and rolled for a quarter-mile. All that was salvaged was the engine and propeller.

Subsequent to this, returning World War I flying aces would set up shop for barnstorming out of Bowness, using an old wagon track as a runway. They held aerial stunt displays and gave rides for a few dollars. The area just east of the present Bowness Road, in the central part of Bowness, became known as Bowness Flying Field. In August 1919, there was great excitement as the first flight across the Rockies, by Captain E. C. Hoy of Vancouver, was scheduled to land there. He arrived at 8:55 after 16½ hours of flying. Hoy set off to return to Vancouver on August 11, stopping in Golden, B.C., to refuel. However, on takeoff a couple of

Boating at Bowness Park, 1892, Glenbow NA 1496-4

Bowness streetcar, 1847, Glenbow NA 2935-6

Urie recalls: "Bowness developed in fits and starts. First came the wealthy and the middle class, to be joined and later outnumbered by those pushed out of the city by high taxes and expensive housing. They squatted on the open prairie, building huts, shacks, and small dwellings, often with their own hands. All melded together on the streetcar – squatters and businessmen, professionals and tradesmen, stockbrokers and the unemployed. All rode the streetcar. It was the ultimate leveler – a club where no one was excluded."[2] By

boys ran into his path on the runway and he had to swerve to avoid them. His plane was gravely damaged and Hoy made the rest of his journey home by train.

In 1919, the Air Board was created to regulate flying in Canada. It then created the Canadian Air Force (CAF) and, as a public relations effort, undertook a trans-Canada flight. The pilot started in Halifax on October 7 and arrived in Vancouver 10 days later, having made a stop in Bowness to great public hurrah. Interest in aviation was growing with exposure at these aerial events.

Part of the CAF's mandate was to promote local flying clubs. In 1919, a promotional tour by Major John Inwood entitled The Commercial and Pleasure Possibilities of Aerial Navigation in Canada led to the formation of the Calgary Aero Club. Some flying instruction ensued, but interest soon waned and the club faded away for the time being. Still, commercial interest in flying continued.

Two companies were established out of the Bowness Flying Field in 1919. George Webber set up shop and bought a Royal Air Force Curtiss JN-4 when these planes were made available to the public. But his enterprise ended when pilot Frank Donnally crashed that plane in May. Captain Frank McCall, a World War I flying ace, set up McCall Aero Corporation in August of the same year. He floated advertising streamers and offered passenger services, but the majority of his business was stunt flying and joy rides. A commercial flight was initiated to Nanton, dropping off a bundle of newspapers over High River en route. At its peak, McCall Aero operated three planes and toured around local fairs doing stunt shows. But two of the planes were lost in accidents, and interest in flying waned in the community as attention turned to bringing in the harvest. The introduction of wing walking piqued interest for a while, and spectators were awed as Alf Maybee performed his aerial acts on weekends in the fall of 1920.

But McCall's operations were no longer viable, so in 1921 his business was purchased by P. Flemming. That ended in June of that year when they crashed on landing after a wing-walking performance. Maybee was killed and Flemming suffered a broken leg and head injuries.

About half a dozen fledgling aviation companies flew out of this rutted stretch of cow pasture over the years between

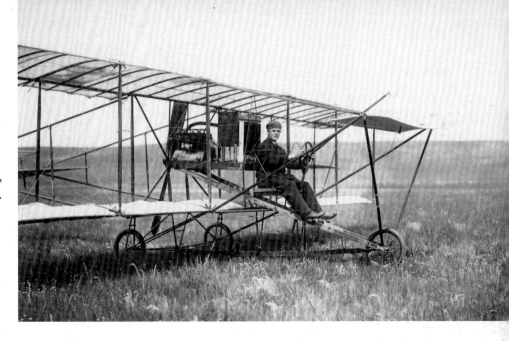

The West Wind, no date, Glenbow NA 2825-4

the end of the war and 1928. Recreational flying received a boost in 1927 when the Canadian government (through the Department of National Defence) introduced a program encouraging the formation of local clubs, with cash subsidies for training and loans of planes. The Calgary Aero Club was revived, once again out of the Bowness Flying Field. However, as newer planes came along that required longer and better runways, the site became impractical. So, in 1928, the aerial activity moved further west, by the Banff Coach Road.

Paskapoo Slopes

On the south side of the Trans-Canada, southwest of the Sarcee Trail intersection, is an escarpment that rises about 150 metres from the valley bench to the upland plateau. This area is known as Paskapoo Slopes. The name *Paskapoo* is said to come from a Cree word meaning "Blind Man," which is from a native story about the occurrence of snow blindness in the area. The term is connected to a geological feature, the Paskapoo Formation, which is a layer of buff-coloured sandstone and grey shale up to 600 metres thick that formed in the Paleocene (about 60,000 years ago) and covers much of the slopes overlooking the Bow Valley.

Paskapoo Slopes have great importance for both ecological and historical reasons. Within this area, stretching about four kilometres along the highway, there are six distinct significant habitat areas, from aspen parkland to balsam poplar

stands to riverine tall shrub areas and rare native grasslands. The area is even more valuable because of the proximity of these different habitats to each other, which greatly increases its usefulness for wildlife. There are numerous ravines cutting through the vegetated slopes, and many fresh springs provide wetland areas. This scenario adds up to huge diversity in habitat and the wildlife that it supports.

As people in the area became aware of the threat posed by rapidly encroaching development, Paskapoo Slopes became the focus of a prolonged battle between developers who viewed this spot as having excellent residential potential, and Calgarians who saw its value primarily as important natural habitat, a refuge for wildlife within the city limits, as well as for urban human inhabitants. Paskapoo Slopes have the added dimension of encompassing an area of high archeological significance (next section).

So, the fight was on. The Paskapoo Slopes Preservation Society was formed in 1991, and this group put a tremendous amount of energy into informing the public, lobbying City Hall, and collecting data that presented the true value of the slopes in their natural state. The society fought for the recognition of the area's value as an environmental, recreational, educational, historical, and even spiritual resource. In spite of this, in 2000 the City of Calgary approved residential development on 165 acres within this area. However, the city gradually became more receptive to what the society was

presenting, and it commissioned a number of studies on the area that led it to revise its plans. In 2006, the city stated in its Structure Plan that "the forested hill is a magnificent sight – a landmark on the city's gateway from the west, similar in significance to Nose Hill Park in ecological quality and visual prominence… Because of its prehistoric context, Paskapoo Slopes could (even) be of provincial significance."[3]

The outcome of this has been a plan for Natural Area Management that leaves the 165 acres in a largely natural state, preserving contiguous open space for wildlife corridors. Areas of significant natural habitat are to be preserved or enhanced, maintaining the integrity of the area's ecology. Walking, cycling and cross-country ski trails will be laid out in the area, in consultation with interested groups such as the Mountain Bike Alliance. These will incorporate an interpretive program to inform people of the archeological finds in the area.

Of course, not everyone is satisfied with the outcome of this plan. The developers, most obviously, are disappointed. Some Calgarians felt that the area should have been simply left untouched, without even the pathways and interpretive additions. But the city seems to have found a satisfactory middle road through this issue that involves many of the stakeholders. It will be a true asset to the city, a source of pleasure and interest for the citizens, and an area of refuge for wildlife under increasing pressure from urbanization.

Early Human Presence in Southern Alberta

One of the strongest impetuses for preservation of the Paskapoo Slopes has been the important archeological finds that are associated with this area. The records of early human activity in this area are fascinating, and probably illustrate the nature of human activity in much of southern Alberta. It seems appropriate that the very start of our journey along the route of the highway includes a look at some of the very first records of human presence in this part of the world. We really are beginning at the beginning.

To put this discussion in perspective, it is necessary to step back a bit and look at the larger story of early human history in North America. Some of the earliest records we have of human activity on this continent have been found in the Yukon, in an area known as the Bluefish Caves located in the Keele Mountain Range. These remains have fairly vague dating, but are probably 18,000 to 14,000 YBP (Years Before Present). Another very old and significant site is found far to the south, near Clovis, New Mexico. This site has been dated back to about 11,500 YBP, and is associated with a particular type of manufactured stone tool known as the Clovis Point. Stone tools themselves cannot be dated. But once they can be associated with something that *can* be (such as bone fragments or carbon remains from campfires), they are a useful marker. This is one of the primary methods that archaeologists use to date the sites of early humans – tools tend to have distinct characteristics that can help locate their users in both time and geography. So we know that there were people in the Yukon possibly as early as 20,000 years ago, and in the Southwestern United States by 11,500 YBP. But how did they get there? And when were they first in the Bow Valley?

Getting a picture of how this happened brings us to a discussion of the great glaciation that affected North America. This occurred in several waves, with the ice sheets advancing and melting back across the continent over long periods. The last great advance of the glaciers, during a period known as the Wisconsinan, occurred between 25,000 and 10,000 YBP. During the periods of peak glaciation, much of the earth's water was concentrated in the ice sheets, and the level of the oceans consequently dropped as much as 100 metres. This

would have exposed a land bridge, now known as Beringia, between Siberia and Alaska – a gap of only 100 kilometres even at modern higher ocean levels. People could easily have walked across this, following game or seeking new hunting territory. This land bridge theory is now generally (but not universally) accepted – and it could explain the arrival of humans at Bluefish Caves.

The question remains how and when these people might have moved down the continent to account for the evidence of human presence in Clovis about 5,000 years later (give or take a thousand years or two). We know that the ice was a formidable barrier at the time these people first arrived in the north. Some theories support the idea of an ice-free corridor to the east of the Rocky Mountains, allowing people to move to the south between the ice sheets. Others claim that this wasn't possible, and people must have moved south some other way, perhaps along a coastal route. Either way, the Clovis site informs us that they had somehow made their way south during a period of heavy ice cover.

Archaeological Finds on Paskapoo Slopes

There have now been over 100 sites located and excavated across Paskapoo Slopes, creating a picture of a complex that was used over an immense span of time. The oldest evidence turned up in the area of Paskapoo Slopes is dated back to 7,000 to 8,000 YBP. There are other, older sites not far from this location: Clovis-style points have been found to the east of Calgary near the Marquis of Lorne Trail, and points from the slightly more recent Cody Complex from about 9,000 YBP have been found in the Calgary area. These older sites are clearly earlier than 6,800 YBP, because they lie beneath a layer of ash – called the Mazama Ash Layer – that resulted from the massive volcanic event that created Crater Lake in Oregon in 6,800 YBP. So we know that people arrived here very early. Still, there have been only a few very old sites found at Paskapoo Slopes. Most of the finds are much more recent, the majority from between 3,000 and 2,000 YBP. There are some sites as recent as 200 years ago, which puts them into the period of the fur trade. These most recent sites include metal objects, trade beads, and other evidence of exchange

Crystal point found during Paskapoo Slopes excavation,
Lifeways of Canada Limited

Bone bed excavation on Paskapoo Slopes,
Lifeways of Canada Limited

Bison or Buffalo?

I am sure that you have heard these shaggy beasts referred to by both names, so which is correct? Technically, the beasts that roamed the plains of North America were bison – scientifically called *Bison bison*. True buffalo exist in Africa (the Cape buffalo, genus *Syncerus*) and Asia (the water buffalo, genus *Bubalus*). Both bison and buffalo are members of the family *Bovidae*, which includes all ungulates (including antelope, sheep, goats, and our familiar bovines or cows). The main differentiation from buffalo is that the bison possess a hairier coat, a larger hump, and shorter horns – as well as a more aggressive disposition, which makes them unlikely candidates for the domestic tasks that the large-horned, short-haired water buffalo is used for. However, both names have come into such common use that they are employed almost interchangeably now. The term buffalo is long associated with the Indians, and so I will use it, even if inaccurately…

Cree buffalo pound near Fort Carlton, Saskatchewan. Original artwork by Lieutenant George Back, 1820; Glenbow NA-1344-2

with the new white arrivals, if not direct contact.

Looking at the finds from all the most common sites, dating from about 3,000 YBP, gives us a picture of a lifestyle in this prairie region that has common general characteristics across the centuries. The people hunting here made elaborate efforts to exploit the terrain to capture buffalo. The Paskapoo Slopes contain a huge complex of kill sites, which probably represent one of the largest known in Southern Alberta, and which is of at least the same level of use and importance as Head-Smashed-In further to the south. Digs have uncovered kill sites, camp sites, and what are called processing sites. Some of these kill sites are huge – one excavation over an area of about 10 by 15 metres contains the bones from an estimated 200 buffalo. That is a tremendous number of beasts to capture, kill, and harvest for meat and hides. Archaeologists feel that this indicates a group of about 100 people working together in an organized way to maximize their ability to harvest and preserve the buffalo bonanza.

The method of hunting these huge numbers of buffalo largely remained the same across the prairies over thousands of years. The types of weapons changed from the spear thrower (the atlatl) in the earlier records to the bow and arrow at about 1,600 YBP, but the general strategy was probably consistent. The early hunters realized that they could capitalize on the herd instinct of these animals to induce them to move as a mass in a direction orchestrated by a group of people working together. These hunters frequently built what are called "drive lanes": a route across the featureless prairie that indicated a

direction leading to a drop. Working on foot (this was prior to the arrival of the horse) as a co-ordinated team, the people encouraged the herd to move down the drive lane, probably gaining in speed and alarm as they progressed, until they met their end in one of two ways. Often the drive lane ended up at the lip of a cliff and the momentum forced the beasts at the cliff edge to tumble over to their death, followed closely by the rest of the herd. If an appropriate cliff arrangement was not part of the terrain, the buffalo were driven into an enclosure called a pound. This was a large corral, probably constructed of brush covered by hides and other materials to make it look impenetrable. As long as no gaps showed, the beasts seemed to have regarded it as a solid wall and would have milled around in the enclosure while the hunters picked them off one by one. Most of these sites along Paskapoo Slopes were probably pounds.

Who were these people? And how might they be connected to the indigenous people who lived in this area in historical periods? We cannot be sure of a continuity in the population groups, but there certainly is a continuity in their lifestyles. They probably lived in small family groups of about 10 to 15 people most of the time, but periodically came together into larger hunting parties to stock their larders for the winter with buffalo – something that could only be effectively done in an organized group. Their very existence in the harsh environment of the prairies would have depended on being able to pull off these events successfully. Gail Helgason describes the dynamic of organizing for such a hunt:

"Buffalo only look like lumbering dolts. Actually, they are skittish, speedy, and relatively agile. They can detect humans up to six kilometres away. They have been clocked at speeds (of) 60 kilometres an hour. Not exactly lumbering… From historic accounts, we know that (the hunters) levied harsh punishments against persons who disrupted herds before communal hunts. Such 'criminals,' in Native justice systems, were often whipped or had their tipis destroyed. The point was to publicly humiliate the wrongdoer, though the tribe might replace destroyed possessions within a few days."[4]

These were big events. Base camps would have been set up nearby (probably more in the valley bottom near Bowness), and a few on-site camps located near the working area (near the springs on Paskapoo Slopes). The task of killing the

Facing page: Buffalo, S. Ditchburn

buffalo was just the first step of a process which required a high level of organization. Once you had a large number of dead beasts lying under the prairie sun, your work was just beginning. The presence of specific bone-disposal areas at the kill sites indicates that there was a level of co-ordination in the butchering. The rough butchering would have been done at the kill site. Then the harvested animals would have been moved to a processing area for the more refined work, with only the worthless bits relegated to the disposal area. The meat was cut up and set out to dry for the winter, fat and marrow was extracted from the bones in boiling pits, hides were tanned using the brain as a processing agent, sinews were carefully collected to use as thread, etc. All parts of the buffalo were used – even the horns for containers, bones for tools, and hooves for rattles.

The movements of these early Indians were probably organized around the seasons and the buffalo herds. Locating the group near shelter, fuel, and food for the winter would have been important. We have no way of knowing the nature of their social organization other than the size of their groups (often determined by the number of tipi rings in a camp site), and archaeologists are cautious about assumptions regarding their relationship to each other and even tribal organization. We don't know if these finds represent one continuous group of people, or waves of different people who used a similar hunting method. Periodically the nature of the tools changed, but did that represent a new group of people in the area or just the arrival of a new technology or trade relationship? There are many questions that remain to be answered…

By the end of this pre-contact period, we can start to make a few more tentative assumptions about the people living west of Calgary. The refinements in the style of points found on Paskapoo Slopes, products of the group who used the site over the last 1,000 years, makes a connection to the *Natsitapii* (Blackfoot-speaking) people. This is consistent with references in the oral tradition among the Blackfoot that this area was part of the northern wintering ground of the *Piitani* band (what we now refer to as Peigan) from the late 1700s into the 1800s. This particular group, the North Peigan, was severely affected by the early waves of smallpox that swept through the native population, and this band eventually died out.

Canada Olympic Park

From ancient Alberta we move on to quite recent history – the site of Canada Olympic Park, which is a legacy from the XV Olympic Winter Games of 1988. In its previous incarnation as Paskapoo Ski Hill and now, as an Olympic athlete training centre, it has been a popular facility for citizens of Calgary and for visiting athletes. Driving west at night during the winter, the eerie effect of snow making set aglow in the illumination for night skiing is a common sight.

Back in 1957, Clarence Haakenstad, whose family had come from the Norwegian village of Lillehammer (site of the 1994 Winter Olympics), noticed an article in a ski magazine describing the new technology for artificial snow. He, Fred Cummer, and Bob Elias had been casting about for a hill near Calgary that would be suitable for the development of a small ski hill. But up to this point, the challenge of consistent snow cover had been prohibitive. All of a sudden, it looked like this problem could be overcome. Haakenstad arranged for some equipment to be sent to Calgary for testing:

"We rigged them up, went down to east Calgary, at Evergreen Irrigation Sprinklers, where we had to have water at a certain pressure and volume, and air at a certain pressure and volume. It was really quite simple. We set up this device one evening, and started pumping snow out over the ground and across the ground and the road."[5]

Two more partners were added to the equation, 18 acres were purchased to the west of Calgary (which then had a population of 240,000), and on Boxing Day of 1960, Paskapoo Ski Centre opened for business. The facility had a lodge (an abandoned military hut), three rope tows, and one run. The *Calgary Herald* responded with a statement that "Bowness skiing is for the birds, you might as well go skin diving in the Sahara."[6]

Despite its negative review, the *Calgary Herald* soon got involved by sponsoring a ski school, and by February of that year 500 skiers were registered. The little ski hill became part of the Calgary winter scene. Debentures were sold to members of the Paskapoo Ski Club to finance improvements – a T-bar, lodge expansion, more lighting…. However, in 1968 Haakenstad decided that he'd had enough, so he sold his interests in the operation. It had been a very demanding

project for him – often involving trips to the hill at 2 a.m. to set up snow-making machinery. Joe Coulliard was hired as manager, and he brought great ambitions for the little hill.

In 1978, the first chair lift was installed, as well as the first summer facilities (an Alpine Slide, GoKart Track and golf driving range). All of these helped make the operation more economically viable. Ongoing improvements were made to the facilities, and by 1979 the site covered 210 acres, had a quarter-million skiers a year on its slopes, and about 500 racers in training. It was time to look on to greater things.

In 1981, official word was received that the International Olympic Committee had chosen Calgary for the XV Winter Games, to be held in February 1988. Several locations had been proposed for development for the games – even little Pigeon Mountain, which we will encounter in Chapter 12. Some of the sites were quite remote and would have required extensive development even to access them. Finally, Paskapoo came to the attention of the OCO (Olympiques Calgary Olympics) Committee. But when Brian Murphy proposed it as a selection, President David Leighton is said to have responded with, "Murphy, there is no way we are putting an Olympic venue on that pimple of a ski hill west of Calgary."[6] However, the little ski hill won out as the final choice for the bobsleigh, luge and ski jumping events, and in 1983 Paskapoo officially became Canada Olympic Park, the facility was sold to the federal government and preparations began for the huge event.

Development proceeded for a ski jump complex on the eastern edge and bobsleigh and luge on the western side, with a new lodge and additional facilities that would make it a valuable training facility in years to come. It opened in time for the 1986-87 season of pre-Olympic events.

There had been considerable concern about the effect of the famous chinook winds that occasionally blow in and melt all the snow. A famous local story goes that if you were driving a team of horses pulling a sleigh towards Calgary during a chinook, you would have to whip them along at speed in order to stay ahead of the warm winds from the west and melting the snow as you went. It was said that the driver in the front risked frostbite, while the passenger riding in the back could suffer from sunburn. The chinooks did indeed cause postponement of some events during the Games. Ski jumping was postponed due to very high wind speeds after one jumper was sent flying into a camera tower, and bobsleigh was delayed as well when dust was blown onto the track. But all the events eventually went ahead.

Among the highlights that Calgarians will remember from the 1988 Winter Games was the Jamaican bobsleigh team, which lacked in training but made up for it in enthusiasm. Their story eventually led to the Disney movie *Cool*

Runnings, which was shot at COP. Britain's ski jumping entry, Eddie "the Eagle" Edwards, became famous for his fogged-up coke-bottle glasses, his lack of experience, and his unathletic physique. But he was nevertheless beloved by onlookers for his indomitable attitude and became a favourite among the media. He came in 55th out of 56 in his event (the 56th competitor was disqualified). Even though no Canadians won gold medals in 1988, the Games created many great memories for Calgarians who were involve either as spectators or among the 9,500 volunteers who helped the events run smoothly (and on budget!).

Once the Olympics were over, ownership of COP was transferred to the Calgary Olympic Development Association (CODA), which decided how the post-Olympic facilities could become a viable operation both for recreational skiers and athletes in training. After 1988, the number of recreational skiers using COP dropped dramatically. Fortunately, the growth of snowboarding in the 1990s brought the younger generation back onto the ski hill, and COP developed a new snowboarding facility. About 300,000 skiers and snowboarders now use the facility over the course of a winter season.

But the challenge of keeping the facility current and competitive is an ongoing struggle. Efforts were made to diversify the facilities at COP, encouraging tourists to visit the Olympic Hall of Fame and Museum and to try a tamer-and-safer version of some of the sports, as well as the development of summer facilities such as mountain biking, a climbing wall, mini golf, etc. The site also took on another role as a conference and event centre. The Bob Niven High-Performance Training Centre opened in 1987 and was expanded in 2006. In 2007 the Alberta government committed funds to CODA to help upgrade the facilities and construct a Centre of Sports Excellence.

In 2009, the announcement was made that CODA was rebranding itself as the new Canadian Winter Sport Institute (WinSport), with an injection of $300 million (of which $130 million came from various levels of government) to add a 500,000-square-foot Athletic and Ice Complex within the COP facilities. This building is set to open in 2011. The concept behind this initiative is to pool all athletic facilities and services for the full range of winter sports under one umbrella. The Nordic training centre in Canmore, the Olympic Oval at the University of Calgary, and other training initiatives will all be channelled through WinSport as a co-ordinated effort.

The facilities at COP from the west, summer season, 2009

The scene from
Artist`s View

Moving west, we pass a whole series of new residential developments and acreages. To the south, on the bluff above the new community of Crestmont (which encompasses the western stretch of the buffalo jump/pound complex), is a landmark known as Artist's View. Many local artists have found inspiration in the commanding view of the mountains to the west. In 1881 the Góvernor General of Canada, Sir John Douglas Sutherland Campbell, a.k.a. the Marquis of Lorne, a.k.a. the Duke of Argyll was en route by wagon from Calgary to Banff along the Banff Coach Road. His party stopped on the edge of this hill and Sir John stepped out to stretch his legs and take in the view across the rolling land west toward the Rockies. He was awestruck by the vista laid out before him, and in response to this inspiration, being a religious man, he wrote the hymn "Unto The Hills Around Do I Lift Up My Longing Eyes."

The view does not spread out before the driver on the Trans-Canada quite yet – but it will soon, I promise. Meanwhile, I should try to clarify the rather confusing collection of names that have been attached to the various roads heading west from Calgary. The Old Banff Coach Road, or simply the Banff Wagon Road, or Banff Tow Road, was the original road for wheeled traffic heading west. Previous to this, there was an Indian trail, known as the Morley Trail, which meandered between Morley and the southwest corner of the City of Calgary. This was just a pony trail, not suitable for wagons or other wheeled vehicles. It had a number of alternate routes, as described in *A Frontier Guide to Calgary*: "One road led from the N.W.M.P. barracks north, fording the Bow River, and climbing the embankment to the prairie above. Here it branched off from the Edmonton-Benton trail (which went south to Montana) and followed the north bank of the Bow

River to Morley. Once on the open plain this road wandered and dipped with the terrain – depending on weather and whimsy. The second road to Morley led westward from the police post, mounted *Shaganappi* Point and meandered at will across the prairie on the south side of the Bow River. It crossed to the north side of the river at one of numerous fords between Cochrane and Morley. From Morley, the two roads became one and entered the mountains over the ancient Stoney Trail by way of the Ghost River and Lake Minnewanka."[1]

Banff Trail, which ran along the north side of the Bow River from Calgary, had also been a horse trail before the advent of vehicular traffic. It gradually became the dominant route west, and evolved into what is now Highway 1A. The earliest record of someone taking a car over the Banff Trail was in 1898 – a tiller-steered White Steamer owned by Mr. W. F. Cochrane, who probably went only as far as Morley.

The route of the Trans-Canada became the main strip to get to the mountains in 1957. The Old Banff Coach Road now dissolves into local roads on the outskirts of Calgary.

Red River ox cart, ca. 1880-1900, Library and Archives Canada / C-001517

The stories of this area are of the struggles of the first settlers, the huge challenge of making a living from this land and the rewards of community building. The first to come west also faced a human relations dilemma. The people who had always lived on these lands, the Indian tribes of the plains and foothills, met the arrival of these white folk with an understandable level of alarm and, in some situations, hostility. These were tough times for the Indians – those who lived on the plains were beginning to feel the loss of the large buffalo herds on which their livelihood was based, their autonomy and strength was being undermined by the traders of firewater moving into the country, and their numbers had already been decimated by the white man's diseases, particularly smallpox. Smallpox epidemics in 1869 and 1879 had wiped out a huge number of the native population.

The earliest folk to arrive in the West with the intention to stay had to come to terms with their indigenous neighbours. Some, like Sam Livingstone – a colourful character who arrived in the West in 1873 and set up a trading post on what would become the western outskirts of modern Springbank – made their living through trade with the Indians and depended on establishing a good business relationship with them for their mutual benefit. Others, such as the MacDougalls of Morley – who we shall meet when we get further along the highway – came west on a missionary calling, with the intent to "civilizing" the Indians. But by the time that the main surge of settlers started to head west, the "Indian problem" had been solved, and treaties had relocated the indigenous people onto reserves and largely tamed their animosity through starvation and the loss of their known way of life. We look further into that can of worms in the section of the highway that traverses the Stoney Nakoda Reserve further west, in Chapter Nine.

Interestingly, the *Dominion Lands Act* of 1872 predates the "acquisition" of the land that it made available for settlement in this area by five years – it was only in 1877 that Treaty 7 moved the Blackfoot and Stoney tribes of the area onto reserves. The government was already giving away land that was not yet "theirs." The railway had been promised to British Columbia when it entered confederation in 1871,

Municipal Districts

As the West began to achieve some population density the federal government decided that it needed a provision for some form of local organization, so in the 1890s it passed a series of ordinances allowing a region of 144 square miles or less, with 50 residents or more (that is to say, males of 18 to 60 years... women didn't count) to create a local government and collect taxes to provide local services. To encourage the construction of roads and firebreaks (prairie fire was a real concern to settlers), landowners could apply work done on these developments against their taxes. Then, in 1903, the areas were enlarged and legislation was passed to create Local Improvement Districts. In 1912, the *Rural Municipalities Act* scaled these districts back to smaller areas (encompassing about nine townships), and in 1918 they were renamed Municipal Districts. In the 1940s, the boundaries were overhauled in many areas to provide for fairer taxation and to bring the school divisions and the Municipal Districts into alignment, and that is how the system remains today.

Having said all of that, The MD of Rocky View, which covers most of the area west of Calgary to the mountains, changed its title to the County of Rocky View in 2009, with the expectation that this would open up more opportunities for economic development.

and a settled population would be a necessary adjunct to operating a railway line across the country. Development was the *modus operandi* of the time, and people had better start heading out into the hinterlands and getting on with it.

The train brought thousands of settlers west, but many still crossed the expanse of the prairie by wagon. In the case of couples, the men often came first and then sent for their wives – but not always. Many young women married and then immediately set forth on the bouncing seat of an ox-cart. The early trains had "colonist" cars – which had rudimentary cooking facilities where the women could patch together some simple meals en route. But often the men in the family travelled separately, in the car with the animals, tending to them and making sure their stock arrived safely.

The Pepper family was one of the earliest to arrive in the Springbank area, and their story probably echoes that of many who made the journey by cart in the early days. William and Harriett Pepper set out in 1884, bringing with them two children and William's widowed mother, Hattie Pepper. They joined up with Bill Parslow, Ebenezer Healy and the Frarey family for strength in numbers, and the group travelled westward by covered wagon and Red River cart, bringing a small dairy herd with them.

The group had to travel with extreme caution in the area around Regina, because the Riel Rebellion was taking place at the time and tension was running high among the Metis and the Indians. At that point, the Healys and Frerys decided to proceed by train, and so it was a smaller group that straggled on across the prairie by cart. In the Regina area, they found that they were unable to ford the river, and so they had the expensive and time-consuming necessity of unloading all their goods from the wagons, reloading them and their cattle onto a CPR flatcar, making the shuffle across the river, and then reassembling all their goods on the other side before they could continue their journey.

At about this point, Harriet gave birth to the family's third child, Fred, and the party proceeded with a newborn infant in its care. They made it to Calgary in the spring of 1885, where another child was born. There, Harriet set up a boarding house in a rental house in town while William sought work as a carpenter west of Calgary in order to scout for land in that region. Having selected a promising looking parcel, they found that it was unavailable for homesteading because of the grazing leases, so they squatted on the land and set up their farm anyway. A huge swath of the land in the area was then leased by the British American Ranching Company and it was quite hostile to the arrival of settlers wanting to homestead. The Pepper family bided their time, running a livery stable and lodging for the stream of men passing through en route to the northern gold fields. Finally,

Grazing Leases and The Dominion Lands Act

The grazing-lease issue became an increasingly confrontational situation as settlers arrived in the West. Even though the *Dominion Lands Act* had provided the structure by which homesteaders could gain a holding of land in the West, the government had seen fit to amend the Act in 1876 to allow large grazing leases without the requirement of homesteading (known as the "no settlement clause"), as was mentioned in the section on Bowness regarding Cochrane Ranche. The government somehow failed to foresee the situation of conflict it had set up by making this amendment.

Part of what had motivated the Canadian government to provide the grazing leases was its observation of the situation that had developed in the United States. In the Great Plains south of the 49th, vast cattle kingdoms had formed, but without any clear definition of where owners were legally allowed to range their cattle or who held water rights. Range wars and a form of vigilante justice had become the way of establishing territory in many parts of the American West, and in some areas overgrazing was already becoming a problem. In Canada, this was going to be controlled through defined leases that required the leasee to stock the land with one head per ten acres within a period of three years (a measure to avoid land speculators profiting from the situation). Furthermore, the British government was threatening to impose an embargo on cattle imports from the United States, which would mean increased opportunity for Canadian cattlemen. The Canadian government further encouraged the development of ranching north of the 49th by waiving the duty on cattle being imported from the U.S. – mostly coming up from Bozeman, Montana at that time. This all resulted in huge cattle companies, often backed by a group of wealthy easterners who might never even lay eyes on the land being leased. Pretty soon, independent ranchers did not have a hope as much of the land had been scooped up into leases and removed from the pool for homesteaders.

Friction between the homesteaders and the cattlemen grew steadily. Settlers' rights associations were formed and protests held (including one headed by Sam Livingstone), and petitions were sent to Ottawa. At one point, potential settlers even threatened to join the Riel Rebellion. But Ottawa finally began to listen. By the turn of the century, the federal government was strongly encouraging population growth in the West, and in 1896 the grazing leases were closed. Land was becoming increasingly available, and the main flood of settlers poured west from 1900 until the outbreak of World War I in 1914. In 1905, a provision for 21-year grazing leases was made, but the selected land had to be proven unfit for agriculture before it was leased in this way.

in 1898 the grazing lease problem was settled and they were able to take out homesteads on NE 2-25-4-5 and pursue their dream of farming their own land.

So, more land was back on the plate for homesteading – but even then, a lot of it was unavailable. As part of the Dominion Lands Act, certain portions of every township were set aside for special purposes. As part of the settlement with the Hudson Bay Company, in which HBC sold Rupert's Land to the Canadian government (all lands draining into Hudson Bay had been granted to the company in 1670 in a charter by King Charles II), HBC was allowed to keep 5% of the "fertile belt" as part of the deal. To account for that, all of Section 8 and part of Section 26 on each township were retained by the Hudson Bay Company. Furthermore, all odd-numbered sections (except 11 and 29) were given to the railway, to encourage their participation in the development of the West and raise funds for their construction efforts. Sections 11 and 29 were reserved as "school sections," which provided for the development of schools when the population warranted. Schools were seldom actually located on these sections, but they could be traded for another suitable site, or simply sold to raise money dedicated to schools.

In fact, once a quarter section had been homesteaded and put into cultivation, settlers quickly found that this amount of land was seldom enough to provide a living in this region. They then had to find additional land available for purchase – either from the railway, the HBC, school divisions or other settlers. They also had to scrabble together the means by which to purchase it. So there was a period of land being shuffled among owners as parcels were sold or traded to make a contiguous piece. While newer homesteaders were trying to assemble the cash to purchase more land, in addition to farming their own homestead they would work for those who had become sufficiently established to require extra help. In 1902, it was estimated that only half of the settlers were living on land that they had homesteaded themselves. Thus the community slowly started to establish itself.

The story of the Youngs is one that encompasses many of the common tales of the budding new community in this area. The two Young brothers, James and William, came west from Ontario in the summer of 1886, selected pieces of land, and then returned to collect their wives, Lily and Mary, to return by train in November. Having seen the area that would become Springbank in the middle of the summer, looking green and promising, and having heard how the chinook winds kept the region warm and snow-free throughout the winter, it was with some consternation that they closed the year of 1886 with 45 centimetres of snow on the ground and temperatures of minus 35 degrees Celsius! Furthermore, the simple one-room log houses that they had contracted to be built in their absence proved to have been constructed of green logs rather than dried ones, and the winter wind whistled in through the gaps as the logs shrank. The barn had been built with a door that was hopelessly too small for their team of horses. Things didn't look too promising at the beginning. But they were determined, and

as well as starting work on their land, they set about cultivating a community.

The family worked hard to help their neighbours and to contribute in areas of common concern. Lily Young was particularly loved for her support for the women of the area. After struggling through the birth of their son Alan while all alone in the house (James was off desperately seeking a doctor), Lily swore that while she lived in that area, no other woman would have to go through what she had. She served as midwife for the arrival of well over 100 new members of the community, and many of the young people would always refer to her as Aunt Lily. A gift was once made to Lily of a hand-made quilt, carefully embroidered with all the names of the many children she had seen into the world.

Their story has its share of struggle and tragedy as they experienced being hailed out, fried by summer drought, and the effect of early killing frosts. Further, their family suffered the loss of their son Arthur, who was killed in a farm accident in 1911, and their daughter Mabel, an epileptic, who died in 1914. Two sons were lost in World War I. But despite all the hardships and grief, the family stood as a pillar of strength in the community from the beginning.

Many of the settlers in the area had young families, so the question of educating the children became a concern to the community. In 1887, a meeting was held among the Young brothers and several other homesteaders to talk about forming a school district. By now, there were three Young brothers with land in the area. The third brother, Thomas, had joined William and James, and had set himself up on a parcel of land purchased for $3.75 an acre. He offered to donate a part of that land as a site for the school to be built.

Once the decision had been made to create a school

Mrs. James Young (Lily) and grandson Rex, 1920, Glenbow NA 3204-2

Chinooks

The area west of Calgary is famous for its chinook winds. This phenomenon had been noted at the time of early settlement, and new arrivals were often attracted to the area by a promise of a mild winter. As those who live in the area know, these mild periods do occur – but are often interspersed by periods of extreme cold!

Looking west toward the mountains in the winter, you might spot a bank of cloud overhead that ends in a sharp line to the west – the chinook arch. This occurs where the winds streaming over the mountains meet the stratus clouds, creating the sharp edge on the clouds, which appears arched as it follows the curvature of the earth. The mountains themselves are often shrouded in cloud, giving the impression that bad weather is approaching. But those clouds tend to stay in the mountains, often creating whiteouts for skiers who have headed west hoping for a sunny day on the slopes.

In meteorological terms, chinooks are caused when moist winds come in from the West Coast and are forced to rise up on the westward side of the mountains, where they cool and drop their load of moisture. Hence, the windward (westward) side of the mountain ranges receive a much deeper snow pack and are greener and lusher in the summer. Once over the mountains, the now-dry wind drops down the eastern slopes, gaining momentum and rising in temperature as it loses altitude. As a rule, the dry air warms up by about 5 degrees C for every 300 metres of elevation drop – which means that it can have gained 25 to 30 degrees C by the time it blasts out onto the flats on the leeward side of the mountains. Air temperatures have been known to warm from the -15 degree C range up to the +15 degree C range in less than one hour during strong chinooks.

The second school at Springbank, 1905, Glenbow ND 42-1

district, one of the next obvious questions was what to call it. After some consideration the group decided on the name "Spring Bank" for the plentiful springs that fed the area. They specifically indicated the title as two words, in order to differentiate it from Springbank, Ontario, but over the years the name has morphed into the one-word version.

The school building was constructed in 1887. It was a simple one-room log building, but it gave the 10 students in the community a place to study. They attended their first classes there on July 3, under the supervision of Miss Lottie Cowan. The amenities were simple. The school was furnished with a blackboard, a rocking chair donated for the teacher's use, and some simple chairs for the students to sit on. It was recorded later in the year that a desk had been procured for the teacher, that the students had proper seating – and even a globe had been added to the teaching aids in the school.

By 1898, the student population had grown to 25, and by 1903 it had outgrown the little log schoolhouse. A new frame schoolhouse was built, and in 1928 a second room and a second teacher were added. The teachers were usually boarded with local families, and there are the expected stories about worms being added to their bath water, ducks being secreted in their closet, or their underwear being tied like a flag to the back of the wagon. Some teachers found the transition from city to country living too difficult – one stayed only a single week – but many taught at the school for a number of years. Some of the second generation of Youngs, Fred, Frank and Harold, are found on the teachers' roll.

As soon as there was a school building, it became the location for social events – the Christmas concert, musical galas, literary and dramatic productions, which gave the the community a welcome new outlet. The early settlers were eager for opportunities to gather, share their stories, exchange news, and support each other in carving out new lives in this sometimes hostile and isolating country. The school gave a focus to their assembly and a venue for their activities.

Students who were not fortunate enough to live where they could get to school on foot either rode or drove a cart to school. Until a barn was constructed, the horses were tied up to wait patiently to take their charges home. One of the popular pranks was to turn a schoolmate's horse loose and force the victim to either borrow a horse or face a long, long walk home. Tasks assigned to students included carrying water from the nearby spring and tending the fire in the winter. Understandably, weather frequently interfered with attendance for several months of the year, but most students attended regularly. Some were called on to work on the farm during the most hectic parts of the year, but generally support for education in the community was strong. One note in the early school records asks that parents ensure that students attend more regularly, while another note makes a request that the teacher assign more homework for the young scholars. By 1937, Springbank School had 60 pupils. Several new schools have been built in the area since, and the old two-room schoolhouse, now known as the "Cottage School," is still on the grounds of Springbank Middle School, which was built on the site of the original log structure.

To turn our attention back to early community needs, the Young families were all strongly religious and felt the lack of church services in their new community. In 1886, James and Lily initiated church services in their home. No ministers were available in the area, so laymen shared the task of conducting the services, and occasionally travelling

North Church, Springbank, 2009

ministers would come out from Calgary. Someone would ride around the community and let all the families know whenthere would be a service with a proper minister. Once the school was completed, services were held there, and in 1894 a log church was built nearby, known as the Spring Bank Union Church. It serves all denominations – offering Church of England, Presbyterian and Methodist sevices…

The construction project was a community effort, and as these projects do, it had its rocky moments. Helen Hutchison reminisced about the controversies: "From the day the church was started until it was finished, it was the one never-failing topic of conversation. I had no idea that amongst so few people such a difference of opinion could exist. One wanted this, another wanted that. One woman even went so far to say that the devil's money helped build it." [2] Once the church was built, on Sundays the Youngs would load their piano into their wagon to bring it along to play at the services.

A Sunday school was organized, and the church became the locus of many adjunct activities such as the Ladies Aid Society, the Women's Missionary Society, church suppers, annual picnics, concerts, bible classes, etc

By 1900, the church was becoming a tight squeeze for its community, so an addition was built, which added a kitchen and a space for the Sunday school. A division among the denominations was beginning to be felt in the community – not only in Springbank but in the neighbouring town of Calgary, and the ecumenical nature of the church was being tested. In 1909, the Canadian Methodist Church took the situation in hand and built a new church a bit further to the north. This created a challenge for Springbank, for it was not really large enough to support two separate churches. It soon became evident that the situation was impractical, so a move was initiated to unite the Methodist and Presbyterian congregations to a more efficient shared arrangement. In 1916, the Presbyterian church resolved that "it is in the best interest of all the people in the community, morally, socially and spiritually, that the two congregations of Springbank unite into one body." The Presbyterians invited the Methodists to "take such steps as are necessary to consummate such a union." The Methodists accepted, and for a period, services were held alternately back and forth between the two churches. This all took place about a decade before the official creation of the United Church of Canada in 1925.

But the community really could not support two churches and finally, in 1947, the older church was closed. The cemetery at the South Church site continued to be used for burials until the 1970s, when it was also closed and turned into a historic site.

The North Church has been expanded and updated over the years since, and it continues to be an active force in the Springbank community. It lies just north of the Trans-Canada, if you want to turn off at the Springbank Road exit and visit it.

Recreational Pursuits

Once the business of breaking land and looking after the necessities of life was under control, the settlers looked for ways to enjoy any free time they had. Church suppers and box socials took care of some social needs, but leisure activities developed in ways much beyond this.

For a ranching community, rodeo was an obvious pursuit where some friendly competition could be enjoyed. A sense of good-natured rivalry developed between cowboys working on the ranches and skilled men would pit themselves against each other in impromptu competitions. These developed into more organized "Jack-Pot" rodeos, in which steep entry fees were collected to provide prize money. A more formal Stampede was held in Jumping Pound in 1922 and 1923. The XC Ranch offered the use of their corrals, and horses and steers were gathered from surrounding ranches. Events included saddle bronc, bareback riding, steer riding and calf roping. By this time, rodeo was becoming a more serious business in the region, and many of the men moved on to compete in the Calgary Stampede which started in 1912.

Another popular pursuit was the hunt. This gentlemen's form of recreation was initiated by Captain Gardner. From an English family with a noble history, Meopham Gardner came to Canada in 1879 with the intention of joining the army. He served in the Riel Rebellion and eventually ended up in the Springbank area. There, he indulged his love of breeding and showing fine horses, and he organized his neighbours to join him in an informal hunt club. He acquired a pack of trained hounds and, lacking an abundance of foxes, chased after the coyotes. In the days before extensive fencing, the group of riders participating in the hunt, with the women in side saddle, would race across the country with each rider in pursuit of the brush (the tail) as a trophy of the day.

Polo was another passion that took hold in the rural areas around Calgary. Captain Gardner was also an active participant in this and played for the Elbow River team for many years. A polo club had also formed in Turner Valley and Cochrane, and teams took their competition seriously. This sport has continued to find active support in the Calgary region, and has since entered the realm of international competition.

These sporting events lent a sense of gentility to a sometimes rough and arduous life in the West. The rodeos, hunts and polo matches must have been a welcome break from the grim day-to-day business of ranching, and were anticipated with excitement by both participants and spectators.

Springbank Airport

Almost directly across the highway from Calaway Park is one of the busiest little airports in the country.

On November 1, 1927, six months after the first trans-Atlantic flight by Charles Lindbergh, a group of Calgarians interested in flying met and initiated what was to become the new incarnation of the Calgary Aero Club. The previous club had faded into oblivion, but the experiences of World War I had encouraged the Canadian government, through the Department of National Defence, to offer cash subsidies and loans of aircraft to groups that were willing to commit themselves to training pilots. The new club elected Frank McCall as its first president, and the first ground school was in place by the middle of November, with an enthusiastic group of more than 100 students enrolled for pilot training. By the end of that year, members had a total of 349 hours of flying on record, and one commercial and nine private pilots had been certified. Membership in the club was growing rapidly.

By this time, the Bowness Flying Field had proven inadequate to the demands of newer aircraft, so this activity was based out of the Banff Coach Road Airport, and later the Calgary Municipal Airport, northwest of central Calgary.

Calgary International Airport was opened (at the time named McCall Field) in 1938, and club activity relocated to that site. In 1946, the group changed its name to the Calgary Flying Club. But McCall Field was becoming increasing busy with large-scale international flights, and accommodating a busy schedule of small aircraft was becoming a challenge. The solution came in 1969, when the federal government selected a site in Springbank for a "reliever" airport to handle the light-aircraft traffic coming into Calgary.

The establishment of the airport meant the expropriation of a farmstead. The MacLaurin farm was purchased, their land becoming property of the Crown as Transport Canada set up shop. By 1971, the airport was open for business, and

One of the improvements that Springbank pursued was the extension of the north-south runway. The airport is 1,200 metres above sea level, and aircraft performance drops considerably with elevation. So on hot days many planes could fly only with limited loads, because the runway was too short for takeoff in those conditions. Thus a flight to Seattle, for example, which would normally be a direct flight, would have to be interrupted for a refuelling stop.

The runway extension also allowed for the exception to the Code B traffic limit that permitted a single category of larger planes to use the Springbank runway. Up to that time, the Alberta government had leases for its Forestry Air Tanker Bases in Pincher Creek and Rocky Mountain House, but it had found that it could not effectively fight fires in Banff and Kananaskis from these locations. It was seeking an additional location midway between them. Springbank was perfectly situated, and it became the third site for firefighting operations, using large Code C tanker aircraft. In wet years, these large craft may fly very infrequently, but in dry years the Forestry Air Base can be active 16 hours a day, every day. The current spread of the pine-beetle infestation from B.C. into Alberta and the controlled burns that are being conducted in connection with this puts the Forestry Base on an even higher level of alert.

Besides the runway extension, two other recent developments have upgraded the Springbank facilities considerably. The installation of an instrument landing system allowed

Aerial view of Springbank Airport, Calgary Airport Authority. Note the extended north-south runway, for the Forestry Air Tanker Base, located on its north-east corner.

the Calgary Flying Club based its activities from this new location.

By the 1980s, the federal government had become interested in getting out of the business of operating airports and commenced an airport divestiture program, and in 1997 Springbank was transferred from Federal control to the Calgary Airport Authority. It was designated a "Tier 2" Certified Aerodrome, which established certain standards for how airport operations would take place at the facility. In subsequent airport master planning the airport was limited to Code B type aircraft, which means planes smaller than the Dash 8 typically flown by Jazz Air, with one exception – read on...

all weather operations to take place under instrument flight conditions. Also, in 2003 Springbank became a border facility that provides Canada Customs services. How these services came into effect is interesting. Prior to the 9/11 terrorist attacks in the U.S., the airport had been testing management of entry into Canada through a program called CANPASS, by which a pilot could apply for special ongoing clearance status that is usually confirmed with a phone call on each entry. But 9/11 put that out the window. A method of international entry was still needed to meet demand, since Alberta had only four ports of entry (while B.C. had about 20), so it became necessary to add full Canada Customs services to the Springbank facility.

The airport now covers an area of 1,040 acres and has two paved runways of 1,524 and 1,043 metres, respectively. It operates 24 hours per day, year-round, seven days a week. In 2007, it was the seventh-busiest airport in all of Canada, and the second-busiest (after Calgary International) in Alberta. The original MacLaurin farmhouse still stands on the site, just behind the new control tower. It is now operated as a fly-in accommodation, called the Tie Down B&B.

Springbank
Airport control
tower, 2009

The Elusive Outlaw

For a period in the early 1900s, Springbank and the surrounding area were kept in a state of fear by the desperate actions of a slippery criminal who passed through the region several times, leaving a series of households gripped by terror. Ernest Cashel had started life as what we would now term a troubled youth. Born in Kansas, he was abandoned by his single mother when he was 14. He fended for himself on the streets and became a great aficionado of the popular dime-store novels about Nick Carter, a rough-and-ready western version of Sherlock Holmes. Cashel's other obsession was Jesse James, the American outlaw of the Wild West. As a writer in *Canadian Cattlemen* magazine commented, "He could not handily emulate the fictitious super-sleuth, Mr. Carter, so he compromised by doubling for the Missouri bandit, on a penny-ante scale."[3] Cashel moved around the American Midwest, gambling and stealing, and soon found himself in jail for larceny. Thus the pattern of his life continued. In 1901, he broke out of jail in Buffalo, Wyoming, was rearrested, broke out again, and headed for Canada.

Once in Canada, Cashel initially seemed to try to turn over a new leaf and abandon his criminal ways. He worked as a ranch hand, and also tried his hand at barbering. Yet Cashel soon returned to his old tricks and started forging cheques. One of his victims put together a few pieces of information and realized that the new barber in town was behind the forgeries, and the victim reported this to the police. Cashel was located, by then working on a ranch near Ponoka, where he had contacted his mother, who was working as a camp cook in the area. He was loaded on a train in shackles to be returned to Calgary. On the trip back, the North-West Mounted Police (NWMP) constable was impressed with Cashel's courteous demeanour and co-operative attitude, so the constable removed Cashel's shackles at a stop in Red Deer to allow him to walk into town for a bite to eat. Cashel continued to demonstrate co-operative and docile behaviour over dinner. Once they were back on the train, Cashel told the constable that he needed to use the bathroom and was released to do this. The constable eventually concluded that Cashel seemed to be taking a very long time to go about his business and return. On investigation, the NWMP in charge of Cashel forced the door on the carriage bathroom and found only some bits of the prisoner's clothing inside. Cashel had jumped from the window of the moving train and was long gone.

He was free again, although somewhat battered from his landing from the train window. Cashel approached a farm near Lacombe, where he introduced himself as Bert Ellsworth and claimed that he'd been injured by being thrown from his horse. The family put him up for the night, fed him, and gave him fresh clothing, then loaned him a horse, which he promised to return the next day. Of course, there was no sign of Cashel or the horse the next day – or the following week. By the time the family finally reported the incident to the police, Cashel had headed east. This time he stayed with Isaac Rufus Belt, a quiet man of about 60 who farmed alone in that region. The next appearance made by Cashel was back in Lacombe to trade a saddle, bridle, and $10 in exchange for a horse and cart. Unfortunately for Cashel, the saddle had "I R Belt" stamped on it, so when Belt's brother-in-law reported a week later that Belt was missing, the connection was made. A search proved that a gun was also missing from Belt's farm, as well as a $50 U.S. note that Belt was known to have kept handy for times of need.

A manhunt was then on for the suspected murderer. The man who had bought the monogrammed saddle recalled that the seller had inquired about the most direct route to the U.S., and another man connected a man of Cashel's description with a purchase of a train ticket to the coast. Constable Alexander Pennycuick of the NWMP was put on the case,

and he chased a man first to Vancouver, next to Seattle on another clue, and finally to a town in Oregon. There, it turned out that his quarry was indeed similar in appearance to Cashel, but different in height and age. This poor soul, captured and interrogated in a jail in Oregon, explained that he was simply on the run from some "woman trouble" in Alberta and knew nothing of Belt's disappearance.

It turned out that Cashel had stayed much closer to the scene of the crime. He had turned up briefly near the Sarcee Reserve, calling himself Nick Carter (after the protagonist

of his favourite tales), and he had used the $50 U.S. note to have some young Metis lads buy him ammunition. From there he moved into the Springbank and Jumping Pound area, where he roamed around for some time. He stopped at the Thompson farm and asked to be put up for the night, heading out again first thing in the morning. He is said to have stopped at the homestead of Charlie Smith (now Rudiger Charlais), where he was almost caught. Yet he eluded his pursuers once more. Cashel's horse went lame, so he stopped at the ranch of Glen Healy to borrow another, saying that he needed it to catch his own mount, which had taken off. Of course, the borrowed horse was never returned. Next, Cashel moved further west, where he broke into a house, stole a diamond ring, and jumped onto a train to the Canmore area. There he was recognized by the stationmaster when he tried to cash a cheque. Cashel was again arrested – to the great relief of Constable Pennycuick, who had been under escalating pressure to get his man. Cashel was then returned to Calgary, where he was found to be in possession of the missing diamond ring and a pair of trousers resembling ones owned by the missing Belt. Although Cashel was strongly suspected of killing Belt, no body had been found. What evidence did exist was not sufficient to nail him for murder, so he was charged only with theft and given three years of hard labour. But shortly after this, a headless corpse was found in the Red Deer River and identified as Belt by a deformed toe he had suffered due to an axe wound. The bullets in the body matched those of the gun Cashel had been carrying, so Cashel was brought back to court on a much more serious charge. The jury deliberated for all of 35 minutes before finding him guilty, and Cashel was sentenced to hang on December 15, 1903.

But, astonishingly, the story still wasn't over. Rumours soon spread that a group of mobsters was coming north to spring Cashel. Some even claimed that Butch Cassidy and his Hole-in-the-Wall gang were part of the rescue posse. But the only person who turned up was Cashel's brother John, coming to say farewell to his sibling in jail. Still, that was all Cashel needed. John managed to slip his brother a pair of pistols, and the prisoner made quick use of them to free himself. "Nick Carter" Cashel was at large once more.

A huge search was organized. The NWMP called in men from other detachments, and even swore in local ranchers and Indians as "special constables" to assist in the hunt. A reward of $1,000 – a small fortune at the time – was posted for Cashel, dead or alive. The *Calgary Herald* covered the event extensively, and Cashel became a kind of media star. According to some reports, Cashel seemed to revel in the attention and started leaving notes at the houses where he stopped to steal things. He was said to have even written a letter to the *Herald*, saying that they should send the hangman home because Cashel expected he would be living a little longer. A state of hysteria reigned in the area where Cashel had made his presence felt. Women in Springbank barred their doors, and farmers made sure that their guns were working and handy.

The outlaw was free for 45 days before someone reported a man of his description hanging around an abandoned building east of Calgary. The site was surrounded and an officer went in to look for Cashel. A bullet zinged by the head of the officer, who beat a hasty retreat. Then there was an exchange of gunfire. Cashel refused to come out, so finally the building was set on fire. This forced him out of the building, and Cashel claimed loudly that he was sick of the whole business. He was hanged in Calgary on February 2, 1904 at the age of 21. It is said that after the event the hangman went to a local bar and sold souvenir pieces of the rope he had used to hang the notorious criminal.

The comments in Cashel's last letter reflect sadly back to the rough start he'd had in life. He may have felt this had given him no opportunities to avoid this destiny, because of how

---

Cashel wrote in a letter a few days before his hanging:

"People in General
On the day of account it will be found that men have cared more in judging the honesty of others then an any one thing else. Not even religion accepted. Many a man has been condemned and had the stigma of dishonesty fixed upon him because misfortune disabled him from paying his just debt. Will stand acquitted by the judge of quick and dead whilst others often dishonest hearts and actions undetected by man.

E. Cashel
N.W.M.P. Police Barracks"[4]

Richardson's ground squirrel

"misfortune disabled him" from making a better go of it. The comments of NWMP Constable Neil Nicholson supported this view. He wrote in his recollections of the event: "I sat in the cell with him as death watch on at least one occasion, and he talked with me very freely about his escapades. I may say here that Cashel didn't have the appearance nor the manners of a criminal. He was boyish looking and friendly. When he stayed with the Driggs family, he must have impressed them as an honest boy. Also, his staying with Mr. Belt would indicate that he had made a favourable impression on him, too. After his escape, he was able to impress the rancher at Springbank to the extent that he and his wife left him at their house when they went to church in Calgary. In my opinion, Cashel was not a born criminal, but being brought up in an environment of crime, he thought it was smart to be a killer."[5]

Wildlife Spotting: The Little Critters By (and On) the Road

During the spring and early summer, the drivers face the hazard of dodging little critters that seem set on making-suicidal forays onto the road. The remains of those that lost this game of chicken mark the asphalt, and lure scavengers such as crows or ravens to play their own game of chicken. People commonly refer to these animals as "gophers," and sometimes as "prairie dogs." They are neither. The only real gopher in this area is the pocket gopher (*Thomomys talpoides*), which lives its short life almost entirely underground and is seldom seen. And prairie dogs don't live in this region at all. Our roadside critters are Richardson's ground squirrels (*Spermophilus richardsonii*), a member of the squirrel family. They are common throughout the foothills in open grasslands, and particularly on the grassy verges of roads. They are about 28 cm long, and are frequently seen standing in "tent peg" position, upright on their haunches, surveying their surroundings. They are wise to keep a sharp eye out, for they are a preferred food for many birds and other animals.

Richardson's ground squirrels are a brown-buff colour with a slightly peppered effect over their head, back and tail. They do not live in colonies, as some other ground squirrels do, but are highly social and are commonly seen in small groups. After the young have grown and gained some independence by late spring, they are encouraged to leave home and set up their own digs. So they start looking for a hard, even surface to start their burrow. To these animals, roads look as if they might offer some good terrain – seeming to be worth checking out – with predictable results...

The hibernation pattern of Richardson's ground squirrels is interesting. They store seeds and grasses in their burrows. But being true hibernators, they probably don't eat much through the winter, instead retaining these reserves for a good start in the spring. You may observe a great decrease in their numbers by mid-summer – and that isn't just because so many have been smeared on the road. The adult males go into a sort of early retirement at the end of July, called "estivation," while the adult females head underground about a month later. Biologists theorize that there is more benefit from hibernating longer and thereby surviving to breed the next year than from remaining active and taking a greater risk of becoming dinner to a hawk or coyote. The juveniles have longer to play on the roads, and those that survive don't go into hibernation until mid-fall.

Wildlife Spotting: Better Buteo Recognition

A hawk on a fencepost or soaring above a field is a common sight along the highway, and you can be fairly certain that it is one of two species: Red-tailed (*Buteo jamaicensis*) or Swainson's (*Buteo swainsoni*). There are other possibilities, but they are much less likely. The Ferruginous hawk (*Buteo Regalis*) is rarer and tends to be further southeast, and the Rough-legged hawk (*Buteo lagopus*) only migrates through in March and October.

To make things difficult, both of our most populous hawks are similar in size (about 22 inches long, with a wingspan of about 50 inches). Also, both have a number of different colour variations, or "phases", which adds to the challenge. But here are some general points to consider in making an identification…

The Red-tailed hawk, as its name suggests, has a reddish upper tail. It is lighter when seen from below, with a discrete white band on the base. The Swainson's tail is creamy with fine dark barring. The Red-tailed hawk frequently has a belly band of darker streaks around its middle, while the Swainson's commonly has a dark bib on its chin and upper chest. If you are watching them soaring above you, look at the leading edge of the wing – the Red-tailed hawk generally has a more evident dark bar here. Also, the Swainson's wings are a bit more pointed, and it tends to hold them in a slightly more upwardly tilted posture in flight. Subtle differences – but lots of repeated observation and checking key identifying points helps you get familiar with the big birds.

These hawks may share a summer habitat, but they head to different destinations for the winter. Red-tailed hawks only fly down to the U.S. for the cold months. Swainson's hawks make a truly marathon migration all the way to the southern part of South America. Sadly, their numbers have been badly impacted by insecticides on their wintering grounds.

Top left: Red-tailed hawk, Tso Dho Nimh (SXC Images)

Top right: Swainson's hawk, D. Ditchburn

Hawks in flight: Red-tailed on left and Swainson`s on right

Roadside
Memorial, 2009

Roadside Memorials

One of the challenges in writing about sights along the highway is that some of them are transient. If a mountain is pointed out, it is likely to be there for as long as this book is available. But cultural phenomena are more subject to change. I inject this discussion of roadside memorials here because at the time of writing one was located here.

I do not recall seeing these memorials along highways in my youth. They seem to have sprung up a couple of decades ago. They may have originally had Catholic connections, and in North America first appeared in the Latin American cultures of the American Southwest. "The purpose of these small, white crosses at the roadside was to mark the rest areas for funeral procession pallbearers travelling by foot from the church to the graveyard. These sanctified, holy rest areas, which are called *Descansos* (Spanish for "resting place"), have since evolved into markers of the location of traffic fatalities by the side of the road."[8]

Roadside memorials recognize the death of someone as due to a traffic accident. They are not restricted to highways – I have noticed a number of them at intersections in the City of Calgary as well. They generally consist of a wreath or flower arrangement, and sometimes mementos such as stuffed animals or figurinesand possibly a written message.

A number of sociological studies connect the rise of these sites with the decline of organized religion, the theory being that they are erected as a secular way to manage the grief of a sudden and violent loss. Although this may be true in some cases, many of the memorials incorporate direct religious references. Other studies link this phenomenon to the increased tendency toward very public displays of emotion (particularly grief). Perhaps this is the response of a society accustomed to expressing every thought and feeling in a blog or through Facebook. People may be interested in making their loss public to give it greater significance, and to tmake it more communal in nature. At some sites, the public does participate by adding elements to the memorial, scattering flowers and other "offerings". Or perhaps families and friends who have suffered the loss of a loved one in a violent incident simply want to erect a visible warning to others.

Do they serve to encourage drivers to attend to their own driving safety? Or do they offer a distraction that increases the hazard? A study conducted by Richard Tay at the University of Calgary examined this question with the intention to advise policy-makers on the subject. He erected a number of mock memorials and observed the results. His data indicated that the number of drivers indulging in risky behaviour decreased noticeably in the presence of a memorial. An online survey found that 60% of the respondents supported the memorials.

Some regions have implemented restrictions on roadside memorials. British Columbia has a policy that states that "the Ministry of Transportation allows placement of roadside memorials within provincial right-of-way at, or near, the accident site. Roadside memorial markers should not be a hazard to those using or maintaining a highway. The sole authority to remove a memorial marker resides with the District Manager, Transportation."[6]

Most Canadian provinces are still pondering how to address the issue, but several American states have taken a stand. Montana and California allow them only if alcohol was involved in the incident, while other stateslimit the length of time they can be left in place. Ironically, much of the concern in establishing policies centres on the risk to the individuals who are erecting the memorials, and may expose themselves to danger in high-traffic zones that have already been proven dangerous.

Our route west on Highway One does not go through the reserve of the *Siksika* (Blackfoot) – their reserve lands lie to the east of Calgary. The Trans-Canada runs about forty kilometres north of the *Tsuu T'ina* (Sarcee) reserve west of the city. However, the land between the city and the mountains was part of the territory occupied by these and other tribes in the past. In more recent history, the Stoney Nakoda lived and hunted over this region, and I will discuss this tribe as the highway crosses through their reserve further to the west. The *Ktunaxa* (Kootenay) once occupied both the eastern and western slopes of the Rockies, but the combined pressure of the warlike Blackfoot and the arrival of the Stoney Nakoda pushed them west of the divide. The *Ktunaxa* now live mainly along the Rocky Mountain Trench area of eastern British Columbia. Understanding something about the different tribal groups and how they affected, and were affected by, the arrival of white people and settlement of this area is integral to understanding the history of this region.

It is hard to specify the boundaries between traditional tribal lands. They probably varied with the seasons as groups moved among hunting and camping grounds, and according to the current relationships among the tribes. Most tribes gave a wide berth to the lands occupied by the Blackfoot, whose society occupied much of the open grasslands where the buffalo thrived. They were a populous, aggressive people who violently opposed any incursion into their territory. Even early fur traders met with a cool reception. One of the reasons that early trade and exploration routes through the west tended to go further north through Fort Edmonton and the Athabaska or Yellowhead passes was to avoid the hazards of travelling through Blackfoot lands. The Stoney Nakoda stayed well into the foothills and avoided confrontations. And the *Tsuu T'ina* also tended to hug the eastern plains, and maintained a cautious truce with the Blackfoot.

The Blackfoot Confederacy

Marius Barbeau, who spent a great deal of time among the Indians in the early 1900s recording their stories and observing their customs, made a very descriptive comment about the Blackfoot. He said that "the Blackfeet were the Bedouin of the prairies. Their numbers and boldness gave them the ascendancy over other nations, and they never relented in the defence of their vast domains."[1] They were indeed a fierce people, closely tied to the plains, entering the mountains only rarely to collect poles for their tepees or

Siksika warriors on horseback, 1907, Canada. Patent and Copyright Office / Library and Archives Canada / C-019089

Piikani on horseback, no date, Edward S. Curtis / Library and Archives Canada / C-019988

to gather coloured earth for paint. The coloured pigments were important to their culture, as they developed a complex pictographic art form and decorated many items such as their tepees, skins, and other objects with elaborate designs. Many of these designs tell detailed stories of the exploits and conflicts of their braves and chiefs. The Blackfoot were less affected by the fur traders because their hostility largely kept the traders away, and also because they lived in an area that did not provide a richness of furs. There were not a lot of beaver pelts to be had on the bald prairie, so there was little motivation for the traders to push the issue.

The Blackfoot speak a language of the *Algonkian* group. They are thought to have moved west from the Great Lakes region and are probably one of the earliest of the modern tribal groups to move into Southern Alberta. In their own language they are the *Saukuitapix*, but they are most commonly known by the names of the individual bands, which have a great deal of autonomy. These are the *Siksika* (Blackfoot band), *Kainai* (Bloods), and *Piikani* (Peigan).

The origin of the different bands is accounted for in a Blackfoot legend. At one time, this group of people was constantly under attack from all other tribes around them. In order to effectively deal with this harassment, they decided to divide into three groups, each of which would concentrate on fighting back against enemies coming in from one of the three areas. One of the groups headed north to confront the Crees. A second group went south and into the mountains to fight against the tribes there (probably the *Ktunaxa*). Finally,

a group moved to the southeast and headed off the combined forces of the Crow and Sioux coming from that direction.

Time passed, and a man who had been with the group fighting the Crees in the north decided locate the other two groups. He made his way southeast first, struggling through prairie fires that ravaged the area. The man found the band of Indians that had been sent in that direction, but an atmosphere of anarchy had invaded the group, for each person he met there claimed to be a chief. So he called that group "Many Chiefs" – or *Akainai*, which evolved into the name *Kainai* (Bloods). They, in turn, called him *Sik-sikah'* ("Blackfoot") because the fire had blackened his moccasins. The traveller went on to find the group that went to the mountains and discovered that they had become slothful. The women were no longer tanning the hides correctly, and thus many of the garments were made of poor leather with bits of hair and meat still stuck to it. Thus the traveller gave the name *Apikuni* (or "Scabby Hides") to this disappointing group. This morphed over time into *Piikani* (Peigan).

The vast lands of the Blackfoot territories were loosely divided into areas in which each band tended to concentrate. The *Siksika* used the vast area over the plains to the east, while the *Kainai* were the group found most commonly in the strip nearer the mountains, generally to the southern end of their lands. The *Piikani* area also moved between the plains and the foothills. The population of this band was most drastically reduced over the years by introduced diseases. At the time of Treaty No. 7 in 1877, there were only about 700 of them left, and after the influenza epidemic of 1918-19, the number of *Piikani* living on the reserve numbered only about 250.

The Tsuu T'ina (Sarcee)

The *Tsuu T'ina* people are a part of the *Athapaskan* language group, and it is believed that they were once connected to the Beaver tribe in the north, moving south several centuries ago. We know that they were in this area by the end of the 17th century. There is a legend among the *Tsuu T'ina* of a time when they were travelling in the north and had to cross a great frozen lake. A young boy in the group spotted something sticking out through the ice in the middle of the lake and decided that he wanted it. His grandmother grasped the object and with a great heave pulled it free from the ice. To the group's horror, it turned out that the object was one of the horns of a gigantic monster that lived in the lake, and the people all scattered to try to save themselves. Some of them ran to the north and made their way home. Others fled south, were then unable to reunite with the others and had to make a new life for themselves in the lands to the south.

Once on the plains, they would have had to contend with the powerful Blackfoot, with whom they were fortunately able to form an alliance that gave them some protection from other hostile tribes. The nomadic tribes of the prairies, whose lives followed the buffalo and depended on these animals that provided for all their needs, were very territorial. Confrontations between competing enemy groups frequently led to violent conflict. Complex alliances were formed, and organized raids and outright warfare were not uncommon. Coming under the shelter of what came to be known as the Blackfoot Confederacy was a huge advantage for the *Tsuu T'ina*.

The *Tsuu T'ina* population was never large. Their numbers were estimated to be about 1,400 when Captain John Palliser arrived to explore the area in 1857. By 1877 (according to the population count for the signing of Treaty No. 7), the *Tsuu T'ina* had dwindled to only 255 individuals. When they were forced onto their reserve in 1880, they were only 160 people. Gradually their population began to increase again, and by the 21st century there were more than 2,000 people on the reserve, and more living away from it.

Known as the Sarcee by the white people from early contact, the people have reclaimed their own name for themselves: *Tsuu T'ina*, which means "Many People." The word "Sarcee" came from the Blackfoot word for "hardiness."

Plains Indian Culture and the White Man's Arrival

As already mentioned, the tribes that lived on the Great Northern Plains were totally dependent on a buffalo-based economy. When you consider the list of items that were derived from the buffalo, it is easier to understand how

Tsuu T'ina Indian Assinaitappi and his wife, ca. 1903-1936, C.W. Mathers / Canada. Dept. of Indian Affairs and Northern Development/ Library and Archives Canada / C-006934

essential they were to the plains peoples. Obviously, buffalo meat was the main source of food. Their hides became clothing and shelter, rawhide became containers and a robust twine, and their bones made tools and handles. The horns were carved into spoons, hooves were turned into rattles for use at ceremonies, and even the tail was used as a fly whisk. No part was wasted, and the people regarded the buffalo as a great gift from their sun spirit.

All the plains tribes competed for access to hunt the buffalo, which at the time were spread all across the prairies. Buffalo jumps and pounds were used into historical times, but the advent of guns and horses (which arrived in Alberta through trade and raiding by the early 1700s, even before the white man had started to move in to the area) changed the way the Indians hunted. With horses and new weapons, the massive effort of organizing a communal hunt and then the huge task of processing a great number of buffalo at once began to shift toward hunting individual buffalo by running them down and shooting them, one at a time. This was one factor that changed the social dynamic of the plains.

Besides hunting methods, the traditional patterns of rivalry and occasional warfare among the tribal groups became more lethal with the white man's weapons. Though there had always been warfare among the Indians, when

Kitsipimi Otunna, Tsuu T'ina, ca. 1903-1936, C.W. Mathers/ Canada. Dept. of Indian Affairs and Northern Development / Library and Archives Canada / C-006933

As a final blow to the plains Indians, by the 1870s it was becoming apparent that the buffalo were rapidly being. Many scholars are quick to blame the Indians with their new rifles, but the white "hunters" shooting buffalo in massive numbers from moving trains for easy cash were the greatest cause of these animals' demise. There was a huge demand for the buffalos' tough hides to serve as drive belts for the booming industrialization of Eastern North America and of Europe. Their bones were collected and ground up for fertilizer, and people reported piles of bones the size of houses stacked beside the railway tracks awaiting pickup. The plains Indians, having no other food source to turn to, were becoming desperate, and some were beginning to starve to death.

The Indians were staggering under the combined effects of warfare, disease, alcohol and starvation. Their dire situation was sadly described by a Salish chief (whose people lived further to the west) to the explorer David Thompson in 1812: "We have now twenty tents of women who have no husbands, with their children whose fathers are in the Land of the Spirits, and as many tents of aged women whose sons have fallen in battle."[3] The Indians were demoralized, dispirited, frightened and angry, which made the situation increasingly volatile. Something had to be done.

limited to hatchets and bows and arrows the consequences were less horrific. Also, the concept of personal ownership and individual possessions was a new factor in tribal societies, which had operated more communally in the past. Raids to steal horses became a new dimension in tribal conflicts.

Adding to this were the waves of epidemics – mostly smallpox, but measles, scarlet fever, and other diseases killed many as well. There was a terrible smallpox outbreak in 1780, and again in 1837, with the latter wiping out two-thirds of the Blackfoot population and large numbers of people in other tribes. By the late 1830s, the Hudson's Bay Company had initiated a vaccination program against the disease, but much damage had already been done.

As well as warfare and disease, the whiskey trade in Western Canada in the early 1870s was a disaster for the native population. Enterprises such as Fort Whoop Up in Southern Alberta provided firewater in exchange for furs. Father Constantine Scollen, a Catholic missionary who worked among the Blackfoot, described the effect of the whiskey trade: "The fiery water flowed as freely as the streams running from the Rocky Mountains, and hundreds of the poor Indians fell victim to the white man's craving for money, some poisoned, some frozen to death whilst in a state of intoxication, and many shot down by American bullets."[2]

Treaty No. 7

In 1875, Rev. Scollen of the Calgary mission wrote to Alexander Morris, Lieutenant-Governor of Manitoba:

"In the summer of 1874, I was travelling amongst the Blackfeet. It was painful to me to see the state of poverty to which they had been reduced. Formerly they had been the most opulent Indians in the country, and now they were clothed in rags, without horses and without guns. But this was the year of their salvation; that very summer the Mounted Police were struggling against the difficulties of a long journey across the barren plains in order to bring them help. This noble corps reached their destination that same fall, and the magic effect put an entire stop to the abominable traffic in whiskey with the Indians. Since that time the Blackfeet Indians are becoming more and more prosperous.

They are now well clothed and well furnished with horses and guns. During the last two years I have calculated that they have bought two thousand horses to replace those they had given for whiskey. They are forced to acknowledge that the arrival of the Red Coats has been to them the greatest boon. But, although they are externally so friendly to the Police and other strangers who now inhabit their country, yet underneath this friendship remains hidden some of the dread which they have always had of the white man's intention to cheat them; and here, excellent governor, I will state my reasons for believing that a treaty should be concluded with them also at the earliest possible date.

1.   The Blackfeet are extremely jealous of what they consider their country, and never allowed any white man, Half-breeds, or Crees to remain in it for any length of time; the only reason they never drove the Americans off, apart from their love of whiskey, was their dread of the Henri rifle.

2.   They have an awful dread of the future. Their think that the Police are in the country not only to keep out whiskey traders, but also to protect white people against them, and that this country will be gradually taken from them without any ceremony. This I can certify, for although they may not say so to others yet they do not hide it from me.

3.   Numbers of people are settling around Fort McLeod and Fort Calgary in order to farm, raise stock, etc. This will probably drive the buffalo away through time from the ordinary hunting grounds, and if so, the Blackfeet, being the most helpless Indians in the country, and unaccustomed to anything else but hunting buffalo, would suffer extremely.

4.   The settlers also are anxious that a treaty be made as soon as possible, so that they may know what portions of land they can hold without fear of being molested.

5.   The Blackfeet themselves are expecting to have a mutual understanding with the Government, because they have been told of it by several persons, and namely Gen. Smyth last year.

P.S. – I am also aware that the Sioux Indians, now at war with the Americans, have sent a message to the Blackfeet tribe, asking them to make an alliance offensive and defensive against all white people in the country."[3]

In Central Alberta, the situation with the Indians had been settled with Treaty No. 6, signed in 1876. This agreement had been made with the Cree, *Chipewyan* and Assiniboine tribes. Other tribes in the area had watched the process with interest. The Indian population was fully aware that they were in a desperate situation. They knew that unless some form of agreement could be reached, they were likely to starve for lack of a means of making a living without the buffalo, and ultimately to lose their land to the encroaching settlers. They were motivated to protect their culture, to establish peaceful relations with the government of the white man, to protect their land from settlement by the newcomers, and to find a new means of sustenance for themselves. They had a large and worrying list of concerns for their future.

Furthermore, many of the groups had lost their strongest leaders through the epidemics of previous years, and were being led and counselled by new and inexperienced leaders. Their disadvantaged position must have been hugely apparent to the treaty negotiators – thesituation could not possibly have been perceived as proceeding on a level playing field.

The three tribes of Southern Alberta came together in the fall of 1877 – the Stoney Nakoda, the Blackfoot and the *Tsuu T'ina*. It took some time to assemble enough of the Indians

Buffalo bones gathered from the Prairies, ca. 1880 – 1890, Library and Archives Canada / PA-066544

Crowfoot addressing the Marquis of Lorne; pow-wow at Blackfoot Crossing, Bow River, September 10, 1881, Library and Archives Canada, Acc. No. 1984-45-213

The references that the Indians brought to Blackfoot Crossing in 1877 for the negotiation and signing of their treaty were a world apart from those who were orchestrating the treaty.

In terms of material promises, the treaty would grant $12 per man, woman, and child at the time of the treaty signing; $5 per person annually into the future (the amount still paid today); for every chief, a suit of clothes, a silver medal, a flag, more money and a new "treaty suit" every three years; and land of one square mile per five persons as a reserve. The terms were rather incomprehensible when translated into the native languages, but the Indians were in a desperate situation and the white negotiators held all the good cards.

Most of the Indians at the negotiations looked to Chief Crowfoot of the Blackfoot for leadership, and he deliberated long and hard on the best action for his people. Finally, after five days of deliberation, on September 22, 1877, Crowfoot said to the white officials: "I hope that you look upon the Blackfeet, Blood and Sarcees as your children now, and that you will be indulgent and charitable to them. They all expect me to speak now for them, and I trust the Great Spirit will put into their breasts to be a good people – into the minds of the men, women, and children, and their future generations. The advice given me and my people has proved to be very good. If the police had not come to the country, where would we all be now? Bad men and whiskey were killing us so fast that very few, indeed, would have been left today. The police have protected us as the feathers of the bird protect it from the frosts of winter. I wish them all good, and I trust that all our hearts will increase in goodness from this time forward. I am satisfied – I will sign the treaty."[5] The other chiefs also accepted the terms of Treaty No. 7, as they understood them, and one by one each agreed to the document by signing an X. The agreement freed about 130,000 square kilometres for settlement, and gave about 3,600 square kilometres in return as reserves among the different tribes.

Father Scollen, witness to the events at Blackfoot Crossing, reflected on what had transpired: "Did these Indians, or do they now, understand the real nature of the treaty made between the Government and themselves in 1877? My answer to this question is unhesitatingly negative, and I stand prepared to substantiate this proposition. It may be asked: If the Indians did not understand what the treaty meant, why

to make a reasonable representation because the meeting had been called during the peak of the fall hunt. They gathered on the banks of the Bow River, at Blackfoot Crossing near the present site of Cluny on the Siksika Reserve. There they heard the presentation of what they were being offered. David Liard, Queen Victoria's representative at the treaty, addressed them: "… now the Queen has sent Col. [James] McLeod and myself to ask you to make a treaty. But in a few years the buffalo will probably all be destroyed, and for this reason the Queen wishes to help you to live in the future in some other way. She wishes you to allow her white children to come and live on your land and raise cattle, and should you agree to this she will assist you to raise cattle and grain, and thus give you the means of living when the buffalo are no more. She will also pay you and your children money every year. Which you can spend as you please. By being paid in money you cannot be cheated, as with it you can buy what you think proper."[4]

The number of language groups that came together to negotiate the terms of the treaty was cumbersome enough to make adequate translation a formidable task. Also, these were a people who had no tradition of legal contracts, and no concept of a binding legal document that could be carefully phrased to mean certain things and not others. They came from an oral tradition. And they had a history of communal mutual dependency, one in which negotiations about their affairs were worked out among the community, and in which what was stated had to carry great weight and commitment.

Left: Chief Chiniquay (signatory for the Chiniki band of Stoney Nakoda), Glenbow NA 662-1

Crowfoot, Chief of the Blackfoot Indians, 1886, O.B. Buell / Library and Archives Canada / C-001871

did they sign? Because previously to the treaty they had always been kindly dealt with by the Authorities, and did not wish to offend them; and although they had many doubts in their mind as to the meaning of the treaty, yet with this precedent before them, they hoped that it simply meant to furnish them with plenty of food and clothing, and particularly the former, every time they stood in need of them; and besides this, many outside influences were brought to bear upon them."[6]

In the assignment of reserve lands, the Blackfoot (*Siksika*) tribe was given land at Blackfoot Crossing, 100 km west of Fort Calgary (near Gleichen). The Bloods received land between the St. Mary and Belly rivers south of Fort McLeod, and the *Piikani* were located on the Oldman River, 25 km west of Fort McLeod. The *Tsuu T'ina* were initially lumped together with the Blackfoot and given a part of the land within the latter tribe's reserve. This was a source of great friction between them. But Chief Bull Head persisted until he managed to negotiate a separate reserve for the *Tsuu T'ina* west of Calgary in 1881.

The Stoney Nakodas had representatives from their three bands at the treaty negotiations, and all three of their chiefs had their names recorded in Cree in the document. *Che-ne-ka* (John Chiniquay) signed for the Chiniki, *Mas-gwa-ah-sid* (Jacob Bearspaw) for the Bearspaw, and *Ki-chi-pwot* (Jacob Goodstoney) for the Jacobs band (later renamed the Wesley band). However, despite being distinct groups, they were all lumped together on one reserve west of Calgary, something that would cause ongoing grief for the Stoneys. We will examine their situation in more detail in Chapter 9, where Highway One passes through their reserve.

Settlers with covered wagons, 1910, Carl Engler / Bibliothèque et Archives Canada / PA-018755

The Settlers and the Indians

The period when settlers began to move into the area west of Calgary was one of huge adjustment for the Indian population. They were still reeling from the effects of starvation, alcohol, disease, and displacement, and the massive changes to their culture and lifestyle, as they were resettled into reserves. Within the lifespan of the elders, the white man had arrived on the scene, the Indians' traditional means of providing for themselves had diminished greatly, and they had found themselves struggling with forces such as completely unknown diseases and the whiskey trade. Then the North-West Mounted Police arrived in their midst. The Indians must have felt a measure of relief that some order was being established, but also awareness of the loss of control over their own lives that arrived with this force. The recognition that things would never again be as they had been, that the Indians' way of life was gone for good, and that their only hope was to agree to some form of contract with these foreigners, must have been a heart-wrenching process at the deepest imaginable level. The Indians were struggling to find a new way to live. Into this situation came the new arrivals wanting to set themselves up on their own plots of ground.

Considering this context, it is amazing how conflict-free the final two decades of the 1800s were. The settlers and the Indians seemed to regard each other more with mutual curiosity or fear than hostility. In the perception of the new arrivals, the Indians were a wild card in the already formidable land that the newcomers wanted to tame and make productive.

The Indians moved around the region being opened up for settlers as they continued to use their traditional routes between the newly established reserves and other communities. Jane Larrington and Jennie Stuart reminisced about their first encounters with Indians passing by their new homestead: "The Indians went along the trail and often camped on a spot across the Jumping Pound. They would sometimes come to the house and peer in the windows. In those days they looked very strange, and Uncle Will said they would take my brother. So I would try to hide him, sometimes in a big clothes basket, and cover him with newspapers. He yelled and resisted, so there was no doubt where he was."[7] Eventually, the old Morley Trail through Springbank was gravelled and became too hard on their horses' hooves.

Sometimes the Indians would approach the homesteads hoping to make trades for food. Food rations that had been provided under the terms of the treaty (and had initially saved the Indians from outright starvation) had gradually been discontinued. Many Indians were going hungry again. They would offer to trade moccasins, homemade buckskin gloves, or even fish they had caught in local creeks, for eggs, flour or other staples – or, best of all, salt pork.

Gradually, both parties became used to each other, and the Indians began to pick up employment on farms and ranches in the area. Many became proficient cowboys who were greatly valued by their fellow range men. Some individuals became particularly respected contributors to the ranching community and many were serious competitors on the rodeo circuit. Other opportunities were found by some of the Stoney Nakoda farther west, where they found employment in the lumber or mining operations, or with outfitters in the Banff area. They became an essential part of the fabric of the Bow Corridor.

"Driving the highway from Calgary into the mountains can be a dangerous experience. The highway itself is new, superbly engineered, adequately posted – the hazards are scenic rather than technical. The temptations to take your eye from the road ahead are frequent and almost irresistible, but resisted they must be, for the flow of traffic is sure to be heavy. Tourists swarm across the border into Southern Alberta and up the Fort McLeod-Calgary Trail to join the hordes from the East already pounding towards the mountains at 70 miles an hour. Unfortunately – and this is the only possible criticism of the Trans-Canada Highway between Calgary and Banff – lookouts are few, and the man behind the wheel must be content to observe in disconnected snatches the stupendous wall of mountains ahead." [1] *

As you drive over the first significant ridge, 16 kilometres into our trip west of Calgary, you crest the top to behold the first great panorama of the eastern edge of the Rocky Mountains. Spread before you is the great wall of peaks that must have been held in awe by the early inhabitants of the open plains, and must have thrilled and rather intimidated the early explorers.

This crest of land is called Towers Ridge, named after Frank Towers, who homesteaded in the area. He was born in England in 1848 and worked his way to Canada on a cattle boat at the age of 18. He got a job with the CPR and came west to lay rails across the prairie. He and his wife, Elizabeth, led an isolated life on their land for the first years, coming into town by wagon every six months to buy provisions.

* quote from Edward McCourt, who grew up on an Alberta homestead, taught literature at the University of Saskatchewan, and made a trip across Canada by car with his wife Margaret in the early 1960s. Some of his observations will appear occasionally in this book

Who was the First Non-native to See these Mountains?

As you crest this rise and look west toward the magnificent mountain vista, you may wonder, who was the first white man to be faced with the view of this magnificent wall of mountains rising so abruptly from the plains?

As usual, the hope of wealth was behind the first probes by the white men into the west. At the end of the 17th century, the Canadian West was still largely a blank on the map, and there were several different parties interested in exploring and exploiting what was to be found there. The French had already made some inroads, and their traders were benefitting from the flow of furs into the market. The Hudson's Bay Company (originally called The Governor and Company of Adventurers of England Trading Into Hudson's Bay) had been granted a Royal Charter by King Charles II in 1670 giving the new company "all lands that drained into the Hudson Bay." But the HBC was feeling a great deal of pressure, as other interested parties were making their presence felt. The company had to get out into that land soon. The HBC began sending explorers out to map the West, make contact with the Indians, and keep an eye out for alternative avenues for trade such as "mines, minerals, or drugs."

There is some controversy around the first possible sighting of the Rockies by a white person, but both possibilities are associated with the Hudson's Bay Company. Henry Kelsey, born in Greenwich, England, in 1667, entered service with the HBC while still in his teens, and over 30 years of service worked his way up from cabin boy to governor of various trading posts. We know from his journals that he was travelling into the prairies between 1690 and 1692. He was certainly the first white person to enter the lands that would become Alberta. His journals report the masses of buffalo and his encounters with grizzly bears – the first such accounts recorded by a white man.

How far west did Kelsey get? His journals are rather cryptic when it comes to descriptions of geography, and it does not help that some of the writing is done in poetic form, which makes it no easier to interpret. For example, the introduction to his 1691 journal reads:

"Gott on ye borders of ye Stone Indians country
I took possession on ye 10. Inst. July
And for my Masters I speaking for ym all
This Neck of land I Deering's Point did call
Distant from hence by Judgment at ye best
From ye house [York Factory] 600 miles south west
Through rivers wch runs strong with falls
Thirty-three Carriages [Portages] five lakes in all
The ground begins for to be dry, with wood
Poplo [Poplar] and Birch with Ash that's very good
For the Natives of that place wch knows
No use of better than their wooden Bows."

His mention of the Stone Indians, and in other places the "country of the Assiniboines," seems to imply that he was as far west as the lands of the Stoney Indians. Kelsey's journals mention learning of a "great wall of mountains," but he stopped short of saying that he had actually witnessed these mountains himself. The mystery remains.

Our second candidate, Anthony Henday (Hendey? Hendry? He was born on the Isle of Wight in England and worked as a fisherman – and, it is suggested, a smuggler. Charges against him for the latter may have encouraged to Canada. In 1754, Henday was taken on by the Hudson's Bay Company to join the HBC's ranks of explorers. (Presumably the company did not know about his criminal record.)

Henday was sent west with a group of Cree, who were returning that way after delivering furs to Fort York. They paddled up the Saskatchewan River, then proceeded along the Battle River on foot. Henday worried about encountering French traders – who might take him to be a spy. When he finally encountered some, they did threaten to seize him and send him to France, but were probably deterred by the large party of Indians in his company.

From here, Henday's route farther west is a little vague – partly because his original journals no longer exist, and the four existing copies are somewhat inconsistent. Also, an observation was made by his London employers that, "We apprehend Henday is not very expert in making Drafts with Accuracy or keeping a just Reckoning of distance other than by guess . . ."

Through this section of the trip, Henday wrote of encountering massive numbers of buffalo in herds so dense his party had to force its way through them. He was seeking to make contact with a group of Indians that he referred to as "*Archithinues*" – thought to be either *Atsinas* (Gros Ventres) or *Siksika* (Blackfoot). Henday met them in a location that would be just south of modern Red Deer. They smoked the peace pipe, sat around the fire, and dined on buffalo tongue. However, they were clear that they had no interest in trading, for their needs were already well provided for by the buffalo.

From here, Henday's party moved farther south toward what scholars have identified to be the present location of Innisfail. The mountains would have been visible from this point, but the copies of his journals bear no comment about such a vista on the horizon. This is a great mystery, because it seems certain it was within sight. Perhaps it is an omission of transcription, for we know that many things were left out. On December 24, however, Henday wrote of a view of the mountains: "I had an extensive view of the *Arsine Watchie* which will be the last this trip inland."[2] *Arsine Watchie*, or *Usine Wurche*, is the Cree name for the mountains, meaning "Shining Mountains."

Henday wintered by the camp of the "*Archithinue*," and by the following June he was back in Fort York to report unfortunately little success in drumming up trade for the company. He returned to the West several times in the following years, but seemed to be plagued with ill health, and, after one final sojourn in 1759, he had to curtail his travels. In 1762, Henday left the Hudson's Bay Company, feeling that he had not been granted sufficient recognition for his efforts.

These two men were followed in 1792 by Peter Fidler, who, although he may not have been the first white person to lay eyes on the mountains, was the first to mark them on a map and attach names to a few peaks. Fidler also came west in the service of the Hudson's Bay Company as a surveyor, and remained in the Company's service for many years. His journals note observations regarding such details as the tar sands in Northern Alberta, the chinook winds, and the use

of buffalo pounds by the Indians. Fidler collected extensive information about natural history as he travelled.

He met with great animosity from the rival North West Company, which made Fidler's efforts much more difficult by destroying his canoes and intimidating his crew. Much of his career was marked by the struggle to do his work in the face of the NWC's aggressive opposition. After years of dedicated service, in 1821 Fidler was informed that he was being retired as part of the merger between the HBC and the NWC. His health quickly failed and he died in 1822.

Fidler wrote of the mountains as being, "Awefully grand, stretching from s.s.w. to w.s.w. by compass, very much similar to dark rain like clouds rising up above the horizon in a fine summer's evening."[3] He assigned the English translation of the Indian name to Devil's Head and gave what we know as Mount Glasgow the name The Pyramid.

How Do Mountains Get Their Names?

Before starting to discuss specific mountains, let us consider how these peaks received the names by which they are now known. Names can be quite controversial, and can even become contentious enough that they are changed years after the original name was assigned.

Of course, most of the geographical landmarks had names long before anyone drew up official maps, but these were seldom officially assigned. Using the native name for a given peak was somewhat complicated because different Indian tribes had, of course, named the same place in a variety of languages – which one would be selected? In a few places, the early explorers noted Indian place names in their records, and those eventually became official. In other cases, a mountain might be named for the first person who had climbed it. Early surveyors are responsible for a great number of names.

Today, there are very specific procedures for assigning geographical names. In 1897, this process became governed by the Geographic Board of Canada. It is now under a provincial mandate, under the jurisdiction of the Alberta Historical Resources Foundation.

So what are these official criteria? Primary consideration goes to accurate identification – does the name fit the feature it describes? You can't name a pond a sea, or a hill a mountain. Effort is made to retain names that are established in local use. Duplication of names is avoided. And, although many of the peaks have historically been named after people, personal names are no longer considered, unless in exceptional circumstances.

Many of the names we know were applied by the men sent out to chart the wilderness and generate maps of the new regions in the West. These were people such as David Thompson (sent by the North West Company), members of the Palliser Expedition (such as James Hector), and George Dawson (of the Government of Canada Survey).

The Vista

Many of the mountains you can see from this vantage are identified on the drawings on these pages. A few of the peaks are worth more detailed examination here, as they will not be visible as we move farther west. I will discuss them in order from south to north. Some are not mentioned here because they will turn up in views from the highway later in the book.

Plateau Mountain — 2,514 m

Locally known as Flat Top, this mountain is named for the long surface that runs eight kilometres from north to south. The top surface is covered with patterned rock that takes the form of polygons of coarser material, a phenomenon thought to have resulted from cracking during cooling, causing the finer material to sift away from the cracks toward the centre of the shapes. This probably dates to the most recent ice age. There are two oil wells on the top of Plateau, drilled by Husky Oil.

Mount Burke — 2,545 m

Burke lies south of the Highwood Valley and is the second-tallest mountain in the Livingstone Range. It was named by a survey crew in 1919 for Denis Charles Burke, an NWMP veteran who ranched near the base of this mountain. An Alberta Forest Service fire lookout was built on the summit in 1929. David Birrell tells an interesting story about an incident there: "To protect the building and its inhabitant from lightning, steel cables ran from a post on the roof to a main cable which extended a mile [1.6 km] down the mountain to be grounded in moist earth. Thus the building was said to be safe if the telephone line which connected the lookout with the Forestry Station building below was disconnected. One lookout forgot to disconnect the phone. Entering through the phone line, a charge of lightning exploded the bed, leaving it in small pieces, and broke a hole in a window as the forgetful resident sat beside it. It is said that the lookout, who had admitted to being afraid of lightning before he went up, burst out the door and descended Mount Burke as quickly as possible, never to return."[5] This lookout was replaced by those on Raspberry Ridge and Hailstone Butte in 1963.

Holy Cross Mountain — 2,667 m

The reason for Holy Cross's name is better understood if you view it from farther south, where, given certain conditions during snowmelt, a cross of snow can be seen on the mountain face. The effect is rather fleeting and is not visible every year. Raymond Patterson, who was so critical of the names of many of the mountains in the Rockies, had his Buffalo Head Ranch at the base of this mountain.

Mount Head — 2,781 m

Connected to Holy Cross by a ridge, Mount Head was identified by this name on his 1860 map by John Palliser. The name refers to Sir Edmund Head, who was Governor General of the Province of Canada (present-day Ontario and Quebec) and was very supportive of Palliser's expedition. The name is coincidental, because when viewed from the prairies farther to the south, a profile of a head can be detected in the cliffs of the more eastern of the two summits.

Junction Mountain — 2,650 m

This mountain can be picked out by the triangle of white formed by the snowfield on its slopes. It was probably named after Junction Creek and has a fire lookout on its eastern end.

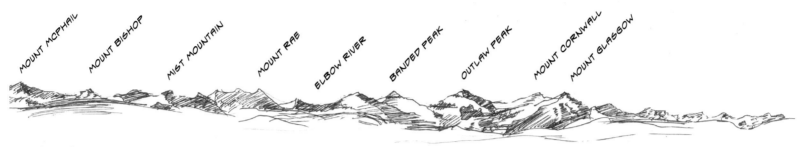

Gibraltar Mountain — 2,665 m

This peak was named for its supposed resemblance to the Rock of Gibraltar, the British territory that guards the entrance to the Mediterranean, because of its dramatic 700 metre cliff to the south side.

Mist Mountain — 3,138 m

Mist marks the southern end of Misty Range. It was named by G. Dawson in 1884, probably reflecting on the weather he endured while in the area. The name Mist may also be associated with the hot springs in Mist Creek Valley. The slopes are rich with fossils, especially horn coral.

Mount Rae — 3,225 m

This peak is named after British Arctic explorer Dr. John Rae, who made four trips into Northern Canada between 1833 and 1854 for the HBC, covering an amazing 36,000 km on foot. Rae located the final link (Rae Strait) to complete the Northwest Passage. While in the North, Rae lived off the land and learned from the Inuit – in contrast to many of the early explorers, who did not see the natives of the North as a helpful resource. In fact, Rae was the first one to learn of the fate of the Franklin Expedition (whose members had not benefitted from local knowledge) from the Inuit hunters, and reported their sad fate back to England. His news was ill received, especially the evidence of cannibalism among the party. Until Rae's report was verified by others, he suffered from being the bearer of this tragic news. In 1857, Rae moved to Canada and settled in Ontario. In 1864, he travelled west into the Rockies, surveying for the proposed telegraph line.

Mount Rae was said to have been named by Sir James Hector, but some think that because of its location it was more likely named by John Palliser. On its slopes is the most easterly mass of ice in this area of the Rockies, and the morning light on this white area makes the mountain stand out from its neighbours. The distinctive notch and northern triangular summit also help make it identifiable.

Banded Peak — 2,934 m

From this vantage, Banded Peak is the southernmost of the Glasgow Group, which also includes Outlaw Peak, Mount Cornwall, and Mount Glasgow. These mountains are located between the Elbow and Little Elbow rivers and, being joined by ridges, make a challenging four-summit day for ambitious scramblers. Banded Peak is one of the easiest mountains to identify, thanks to its sharp triangular shape and the black band created by the 30 metre cliff below the summit.

On his trip west in 1881, as well as writing a hymn inspired by the view (see Chapter 3), the Governor General of Canada, the Marquis of Lorne, sketched the Glasgow Group and published the image in his book about his trip west.

Outlaw Peak — 2,850 m

Unofficially named (you won't find it on the government maps) by Don Forest in 1974, Outlaw is the result of an error. Thinking that Banded Peak was actually "Bandit Peak," Forest thought that Outlaw would be an appropriate title for its neighbour. It used to be unofficially called Rustler Peak as well.

Mount Cornwall — 2,978 m; Mount Glasgow — 2,956 m

Next in line in the Glasgow Group, these two mountains are most easily talked about together. Both are named after British World War I warships, as are about 20 peaks in the Kananaskis region. Most of these names refer to ships that were a part of the Battle of Jutland in 1916 – but not these two cruisers. Their fame is from the Battle of the Falkland Islands in 1914 – where, together with *HMS Kent*, they pursued three German warships that were trying to escape toward Tierra del Fuego at the southern tip of South America:

Mount Putnik — 2,940 m

This peak was named in 1918 for Field Marshall Radomir Putnik of the Serbian Army, the Balkan country's Chief of General Staff during World War I.

Fisher Peak — 3,052 m

Fisher Peak is the highest peak in the Fisher Range, located between Barrier Lake and the Little Elbow River. It was named by Captain John Palliser for John Fisher, who was active in the Royal Navy prior to World War I.

Moose Mountain — 2,473 m

This is the closest mountain to Calgary of any visible in this panorama. It looks even larger from here than it actually is because its ridge runs perpendicular to the line of sight, on a north-south orientation, for six kilometres. Thomas Blakiston of the Palliser Expedition named it "The Family," but the name attached to it in 1949 is the one that gained official recognition. The Alberta Forest Service established a fire lookout here in 1929, and the present one is the third of the lookout buildings, still operating after 80 years. Moose Mountain Dome is a productive gas formation, and there are several gas wells on the mountain and in the valleys around it.

Moose Mountain is known for the extensive cave system contained in its rocky bowels. Over half a kilometre of passages have been mapped. It was discovered by Stan Fullerton in 1905 on the southern face of the mountain. At certain times of the year, spectacular ice formations decorate the interior of the cave system.

Mount Kidd — 2,958 m

Stuart Kidd arrived in Morley in 1907 to run the Scott and Leeson Trading Post. The Stoney Nakoda made him an honourary chief and gave him the name *Tah-Osa (Ta Otha)*, or "moose killer." The name was assigned to the mountain by geologist D. Bogart Dowling, who was part of a survey party that was provisioned by Kidd. Mount Kidd has two summits, 2.5 kilometres apart. There was a fire lookout on the ridge to the north, just below the summit, but it was removed in 1997 because of funding cuts and redundancy.

Mount Bogart — 3,144 m

Mount Bogart tends to hold the snow on its slopes, so it frequently shines white when its neighbours do not, making it stand out from the crowd. It is the second-highest peak in the Kananaskis range, and was called "The Pyramid" in 1858 by Thomas Blakiston of the Palliser Expedition. However, the name that has become official is the one honouring Dr. D. Bogart Dowling, a geologist with the Geological Survey of Canada who examined this area for coal and oil reserves. Dowling was equally interested in other topics, such as flora and fauna, and native history. He recorded a great deal of information about these topics, as well as notes about the rocks and minerals.

Bogart was first climbed by Katherine (Katie) Gardiner, daughter of an accomplished climber, who had cut her teeth in the Alps. She first came to the Rockies in 1929, and hired Walter Feuz as her guide. Gardiner returned to the Rockies for many years and climbed the peak now named after her in 1930.

Mount Sparrowhawk — 3,121 m

Connected to Bogart by a long ridge, Mount Sparrowhawk is not named for the falcon of that name but for another British warship, the *HMS Sparrowhawk*, a Royal Navy destroyer in the Battle of Jutland in World War I. The battle she was involved in was something of a fiasco. *Sparrowhawk* ended up being damaged by her sister ship, the *HMS Contest*, and had to be rescued. She was subsequently retired and sunk.

Mount Sparrowhawk was considered as a site for the 1988 Olympics but lost to Mount Allen. It remains a popular destination for backcountry skiers.

Mount Allen — 2,819 m

Made up of the Mesozoic rock that hosts rich coal formations, this mountain was appropriately named for Dr. J. A. Allen, who in 1912 became the first professor of geology at the University of Alberta. It was called *Chdse Tida Baha* (*Châ se Tîda*), or "Burnt Timber Hill," by the Stoneys. It was the site of a coal mine started in 1947, and a community called Kovach of about 100 miners and their families grew up on the banks of Ribbon Creek. Operations stopped in 1952 as coal prices fell, leaving a mine scar on the mountain's eastern side.

In Canada's centennial year of 1967, the Rocky Mountain Ramblers established the Centennial Trail traversing the summit of Mount Allen between Dead Man's Flats and Ribbon Creek. This site was selected over Sparrowhawk and other proposed sites as the location for the 1988 Olympic events. The Centennial Trail is closed each spring to protect lambing areas of bighorn sheep, who favour these slopes because they tend to remain free of snow. (I shall make no comment on the implications of this fact for the viability of a ski resort…)

Mount Fable — 2,702 m

This peak was named in 1947, based on a story about difficulties that were encountered during an attempt on the summit, but which were later disclaimed as a fable by a subsequent, successful party. Enough said.

Association Peak – 2,322 m

Nobody seems to know which association this peak might be named for. It is located between the headwaters of Old Fort Creek and the South Ghost River.

End Mountain – 2,420 m

Farther along the ridge from Association Peak, End Mountain was named in 1884 by surveyor J. J. McArthur for its obvious location – at the end of the ridge…

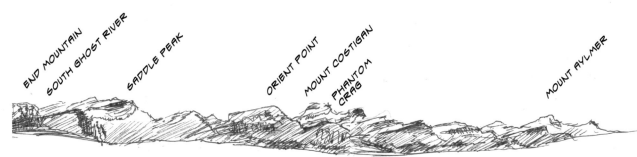

Saddle Peak – 2,831 m

There is some discrepancy about the name of this mountain, located between the valleys of Lake Minnewanka and the South Ghost River. Some claim that the name is for the saddle-like shape of the peak itself (as several other mountains in Southern Alberta have been named), but others claim that it is because of an abandoned saddle found below the summit.

Orient Point – 2,636 m

Although the story behind its moniker is undocumented, this peak must have been named for its significant location at the entrance to Devil's Gap, an important route into the mountains used frequently by the Indians for centuries.

Mount Costigan – 2,980 m

This peak is named after John Costigan, a senator from New Brunswick who visited the area. It is better known for its northeast buttress, Phantom Crag.

Phantom Crag – 2,332 m

This is a popular climbing destination, offering a fine multi-pitch route over broken limestone cliffs. It was named in 1958 in keeping with the ghostly theme of the Devil's Gap area. It is also known as the Devil's Fang.

Mount Aylmer – 3,162 m

Part of the Palliser Range, Mount Aylmer is on the northwest shore of Lake Minnewanka. It was named by Dominion Land Surveyor J. J. McArthur after his hometown of Aylmer, Quebec. McArthur worked as a surveyor between 1886 and 1893, made many first ascents in the Rockies, and probably had the most intimate knowledge of these mountains of any person at the end of the 19th century.

As you tear your eyes away from the mountain vista and focus back on the road, you soon reach the interchange with Highway 22 – also known as the Cowboy Trail. This road runs through the heart of ranching country, and at certain times of the year travellers are likely to see cattle drives and other ranch activities along this route. Highway 22 offers great exploration opportunities in both directions. Sites and events along the way emphasize the western theme and the associated cowboy culture and hospitality.

The Road to Bragg Creek

If you were to travel south of this intersection for about 15 kilometres, after crossing the Elbow River you would come to the hamlet of Bragg Creek. This community was named after brothers Albert Warren Bragg and John Thomas Bragg of Nova Scotia, who homesteaded in this area in 1894. It has long been a cottage community for Calgaryians, and it is a popular weekend destination for access to Kananaskis Country and Bragg Creek Provincial Park, and offers shopping and restaurants for visitors. Bragg Creek is also known for being where the popular CBC-TV series North of 60 was filmed during the 1990s.

Bragg Creek was also the location of the first Youth Hostel in North America. Started by sisters Mary and Catherine Barclay in 1934, the facility operated out of a tent for a few years before simple cabins were established on the site.

Our Lady of Peace Mission

Along this stretch of Highway 22, almost as far south as the Elbow River and a bit to the west, is a cairn that marks the location of the first church in Southern Alberta. (It's located at 10-24-4-5, for those who wish to practice their township and range skills.)

Catholic missionaries had been active farther north, where they ministered to the Indians near Hudson's Bay Company trading posts in what is now the Edmonton area. However, the area to the south, Blackfoot country, was considered too dangerous for the church to establish a foothold. Still, in 1845 a Jesuit missionary came north from the United States – "as far as the Bow River," according to his journals – and worked among the Blackfoot. He continued on up to Rocky Mountain House, pausing en route to baptize a group of Indians that he referred to as Stoneys in his journals. In 1862, Father Albert Lacombe was in the area – "as far as the Bow River," according to his notes – assisting the Blackfoot during one of the many waves of smallpox that swept through the native population in the West.

Even before the North-West Mounted Police arrived to stabilize an increasingly desperate situation, resulting from the combined effects of alcohol, disease, famine, and new weaponry, there were already a few individuals working among the Indians and trying to offer them some form of order to their lives. The missionaries posted to the early West must have possessed strong, independent, and courageous natures, as they entered what could easily have been hostile situations. They were very committed to bringing the word of their God to the native population and they must have presented themselves as a preferable alternative to the destructive influence of the opportunistic traders. Also,

Drawing of Our Lady of Peace mission by Richard Barrington Nevitt, ca. 1875, Glenbow NA 1434-40

the priesthood in 1873 and immediately set out among the Blackfoot. He baptized 67 of them that summer.

Alexis Cardinal, a Metis lay helper to the church, had been sent out the previous summer to build a log structure that would be used as the first mission, located where many of the Indians forded the Elbow River and near where they often set up their winter encampment. The mission was a simple building, with canvas-covered windows and a dirt floor. It was no more than 4½ metres in either dimension, and had a cross surmounting its rough roof. Later a tiny addition was made to serve as a chapel. The church was named Notre Dame de la Paix (Our Lady of Peace). Father Scollen ministered from this simple structure for two years.

In 1875, Father Scollen learned that the NWMP's "F" Troop was to be sent west to establish a post by the junction of the Bow and Elbow Rivers (which that year would become Fort Calgary). Understanding that this would become the focus for the local population, Scollen made the decision to move the mission near this spot. He loaded up the material goods from the original Our Lady of Peace mission and floated them down the Elbow to the Bow. When the NWMP troop arrived, they found Scollen already on the site, ready to set up his mission there.

It seems that the "Old Mission" was not entirely closed right away. Occasional use was made of the structure until it was fully abandoned in 1882. Nothing now remains of the old mission building except the chimney stones, which were used to build the memorial cairn. The place was declared a historic site in 1976, and the plaque on the cairn honours Father Scollen: "A zealous servant of God, he ministered to the dwellers of the plains during the hard times that saw the passing of their old ways of life. His name is affixed to Treaty No. 7, signed by the Blackfoot Confederacy in 1877." Scollen served at the Fort Calgary mission until 1882, then was sent to Edmonton, next to the Hobbema area, and finally to the U.S. He died in Idaho in 1902.

much of what they preached was not altogether foreign to native spiritual concepts. The Indians held a belief in an overall protective spiritual figure, and it was not too much of a stretch to harmonize the new religious ideas with their traditional legends and beliefs. The Stoneys were particularly receptive to Christian teachings, and they were quickly brought under the umbrella of the church by a Methodist missionary working in Morley. But that is farther down the highway from the site of Our Lady of Peace by the Elbow…

Records are unclear whether Chief Crowfoot of the Blackfoot made a request to Bishop Vital-Justin Grandin to send priests to his people, as is stated in some writings, or whether the initiative came from the Council of St. Albert Vicariate in 1869. The result was that Father Constantine Scollen, O.M.I., was selected to open a mission in the area and minister to the surrounding tribes. Scollen had been born in Ireland in 1841, and at the age of 17 entered the Congregation of the Oblates. He was called to Canada by Bishop Grandin in 1862 and helped establish a school at Fort Edmonton. He quickly learned to speak several native languages, and in 1873 published a Cree grammar and dictionary – a monumental work. Scollin developed a great interest in taking a mission further afield. He joined

Alberta's First Cheese Factory

Also located near the intersection of highways 1 and 22 was Alberta's first cheese factory. This was run by Ebenezer Healy, who had grown up on a dairy farm in Nova Scotia and headed west to try his luck in 1882. He initially landed in the Winnipeg area, but soon moved on to homestead north of Regina. However, Healy found that area too dry to be conducive to dairy production, so he was soon moving west again. Healy, his wife, five sons, and one daughter travelled by ox-drawn wagon, bringing along a herd of 20 milk cows. After settling in the Springbank area, Healy rapidly expanded his dairy operation and was soon one of the many farmers supplying the growing town of Calgary with milk and butter.

Farmers in this area maintained about 300 dairy cows in total to meet the local demand, but the small-scale industry had its own set of challenges. Production of fresh milk was accompanied with issues around delivery of the product while it was sufficiently fresh. Most farms dealt with the abundance of cream by turning it into butter, which was less delivery-sensitive. However, this involved a great deal of labour and was harder to market.

Healy met with his neighbours and proposed the idea of a cheese operation to make use of their cream. His idea met with enthusiastic support. Healy's facility consisted of a log building with a sod roof, with a storage room sectioned off inside for ripening the cheese. The operation had no running water, but Healy accessed a nearby spring, which he enclosed in a wooden structure that doubled as cold storage.

Healy's first products were sold to the I.G. Baker store in Calgary in 1888 for 20 cents per pound, and the general response pronounced his product to be of excellent quality. Over the next few years, Springbank Cheese increased production from three cheeses a day at startup (which totalled about 165 pounds in a season) to production totalling 10 tons of cheese by the 1890 season. Healy even shipped some of his cheese to the Chicago Fair, where it won an award.. By this time a number of other dairies around Calgary had also entered the cheese business. Healy tried to expand his business by selling cheese to the Vancouver market, but that proved unprofitable. In 1896, he therefore made the decision to convert his operation to a cream-separating station, and later he moved on to ranching. Other cheese factories that had started up in the area struggled on for a while. But with cheese selling for 11 to 12 cents a pound and butter bringing in 30 cents, there was little incentive for local cheese operations to continue.

Ebenezer Healy retired from ranching in 1907 and died in Calgary in 1937 at the age of 92. A stone cairn was erected by the Dairymen's Association on the site of his cheese factory. But even that remnant of his entrepreneurial efforts is now gone: the cairn now resides in Heritage Park Historical Village in Calgary.

Cochrane

About ten kilometres north along the Cowboy Trail is the town of Cochrane. It's one of the fastest-growing communities in Alberta, as many families have chosen to live here rather than in the busy city of Calgary. The community became a village in 1913, and achieved town status in 1971. Cochrane has worked to preserve its western flavour in its architecture as well as cultural activities such as the Labour Day Parade and the Old Tyme Country Fair held the last weekend of August. Over the town looms the Big Hill (sometimes referred to as Cochrane Hill) – called *Manachaban* in Cree, for "Big Mount." It has always been a dominant landmark in the area, and today is popular with paragliders and hang-gliders. Another draw for visitors to Cochrane is the popular MacKay's Ice Cream, which has operated in the town since 1948.

Cochane Ranche

The town of Cochrane takes its name from the historic Cochrane Ranche, which was briefly mentioned in the section about Bowness in Chapter 2. This huge enterprise extended west from Calgary's current city limits to cover the area where the town now lies. To review the situation briefly, Western Canada in the early 1880s was open for business. The presence of the North-West Mounted Police ensured order in the area. The various Indian tribes had, for better or worse, signed treaties and been relocated onto reserves. The Canadian Pacific Railway was making its way westward to the Pacific coast, and the federal government had established a system for distributing land in the *Dominion Lands Act* and the subsequent grazing leases. The government of Sir John A. Macdonald had set the stage for the civilized settlement of the area, and particularly for the establishment of grand ranches backed by wealthy investors who would hold up the British values of supporting the establishment and gentleman entrepreneurs.

Senator Matthew Cochrane of Montreal was exactly the type of character who Macdonald foresaw as a desirable sort for colonizing the West. Senator Cochrane was well connected to the movers and shakers in the federal government, had friends and finances to back his enterprise, and was eager to take advantage of emerging opportunities. Also, the situation in the West was creating huge demands for food supplies for the Mounted Police posts, railway employees, and new settlers – and, increasingly, the Indians, who had lost their food source with the disappearance of the buffalo.

Senator Cochrane also recognized that the scene was set for financial gains, as demand for land in the West would grow and the resale value of property was sure to skyrocket.

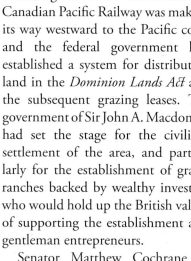

Senator Matthew Cochrane, 1889, Topley Studio, Library and Archives Canada, PA-026580

It was a perfect moment for a speculator – having the first choice of ideal locations, with opportunities near the railway transport link, communities where services would develop, and good water sources. Senator Cochrane entered into the deal to create a ranch named after him without ever having set foot on the land.

He was encouraged by what he had heard about the warm chinook winds that guaranteed mild winter temperatures and snow-free grazing that would be ideal for raising cattle. Before the legislation allowing for grazing leases had even passed Parliament, he had already assembled a group of investors and started accumulating the land and leases. He ended up with leases on territory that spanned the area between the North-West Mounted Police post in the new community of Calgary and the Morley mission to the west, and which straddled both the Bow River and the route that the railway would take through the area. This was choice land indeed. Lieutenant-Colonel James Walker, who had been a Superintendent with the NWMP, was hired as Senator Cochrane's first ranch manager. Walker oversaw the construction of the ranch house, complete with library and wine cellar, located in a sheltered spot at the base of the Big Hill where Big Hill Creek flows into the Bow River.

Acquiring the cattle for the ranch ended up being delayed until the fall of 1881, when Senator Cochrane purchased 6,700 head to be brought up from Montana. Because of the late purchase, the cattle were forced to travel north fast, through deteriorating early-winter conditions. "The stock was shoved along at a merciless rate, the steers in the dry herd averaging fifteen to eighteen miles every day, while the cows often did fourteen. This drive has remained the criterion for hard driving, as no such great numbers of cattle have ever since been moved so rapidly by trail. The poor animals were 'tin-canned' and 'slickered' from morning until night, kept on the move from daylight until dark, and were usually so weary when darkness came that they preferred resting to eating. Then, too, they were herded so closely that there was little chance of a square meal even if they did have the energy to look for it."[1] Many of the animals died en route. Because of the belief that the chinooks would keep grazing clear all winter, no winter feed had been provided. Unlike horses, cattle do not paw through snow to graze, and many more of the weakened cattle died during the winter when they could not get through the crust of ice which formed after the warm winds blew through.

The next year, to boost the numbers, another 4,300 head were purchased. But once again, despite the previous year's experience and advice from local people, the beasts were moved in the late fall. "Driven fiercely, they forced the herds to the Big Hill, and then Poindexter, riding to the head, said to Major [sic] Walker: 'Here they are. I have carried out my contract and delivered at the Big Hill. Count 'em now, because half of them will be dead by tomorrow!' By this time there was no chance of feed on the Cochrane range, the snowstorm lasting until October 15. Following this came a thaw that merely softened the snow. Then the bitter weather came down, forming a crust on the snowbanks that was strong enough to hold up a team. The cattle, with their hoofs worked to the quick, moved only with difficulty…"[2]

Better grazing conditions were available just to the east, near Blackfoot Crossing, but again the absentee owners gave instructions that were ill advised, insisting that the cattle be kept within the Cochrane Ranche lands. Despite persistent efforts by the cattle to head in that easterly direction, they were pushed back by the cowboys, and "every morning the longs strings of bawling cows and steers could be seen by the people of Calgary walking downstream along the tops of the riverbanks; every evening the people of Calgary saw the Cochrane cowboys shoving the reluctant beasts back on the iron-bound range."[3] By the spring, only 2,000 animals remained from the total of 11,000 purchased. Lieutenant-Colonel Walker resigned in disgust.

The Cochrane Ranche's owners assessed the situation and decided to cut their losses. They acquired a different stretch of land farther to the south, to be known as the South Cochrane Ranche, and moved their operations there. Much of the land between Calgary and Morley became the British American Ranche Company, which focussed was on raising horses, which were in high demand at the time. By 1887, under settlement pressure, these lands had been divided along the Bow River. The area to the south was opened up for homesteading, while the Ranche on the north side was converted into a sheep operation.

Today, if you visit the site of Cochrane Ranche, at the foot of the Big Hill you will find interpretive material, walking trails, and picnic grounds. Confusingly, the location called the Cochrane Ranche House is not the old home from the Cochrane Ranch but a modern facility with conference and event spaces, the town administration offices, and the Stockmen's Memorial Foundation.

Brushy Ridge

The area between the town of Cochrane and Highway One was historically known as Brushy Ridge. Having come under heavy cultivation, it is much less brushy than it used to be, but the rolling hills were once covered with thick, short clumps of bushes.

One of the characters who homesteaded in this area was Sykes Taylor. He had been born in Yorkshire, England, and his family moved to Massachusetts when he was 14. Taylor came west in the mid-1880s with his brother, and they scraped together a living by gathering buffalo bones off the prairie and piling them by the railway line for collection and use as fertilizer and in the sugar refineries. By 1886, the rest of the family had joined Taylor and his brother. The family settled in Morley, where his mother ran the stop-off house, feeding railway workers and travellers who came through.

Taylor met his future wife, Annie Smith, when her family stopped in Morley in 1893. They were married by Rev. McDougall in Morley, and the couple settled on land owned by the wife's brother just north of the present Old Banff Coach Road overpass. But they really needed a bigger property to reliably grow a hay crop, so they homesteaded a section further west in Brushy Ridge and purchased the adjoining "school land" to add on. Their story is probably typical of many stories of a struggle to get by. The Taylors bought and sold horses, cut firewood to sell, and ran some milk cows (initially producing over 100 pounds of butter a year from home before starting to sell their cream to the cheese factory).

Once his family had achieved some comfort and stability, Taylor became interested in the new cars that were turning up in the Calgary area. His daughter, Marjorie, had learned to drive during a visit to Ontario, and on this inspiration he purchased a 1918 Model T Ford – the first car in the Brushy Ridge area. Sykes never drove it much, and even that came to an end when he drove the car into the garage one day – and on through the back wall. He wasn't hurt, but the car didn't fare too well.

The most newsworthy event that happened in Brushy Ridge was the great fire of November 18-19, 1936. There are claims that it got started when somebody tried to burn out the Jumping Pound Forest Ranger, but this story can't be verified. It might have been a lightning strike or a careless campfire. For whatever reason, the fire came through the area of Sibbald Creek to the west and moved through Jumping Pound, spreading until it covered a huge swath of Brushy Ridge.

There had been a series of dry summers, and late on the afternoon of November 18, smoke was noticed to the west. Around midnight the local party-line phones rang with the one long ring that signalled an emergency and the worst was confirmed – fire was sweeping toward Brushy Ridge. By 4 a.m., when Jack and Percy Copithorne headed west on horseback to assess the situation, flames could be seen reflected in the low cloud cover. As the wind picked up and the flames became more visible, it became apparent that there was nothing they could do by continuing in that direction. They turned back to get tractors and plows to attempt to get a fire break in place before the wall of flames reached the area. By then, winds of 150 kph were making things happen fast. Haystacks would catch fire, then get picked up by the wind and carried ahead to start a new fire.

Trudy Copithorne recalls the events of that day: "They could see some calves in Section 2 (at the Bennetts' place) that were directly in the line of fire. The fire was building up such momentum because of the wind; they could see a broad front of flames shooting 20 feet [6 metres] in the air about to engulf these calves. They had to leave them, but opened gates and fences in order that some might escape. There were 20 or 30 calves lost in this bunch – burned in their tracks…

"The people of the district knew they had to move quickly. Mr. Ernie Crowe phoned around to the women to tell them to go to the Jumping Pound Creek. People started placing worldly goods in potato patches or wells. Many left their homes with only the clothes they had on. Men started to try to plow fire guards around haystacks and buildings, but they were faced with an almost impossible task…

"Edna Copithorne, then pregnant with her son, Marshall, thought it unwise to go to the creek with her neighbours. She started off in her car to try and reach the safety of Cochrane or Calgary. The burning fence posts were her only guide, showing her that she was still on the road allowance, as it was as dark as night. She bumped into several cows and saw many other animals race by – just balls of flames. Suddenly, she crashed into the centre of a huge pole that had blown across the field and through the fence and lodged on the road. She was forced to sit there until Sam Copithorne drove down that road and found her and 2-year-old Sheila…

"When the fire struck the Brushy Ridge area, school was in. Without the bravery of Ted and Alfred Callaway, 14 children and their teacher, Miss Grace Davis, might have perished. These men rushed to the school and, amidst the smoke and dust, were able to pile the children into their cars and drive them to Cochrane and safety…"[4]

The entire Coelen farm burned to the ground. Next in line was Harry Johnson's. He took his mother and father out into the middle of a plowed field for safety, then tried to rescue the 16 cows and the pony that had been put into the barn because of the terrible winds. But all the animals were lost when the barn and all the buildings except the house burned. Every building at Johnny Arnell's burned, including the pen of hogs he was preparing to take to market. At Billy Vowles' farm, all the buildings and pigs were lost. Ted Callaway was luckier: his house, garage, and grainery survived, although he lost some outbuildings. Callaway had rushed into his barn to free his animals, and had managed to get the horses and cows out. The bull had gotten itself wedged behind the manger, so had to be left. But it was later found among the cows, having somehow managed to free itself.

There were many other sad stories, such as the one about the horse belonging to one of the Wallace kids that had managed to escape from the burning school barn. It had been wearing the harness collar used to pull the cart full of kids to school. The collar had caught fire, so even though the horse escaped the building, it had to be put down because of the terrible burns around its neck.

All of Jergen Messer's buildings and pigs burned. The fire continued to the homestead of Sykes Taylor, who, at 68, was home in bed ill with pleurisy. He was rescued and taken to Cochrane. Sadly, complications from the pleurisy coupled with the shock of the events caused Taylor to succumb two weeks later.

The desperate efforts to stop the fire – all the water poured on it, all the fire breaks plowed in its path – failed completely. The fire continued to spread, burning almost to the outskirts of Bowness. It was stopped only because it started to rain, as nature finally stepped in and saved the situation from becoming even worse. In the end, over 100,000 acres of farm land had burned. There are no figures for the losses in horses, cattle, and other domestic animals, or for the wild animals that were killed.

To make a horrendous situation even worse, the affected families learned that their insurance would not cover their losses. This was because their policies specified that, in order to be covered, a fire must "originate within the boundaries of the farm in question." The *Calgary Herald* responded by sponsoring a Bow Valley Fire Fund that raised about $4,000 for the farmers. The CPR moved stock to other areas so they could winter where surplus supplies were available. The community stepped forward to help each other out, and rebuilding started almost immediately.

Brushy Ridge School, which had opened along the road to Cochrane in 1906 with 20 pupils, operated temporarily from Wellington Barkley's bunkhouse. A new school was built and opened in June of the following year. That school continued to serve the area until 1962, when it was closed and the building was moved away.

Top: Brushy Ridge fire, 1936, Glenbow NB 16-648

Bottom: Aftermath of the Brushy Ridge fire, 1936, Glenbow NB 16-650

Wildlife Spotting: What's That Terrible Smell?

Driving along the highway, you may detect the penetrating aroma of skunk, often because the poor little critters have been hit by cars. Mostly nocturnal, they are hard to see on the asphalt and almost impossible to avoid at highway speeds. Their famous smell can carry a kilometre if ejected by choice – and it seems to go even further if released by trauma.

These furry black animals with the double stripe down their back are a member of the weasel family – hence the scent glands at the base of the tail that produce an odorous, oily substance. (All weasels are somewhat pungent.) Skunks' scientific name, *Mephitis mephitis*, is Latin for "bad odour." About 60 cm long from nose to tail tip, they prefer to live in mixed brush and open meadow. They eat mice and insects, and grub up whatever they can from the ground with their sharp claws.

The skunk's scent is produced by sulphur compounds called mercaptans. When the animal feels threatened, it will warn the intruder by growling, hissing, and stamping its hind feet. If the intruder pushes the point, the skunk curls its body around to aim its posterior at the threat. It can shoot its smelly musk up to five metres. The glands contain about a tablespoon of the substance, and that can provide several "firings", so it is amazingly potent stuff. The musk is also an irritant, so an animal getting it full in the face suffers from physical discomfort, as well as the agony of living with the smell for a week or so.

Skunks get through the winter by hibernating, the only weasel other than the badger to do so in this region. A group of several animals, or a few families, will huddle together in an old coyote den or other protected spot for the winter months.

Top: Porcupine, D. Ditchburn

Bottom: Skunk, T. Roberts (SXC Images)

Another frequent victim of the automobile is the slow-moving porcupine *(Erethizon dorsatum)*. These animals are semi-nocturnal and prefer open woodlands. Porcupines are rodents, our second-largest after the beaver. They have a rodent's continually growing teeth, which are kept honed back by continual chewing. They dine on the inner bark of trees through the winter, and enjoy leaves and conifer needles in the summer months. Porcupines seem attracted to salty flavours. Around human habitations, they love tool handles, old boots, outhouse seats… as well as the grips of walking poles. At some trailheads, hikers cage off their vehicles with chicken wire before before hitting the trail so that they do not return to chewed tires (or worse, brake lines) be porcies attracted by the road salt residue.

All of a porcupine's body, except its face and underside, are covered with quills from 2 cm to 12 cm long. These quills have a cream-coloured shaft with a black tip. Interspersed with the quills are a thick woolly undercoat and long guard hairs. Contrary to popular belief, porcupines cannot shoot their quills. But they *do* lash their tails ferociously, which gives them a surprising range. Like the skunk, they usually give fair warning before employing their artillery.

The question that naturally comes to mind when pondering porcupines is how they manage to maintain their species. Isn't mating a rather hazardous affair? The process starts with an elaborate ritual in which the animals circle each other, rise up on their hind legs, and sometimes link forepaws in a sort of waltz. Perhaps that is part of working up their courage for the next step. The female turns, flattens her quills down, and cranks her tail around to expose the quill-free underside. Once the act has been successfully performed, the question is, how do these prickly critters emerge into the world? The young are born with soft, barb-free quills, which harden only after they are exposed to air.

Porcupines remain active throughout the winter. Their tracks leave a sinuous mark from their pigeon-toed waddle.

A little farther west from Brushy Ridge, another community formed as settlers moved into this area, taking its name from Jumping Pound Creek. The word "Pound" probably refers to a buffalo jump and pound complex on the banks of the creek farther to the north, where the creek enters the Bow River.

While Springbank looked to Calgary for services, the communities of Brushy Ridge and Jumping Pound tended to go to Cochrane when they needed to shop or run errands. These areas, particularly Jumping Pound (which is now about 40 kilometres from the centre of Calgary), felt much more isolated in the early ranching days. They had to be even more self-sufficient and had more complex problems for provisioning themselves and shipping their products to market.

Jumping Pound residents got together and established a school very early on. The first one was built in 1893, called the "Jumping Pond School," a misspelling that was also applied to the post office for a period. The name was finally corrected in 1910. The first school was a simple log structure that operated until 1928. Two other schools were subsequently built in the area, in 1899 and 1943. None of the old school buildings remain.

As well as a school, a community needs a space for meetings and socials. There were plans for a hall to be built on Pile of Bones Hill before World War I, and logs were even collected and prepared for it, but too many of the men involved in this project were lost in the war. It was never completed. In 1927, a fine clapboard hall was built on land donated by John Copithorne on the east side of the creek. It had a hardwood floor, which was good for dances, and benches built along the sides. Electric lights were added in 1947, and propane heating replaced the old wood stove in 1967.

Margaret Bateman recalls the hall's initiation: "The opening night of the Hall was a gala affair – the walls were decorated with bear, wolf and deer hides loaned by Mr. Frank Sibbald.

A huge crowd attended and Mr. Sibbald was floor manager. Over the years the hall has been decorated in different ways, at one time Kleenex flowers were attached to shutters painted green and adorned the windows… In those days if one chose to have a nip or two, the bottle was cached behind a willow bush or down a gopher hole. The police sometimes came out and checked on the dances. A few times there was a fight or two, no one was seriously hurt just their dignity. Lunch was served at midnight – a good one, sandwiches, homemade cake and real good coffee."[1]

The Jumping Pound Hall is still in active use for community events.

Jumping Pound Creek

The Copithorne Family and Early Ranching

Much of the land in the Jumping Pound area has been the domain of the Copithorne family. The ridge to the east of Jumping Pound Creek on the north side of the highway is called Copithorne Ridge, a tribute to the family's long presence here. Over the years, they have become something of a local ranching empire.

John Copithorne was born on a dairy farm in County Cork, Ireland, in 1862, to a family of 15 children. "Whether it was the cows or the call of adventure that drove him from

the 'Owld sod' or the fact that there were six sons in the family each having to make his own way in the world, it is hard to say. Anyway, after being caught cheating on an examination paper he was expelled from school and his outraged father put him to work digging drainage ditches. After a couple of days of this back-breaking labour, he stuck the shovel in the ground and announced at the supper table that he was going to Canada."[2]

When John arrived in Canada in 1883, there was growing unrest among the Metis that led to the Riel Rebellion two years later. John was employed by the federal government to head west and observe the Crees, taking a measure of how far the rebellion was likely to explode.

Top left: Pupils at Brushy Ridge School, 1909, Glenbow NA 1288-1

Bottom left: Jumping Pound hall in 2009

Right: Richard Copithorne, 1886, Glenbow NA 3033-7

Trumpeter swans, M. Zimmerman

Wildlife Spotting: What Are Those Big White Birds?

In the curve of the bend where the highway approaches Jumping Pound Creek, there is a body of water where swans are frequently spotted for a few weeks in the spring. These big birds move through Alberta in large flocks in the spring migration. Most of them are Tundra swans (*Cygnus columbianus*). They are slightly smaller than the Trumpeter swans (*Cygnus buccinator*) that may also be found in the ponds in mixed flocks. If you have binoculars, look for a small yellow oval mark between the eye and the bill of the Tundra swan.

This pond (and a few others that swans favour – look for them also at the Sibbald Flats turnoff and on Lac des Arcs) is an important refuelling stop for these migrants as they head back north to the Arctic for the breeding season. Swans are quite particular about the nature of the ponds they select for breaks on their journeys – the ponds must be mostly free of ice and have an abundance of the swans' favourite weeds and invertebrates. You are less likely to see swans during the fall migration because they take a different route back south as they head for their wintering areas on the west coast of the United States and along the border with Mexico.

Listen for any vocalizations that these birds make. The Trumpeter is well named for its bugle-like voice, while the Tundra makes a softer, higher-pitched call. Swans have an extra-long trachea (windpipe) coiled behind their sternum (breastbone), and this is what makes their sound so resonant.

The presence of Trumpeter swans is a feel-good conservation story. In the early part of the past century, they almost became extinct through hunting and habitat loss. Just two small populations remained, near Grande Prairie, Alberta, and in Yellowstone Park in the U.S. But a number of protective measures such as the Migratory Bird Convention were put in place, and efforts were made to develop refuges for species in danger. Relocation programs have ensured that flocks have become more geographically diverse. While not back up to their original number, the species is now thought to be out of the woods.

First ranch house, CL Ranch, c.1900, Glenbow NA 3017-5

John Copithorne and family, 1910, Glenbow NA 3033-1 Back row, L-R: Jim, Jack, Claude, Ernie Centre row, L-R: Ethel, John, Susan, Bert Front row, L-R: Harry, May, Charlie

During 1886 and 1887, John worked delivering rations to the Sarcee and Stoney Indians, who were now suffering greatly from the loss of their traditional food sources. This is how he became familiar with the Jumping Pound area. Finding it appealing, he left his job and started a homestead on the banks of Jumping Pound Creek at SE ¼ 6-25-4-5. Soon his older brother Richard arrived and bought some additional land from the CPR. Together the brothers built a log house with a sod roof as well as a stable on John's property, and then a house on Richard's land. The brothers farmed together on what became known as the Lone Star Ranch, using the Lazy J brand. In 1895, Richard received his own brand, and the CL Ranch was born.

Those early years of ranching were hard. John's son Harry comments on his impressions of their struggles: "The cattle losses through the winter and spring seem unbelievable to us now. Not too many people are still around who remember the strident screech of wagon wheels on a cold winter morning and the cows coming on the run bawling their heads off, to snatch at bits of hay falling from the rack. Only the scrawny animals were fed, and just enough to keep them alive. The ones in better shape were kept in a separate field, nosing through the snow to get at the prairie wool underneath. No wonder the bone pile hidden behind a hill assumed gigantic

proportions by spring. The coyotes undoubtedly lived high in those days; perhaps not on meat but on the hides and bone marrow, and unborn calves the mothers were too weak to deliver."[3]

A third brother joined them in 1904: Samuel Copithorne, who set up his homestead closer to Springbank. He married Beatrice Ethel Blache and operated Mountain View Ranch, where they built a home known as the Stone House on the banks of the Elbow River. After having a four children arrived, they moved closer to the Springbank School. Samuel became known as a great "axe man" and was in much demand for constructing log buildings. He was also known for his love of a good coyote chase and kept a pack of hounds for the sport.

John Copithorne married Susan Toole in 1887. After doing mixed farming and dairy with Richard, in 1898 they switched over to beef ranching, running mainly Herefords. They had nine children: James, Jack, Claude, Ernest, Ethel, Albert, Charles, Harry, and Georgina. John and Susan retired to Victoria in 1912, and Jack took over running the Lone Star Ranch with his brother Claude.

Richard Copithorne married Sophia Wills, and they had five boys and two girls. The CL Ranch expanded over the years to include 26 sections of land, on which they raised Herefords and Clydesdales.

Mange dip

Very little hay crop was taken in. The native grasses were fairly nutritious, and there was not the expectation that cattle would be fattened and sent to market as fast as they are these days. Ranchers kept their steers until they were three or four years old before sending them to market weighing around 1,200 pounds. Today, cattle are expected to achieve that weight in just a year and a half.

For a while, horse ranching became more profitable than cattle. In the 1880s, the price of a good saddle horse spiked to more than $125 – a fortune compared to the price of cows. At first, the draft breeds were in demand for breaking soil, hauling wagons, and other heavy work. Then, in 1898, the Klondike gold rush created a market for saddle and pack horses as men poured north into the Yukon gold fields. This was followed by the Boer War from 1899 to 1902, when lighter horses were sought as cavalry mounts. And during World War I, horses were shipped to Europe for the troops. But by the 1920s machinery was taking over from the horse, so the ranchers turned back to cattle.

Besides blizzards, droughts, and other natural challenges, cattle illnesses were a constant worry. Alberta suffered from a series of outbreaks of mange at the turn of the 20th century. The federal government finally took steps to get it under control by making cattle dipping compulsory across the southern part of the province. A dipping tank was constructed at SE 12-25-5-5. The water was heated by a wood fire, then

Cattle in a mange dip, pre-1908, Glenbow NA 3929-6

Sam Copithorne and his son Louis with coyote hounds, no date, Glenbow NA 3420-11

Ranching was a rough and sometimes grim affair. In those days, it was estimated that a rancher needed 10 acres per cow, so the cattle roamed over vast areas. The free-ranging cattle were wild and hard to handle. During calving in April and May, the men had to be out among the cows several times a day to help the ones in trouble and collect any orphans. A survival rate of only 60% was considered not too bad in those days – pretty harsh statistics compared to the contemporary rancher's expectation of a more than 90% survival rate.

the cattle were driven into a 10-foot trough of water. The trough started at only four inches deep, but then dropped off, forcing the beasts into full immersion before they could clamour up the ramp on the other side. The problem was thus brought under control.

In the days before fencing, cattle had to be rounded up in the spring for branding, then again in the fall for sending stock to sale. So outfits forayed out to roam the range, each seeking out its own cattle. Each ranch had its own wagons with provisions for the cowboys, and this mobile operation could be out on the range for weeks at a time.

Branding was a community event. In mid-June, all able hands would be called on to help out. Trudi Copithorne recalls the atmosphere on branding days: "About 5:00 a.m., before the flies are out, the cowboys, including the rancher's children, saddle up and ride out to the cow pasture where the cows are grazing in the early morning sunshine. The boss instructs his men on how he wants the cattle brought in and the big drive is on. Barking dogs flush the cattle out of the underbrush, cows bellow for their calves, cowboys whoop and horses sweat. By 7:30 a.m., the din of cattle bawling, dogs barking and cowboys shouting can be heard at the ranch buildings. In a cloud of dust and noise, the herd heads across the creek and into the corrals. A handful of calves balk at the creek. One makes a dash back for the pasture. A cowboy on horseback lunges after it. His lariat snakes through the air but the calf jumps through the loop and is gone. Two or three fences and 15 minutes later when the corral gates are shut on the rest of the herd, we see our famous cowhand walking toward the creek leading his lathered horse and prodding the exhausted calf ahead of him, this time with the rope around its neck."[4]

Once the calves had been separated from the cows, the serious work started. The branding irons had been heating in a fire for some time, and the calves were thrown and pinned down while the hot iron was applied. While they were immobilized, the animals were also castrated, dehorned and vaccinated before being allowed to race back to their mothers.

"By the time the sun is high in the hot June sky, the cloud of dust over the corrals should be settling and the breeze from the West blows the smell of wood smoke, burned hair, sweat, blood and manure away from the branding corral and the group of grubby dusty cowboys head to the ranch house where the ladies have heaping platters of mashed potatoes, roast beef, buns, pies, and hot coffee waiting."[5]

Modernization has changed the face of ranching beyond recognition. The science of genetics has improved many breeds and caused others to almost disappear. The practice of simply sending the bull into the field with the cows has fallen out of favour, replaced by artificial insemination. The business side of ranching has mushroomed and ranchers are forced to become involved in politics, lobbying for their concerns. John Copithorne would hardly recognize ranch life today.

Early Mail Service

Communications were difficult but highly valued in the early settlements, so one of the first things the homesteaders organized was mail service. Springbank started up a local post office in 1891 and weekly mail service commenced in Jumping Pound in 1892. The service was run from the two-story log home of William Stuart, who also ran a small store out of his home with a few non-perishable items and took orders for things to bring back from town on his mail run. With this mail service came the job of cream delivery, and up to 35 two- or five-gallon cans were collected along the route. These runs to Calgary were gruelling in the winter, travelling by sleigh, wrapped in robes packed with hot bricks to keep warm. If the snow was deep, the horses were doubled up so that four beasts could power the sleigh through the drifts. If a chinook had melted the snow, the sleigh was switched for the wagon and the driver hoped to get back home before it snowed again. In 1916, the horses were retired and the route

W. Stuart house and post office, built in 1892, 2009

The "new" Jumping Pound post office, built in 1913, Tom Bateman in doorway, no date, Glenbow NA 946-1

was covered by automobile, which was still very challenging in poor weather.

Certain times of the year involved a heavier mail load, such as when the Eaton's catalogues were delivered in the fall, and later when the mail-order purchases started to arrive. Registered and first-class mail was delivered for the rural post offices in a locked bag. On one trip, the key to the bag was lost, so all the recipients had to wait for the next week's delivery to be made with a new key. The key arrived – locked safely away in that week's bag – so they resorted to cutting the bag open to get it.

In 1905, Bill Stuart had to resign from the post-office business because of failing health. John Bateman took it over, building a new one-story log structure to house the post office and store. The Jumping Pound Post Office was finally closed in 1949.

Telephone Service

Communication by telephone arrived about 15 years after the mail service. A line was built between Calgary and Banff in 1907, and a branch was run from there to the Johnston house in Springbank to serve the whole community at 10 cents per call. By 1909, a more general service was installed through a connection to the Cochrane Exchange, and farms were hooked into party lines with a small, local switchboard. The operator used manual plugs to connect calls made between different lines. Calls made to other numbers on the same line could be placed without the switchboard, by turning the crank to produce the required number of short rings to specify the callee. One long ring meant an emergency, and everyone on the line was expected to respond to that.

"Rubbering," or listening in on the party line, was a popular recreation. Certain individuals were well known for indulging in this, and callers would pick up the sound of babies crying, dogs barking, and other identifiable noises from the illicit listener. Margaret Buckley recalls one culprit: "On the seven line we had Stanley Cope, a bachelor, who depended very much on the telephone to catch up on all the news and pass it along. Stanley had a captain's chair under his phone and every evening tipped backwards and

proceeded to listen to all the calls… Many evenings Stanley would fall asleep in this position, chair tilted, telephone to ear, and begin to snore so loudly that the person trying to talk to their other party couldn't even hear. You would have to ring one long loud crank to wake him up, in order to carry on your conversation."[6]

In the 1930s Alberta Government Telephones decided the rural lines were not economical and planned to remove them. Communities responded to this by establishing mutual companies (like local phone co-ops) to maintain service. There were problems with this, because once a line was installed at the mutual's expense, others along the line could subscribe to a private line with AGT, undercutting any profits to the local mutual. This became a highly contentious matter. There were additional problems due to the high cost of maintaining phone lines, and the 1936 Brushy Ridge fire wiped out more than 200 telephone poles in that area. Local volunteer labour repaired most of this damage, but management problems continued to plague the mutuals. In 1969, AGT returned to the scene and took over the telephone service. By 1975, all the lines through the Cochrane Exchange were being transferred as local calls to Calgary.

The Jumping Pound Gas Plant

After you cross the Jumping Pound Bridge but before you climb over the Nicholl Ridge, just ahead look to the right and in the distance you'll see the Jumping Pound Gas Plant. It is almost easier to spot at night when the lights stand out in the dark. The history of oil and gas exploration in the area west of Calgary culminated in the installation of this plant, now a major hub for the region.

By the start of the 20th century, the search for petroleum was heating up in Alberta. Exploration began in the Jumping Pound area in the early 1900s, with the hope of finding a sizeable reserve of heavy crude oil. The area was believed to hold high potential, and the first primitive hole was drilled in 1912, using a percussion-style rig that greatly limited the depth that could be achieved. That effort produced a dry hole. In 1914, with some technological advances, the first rotary hole was drilled. But much of the equipment used for that well was lost down the hole, so it was also a dud. Although no great finds marked these first attempts (the second well's location is now paved over by the Trans-Canada itself), there were still enough indications of high potential to sustain interest in the area. Small, independent companies continued to explore, but did not make any great finds.

In the 1920s, geological maps started to become available, providing more information to direct exploration activity. Dr. G. Hume created detailed maps of this area in the late 1920s that clearly indicated that resource wealth might lie beneath the surface. Throughout this decade, several exploration operations drilled in the area, and many local men found jobs working for these companies. Finds in other areas surrounding Calgary fanned the flames for continuing exploration efforts, and the local media dove into the frenzy with reports of the great wealth coming to those who struck black gold. Reports of dazzling new discoveries were constant headline news. In this heady atmosphere, many small companies were founded and started operations with great hope and enthusiasm, only to disappear just as quickly when their efforts did not turn up the promised great finds.

There were also a number of fly-by-night enterprises taking advantage of the situation. A resident of the area recalled how, "with legitimate oil companies operating in the area and with oil stocks offering a rather attractive investment, some not-so-legitimate operators would attempt to cash in on this golden opportunity. All a 'moonlighter' needed to do was stake out some land, use an impressive company name and start selling shares. If some shareholders began to inquire too closely into the operations, a semblance of activity was created by hauling in some lumber or a bit of piping. If things began to get too hot, the operator could either disappear or declare bankruptcy. Either way the shareholder was the loser."[7]

Much of the early exploration for oil had been frustrated by finds of undesirable natural gas, which were capped over and abandoned. However, a find of sweet gas near Medicine Hat in 1890 was deemed to be worth exploiting, and a pipeline was installed to provide the city with gas – the first such commercial development in Western Canada. Then, in 1909, the Canadian Western Natural Gas, Light, Heat and Power Company struck a sizeable gas field near Bow Island, south of Calgary, and gas began to look more desirable.

Jumping Pound Gas Plant

In Jumping Pound, some of the early wells struck gas in the late 1920s, but finds were of insufficient volume to hold commercial potential. However, a provision in one drilling agreement resulted in the gas pool being tapped for local use in a few homes from the Bow River No. 2 well of 1928. This was a cause for great local celebration, and parties were held to mark each stage of the installation.

The Depression years of the 1930s slowed things down considerably. Then, in the 1940s, the establishment of oil reserves became of top importance to support the war effort, and the increasing use of automobiles was causing demand for fuel to soar.

By now, some of the big international players had entered the arena of oil exploration in the Calgary area. Shell Oil, already actively involved in research into aviation-fuel technology, began to take a closer look at the Jumping Pound area. The company already held the lease on a large portion of land there, so it pooled its resources with R. A. Brown, conducted some seismic work, and drilled its first well in the area in 1942 – the Norman No. 1. Shell had great hopes for this well, which was the deepest drilled in the area at that time – at 12,056 feet, it was well over two miles below ground. Yet it, too, was also unsuccessful. Despite this setback, Shell remained convinced that there was promise in a structure called the Front Fold. So it drilled another well in 1944, making use of more advanced seismic technology

Wildlife Spotting: Is That a White-Tailed or a Mule Deer?

Deer are frequently seen in the fields by the highway through this stretch of ranching country and into the mountains. Mule deer *(Odocoileus virginianus)* and white-tailed deer *(Odocoileus hemionus)* are about the same size, both standing about a metre at the shoulder, so size is no help in distinguishing between them. If you get a good rear view, that is your best indicator. Mule deer have a white rump patch, with a narrow white tail with a black tip. White-tailed deer do not have the white rump patch. In fact, you see white only as a fringe around the larger tail if it is held down, but if the deer is alarmed it raises its tail to display the white underside.

The antlers are also different. White-tailed deer grow theirs with a single main beam curving slightly forward, from which a series of points grow upward and slightly inward. On mule deer, the antlers grow up and out from the head and divide. Then each prong divides again, branching outward in this manner. The doe does not have any antlers. Also, mule deer have larger ears, hence their name.

Something called "stotting" is a good way of identifying whether you are watching a mule deer. When they are startled they will "stot" or move with high four-legged leaps which take then easily over fences. White-tailed deer are less likely to jump fences and can be observed crawling under them. Also, mule deer tend to "stot" off for a short distance and then stop to look back, whereas white-tailed deer simply run away, making them less vulnerable as targets for hunting.

Deer are active both day and night, travelling in small groups. They do not form harems with a single male as elk do, but stay in loose family groups. Elk (which are encountered farther west into the mountains) are the largest of the deer family, and, although they once lived in the prairie habitat, they are no longer found here.

Top: White-tailed deer

Bottom: Mule Deer, B. Creavis (SXC Images)

for the first time in Alberta. This time, instead of the oil the drillers were hoping for, they found natural gas – almost a trillion cubic feet of it, representing about a quarter of all the known gas in the province at that time. Still preferring to find oil, Shell drilled three more holes, which also turned up gas but no oil. So the company mothballed the whole thing.

Although Shell's decision seems unbelievable from our modern perspective, at the time demand for natural gas was undeveloped. The infrastructure needed to transport it was not in place, it had virtually no market value, and the stuff was simply being flared off. (Turner Valley burned off a quantity similar to the reserves in this entire field during the 1920s and '30s.) Shell even put its lease up for sale at one point, only to find that there were no takers – much to the company's benefit in the long run.

Then, in February 1947, a huge oil strike in Leduc just south of Edmonton injected great excitement into oil and gas activity in Alberta. The industry heated up dramatically. This bullish atmosphere, combined with an offer in the mid-1950s by Canadian Western Natural Gas to build a gas pipeline to Calgary, changed the situation completely. Shell was nicely set up for the development of the Jumping Pound gas field. An agreement was made to deliver 20 million cubic feet per day from the reserve over the next 10 years – at a price of 10 cents per thousand cubic feet. (By the fall of 2009, the price was in the range of US$4.)

But being able to provide this gas as a finished product was rather complicated. The Jumping Pound field was sour gas, which contains hydrogen sulphide and other nasty chemicals that need to be removed before the gas can be used. Shell approached Fluor Corporation, an engineering and construction company specializing in the oil and gas industry, to design a processing plant that would remove the hydrogen sulphide and carbon dioxide. The plant was designed and constructed as quickly as possible, and the Jumping Pound gas processor opened on May 7, 1951, with the capacity to treat 20 million cubic feet of gas per day.

Almost immediately the plant ran into problems. The design by Fluor, which was based in California, failed to give sufficient consideration to the potentially vicious environment in which the plant would be operating. "When temperatures during that ferocious winter of 1951-1952 began to plunge,

it was a whole new ball game. And by the ninth inning, the weather was ahead by five runs. Gas hydrates started freezing up everything in sight. The buildings intended to keep things warm hadn't yet been completed, and… crews had to work around the clock with steam hoses, admirably managing to keep the gas flowing to Calgary."[8]

Fluor had built the plant to specifications. But little was known about working with sour gas, and this turned out to be a steep learning curve. Engineer Bill Fisher, who worked to solve the problems, commented that, "We were just developing a knowledge of sour gas… It was a new industry. Other companies came up to learn from us, like the Gulf Canada guys from Pincher Creek. People designing new plants didn't really know sour gas."[9] The plant's operators ultimately did overcome the facility's problems, developing new technologies, and ramping up processing as demand increased.

One of the first new additions to the plant was the sulphur unit. Demand for sulphur was growing for use in newsprint, the production of rayon, and, increasingly, for use in munitions in the Korean War of 1950-53. Originally, the hydrogen sulphide (H_2S) was incinerated to form sulphur dioxide, which was then vented off. The Jumping Pound plant was not only Canada's first sulphur producer, it was the first sulphur plant of its type in the world. Once in production, it turned out 32 tons of the material each day.

Dealing with sulphur is never to be taken lightly. "'I learned to respect H_2S after one day I was taking pressure readings,' recalls Bill Roman, a long-time Jumping Pound engineer… 'I was using the same gauge for two different places [to minimize error], and when I removed the gauge from the first valve there was a small amount of gas trapped in the tiny space between the valve and the gauge. Well, I got a whiff of that and I learned pretty quick. It took a couple of hours to recover.' Roman says he became an unofficial safety engineer after that. 'There was no formal position in those days, but even if there was it would have been useless because you needed to have practical experience with it. We started having safety meetings. It became everybody's business. That's how it grew…'"[10]

The plant was expanded in 1953, and again in 1954, making it the largest network in the country. A third expansion in 1957 brought capacity up to 90 million cubic feet per day, which was by then supported by 11 wells in the area. The years of the Cold War caused another jump in the demand for sulphur, which was needed by the nuclear industry to process uranium, and the plant's sulphur output reached 80 tons per day in the 1950s. More development has involved mprovements to safety equipment and environmental considerations. Currently, attention is directed toward revitalization of the aging facility. A number of environmental controls have been added, and the huge flare that used to be a landmark for drivers heading home on Highway one no longer lights the sky in that area.

Frank Ricks and The Hermitage

The next landmark on the Trans-Canada is the turnoff for Hermitage Road. The name for this road comes not from any recluse, but from the title attached to a homestead located down this road. The reason for the house's name is a bit unclear – some claim that it was so called simply because of its remoteness, while others state that it was named after a location in Scotland.

Frank Ricks arrived in Alberta from California in 1883, when he took a job to drive a herd of 200 horses up from Oregon to the Mount Royal Ranch near Cochrane. He stayed to work as a ranch hand and married Isabelle Jane Potts, the daughter of James and Jessie Potts of Morley. The couple homesteaded a spot southwest of this turn-off. Here Ricks built a grand house, complete with ballroom.

Before arriving in Alberta, Ricks had an illustrious career as a bronc rider in California and Oregon. His reputation only increased with his performance in Alberta, as the following testimony indicates: "An outlaw horse was brought in that was as bad as the worst animal that had ever come into the Province, and that is saying a good deal. He was a fine, active, long-barrelled dark chestnut, a wild horse and an outlaw of some ten years' experience. Not only did he buck in a thousand different and original twists, but he was a man-killer – a savage, untamed brute… One September day Frank Ricks came along on foot and asked for the loan of a horse. "Take the chestnut," offered Kerfoot [manager of the Cochrane Ranch] and Ricks promptly roped and saddled.

Then he rode as the Cochrane hands present had never seen before. Ricks was a superb horseman, riding on weight and balance, not by main strength like John Ware and other hard horsemen. He rode that ugly chestnut until it could scarcely stand, he cut it from tail-stump to ears with his spurs, he temporarily beat the spirit out of it with his heavy quirt. When the session had been completed to Ricks' satisfaction he left a wreck in the place of the thousand pounds of fighting horseflesh he had mounted."[11]

Ricks continued to move around frequently. In 1902, he became involved in the Alberta Hotel in Banff (now The Cascade) with Walter Potts. He was thrown from a horse in 1913 and badly hurt. That may have been a factor in his talking his own life the following year. His family moved into Calgary, and after going through a few owners, the house was allowed to fall into a state of disrepair that finally made it beyond rescuing, and in the 1960s it was burned down.

Why Are There All These Ridges?

The hog's back ridges that you cross repeatedly as you drive from Calgary to the mountains are composed of a harder sandstone rib surrounded by softer crumbled shaley rock and soil. The ridges all run from southeast to northwest, and beneath them lie a complex of faults (fractures in the earth's crust) with a similar orientation. The next chapter will delve into an explanation of the geomorphology (the study of how land forms come about). But, for a brief explanation here, try to imagine the mountains extending from where they end now on across the foothills toward Calgary for many kilometres, gradually diminishing in size. That is what it would have looked like 100 million to 200 million years ago. What you see as these ridges are the roots of these vanished mountains that have eroded away over millions of years, leaving only the remnants of their rocky cores. It is a bit mind-boggling to imagine, but trying to wrap your mind around the immense time scale of the geological history of the mountains is always a challenge!

There are two ridges in quick succession just after the Jumping Pound Gas Plant. Mainly to the north is Nicoll Ridge, another feature named after early settlers. A distinct hill on the north end of this ridge is known as Pile of Bones Hill. For years, bones of animals that had succumbed to harsh conditions, disease, or sometimes old age were hauled here for disposal. A market for bones developed as the many piles of buffalo bones were collected from around the prairie. So the bones collecting on Pile of Bones Hill were dug up and shipped to B.C. for use in refining sugar.

The next ridge, on the south side of the highway, is Bateman Ridge. You guessed it – the Batemans were a pioneering family. This land is now owned by the Copithornes.

Next you'll pass by Noble Ridge – again named for a homestead family. It is more noticeable on the north side of the highway, and has a rocky spine along its crest. These ridges are called "hog's back" ridges for their resemblance to what must be a rather underfed swine's shape.

Remains of a sun-dance lodge at Sibbald Flats

Here we get a bit ahead of ourselves – and, I will admit, a little far off the highway. But trust me, the story is worth the diversion. We will meet Andrew Sibbald more intimately whith the story of Morley. His son, Howard Sibbald, was a rancher in this area (as well as Banff Park's first warden) who used the flats along the road leading southwest as winter pasture for his cattle. He did so because the area was well protected from harsh weather and provided better winter feed in the grassy meadows than much of the surrounding areas did. The area was made a part of the Bow Crow Forest Reserve in 1910, but it continued to be used for cattle through grazing leases, as it is to this day. Watch for cows on the road if you drive through this route. The flats are about 20 kilometres from the turnoff onto Highway 68 from the Trans-Canada, lying in a broad valley that leads into the mountains.

The reasons for Sibbald to turn his cows out here were also good reasons for the ancient inhabitants of the area to themselves settle by these meadows for the winter. When Highway 68 was upgraded in 1980, prompting a survey of the archaeological significance of the location, this is exactly what was found. The area around the flats is rich with evidence of human occupation. The oldest finds included fluted points dating from 11,200 to 10,200 YBP (years before present), and there are uninterrupted indications of occupation right up to historical times. The most recent pre-contact artefacts are plains side-notched points (for mounting on shafts). Historically, there are records of Assiniboine hunters using the area throughout the second half of the 1800s.

It appears that the area was mainly used for winter camps, with groups of four to six families establishing themselves to weather through the cold months. Hearths were found, as well as the charred remains of animal bones heavily marked by stone tools. The only bones found that were marked by metal tools (and hence were from the post-contact years) were not buffalo. This suggests that the bison were largely gone from this area by the time these people started using trade tools.

"Lithic workshops," areas used for crafting stone tools, were identified by the collections of stone chips. People must have passed part of the cold months preparing tools for the richer hunting that spring would bring. The impressive inventory of stone tools collected includes 146 points, 76 biface knives, 14 gravers, 213 retouched flakes (a type of scraper), 80 end scrapers, 20 side scrapers, 38 choppers, a wedge, anvils, abraders, hammers, and much more. This was an amazingly rich find. The density of the artefacts attests to how heavily the site must have been used. There were even ceramic fragments, an unusual find in Alberta. Items such as glass medicine bottles, clay pipes, and trade beads bring the story into the time of the explorers and traders in this region.

This area remains important to the Stoney Nakoda (Assiniboine people). They frequently build a sun-dance lodge or a sweat lodge in the meadows near the flats. Here the Stoney Nakoda carefully pass on their traditions to their young people, teaching them the ways of their ancestors and giving them the opportunity to experience their heritage as a living thing.

Highway weigh scale

Just What is a Highway Weigh Scale?

You may see these Vehicle Inspection Stations along any highway in Canada and the United States. In Alberta, they are operated by the Commercial Vehicle Enforcement under the Ministry of Transportation to monitor commercial and heavy truck traffic. The stations have scales to determine axle weight, but they are also concerned with identifying other potential safety concerns. Truckers may have to present their log books to show, for example, whether they are they driving within the permitted number of hours. The truck may be examined for maintenance and other safety issues, and the load may be checked for whether it is properly secured.

There are load limits for trucks that set the maximum safe weight. During certain times of the year, a "road ban" may be in effect, so the limit becomes a much smaller fraction of the normal allowed weight.

You may have noticed black skid marks on the asphalt of the highways in places. These may indicate that a truck's air brakes have locked – a dangerous occurrence. Or you may have seen chunks of rubber that have broken off the enormous truck tires and flown (hopefully) off the side of the road… Inspections are intended to catch these kinds of dangers before they become a traffic hazard.

As you approach the weigh scale from the west, you'll drive under an apparatus that looks like a white cone suspended over the highway. This device is part of the Partners in Compliance system. If a commercial driver with a record of compliance with regulations can become qualified through the Commercial Drivers Safety Association to bypass the inspection stations. A transponder installed in the truck indicates the driver's status to the weigh station. Roughly a quarter of commercial drivers are part of this system. Occasionally a truck that is required to pull through the station does not, or a driver of a large rented truck, such as a U-Haul, is unaware that he or she must check in. In these cases, one of the enforcement officers has to jump in a vehicle and pursue the driver down the highway to intercept them.

Tree ID: Trembling Aspen

The dominant species of tree in this area is the Trembling Aspen, *Populus tremuloides*, which is the most widely distributed tree in North America. It grows in groves of clones, all of them genetically connected, in which many trees sprout from a common root mass. (They might more accurately be thought of as multiple stems.) The trees grow quickly, then die back relatively quickly as well, resulting in a continually self-regenerating organism.

In fact, the title of "Largest Living Organism" (along with a 1,500-acre fungus in Washington state) has been awarded to a huge trembling aspen grove in Utah. It has even been given a name: *Pando* (Latin for "I spread"). This colony collectively weighs 6 million kilograms (13 million pounds) and is also said to be the oldest living organism at an astonishing 80,000 years. It covers an area of 43 hectares (106 acres) and includes 47,000 tree trunks, with an average individual age of 130 years.[12]

Trembling aspen are so named because their leaves quake and shimmy with the lightest breeze. This is due to the flat shape of the *petioles* (from the Latin for "little feet") or leaf stalk that connects the leaves to the stem. The leaves turn a brilliant gold in the fall and are quite a sight as they dance about.

In the spring, aspen trees produce catkins (its version of flowers), with a different version for male and female trees. The white colony fluff that these catkins generate sticks to everything around them, and makes these trees less popular near dwellings. Another interesting aspect of the trembling aspen is the white powder that covers its white bark, which acts as a protective sunscreen.

Aspen are a popular food for beaver, so large areas of them are mowed down near beaver ponds. Ungulates such as deer and elk eat aspen bark during the winter, leaving black scars as high as they can reach on the bark from scraping it. The bark is also scarred by bears, which seem to like marking these trees with their claws (perhaps a form of communication?), and by ungulates rubbing the velvet off their antlers.

Recently, a dieback has been observed in trembling aspen populations across North America. The cause is not understood, but one theory is that it might be connected with the policy of fire suppression, and that aspen groves need periodic fires to remain healthy. We will have a closer look at issues to do with fire and fire control as we get into the mountains.

Scott Lake Hill

Back on the Trans-Canada, Livingstone Ridge (yes, the Livingstones were early settlers) lies to the south of the highway just before Highway 68. Then you climb a noticeable grade onto what is essentially this ridge's northern extension, known as Scott Lake Hill.

Tom Scott was born in 1854 in the Ontario town of Galt (now part of Cambridge) and came to Calgary in 1883. He first attempted to settle in what is now the Hillhurst area, but ended up trading his prized violin for land farther to the west. He started to work this site, farther west than most of the settlers wished to be, and supplemented his meagre farm income by working for the CPR in Cochrane, pumping water for the water tower. In 1895, he married Elizabeth McBail, who he had met at a party and impressed with his prowess on his new violin. The couple moved from their homestead to Midnapore in 1909.

There is a particularly gnarled old Limber pine to the north, just as you reach the top of Scott Lake Hill. It is a venerable old character, standing among the white spruce along the crest of the ridge.

At 1,410 metres above sea level, Scott Lake Hill is the second-highest point on the entire Trans-Canada. (The highest is B.C.'s Kicking Horse Pass, at 1,643 metres, and the third-highest is B.C.'s Rogers Pass, at 1,382 metres.) Drivers along this stretch of the highway may experience a meteorological phenomenon known as a temperature inversion as they climb over the hill. In this condition, continental polar air from the Arctic meets warm air from the Pacific, and the warmer air flows over top of the cooler air. In the winter, entering this warm zone results in instantly fogged windows and some tense moments until visibility is restored.

Tree ID – Limber Pine

The Limber pine's Latin name is *Pinus flexilis,* which comments on the flexed and distorted shape that they tend to take. These trees are sculpted by their environment, blasted and sculpted by the wind. Their preference to grow in a solitary state on exposed slopes and ridges makes them subject to the blast of the elements. Unlike other pines, the lower branches of the Limber pine tend to be much longer than the upper branches, giving it a graceful, reaching air. The trees reach a mature height of about 10 metres.

The needles of the Limber pine grow in groups of five, each about five to six centimetres long. Their cylindrical cones are the largest of any on the pines in this region – up to 12 centimetres long – and have thick, woody scales. All pine trees have both male and female cones. The ones we notice are the females ones, because male cones are less noticeable, being much smaller and tending to fall off after they have released their load of pollen.

Conifer Needles

You can easily tell which of our conifers you are looking at by examining the needles and remembering this little memory aid:

Pines have long needles of Portentous Proportions, which grow in Pairs (or more…).

Spruce needles are Single and Square, and Spin when rolled between your fingers. But watch out: they're Spiky and Sharp.

Fir needles are Flat and Friendly (blunt-ended).

Limber pine on Noble Ridge

Chapter 8 - Another Vista... and some Geology

Some Basic Geology — Or Why the Mountains Look the Way They Do...

If you are not at all interested in geology and the processes by which the mountains that you are witnessing were formed, then you may wish to skip this chapter. However, if you do read the information outlined here, many of the features discussed in the pages ahead will make much more sense. I will try to keep it very simple and brief. But if you become fascinated by this subject, I highly recommend that you find one of the books on geology I mention in the notes and delve into this topic a bit deeper. You will never look at a mountain the same way again...

To start at the very beginning, let's look at how mountains are formed. To do that, we first have to step way back for a look at the much bigger picture – the entire globe. The continents have not always had the outlines we would recognize on a contemporary map. In fact, they once (almost two billion years ago!!) were part of a single vast land mass, a "super-continent", known as Rodinia. On the surface of this mass, there accumulated a series of layers of rock-forming material or sediments. Their composition varied as forces in the earth raised and dropped the land mass. These allowed the ocean (or an inland sea, if the dropped area was a dip in the middle of the land mass) to flood the area, and sediments to settle and build on the ocean floor. Layers of sediment accumulated and eventually formed rock, which still shows distinct, identifiable layers. Then, about 800 million years ago, this mass of land broke up into smaller sections, or plates, that began to move about the surface of the globe on the fluid layer of molten rock beneath them.

The view from Scott Lake Hill

Eventually, the loose plates rejoined to form a second contiguous land mass, called Pangaea. This supercontinent existed from about 500 million to 200 million years ago (roughly during the geological periods known as the Paleozoic and early Mesozoic eras). All around the coastline of this continent, more land continued to form from sediments generated, in part, by the earliest living things – early corals and other sea creatures. These sediments are a little different from the older rock layers: they are known as carbonates (because they contain calcium and magnesium carbonate), and they formed the limestone and dolomite that make up a great deal of the mountain mass in the Rockies.

Like its predecessor, this supercontinent broke up (starting about 200 million years ago) and the plates floated around on the earth's surface. Accumulation of sediments continued, this time mainly as shales and sandstones. In the course of their moving around, plates sometimes bumped into each other. When this occurred, one of the plates would be lifted up, forcing the other plate down and under it. By now, we are in (relatively) recent prehistory, geologically speaking,

Million Years Ago	Eon	Era	Period	Rock formations		Event
1.6	Phanerozoic	Cenozoic	Quaternary		Sediments form sandstones and shales	Ice Ages begin
66			Tertiary			Laramide orogeny (85 Ma)
144		Mesozoic	Cretaceous	Belly River Kootenay		Columbia orogeny (175 Ma)
208			Jurassic		Formation of carbonates on edges of continents – dolomite & limestone	
245			Triassic			
286		Paleozoic	Permian			
320			Pennsylvanian			
360			Mississippian	Rundle / Banff		Pangaea forms and breaks up
408			Devonian	Fairholme / Palliser		
438			Silurian			
505			Ordovician			
			Cambrian	Gog / Pika / Eldon / Stephen / Cathedral	Formation of slate, gristone, and quartzite through ocean bottom sediments	Rodinia breaks up
590	Precambrian	Proterozoic	Upper			
900			Middle			Rodinia is already very old

Geological time scale

and this is where the land shapes that we are looking at began to be formed.

These collisions between tectonic (from the Greek *tecton*, meaning "builder") plates sound truly cataclysmic, but remember that it all happened very, very, very slowly. In fact, this process is still happening today, for instance as the plate that supports India runs into the Asian Plate to its north True, it doesn't feel all that dramatic. But it *is* a process similar to the one that produced the Rocky Mountains, and it is pushing up the Himalayas at a rate of about 5 millimetres a year (not quite as fast as your fingernails grow).

Each of the layers of sediments that accumulated to form the rock of our earth's crust has individual characteristics that have been identified and named by geologists. By examining and mapping the layers (or "formations"), geologists have managed to get a picture of how mountains were raised.

Mountain building in the Rockies occurred in a series of events between about 175 million and 85 million years ago. The collision that raised them began when the North American Plate was heading westward and ran into the Pacific Plate, which was moving to the northeast. The North American Plate was by far the heftier of the two, so it was harder to deviate from its course and it pushed the Pacific Plate down and under it. But the Pacific Plate did offer resistance, so the material on the surface of that plate started to crumple and be scraped into folds in front of the advancing North American Plate. This, in turn, started pushing the material on the North American Plate back into ripples and folds. The pieces of the Pacific Plate became glued onto the western edge of the North American Plate, forming most of what's now British Columbia. This all happened at the amazingly slow speed of up to 5 centimetres a year. We have begun to understand that this crumpling and folding, as cataclysmic and chaotic as it sounds, actually happened in a somewhat orderly fashion. And this is what created the distinctly different types of mountains that you observe as you move deeper into the Rockies.

After travelling west through the foothills, our route first crosses the Front Ranges, which have a distinctly different form than the Main Ranges that form the central area of the Rocky Mountains.

Think back to all those periods in which sediments were being laid down and forming layers of rock. These layers remained distinct in the earth's crust, and moved together as they were forced sideways, broke, and then slid up and over the layers that had been adjacent to them. This break is called a fault, and when one side of the broken rock is forced (or thrust) up over the other, it is called a thrust fault. The remarkable thing about a thrust fault is that, if the layers are pushed right up over top of those adjacent to them, you end up with layers of older rock sitting on top of younger ones. The result is the compressing of the land surface into a telescoped, tilted, or stacked arrangement, covering a much smaller (narrower) area than the smooth and spread-out

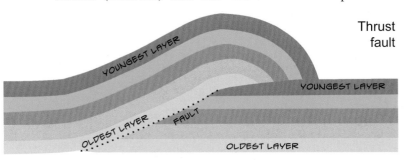

Thrust fault

surface did at the start. In the case of the Rockies, geologists believe that the land area was compressed together by about 200 kilometres!

The first mountains built in the Rockies were the Main Ranges in the central area. The layers were pushed up, faulted, and stacked on top of each other in the fashion of a layer cake stacked on top of another one. The entire mass was moved (extremely slowly) about 40 kilometres from the southwest toward the northeast as tremendous forces played out their strength on the earth's surface. This event, called the Columbia *orogeny* (from the Greek word for "mountain generating") occurred about 175 million years ago.

Then, as the waves of pressure continued to move eastward, more mountains were pushed up to the eastern side of the Main Ranges. But in this case, the faults broke the earth's crust into sections that stacked up next to each other, much like a stack of books piled side by side on a slant. This second event is known as the Laramide *orogeny*, and it produced the Front Ranges (the mountains on the eastern side of the Rockies) about 85 million years ago. Farther east, these ripples did not result in such a complete lifting of the layers, and these became the foothills and ridges between Calgary and the mountains. And even farther east, there is no evidence of tilting, so the layers lie flat and undisturbed on the prairie.

Now, to this picture you need to add the millions of years of erosion that have further sculpted the mountains. The highest mountains in the Main Ranges were once as high as the Himalayas are today, but they have been worn down to lesser remnants of their former selves. Wind, freezing, and, in particular, glaciation have changed the mountains' appearance enormously from the raw, much larger forms they once were. Remember the exceptionally long time during which sediments accumulated to create the rock layers. To understand the effect of weathering and erosion,

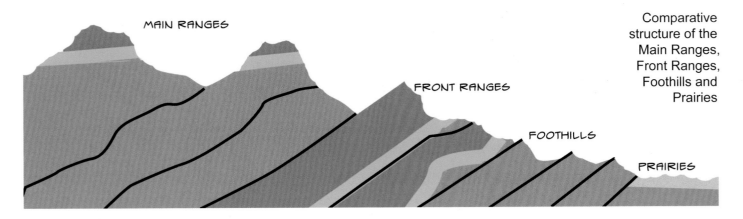

Comparative structure of the Main Ranges, Front Ranges, Foothills and Prairies

Taking Your Eyes Off the Road – The Panorama

This is a particularly impressive view, but there is absolutely no safe place to pull off and enjoy it – such a pity. Stay in the far right lane and try to keep paying attention to the traffic while you take in the wall of mountains in front of you.
Many of these mountains will be discussed in more detail down the road, so just enjoy filling your eyes for now...

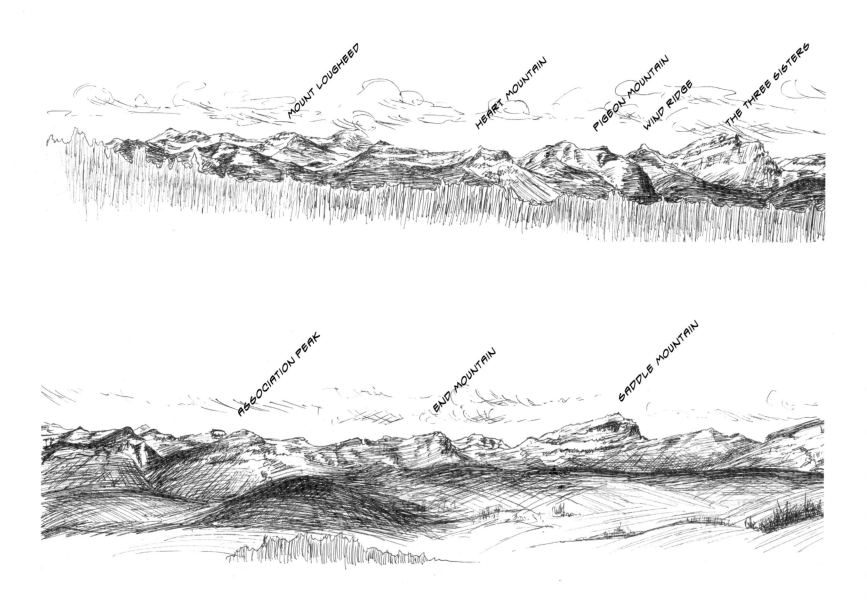

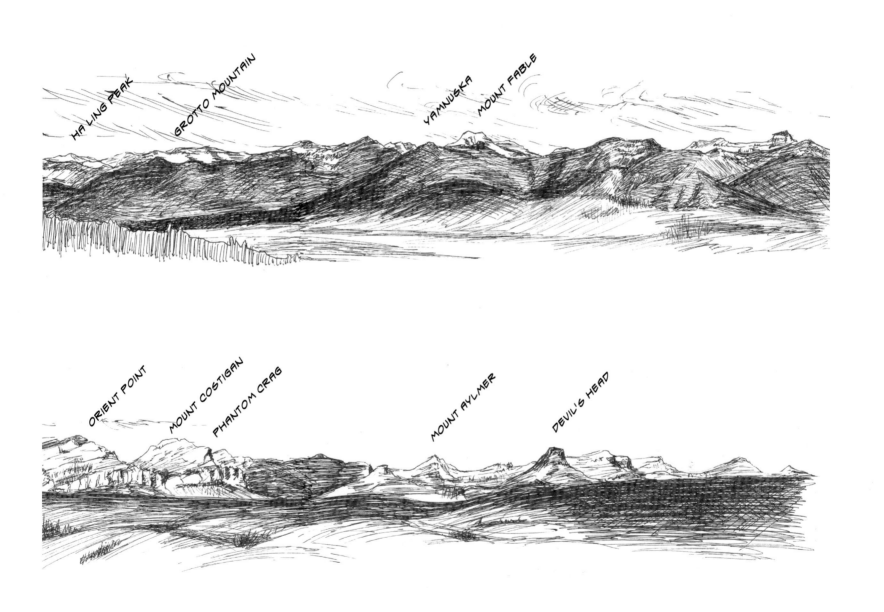

HA LING PEAK
GROTTO MOUNTAIN
YAMNUSKA
MOUNT FABLE

ORIENT POINT
MOUNT COSTIGAN
PHANTOM CRAG
MOUNT AYLMER
DEVIL'S HEAD

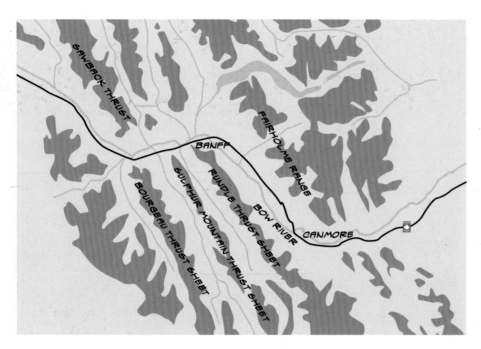

Trellis drainage
pattern

will see a series of diagonally oriented mountain summit ridges separated by regular valleys. The Trans-Canada crosses four of these rows of diagonal summit ridges before the Banff townsite, then follows a drainage valley northwest before crossing three more lines of summit ridges after the highway turns southwest again. These valley drainages are connected intermittently wherever water has found a weak point to erode between the valleys, creating a grid-like effect. This pattern is termed a trellis drainage system.

In contrast to the tilted layers of the Front Ranges, in the Main Ranges the harder layers tend to sit horizontally on top of the softer rock instead of being angled against each other. Thus the Main Ranges do not show the regularity of ridge and valley found in the Front Ranges. The mass of the Main Ranges is more similar in material, as if a single sheet had been thrust over this part of the mountains, then broken up and eroded into distinct peaks. Since the harder rocks tend to somewhat shield the softer layers, the mass tends to remain more intact. The peak and valley organization is more random. These peaks have been stacked up to higher elevations and have higher valleys between them. Being therefore colder and wetter, it is here that you find the glaciers – remnants of the most recent period of great glaciation over the northern part of the continent. The oldest rocks are exposed in places in the Main Ranges, and we will see these layers in the Lake Louise region.

As we move farther west, we will look at some specific examples of this theoretical description. Hopefully, looking at a real mountain and then mentally moving back in time through the processes just described will allow you to envision how that massive pile of rock came to look the way it does today.

you must bear in mind that these layers – laid down over millions of years through different processes and in divergent conditions – have distinct characteristics and vary greatly in hardness. Some layers are very tough and resistant to erosion, while others are much softer and wear away more easily. As a general rule, the older rock is much harder than the younger layers.

So, back to the Front Ranges… As mentioned above, older formations may now be lying on top of younger ones (in some places the difference is as much as 450 million years!). This also means that harder rock may lie above softer rock. The upper layers of older and harder limestone from 500 million to 250 million years old are separated by softer layers of siltstone and shale from 100 million to 65 million years old. Being softer, the siltstone and shale wear away much faster, leaving the limestone even further exposed. The areas that have eroded out become drainage valleys between peaks formed of harder carbonates such as limestone and dolomite. This pattern accounts for the eastern edge of the Rockies, which is about 50 kilometres wide.

If you look at a topographical map of the Front Range Mountains between the foothills and Banff townsite, you

As you crest Scott Lake Hill, you are entering the Stoney Nakoda Reserve. There is a sign on the boundary just after the limber pine on the north side of the highway, and it stretches on across the windswept Morley Flats to the Kananaskis River. Prior to allocation of land to specific tribes through Treaty No. 7, a number of different native groups would have moved through this area. Most of the tribes were of a nomadic nature and may have used this region only sporadically, but they all contributed to the mix of early cultures that tapped the resources of these lands and created a diverse cultural presence. The Kootenay may have made periodic trips from the west for trade; the Blackfoot would have passed through, heading for the mountains to collect tepee poles; and the Cree may have made hunting trips into the area. But now it is exclusively the home of the Stoney Nakoda people, who had traditionally called this area their homeland.

Entering the Stoney Nakoda Reserve

A Brief History of the Stoney Nakoda

As was briefly discussed in Chapter 4, the Stoney tribe – or the Stoney Nakoda, to be more accurate – were relative latecomers into this tribal dynamic. It is speculative to date their exact arrival on the eastern slopes of the Rockies, but it is documented that the Stoney Nakoda were living in the Alberta foothills by the middle of the 18th century. References in the writings of the early Jesuits indicate a split between the Dakota/Lakota nation, to the south of modern Manitoba, and the Stoney-Assiniboine people as early as the mid-17th century. When Anthony Henday (see Chapter 5) made his trek in 1754, he found a people who he identified as Stoneys established in the western plains.

There are a number of theories about why these people moved westward into this part of the country. The push of the fur trade may have been a factor, and it fits with these dates. The Stoneys were certainly among the groups to have made early contact with traders and received guns and other metal objects. We know that the arrival of the fur trade caused extensive redistribution among tribal groups regarding which territories they could claim and hold, as some tribe received firearms and material support and others did not. The Stoneys appear to have moved westward in a similar pattern to the Cree, with whom they were allies and who were active traders of fur.

Other scholars observe that the early smallpox epidemics and other diseases that accompanied the arrival of the white man in the east may also have been a motivating factor for westward migration. Catherine Whyte of Banff, in a letter to her mother in 1945, refers to a story told to her by Stoney Chief Hector Crawler: "The Indians who lived on the plains

or prairies had a great sickness about four hundred years ago. Hector called it a kind of flu, but his son-in-law George McLean said it was smallpox. Many died, whole tepees of people. (They speak of a family as a tepee of Indians.) Sometimes there would be just one boy or girl left in each tepee, and the Indians tried to get away from this great sickness and went off in different directions, but still the sickness went with them and many died. The Stoneys came to the mountains and the sickness gradually left them."[1]

Regardless of the reason, the first wave of Stoney Nakoda are now known as the Chiniki band, and they settled in the area of the Bow Valley. A second wave may have arrived somewhat later, by 1700, via a more northerly route. These people, the Goodstoney or Wesley bank, established themselves farther north, near the headwaters of the North Saskatchewan River in an area now called Kootenay Plains. The Bearspaw band occupied the lands further to the south, around the Jumping Pound, Highwood, and Oldman rivers. These three groups are collectively known as the Mountain Stoneys. There are other groups of Assiniboine Sioux-speaking Indians further to the north, west of Edmonton, who are identified as the Wood Stoneys (and who are part of Treaty No. 6 rather than No. 7). The language dialects are slightly different between the two groups, which linguists suggest indicates an earlier division. Altogether, the Stoneys once inhabited an area from the U.S. border north to the Jasper area, and from the present B.C.-Alberta border across the mountains into the plains where Calgary stands today.

Discussions of Stoney culture tend to treat the three Mountain Stoney bands as one homogenous group, but there are distinctions among them. John Laurie, writing in

Chiniki Chief Calf Child (Hector Crawler), Stoney (Chiniki), Glenbow NA-3878-7

the 1950s, commented that the Goodstoney band was of a different character than the other two bands – which may have been due to its isolation from more aggressive tribes and greater distance from the buffalo. The three bands – the Bearspaw, Chiniki, and Wesley (as the Goodstoney are now called) – tend to be lumped together these days partly because they were treated as a single group in the treaty settlement. More on that later…

The people of the Stoney Nakoda tribe occupied the transitional area between the plains and the mountains, and thus benefitted from the resources in both regions. The tribes of the plains had developed a lifestyle completely oriented around a bison-based economy. But the Stoneys, because they moved between two economic and geographic zones, could take advantage of the opportunities presented by both – though sometimes at the peril of encountering hostile tribes set on protecting what they saw as their unique right to their land's resources. On the principal lands that the Stoneys occupied, along the eastern slope of the Rockies, they could pursue a range of game such as sheep, moose, deer, elk, and goats, as well as smaller animals such as hare and marmots. Here, hunting as an organized group was less important than the individual skill of tracking and stalking, although sharing the wealth from successful hunts was still emphasized among the communities.

But the Stoneys' hunting trips farther onto the plains were always fraught with the fear of running into bands of their enemies, the Blackfoot. Records dating from after the arrival of white settlers indicate that the Stoneys used buffalo pounds as a hunting technique, but in a much more limited way than the Blackfoot. Their lesser dependence on a single food source made a great difference in their transition to the post-treaty world.

These people call themselves *Îyârhe Nakodabi* in their own tongue, which roughly means "Rocky Mountain Sioux." The name "Stoney" comes from their practice of cooking by dropping hot stones into hide-lined pits to heat the contents. Henry Kelsey, exploring west from Hudson's Bay (and probably the first European to see the open prairie) commented on encountering a group of Indians whom his Cree guides called the *Assine-boets*, which means "stone cookers."

First Contact with Europeans — David Thompson

Rumours of white people preceded their actual arrival on the eastern slopes of the Rocky Mountains. There are traditional stories among the Stoney Nakoda of predictions made by their medicine men and of people having visions of strange beings arriving in their lands. The first to arrive were in pursuit of trade – explorers sent west by the Hudson's Bay Company

The first white man of note in this area was David Thompson. This early adventurer, who was born in 1770, had a rough start in life. His father died when David was two years old, and the young boy's mother, unable to provide for David and his brother, gave them up to the Grey Coat Hospital. David excelled in his studies and graduated from a mathematical school, where he had developed an early interest in navigation. In 1784, at the age of only 14, he was accepted for an apprenticeship with the Hudson's Bay Company and moved to Canada. Sent west as clerk on an expedition, in 1787 Thompson first saw the mountains in the distance and recorded in his journal that "they rose in height, their immense masses of snow appeared above the clouds and formed an impassable barrier, even to the Eagle."[2]

A decade later, Thompson had been promoted to the position of surveyor with the HBC. Then, suddenly, he jumped ship in 1797 to join the competition. Thompson hired on with the rival North West Company, which had been formed in 1783 by a group of wealthy Montreal merchants to challenge the monopoly held by the Hudson's Bay Company. The latter had been granted exclusive rights over all lands draining into Hudson's Bay in 1670 by King Charles II. (Hudson's Bay, the body of water, was later renamed Hudson Bay, but the company has retained the original name.) Since the geography of Western Canada was not well understood, this was a rather vague definition, and the North West Company felt that there were trading opportunities to be had outside the grip of the long-established company – and that the HBC's exclusive hold on the vast region's abundant resources was perhaps too stretched to be effectively protected.

The NWC sent Thompson on his first trip west as a surveyor and fur trader in 1798, and in 1800 his explorations took him and his colleague Duncan McGillivray along the Bow River. Thompson's journals record his impressions of the landscape and the dynamics of raiding among the different tribes in the region. In the vicinity of the Bow River, the trading party found itself in the midst of a horse-raiding expedition by the aggressive Peigan against the Kootenay just as the Nor' Westers were trying to make contact with the Kootenay. The European explorers were forced to provide protection for the Kootenays, who returned home westward over the mountains after the Peigans stole their horses and laid plans to ambush the Kootenay party en route to its own lands. Of the Stoneys, Thompson recorded that "the Stone Indians are always in want of horses, which appears to be occasioned by hard usage. They are most noted horse stealers and wherever they appear in small parties, the horses are immediately guarded."[3]

By 1806, the focus of Thompson's task had become the location of a new route to the Pacific. Alexander Mackenzie had made a more northerly corssing to the Pacific in 1793 and Lewis and Clark had travelled across the United States to the Pacific Ocean in 1806. The British needed a more southerly foothold in their territories. Thompson continued his exploration of Western Canada throughout the first decade of the 19th century, mapping the drainage of the Kootenay and Columbia rivers. He finally made it to the mouth of the Columbia in 1811, but only after the Americans had already arrived there and staked a claim to what's now Oregon and Washington state. Nonetheless, the maps that Thompson drew during his extensive explorations remained the standard reference source for many decades of subsequent exploration.

The Establishment of Trade in the Bow Valley

On the north side of the Bow River, 10 kilometres west of the town of Morley, a creek runs down through the hills to join the river. Now known as Old Fort Creek, this is where European traders first tried to establish a toehold in this area. The early trading routes were concentrated farther north, around Rocky Mountain House, largely due to the hostility of the Blackfoot farther south. But by the 1820s, trading posts were being established south of the 49th parallel and there was competitive pressure on the Hudson's Bay Company to increase its presence in its holdings farther south.

In 1832, John Rowland was sent west to establish a presence at a site along the Bow River. However, business did not thrive – the Peigan had just been defeated in a skirmish with the Bloods and were not trading, and other groups were reported to be elsewhere in pursuit of the buffalo herds. There is some speculation that what business was done was quietly conducted on the side by less-than-loyal employees, which cut into the Hudson Bay Company's profits. The HBC again retreated to Rocky Mountain House. What became known as Peigan Post or Old Bow Fort (to distinguish it from the later HBC Bow Fort built at the junction of the Bow and Elbow rivers) soon burned to the ground.

The Arrival of the Missionaries

Soon other Europeans arrived with different intentions than trade – to bring the word of their God to the "savages" of the new lands. Again, there are stories of predictions among the Indians that had paved the way for the missionaries' arrival. William and Joshua Twin described a story to Jon Whyte: "It was a very lean winter, people were starving, and the chief was praying and singing to ask for help for his people. He suddenly heard a voice, telling him to stop singing and to 'watch and listen for a white missionary who will come to this country of yours at the time of the next moon. When the snow is gone and when that missionary comes he will tell you about a Father God in Heaven, and if he tells you about this God, that is very true. You believe in that God and leave me alone for I cannot help you any more.'"[4]

Sure enough, in 1844 a Wesleyan minister, Reverend Robert Rundle, made his way into the area, where he was well received by the Stoney people. They were the first native group Rundle introduced to Christianity, the Stoney leaders *Tchakta* and Two Young Men being his first converts.

Robert Rundle was born in 1811 in Cornwall, England. In 1840, he was one of three missionaries taken into the employ of the Hudson's Bay Company to head west to minister to the Indians and act as company chaplain. The three missionaries set off, having been given a set of printed instructions from the Wesleyan Society regarding their conduct: "Take heed to yourselves as well as to your doctrine. Keep yourselves pure. Keep at the utmost distance from all trifling and levity in your intercourse with young persons, more especially with females. Take no liberties with them… Never be unemployed. Never be triflingly employed. Do not while away time… the completion or frustration of your new mission mainly depends under God upon your fidelity."[5]

Although Rundle worked in the area for about seven years, he never set up a fixed mission. He preferred working in the Indian camps to being based in a fort, and he moved around the area, visiting the various native groups, travelling by horseback with his pet cat. Over the years he performed many marriages and baptisms, keeping careful records of the latter, noting the Indian names of the parents but registering the child with a European name. His diaries record a certain discomfort regarding the rival presence of the Catholic missionary, Father Pierre-Jean De Smet, who arrived in the area in 1845 and made occasional forays into what Rundle had come to regard as his flock.

The mountains held great allure for Rundle, and he eagerly embraced opportunities to explore them. It seems appropriate that one of the most picturesque peaks is now graced with his name – but that is a few chapters away yet…

Of a more enduring influence was the arrival of the Methodist missionaries Rev. George McDougall and his son, Rev. John McDougall, who came to the area in 1873. In the early 1870s, the Stoneys had expressed an interest in support from Methodist missionaries, to minister to their newly acquired Christian beliefs and help them deal with the influence of the aggressive liquor traders. The McDougalls arrived in the area in the same year as the North-West Mounted Police were established – a dual counterattack on the distributors of firewater in the West.

The McDougalls established a site for their mission not far from the previous location of Old Bow Fort. The place came to be known as Morley, or sometimes Morleyville, named for Rev. Morley Puncheon, a Methodist preacher who was a supporter of the new mission. The Stoneys had known the area as *Mînî Thnî*, or "place one takes bows from." It had been a traditional wintering ground, providing a reliable water source, some shelter from the elements, and a supply of firewood, as well as being kept fairly snow-free by the chinook winds that scoured the area. To the McDougalls, it seemed a logical place to encourage their flock to establish a permanent settled community and start to enter a more agricultural mode of existence.

The first site for the mission was on a raised bench, which provided some defensive protection from Blackfoot incursions. Two years later, the troubles with the Blackfoot and whiskey traders had settled down enough for more permanent buildings to be established closer to the Bow River. A log house was built for the three McDougall families (John's brother, David, and his family had joined the endeavour) and a split log church was erected. It was later adorned with a bell tower housing a train bell donated by the CPR.

In 1874, David built a trading post, taking over from an HBC post that had closed shortly after the McDougalls' arrival. A schoolhouse was added in 1876, and was referred to as an orphanage even though most of the students had family in the area. There is speculation that this designation encouraged more successful fundraising back east. The church received various additions and upgrades over the years, but the original building is still there as part of the recently restored structure that stands on the original foundations. It

Rev Rundle, no date, Glenbow NA 589-3

can be visited if you take a short detour north of Highway One through Morley and very slightly east on Highway 1A.

George McDougall tragically died of exposure in 1876. That January, some of the last herds of bison were reported to the east of the mission, and he had gone out with a hunting party to procure some meat. On the return trip, George went ahead to start dinner at camp. But he never made it to camp, and his frozen body was found 13 days later.

Another individual who we met briefly in the previous chapter joined the McDougalls in the capacity of school-teacher. Andrew Sibbald was born in Ontario in 1833 and worked as a carpenter until he lost his left hand in an accident. He then retrained as a teacher and came west in 1875 to teach in Morley – the first school teacher in Alberta. Despite his impediment of being single-handed, Sibbald brought with

him a portable sawmill, which he set up on the banks of the Bow. He became known as one of the best builders in the region in spite of his handicap. Sibbald's wife died in the typhoid epidemic of 1882, but he lived on to the age of 101.

The following year, John McDougall accompanied the Stoney Nakoda contingent to the Treaty No. 7 negotiations at Blackfoot Crossing, as was touched on in Chapter 4. The Stoneys were the only group present that were under the influence of a missionary, which may have affected their position on the proceedings. As was mentioned, all three bands were lumped together and given only one territory under the treaty, which was

contrary to their understanding that each band had been promised its own reserve. How this occurred is unclear. It seems likely that the decision to configure the reserve this way was made by the Indian Commissioner, who instructed the surveyor (possibly in consultation with Rev. McDougall). The surveyor, in his notes, did state that the only band he found camped in the vicinity where he was instructed to work was that of Chief John Chiniquay. That was because Chief Jacob Goodstoney and the Wesley band families were camped by the headwaters of the Red Deer, James, Clearwater, North Saskatchewan, and Brazeau rivers, waiting for surveyors to show up.[6] They never did.

The order in council that created the reserve lists three separate clauses (142, 143, and 144) as if in recognition of three separate entities. In 1892, after Chief Peter Wesley's band had struggled with famine and crowded conditions, Wesley took most of the band's members back to their traditional lands west of Rocky Mountain House. There, they essentially occupied their own homeland as squatters until their claim was recognized in 1947 and 5,000 acres were given to them as the Bighorn Reserve. The Bearspaw band likewise remained on part of its traditional lands at the upper region of the Highwood River until the Eden Valley Reserve was designated there in the 1940s.

But to return to Morley... When the reserve survey was done, it was determined that the lands the McDougalls had claimed for their own homes, trading post, school, mission,

and farm were within the reserve's boundaries. The Methodist mission petitioned for title to this area, which was granted. Thus the most productive land in the area was removed from the official tract of the reserve. This has led to ongoing land-claims disputes.

Meanwhile, the McDougalls were trying to assist the Stoney Nakoda to make the transition from hunting to agriculture. This had been one of the intentions of Treaty No. 7, and McDougall had encouraged the Stoneys to accept farm implements as part of the settlement in place of the cattle that some bands had received to help them set up ranching operations. However, it soon became very apparent that, in addition to the Indians' lack of background or enthusiasm for agricultural pursuits, their lands were hideously unsuited to crop production. This fact was recognized by the land surveyor for the Dominion, who informed the Minister of the Interior in his report that "There is no timber on either portion, other than a few scrubby clumps of small poplar of no value, and a few spruce and pines also of no value except as firewood. The land is very stony and gravely, as a rule and is of little or no value in our agricultural sense."[7] Another surveyor reported that "the climate of this locality is such that I do not think that grain could be raised here at all, and as to other things only those that are hardy, will ever repay the trouble and expense of cultivation."[8]

By the 1880s, most of the Indian tribes, with the loss of the buffalo and restriction to small pieces of land, were starving. The federal government had been forced to institute food rations, but in 1884 Indian agent Magnus Begg informed the Stoneys that because they could still hunt, they would not receive rations except for the sick and widows. This led to another great struggle for these people. They had been better off than the tribes that depended wholly on the buffalo, as they had a variety of game in the foothills and into the mountains. But they were then faced with the demand that they must stay on their reserve (for many years, they were even required to obtain a pass from the Indian Agent to leave the reserve for any purpose), and conform to all game-hunting laws. The Stoneys had understood that, under the treaty, they would continue to have the right to hunt on all unoccupied Crown land. This situation worsened and became an ongoing conflict among various interests.

As the Rocky Mountains Park (later to become Banff National Park – details in Chapter 12) was being established in the mountains, complaints were laid that the Indians were responsible for the depletion of big game. In 1902, Howard Sibbald (Andrew's son) reported, in his capacity as Indian Agent, that the enlargement of the park had encompassed almost all the Stoneys' hunting grounds. And in 1909, park superintendent Howard Douglas named the Stoneys as the most serious threat to game in the national park. One wonders if the pressure put on the natives to stop hunting was coincidental – Sibbald was quoted as saying that "as long as they can hunt you cannot civilize them."[9] Even in 1921, mountain guide and outfitter Jimmy Simpson wrote to the Commissioner for the National Parks and North West Game Act complaining about hunting by the Indians and

Morley Mission, 1875 (Church in background, mission house on left) – drawing by Richard Barrington Nevitt, Glenbow NA-51-2 art dept cat. 59.40.23

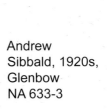

Andrew Sibbald, 1920s, Glenbow NA 633-3

The church at Morley, 2009

claiming that it threatened the positive experiences of visiting sportsmen.

There is some controversy regarding the McDougalls' role in the federal government's efforts to convert the Indian population into a sedentary and co-operative agricultural community that would meekly take guidance from the new leaders of the Dominion and leave behind its traditional ways of life as a semi-nomadic hunting culture. In 1874, John had accepted a commission from the government to tour the region and explain the meaning of the upcoming treaty negotiations and the NWMP's role in protecting the Indians from such negative influences as the whiskey trade. It is probably fair to stay that there is some ambiguity between the mandates of God and government in his activities…

A large segment of the Indian population feels that they were betrayed by the missionaries. The actions of these men must be considered in the context of attitudes at the time, which assumed that the white man knew best which future was advantageous for the native population and that the missionaries were charged with helping the Indians see the light and adapt to the white man's ways for their own betterment. This patronizing attitude is hard to understand from our modern perspective, but it was what these missionaries believed justified them in labelling Indian ways of life and spiritual beliefs as backward and erroneous.

As for the Morley mission, a new boarding school was constructed in 1883 on lots 7 and 8 of the Morleyville Settlement at the present townsite on the north side of the Bow, and it operated until 1908. A new residential school was built in 1925 in the present townsite of Morley (and torn down in 1983 for the modern Morley Community School, which opened in 1986). The Indian Agent office was also located in the "new" town of Morley, and gradually activity began to focus more in that area. The church mission on the north side of the Bow was officially closed in 1921, and a new United Church was built in the townsite.

Morley church, print by Cliff Robinson, 1940s, Courtesy of Ron Robinson

Cultural Notes

Writing about traditional native culture and beliefs is something that I have approached with some trepidation. Addressing the topic from outside the culture, there is a great risk in misinterpreting, in placing an incorrect emphasis, in making the mistake of presenting beliefs and practices as artefacts for a sort of cultural voyeurism… Yet it would be an oversight not to at least attempt a discussion of this subject –so I forge ahead in hopes that I can offer a balanced and adequately informed view…

I use the past tense in this section, in keeping with a historical account. But many of the things discussed here either remain a part of modern Stoney Nakoda culture or have been revived in recent years, so referring to them in the present tense would frequently be entirely appropriate.

Not much has been written about traditional Stoney Nakoda culture. The first, and only, comprehensive scientific ethnography was recorded by anthropologist Robert H. Lowie (titled "The Assiniboine") in 1907. One of the few individuals who did record information on this topic was John Laurie. He was a Calgary educator who promoted

Indian concerns from the mid-1930s until his death in 1959. He held the position of Secretary for the Indian Association of Alberta for many years. Among the files he left are extensive interviews and descriptions of native culture, work on Stoney-language dictionaries, and other valuable records.

This is how Laurie described the traditional dress of the Stoney Nakoda: "The men wore breechcloths or aprons about their middle, sometimes both garments, sometimes one or the other. Leggings, resembling the 'chaps' of the cowboy, covered their legs and were fastened by thongs to a belt. Some men wore skin shirts and most used a fur robe in winter. The women wore a long dress of tanned skins, bound at the waist by a belt, and moccasins whose high tops reached almost to the knee. Often they made an effort to ornament their garments with trade beads, shells, elk or beaver teeth."[10]

The embellishment of clothing and other items reflected the influence of several stylistic traditions. Like the eastern woodland Indians, the Stoney Nakoda employed elements of floral motifs in naturalistic colours, although they also employed the geometric patterns of the plains peoples. In general, their decorative work tended to use brighter colours than those usually found among the plains Indians. One element considered typically Stoney was the use of lines or stripes running the length of the decorated area.

Group of Stoney Indians, 1906, Byron Harmon, National Library and Archives C-015046

The Stoney Nakodas' dwellings, like their garments, were sometimes adorned with patterns and symbols, mostly geometric shapes such as circles, stripes, and triangles. The tent-style tepee was made by stretching new skins over a cone-shaped framework of poles, and a fire was lit inside the structure to cure the hides in this form. Erecting the tepee was traditionally the domain of the women in the tribe. The people did not necessarily live in tepees all year, but may also have erected more permanent structures, perhaps with spruce bark as an external facing.

Sites that were favoured for tepee encampments are evident in the remaining "tepee rings" of stones used to weigh down the tent sides. Archaeologists can identify the age of a site

Stoney travois, 1937, Glenbow NA-1164-1

partly by the diameter of these rings: smaller rings were used in earlier days when, before the horse became a part of native culture, belongings were carried on dog travois.

The travois was a wheel-less trailer of sorts. Shaped in a broad "V" that came over the back of a dog – or, in later years, a horse – it supported a platform to carry the load of belongings (or kids!).

A ceremonial structure that can occasionally be seen from the Trans-Canada is the Sundance lodge. There are a couple of these ceremonial lodges visible at the time of writing 58 kilometres into our trip from Calgary (they are set back in the valley a bit, and are more easily visible if you are driving eastward, from the pulloff on the flats). The Sundance ceremony has had a strong revival recently, after having been repressed in the early part of the 20th century – and even outlawed by the Indian Act until 1957. These elaborate ceremonies were generally held in times of need or if a member of the band had a vision that inspired such a ceremony. It may have been held as an appeal to the Great Creator for good food supplies and good health among the people of the tribe, or as an expression of gratitude for the end of a long winter. The event may have involved the making of vows or pledges by individuals involved in the ceremony, and similar statements of support from other in the tribe.

Once a Sundance ceremony has been called, usually during the early spring, preparations by the tribe's medicine man begin that involve several days of fasting and prayer. A tree is selected to serve as the centre pole for the lodge, and it is cut with great reverence and raised in the chosen location, accompanied by song and prayer. A new site is used for each event, and at the end the lodge is left to fall back to the earth. Offerings of coloured cloth are tied to the central pole and surrounding circular wall, which is about 20 metres in diameter and built of branches to create a sacred space on the interior and screen events from the outside world. Around the perimeter, sweat lodges are built for ritual purifications in preparation for the Sundance events themselves.

After the preparations, the crowd gathers around the perimeter of the lodge. The dancers, their faces painted, enter and start to dance. Traditionally, the young warriors would skew lines from the top of the pole to their chest by pegs and dance until they were pulled through the skin. These days they rarely do so. Dancers blow on bone whistles to get the attention of the Great Spirit. A variety of other dance styles are also performed. Twenty-eight days of preparation lead up to the Sundance, which extends over four days.

The sweat lodge was used on many other occasions besides the Sundance. The lodge itself was a low, dome-shaped structure two to three metres across, made from cut willows and covered with hides. Water sprinkled over hot rocks created a steamy atmosphere. The important elements of fire, wood, water, and stone were all symbolically present. As well as preparation for other ceremonies, the lodge was employed as a place to cure ills or access spiritual knowledge, or simply as we might enjoy a sauna today. Sweetgrass was often burned as a purifying smudge or offering. The pipe may have been passed around the circle, and the participants would gesture with it to the four cardinal directions and address guardian spirits, natural forces, and other symbolic references.

Another ceremony that held great importance for the Stoney Nakoda was the vision quest. This was seen as a sacred personal journey to gain wisdom and make a connection with the Great Spirit; a rite of passage for seekers within the community. After purification ceremonies, a seeker would retreat to a designated location, usually a spot with a commanding view and oriented on an east-west axis with the sun. Here, he or she would fast and pray, seeking visions or dreams that would offer guidance or answers to questions.

Chief John Snow described how the quester might gain knowledge of how to assist his tribe: "Upon these lofty heights, the Great Spirit revealed many things to us. Some of my people received powers to heal. They could heal the physical body with herbs, roots, leaves, plants and mineral spring waters. They would also heal the broken and weary soul with unseen spiritual powers. Others received powers over the weather. These gifted religious men and women could call for a great storm or calm the weather; they could call the winds, rain, hail, snow, or sleet, and they would come. From these mountain-top experiences my fellow tribesmen and women were given unique tasks to perform to help the tribe prepare for things to come."[11]

The role of medicine man was of great importance in the tribal community. These individuals may have received their assignment to this role through a vision quest. They received

Stoney Teepe near Banff, no date, Glenbow NA-714-190

a combination of scientific knowledge and spiritual force, as they underwent long training to add great skill to their gift of insight. Their services were sought for predictions and advice, to oversee special events such as the sweat lodge and preparations for a vision quest, and for their healing talents.

Their role as advisors, using their special vision, was described to Marius Barbeau by Daniel Wildman in a story about a theft of some horses by the Bloods: "The chief

Sweatlodge structure

Sundance lodges on Morley Flats

dreamer [Tchakta] *uhamnigition*, was called to try and find in what direction to go. They gave him some tobacco. They honoured him because they depended on him. So he took his spirit drum, *tihamne gahubi* [a large one], and then he took his *gahnabi*, small medicine rattle or spirit drum [which was four inches across]. Choke-cherry stones were inside the small drum or rattle. He took this drum into the big medicine lodge [tipi]; this tipi is only for the spirits, and the young fellows sing to the spirits, saying, 'Oh, grandfather, come on, we need you! We are up against it!' The medicine man shook his rattle, while he did sing. He said to the singers, 'Stop! It is not difficult to find. There are two large camps east of here. The first stands at *Kahanmehedwow* [Deep-Canyon], Cochrane. It is a Blackfoot camp there, and the other, at *Phaben-wabish*, Paint-on-the-Rock.' On this rock the enemies used to paint signs in the earlier days. Whoever passed there could tell whether Bloods or Blackfeet had been there recently. There was a big Blood camp there."[12]

As well as the medicine man, another important role in the Stoney Nakoda community was played by the pipe carrier. These people also had spiritual duties to the tribe and may have acted as seers. The pipes were carefully protected, passed down through generations, and brought out with great reverence. The pipe carrier oversaw the passing of the pipe, and the act of smoking was viewed like a communal prayer, the sacred smoke from the shared pipe acting through the bodies of the participants.

Probably the most well known event in Indian culture is the powwow, and these festivals of dance, singing, and drumming are popular events among all tribes today. They are a chance to meet, participate, and even compete in various dancing styles, to join in celebrating Indian culture, and to socialize. These events, which may last several days, are often sponsored by one tribe, which invites many other tribes to attend.

Many of the spiritual traditions of the Stoney Nakoda were centred on specific geographic sites. Natural features were commonly associated with spirits, and rituals were conducted to honour these forces and make offerings to them. Places such as mountain hot springs, hoodoo formations, high points of land, and mineral veins were held in reverence and frequented at certain times throughout the year. Many of these places now lie within park boundaries, which has created challenges for native people to maintain or renew their connection to their spiritual heritage.

Chief John Snow, in a key passage of his fine book *These Mountains Are Our Sacred Places*, expresses this connection, and describes how "the Rocky Mountains are precious and sacred to us. We know every trail and mountain pass in the area. We had special ceremonies and religious areas in the mountains. In the olden days some of the neighbouring tribes called us the 'People of the Shining Mountains.' These mountains are our temples, our sanctuaries, and our resting places. They are a place of hope, a place of vision, a place of refuge, a very special place where the Great Spirit speaks with us. Therefore, these mountains are our sacred places."[13] The mountains were a part of the Indians' sacred cosmos, a bridge to the spiritual world, and the home of their ancestors.

Recent History

To bring the Stoney Nakodas' story up to the present day requires a brief (and hopelessly oversimplified) discussion development and politics over the past century. Over the 18th to the 19th centuries (by the white man's accounting…), progress spun itself across the reserve as the railway line was laid through the middle of it. The transaction to compensate the tribe for this strip of land was conducted entirely between the CPR and the Department of Indian Affairs, with the Stoney people being given no voice. Indian Affairs proposed a compensation rate of $2.50 per acre (the going rate for land), but eventually settled for $1.25.[14] The Stoneys received a total of $2,100, which they invested in a sawmill.

The first decade of the 20th century was one of intensive settlement in this area. The new homesteaders bumped up against the edge of the reserve and resented the fact that they could not access what they saw as "unused" land. They put pressure on the government, which put pressure on

Stoney Medicine Man, Banff, 1928, National Library and Archives PA040768

the Stoneys, which resulted in the approval of a sale of the northwest corner of the reserve, shrinking it even further.

Calgary Power built the Horseshoe Dam in 1909, and six years later the Ghost Dam, flooding a portion of the reserve and running transmission lines across the land. In 1911, the route for what's now Highway 1A was surveyed, and that highway removed another strip of land from the reserve. And in 1930, the Ghost Lake Dam flooded 1,234 acres of prime land along the Bow River.

Many of these incursions onto reserve land were done without consultation or adequate compensation. And they left unresolved land claims, many yet to be settled.

The Trans-Canada Highway was built through the Stoney Nakoda reserve in the early 1950s and twinned only a decade later. Since that highway is the thread that ties this book together, a whole subsection could be written on the struggles by the Indians to get proper compensation for that episode. The reserve was now divided by a railway, two highways, power line rights-of-way, and the river into a series of long, narrow strips. The Stoneys, who were trying to build up ranching on their land, found the management, watering, and movement of their livestock increasingly difficult.

The federal government had started building the Trans-Canada without having come to any understanding with

Sawmill on the Stoney Reserve, Watercolour and ink sketch by Cliff Robinson, 1940s, Courtesy of Ron Robinson

the bands, and things certainly didn't get any easier during construction. There were disagreements over whether the Stoneys would be compensated with money or land, and, if the latter, which land. The situation deteriorated until the Stoneys threatened to block the highway during a holiday weekend. The government finally gave the Stoneys some land. But it was rough, unproductive country, rather than the better grazing land south of the Bow.

Well into the 1960s, all services on the reserve were still being run by non-Indians employed by the Department of Indian Affairs, with the exception of the band-operated sawmill the Stoney Nation had purchased. In 1968, huge changes occurred as the federal government granted the Indians of Canada the right to self-government. The Stoneys entered a period of both challenges and growth as they undertook to manage their own cultural, educational, and social programs, and enter into commerce for themselves. The Stoney Nakoda language was introduced in the reserve school. The Stoney Indian Park was opened to offer cultural experiences to young people, and featured a buffalo paddock.

From 1971 to 1985, a series of ecumenical conferences were held at this park. These events brought together not only representatives from numerous North American tribes,

but indigenous people from around the world, such as Maoris from New Zealand and Lapps from Norway. These were heady events, filled with sharing of struggles and the occasional triumph, discussions about assimilation and preserving traditional cultures, and comparisons of spiritual and religious beliefs. The people who came to these events took the energy they experienced back to their homelands and developed their own expressions of the spirit of the conference. These events did much to start to rebuild a sense of self-respect and empowerment among native peoples.

On a much more pragmatic plane, the 1970s brought greater prosperity and opportunity to the Stoneys when natural gas was found under their reserve. As income flowed in from the new wells, the tribe was able to undertake many development incentives. Housing was one of its first priorities, as many people were still living in simple log homes even in such recent times. The YMCA Camp Chief Hector was returned and converted into the Stoney Wilderness School, which was used to pass on traditional learning to the young. The Chief Goodstoney Arena and rodeo grounds were constructed in 1983. Businesses were developed at the Morley turnoff from Highway One, including a gift shop, gas station, and the Chief Chiniki Restaurant. The Two Rivers ranch adjacent to the reserve was purchased in 1976 and turned into a detox centre. Development continued into the 1980s as the Nakoda Institute was established, and a lodge and conference centre was built on the shore of Hector Lake. As well as hotel and dining facilities, it houses a library and cultural centre, and acts as the base for the Stoney Cultural Education Program.

The latest, and most controversial, entrepreneurial effort by the Stoneys is the new Stoney Nakoda Resort and Casino, opened in 2008. With natural-gas royalties beginning to decline, it was hoped that this venture would provide revenue for services and infrastructure on the reserve, and jobs for the population. Some members of the tribe strongly objected to the plan. Three elderly sisters conducted a blockade of the construction site until a mediator was called in and an agreement was finally reached. Further developments are planned: a hotel expansion, more tourist facilities, and an outlet mall designed to tap into the tourist dollars flowing by on the Trans-Canada.

The Stoney Nakoda Resort of the Canadian Rockies

Looking Into The Future

The Stoney Nakoda Tribal Council, which is made up of an elected chief and four councillors from each of the three bands, continues to work toward greater economic independence and prosperity, and find ways to preserve and enhance its cultural traditions and identity. The blending of traditional tribal forms of organization with the formal institutions of the modern western world is an ongoing challenge to the Stoney Nakoda leaders, as they try to honour their cultural ancestry while interacting effectively with the broader political and economic scene in Canada.

The Nakoda people have, over their four decades of self-government within a world dominated by the white man, made great steps in finding a way for their people (who now number about 5,000) to manage the influences from two divergent cultures. John Snow described his vision of how this would play out: "We came to understand that it was not an either/or choice: acculturation to the dominant society or clinging to our old ways in a world where they could no longer offer us and our children a good life. We came to understand that there was a third way – the way of biculturalism. We came to understand that we could still follow Stoney tribal customs but, at the same time, adjust to a technological age on our own terms. Our hope was (and still is) to retain the best in the Stoney culture and to take the best in the dominant culture."[15]

View west from Morley

Some Individuals

Before we leave the reserve, I would like to introduce a few of the interesting and important characters who have made their mark in the history of the Stoney Nakoda people. Here are a few members of the tribe who I personally wish that I'd had a chance to have met…

George McLean (Walking Buffalo)

Born near Morley in 1871, named *Tatâga Mâni* in his native tongue, Walking Buffalo attended the signing of Treaty No. 7 at Blackfoot Crossing in 1877 and subsequently witnessed a period of immense change and upheaval for his people. His mother died while he was very young and he was adopted into the family of John McLean, a Methodist missionary from whom he received his English name. After graduating from the Morley school at 16, George McLean went on to study at the Red Deer Industrial School and then St. John's College in Winnipeg. He worked for the NWMP for a while before returning to Morley to work as an interpreter. He quickly attained a reputation of great status among his people, becoming a medicine man, and being elected a chief of the Bearspaw band.

One of the things McLean is best known for is his involvement in the Moral Rearmament movement, and he travelled the world extensively as one of its emissaries in the 1950s and 1960s. This movement, which was based largely in Europe but spread internationally, pointed to the military rearmament on the eve of World War II and called for a parallel spiritual and moral strengthening. The MRA had Christian origins, but embraced a multi-faith approach and multi-ethnic inclusiveness that appealed to McLean.

This man, who had seen his people lose their traditional way of life but who had personally gained a level of comfort in the international, multicultural milieu, expressed his perspective on the Indian transition into white culture to Marius Barbeau: "Our old father told us that the civilized people were coming from the east. These civilized men were called the white people, Red Coats. The savages were told by the white men to stop slaughtering each other. And then, later on, the white traders told us that the buffaloes were going to be gone. We just laughed at them. We could not believe that. In later years, we saw the preachers coming to western Alberta. Every summer the white people increased in number. Then we heard through the traders that the white people were rulers come to the Western country. Even the white traders did not think the savage Indians would be able to live under the civil law. But they passed a treaty in

Gleishen. They were trying to make a treaty. But most of the Indians wanted to destroy all the police, the Mounted Police. The elders and the chiefs sat united to keep down the Indians. They said, 'Maybe a better life those civilized people live than our lives, because when there is no law, there is firewater which kills a lot of Indians. And a lot of people steal our horses among ourselves; a lot of people steal the homemade saddles and homemade raw ropes, the blankets.' And the elders and the chiefs allowed the policemen to stay, to see what this civilized life really meant. We found now that the life was easier and more peaceful, but we could not be happy as we had been. We were not used to this new civilized life. We were feeling like we were living in captivity."[16]

A man of insight, dignity, and adaptability, McLean also had a keen sense of humour. At an international event, he was introduced to another man, who explained that his own heritage was Scottish. George quickly responded that they had that in common, pointing out his own surname.

George McLean died in 1967, the year before his people gained self-government.

Tchatkta and Hector Crawler

A man known as *Tchatkta* was believed to have been among the first Stoney Nakoda to have accepted Christianity. Despite his conversion to the white man's faith, *Tchatkta* appears to have been comfortable with maintaining strong elements of his native beliefs and practices. George McLean commented to Marius Barbeau of this man: "He was the first to believe in Christianity among the Stoneys. He would not go to war but sat in his tent and just prayed. He believed in Christianity so strongly that when he heard of war or shooting, he would go into a fast, not eating. He was a brave man just the same. In the old days, chiefs were not in general of a bad kind. But because they were brave, they fought. These men were leaders, and they had to face war. They were not afraid of being killed."[17]

Hector Crawler, or Chief Calf Child, seems also to have had a strong mystical inclination. A medicine man, he went into the mountains on several occasions and returned after

having had intense spiritual experiences. His powers of healing were well known among his people. Crawler worked as a guide in the new Rocky Mountains Park, and it is said that he was the one who told Tom Wilson that there were hot springs at the base of Sulphur Mountain – a significant event in the development of Banff Park, as we shall explore in a later chapter. Serving as chief of the Wesley band, Hector Crawler tried to govern his people in a way that honoured their traditions.

William Twin

William Twin – a.k.a. William Hunter, or *Nâ sho da*, meaning "Embers" – was another Stoney who also found work off the reserve. Twin's life characterizes the tenuous balance that some of the Indians achieved, with one foot in his traditional culture and the other in the white man's world. William was, indeed, a twin. His bother, Joshua, also became well known through his work with outfitters in the Banff area.

Born in 1847, William Twin was 30 years old when Treaty No. 7 was signed. He experienced the move onto the reserve, the transition to ranching and outfitting, and all the upheavals that the advent of the 20th century brought to the area. He is said to have met with James Hector when the explorer travelled through Twin's traditional hunting ground in 1858. Twin harvested hay from the Vermilion Lakes area for John Brewster in the 1880s and had a long association with the Brewster family's outfitting business. In 1894, Twin was employed by the CPR at Lake Louise, where he cut trails and guided tourists. Twin was one of the guides hired by Samuel Allen and Walter Wilcox from Yale University as they explored this area.

Tom Wilson and Hector Crawler, Stoney Chief, at Banff, Alberta, 1927, Glenbow NA-673-24

Joshua and William Twin (Hunter) at Morley, 1905, Whyte V701/LC-312

Twin suffered the loss of his wife and all four of his children in the terrible <u>smallpox</u> outbreak in 1893. He was devastated by the loss of his family from the white man's disease. This event may have been a factor in his acceptance of an invitation from the CPR to go to New York to attend (or, perhaps more accurately, be displayed at…) the New York Sportsman's Show. He had been recommended by John McDougall as a true example of a "real Grizzly Bear Hunter" for the event. Twin was a great asset to the CPR – a "typical Indian," but one who spoke good English, had a better-than-average command of how to function in white society, and offered a picturesque element as part of the romantic vision of the Wild West. His image was useful to the CPR in marketing the railway's tourism packages in the Canadian mountains. On his return to Canada from New York, Twin summed up his impressions of the big city as being "not a very good place to camp."[18]

When Peter Wesley led his band back to Kootenay Plains, Twin accompanied him. He returned to Morley in his later life, where he lived to the good age of 93.

Chief John Snow

One of the best known among the more contemporary figures in Stoney Nakoda culture is John Snow. Born in 1933, he was given the name *Îtebigo Mâni*, or Walking Seal, after his great-grandfather, Chief James Goodstoney. He was given the name John Snow, after an uncle, while attending the residential school in Morley. George McLean was his grandfather.

Snow went on to attend the Cook Christian Training School in Phoenix, Arizona, and then St. Stephen's Theological College in Edmonton. He was subsequently ordained as a United Church minister, and he worked in this capacity away from the Morley reserve until 1960, when he and his wife, Alva Townsend, returned to Alberta. Snow was alarmed at the poor conditions in which his people were living and immediately set about making changes. He was elected chief of the Wesley band in 1969 and held that position for 28 years, working to improve housing, social services, and opportunities for his people. Snow was the first director of the Treaty Rights Research program at the Indian Association of Alberta, and worked to address outstanding land-claims conflicts, finally achieving a settlement for the Ghost Reservoir claim in 1991. In 1969, when the Canadian government tabled its notorious "White Paper" proposing assimilation for the country's native peoples, Snow represented the tribal communities the following year when they countered with the Indian Chiefs of Alberta's "Red Paper," which asserted the treaty terms and demanded recognition of aboriginal rights.

Snow was the host for the ecumenical conferences on the Stoney Nakoda Reserve during the 1970s and 1980s, and was passionate about finding a harmonious way for his people to blend their traditional beliefs with Christian teachings. He was an intensely spiritual man, blending strong humanitarian values with a political astuteness that informed his work to improve native rights and respect.

Snow received honourary degrees from the University of Calgary and from Cook College and Theological School in Tempe, Arizona, as well as many other honours for his service to his people. He was dearly loved and greatly missed after he died in 2006 at the age of 73.

You have now driven down from Scott Lake Hill, the last of the foothills ridges, and onto the glacial outwash plain of Morley Flats. Beneath this rocky soil lies the Morley Gas Field, which has been such a boon to the reserve. This can be a blustery spot, where the winds from the west that have been pushed up over the mountains drop again and hit you full in the face. Watch for sudden extreme gusts as you drive through this section. Before we get into the mountains, there are a few other interesting sites and stories to consider.

The Canadian Pacific Railway

To the north, paralleling the highway, are the Canadian Pacific Railway tracks. This is the first time they have been visible since the highway passed under the railway bridge when leaving Calgary. The train line runs along the north side of the Bow River for much of its route toward the mountains, and crosses back to the south bank after Cochrane.

So much of the history of the area has been closely tied to the railway that it is worth giving it some consideration here.

The planning of the coast-to-coast Canadian railroad was surrounded by a feeling of urgency. The Americans were

The railway across Morley Flats

Geological Notes: Drumlins

The word "drumlin" comes from the Irish *droimín*, which means "little hill" – and they are indeed little hills, but very specific ones. Drumlins look rather like an overturned rowboat – they have the rounded shape of a hull, with a pointier (prow) end and a blunter (stern) end. They tend to occur in "swarms" where the tongue of one of the great glacial sheets once covered the land during an Ice Age.

There is consensus that they are a glacial feature, but there is some controversy over the details of how they were formed. The most common theory holds that they were created by water flowing under the ice sheet, which eroded a space under the ice that then filled with debris. Drumlins are all oriented to follow the direction of the ice movement. Those on Morley Flats all sit along a distinct axis with their tapered "prow" (downstream end) to the northeast and their blunter "stern" (upstream end) to the southwest.

It is generally agreed that drumlin formation occurred during the end of the most recent Ice Age, when the ice sheet was retreating. The latest Ice Age event (for there were several), the Wisconsin, started about 110,000 YBP and ended about 15,000 to 10,000 YBP. So these drumlins are probably about 15,000 years old.

Drumlins are only found in a few locations around the globe. In Canada, they are also found in Nova Scotia. As well, there are a number of sites in the Northeastern U.S., Northern Europe, and Patagonia.

Another intersting observation can be made in these photographs – all of the trees are growing on the northern slopes of these small hills. This is a good illustration of how microclimates affect vegetation. The northern exposure tends to be slightly wetter, and that makes just enough of a difference for trees to find a foothold in this harsh climate.

Drumlins on Morley Flats

making rapid strides westward with their own rail lines, and there were concerns in Canada that the Americans might have intentions to move into the territories to their north as well. Further to this, once British Columbia entered Confederation in 1871, the Dominion government was under the gun to fulfill a promise to link the newest province by rail with the rest of Canada within 10 years.

Prime Minister Sir John A. Macdonald believed that the railway was an essential element for unifying the country, and he made it one of his government's top priorities. Ironically, a scandal over railway contracts led to the fall of his Conservative government in 1873, and for the next five years railway development languished under the Liberal government of Alexander Mackenzie. Back in office in October 1878, Macdonald again aggressively promoted the railway, and by the spring of 1880 construction had started in the East.

In the fall of that year, the federal government decided to transfer responsibility for the railway to private enterprise. In a form of early public-private partnership, the government provided land and $25,000 credit toward the project. Then the government got out of the railway business and the Canadian Pacific Railway Syndicate took over the reins to push the ribbon of steel westward.

The company hired an American railroader, William Cornelius Van Horne, to oversee the project, and one of his first tasks was to determine the course the railway would take through the mountains. A northerly route through Fort Edmonton and the Yellowhead Pass had been favoured by Sir Sanford Fleming, chief surveyor for the Dominion government. But the owners of the Canadian Pacific Railway finally chose a more southerly route that went up the Bow Valley. This decision is attributed to a number of considerations. The northerly route would have left all the southern lands vulnerable to American interests that might draw

trade south of the border. Also, the route along the Bow went through lands that had been reported by naturalist John Macoun to be excellent for agriculture, which seemed promising for settlement (although Captain John Palliser had a different opinion, and had reported the lands in this area to be extremely arid). Finally, the southerly route would be considerably shorter.

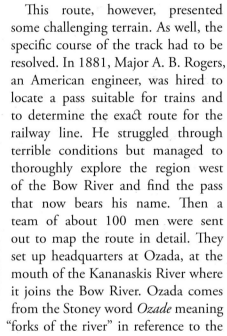

This route, however, presented some challenging terrain. As well, the specific course of the track had to be resolved. In 1881, Major A. B. Rogers, an American engineer, was hired to locate a pass suitable for trains and to determine the exact route for the railway line. He struggled through terrible conditions but managed to thoroughly explore the region west of the Bow River and find the pass that now bears his name. Then a team of about 100 men were sent out to map the route in detail. They set up headquarters at Ozada, at the mouth of the Kananaskis River where it joins the Bow River. Ozada comes from the Stoney word *Ozade* meaning "forks of the river" in reference to the confluence of the Kananaskis and Bow rivers.

Railway construction reached the eastern edge of the mountains in the spring of 1883. By the summer, tracks were in place as far as present-day Canmore, where a construction camp had been established called Padmore, named after the individual in charge of the site. Another camp was set up in the meadows near Banff, called Aylmer Park after Fred Aylmer, the crew chief there. By early December, construction had proceeded to what is now Lake Louise. The story of the progress further west is indeed a fascinating one, but beyond the scope of this book. Suffice to say, the railway was finally completed and the last spike driven into place on November 7, 1885 – four years after the original deadline to meet the commitment to British Columbia. But it was a monumental achievement and would, as Sir John A. Macdonald foresaw, be instrumental in defining and uniting the country.

Once the rail line was in place, there was a need for settlers. Canadian Pacific agents were sent overseas to encourage immigration. They offered a package deal that included passage on a Canadian Pacific ship, travel west on the CPR, and even land available through the Canadian Pacific. Homesteaders and entrepreneurs started to filter West.

The CPR was very aware of the value of the scenery along the rail line through the mountains and sought ways to encourage visitors to the Banff area. Van Horne published an account called "The New Highway To The East Across the Mountains, Prairies and Rivers of Canada" that expounded on the wealth of beauty in the mountains. Artists and photographers were brought out to document the scenery along the railway route. Dining halls and simple accommodation facilities were constructed by the CPR at key stops, and these sites would later grow into magnificent hotels.

The early formation of a park in the mountains supported the company's ambitions. It was to be be "not just any park, but a park that would attract wealthy upper class people. It was not a spa for people of modest means, who, in any case, were not able to pay the first class tariffs. It was important for the CPR to attract visitors with money. A main purpose of the (1887 Rocky Mountains Park) Act was to ensure development would make the West an attractive destination for people with money to spend."[1]

Before we leave Morley Flats, let's look at one more glimmer of excitement that has occurred here since the track's completion. The railway camp called Ozada fell into disuse after the railway was built, but it came alive once more with the establishment of a coal mine in the Ribbon Creek area of the Kananaskis. There was no rail line to the mine, so all the coal had to be trucked out to the train connection.

An area of about one square mile was leased from the Stoney Nakoda, a tipple was built to load the train, and a small town sprang up to house the workers. Electricity was installed, but the people in the area never did benefit from running water – the whole town drew its water from a communal well. About 75 people lived in Ozada from 1947 until 1952, when the mine closed and the site was left to go to ruins. The tipple was finally demolished in the 1970s, and all that remains to show for the place now are some cement foundations, a couple of ruined houses, and a coal slag.

Highway 40 and The Kananaskis

At this point, the Trans-Canada intersects with Highway 40, one of the access routes into Kananaskis Country. Much of the area at the entrance to this broad valley was once part of Rocky Mountains Park (which would become Banff National Park). In 1911 it was taken out of this park, and in 1917 returned to it… Then, in 1930, with the passage of the National Parks Act, which set the guidelines for park status, Kananaskis was again removed from the park. This was because of the impact of forest fires and logging operations, as well as a proposed power-dam development on the Spray Lakes. The area then became part of the Rocky Mountain Forest Reserve (which the federal government had established in 1911, largely to protect watersheds), and administration was passed to the province.

The first rough road into the valley was built in the mid-1930s, and in 1948 the Alberta government improved it as a part of the Forestry Trunk Road between Seebe and Coleman. The coal mine near Ribbon Creek created a small community called Kovach (after the district ranger, Joe Kovach), but it was abandoned when the mine closed in 1952. The Kananaskis road was brought up to highway standards in 1973.

Efforts to give the Kananaskis some sort of protected status started in the 1960s, when Clarence Copithorne (remember the CL Ranch?) and Bill Milne started pushing the idea. The designation of the area as Kananaskis Country finally came about in 1976. "K Country" covers more than 4,000 square kilometres, and includes a number of smaller areas with various designations for protection by the province.

The first non-native person to travel the route through the Kananaskis was probably James Sinclair, a Red River settler, in 1854. He had previously travelled through the Bow Valley by way of Whiteman's Gap with a group of settlers heading for Oregon (see Chapter 13). However, in '54, on the advise of his Cree guide, Sinclair and his group of about 100 settlers, travelling by ox cart, took the valley we now call Kananaskis. This group barely made it over what we know as South Kananaskis Pass after great hardship, abandoning the carts and having to eat some of the oxen.

It is thought that Sinclair was the one to mention this route to Captain John Palliser (there's more on the Palliser

Looking towards the Kananaskis Valley

Expedition in the next chapter). In 1858, Palliser followed what he remembered of Sinclair's directions to access British territory further to the south. By his description, he probably travelled south from the Bow River through Kananaskis Valley and on over a pass that he named "Kananaskis" after an Indian who made a miraculous recovery after from a terrible axe wound.

Logging in the Bow Corridor and The Kananaskis

Ranching, railroading, and industrial growth all generate demand for lumber. Construction created an initial demand, but once the railway was pushed westward the huge demand for fuel for the steam-powered trains generated a lot of logging activity. Early trains devoured fuel through the mountains and, until coal replaced wood for energy, forests were mown down to feed the hungry locomotives.

The federal Department of the Interior sent surveyors out as early as 1883 to assess the timber potential. They found the Bow Valley to be heavily affected by forest fires in many locations, but the Kananaskis Valley and around Castle Mountain were deemed to offer commercial potential. A system was set up to offer logging permits or "timber limits."

The first logging done in the Kananaskis area was in 1883 to provide timber for the Cochrane Ranche. When Colonel James Walker quit his position as manager at the Ranche, he bought its sawmill and set it up on the bank of the Bow River near the mouth of the Kananaskis River. At about the same time, a gentleman from Ottawa, a lawyer named Kutusoff MacFee, was employing consultants from Eau Claire, Wisconsin, to assess the timber potential of the confluence of the Bow and Kananaskis rivers. Their optimistic conclusions led to the establishment of the Bow River and Eau Claire Lumber Company, which received timber grants for the Kananaskis and Castle Mountain areas in 1886.

The new company set up its mill in Calgary and constructed booms across the Bow River to manage the logs. Trees were cut during the fall and summer and stored near the mountain streams. At spring break-up, the high water would be used to flush the logs downstream to the mill. This was a highly hazardous business, as the logs frequently became jammed and the men faced the daunting task of freeing them, often with the use of explosives. In one particularly bad year, six men drowned struggling to free a log-jamb.

Logging continues today in parts of Kananaskis Country. Spray Lakes Sawmills has been active in the area since 1943 and has timber rights to several locations within K Country. This has become quite controversial and has been fought fiercely by conservationists. Also, there is an inherent conflict between two land-use planning documents. The Land-use Framework, established in 2008 by the province's Sustainable Resource Development ministry, states regarding designated areas that "establishing, growing, harvesting and removing timber is to be the primary use thereof." Yet the Water For Life Strategy adopted in 2003 by the Alberta government is dedicated to the protection of watersheds and prevention of degradation of aquatic ecosystems. A Public Advisory Council has been invited into the process and public discussion on this issue continues…

Log-jamb, Eau Claire and Bow River Lumber Company, ca. 1890s, Glenbow NA-1360-8

Ozada Prisoner-of-War Camp 133

During the Second World War, a windy field on these inhospitable flats was transformed into a prisoner-of-war camp. In the spring of 1942, word arrived that lodgings were needed, fast, for men captured in North Africa from German Field Marshal Erwin Rommel's Afrika Korps. So the area to the southwest of the intersection with Highway 40 was transformed into a fortified camp. A barbed-wire enclosure 12 feet high was built around 1,100 square metres of rocky ground, with wooden guard towers dotted around the perimeter. The enclosure was divided into quadrants filled with tents, each to be shared by four prisoners. In May the prisoners started to arrive, and by the end of the summer there were 10,000 men lodged in the camp. Members of the Veterans Guard of Canada, a corps of First World War veterans between the ages of 40 and 65, were called in to watch over these prisoners.

It was a cold and miserable place. There was considerable danger from fires sparked by stoves that prisoners improvised out of tobacco tins to stay warm. The remote location made attempts to escape rare. Still, on one occasion a group of German officers managed to build and occupy an underground chamber about three metres square and one metre high that they had provisioned with food, water, and bedding. They resided there, undetected, until one of the guards noticed the print of a German military boot and followed the tracks to the four men in their hideout.

There was a brief period of heightened tension at the camp, as described by Doug Hogg, who was serving in the Canadian army and was called to work at Ozada: "The government of Canada had been informed that Canadian prisoners of war taken at Dieppe were already, or going to be, shackled in German prisoner of war camps overseas. A reciprocal movement had been ordered for all German prisoners of war in the Ozada camp. This brought immediate reaction from the German prisoners, who threatened to riot if attempts were made to shackle them. Thus our task as the nearest trained infantry unit was to supervise this shackling, and prevent or contain any riotous behaviour by prison inmates… As I saw it at the time, this could have developed into a very messy situation. Ten thousand objecting prisoners, about one thousand heavily armed troops and guards, and a government that wanted its directive carried out. To prevent bloodshed and casualties, somebody had to blink. The Canadian government did blink, and we were given orders to stand down. The story we were told was that our government was given assurances that day by the German government that our Canadian prisoners of war would have shackles removed, and no further shackling would take place. To me this seemed like a comfortable and happy ending."[2]

Fortunately for the prisoners, before the worst of winter hit they were moved to better quarters near Lethbridge, Alberta.

Site of Ozada POW Camp

First guard tower at Ozada prisoner-of-war camp, April 1942, Glenbow NA-4197-1

The Kananaskis River

The Trans-Canada crosses the Kananaskis River as it flows out to join the Bow. This is a heavily controlled piece of water, with three dams (Interlakes, Pocaterra, and Barrier) along its 75 kilometre course to manage the water supply to TransAlta power projects downstream. The steady year-round release of water from Barrier Dam means that the river below this offers great opportunities for paddlers. TransAlta posts a schedule for a consistent release of water from the dam so kayakers can get on the water at optimum times to play in the rapids.

Rafting on the Kananaskis has become a popular activity in the last decade, and several companies offer half-day trips here. The river is classified as II-III whitewater. That means it's on the gentle end of the scale as rafting goes, which makes it good for beginners and small children.

Although the rafting is seasonal, the relatively warm water being released from Barrier Lake means that this stretch of water is open for paddling 12 months of the year, and a section of the Kananaskis has become a real whitewater canoeist's and kayaker's mecca. In 1984, the Alberta Whitewater Association started making modifications to the river. The consistent year-round water release means that the river never freezes up, so the riverbed is more stable than

Rafting on the Kananaskis, Canadian Rockies Rafting

Kayaker working a wave in the freestyle section, riverboarder in background, E. Duggan

most rivers, which are subject to the freeze-thaw cycle. This makes the Kananaskis unusually suitable for improvements. Between the put-in at the "Widow Maker" rapid and the take-out at Canoe Meadows, a section of the river has been enhanced by man-made elements to create exciting runs of big waves, holes, and other features that paddlers love. A 30-gate, 300 metre slalom course was installed that has served as the premier training course in Alberta for more than 20 years. Four National Whitewater Championships and one North American Championship have been held here, and this site is the permanent host for the annual Provincial Slalom Championships. The annual paddling festival, Kanfest, is staged at Canoe Meadows each summer. This results in an estimated 50,000 individual day uses of the river annually.

The Alberta Whitewater Association has worked closely with the federal Department of Fisheries and Oceans, Alberta Environment, and Alberta Parks regarding the development of the Kananaskis River. Because of the flushing from the dam, this is virtually a dead river – no vegetative or invertebrate life will survive in that warm water and daily dry-up, so it will also not be a good habitat for fish. This makes it an ideal candidate for recreational development.

A couple of new river sports are showing up on the Kananaskis. River surfers ride the standing waves in the river. Enthusiasts paddle out, catch a wave, and stand on their board, remaining in one spot as the river travels underneath them. For the other new sport, riverboarding, the participants wear fins for control (as well as protective gear!) and grip a super-heavy-duty flotation board to ride down the river. Edmond Duggan, a kayaking instructor, describes this sport as "armoured flutterboarding." It is growing quickly in popularity, partly because it has a less challenging entry level – no learning to roll a boat or stand up on a surfboard...

The growth of river surfing has generated plans to create in the near future a drop structure that will be ideal for this sport. In the longer term, the section below Canoe Meadows downstream to the Trans-Canada will probably be developed for introductory paddlers, to allow them to develop skills that will take them on the more advanced water in the existing section.

Paddling the Kan, T. Jacklin

Alberta Slalom Team training session, E. Duggan

Billboards and Highway Advertising

One of the sights that borders the highway through this stretch is a string of advertising billboards. The provincial Public Highways Development Act bans this type of signage along major highways, but Indian reserves, which are controlled by the federal government, have no such regulations. Thus, in this stretch where you get the fabulous view of the entrance to the mountains, the foreground is dotted with huge advertising signs.

Billboard by Kananaskis River

Wildlife Spotting — Is That a Wolf?!?

You may spot a large, dog-like animal along the edge of the Trans-Canada. It may very well be a domestic dog out on a spree, or it may be one of the wild canids (member of *Canidae* or the dog family). People who are not familiar with the local fauna sometimes get excited about having seen a wolf, but wolves are very, very, very rarely spotted along the road.

The most likely canid to be seen in the foothills is the coyote *(Canis latrans)*. They live on the local population of small mammals and rodents, although groups will take down a deer occasionally. Coyotes stand 50 centimetres at the shoulder – about half the size of a wolf. They are much more tolerant of human presence than wolves and their population has expanded over the years. They live in loose family groups, becoming more solitary in the summer and then banding together for the winter. In the evening, you may hear them yipping and howling, a shorter, shriller sound than the wolf's more melodic howl.

Coyotes have a finer face than the wolf's more robust features, with a tapered muzzle and small dip between the forehead and the nose, whereas the wolf has a defined change of angle above their square muzzle. Another point of difference is that coyotes tend to carry their tail in a low position when travelling, while wolves carry theirs straight out behind.

While coyotes are fairly consistent in colour, wolves *(Canus lupus)* are highly variable in colour, ranging from quite blond to almost black. Most in the Banff area tend to be quite dark. Their frame is much heftier than the coyote, though their tail is less brushy. The packs tend to stay within the mountains (there are now about four packs within the boundaries of Banff National Park). Packs have a complex social structure, led by a dominant male and female. They are highly territorial, and encounters with other packs can be quite aggressive as boundaries are negotiated.

Wolves almost dissappeared from the area due to an active eradication program in the 1950s. Gradually, starting in 1982, they have returned, but their survival is still tenuous. Their greatest threat now is traffic.

Top: Wolf, D. Ditchburn

Middle: Coyote, S. Ditchburn

Bottom: Red Fox, iStockphoto

The one other member of the dog family you might see is the Red Fox *(Vulpes vulpes)*. They are smaller than the coyote (about 30 cm to 40 cm at the shoulder) and, although called Red, may be brown to grey. They have a lighter underside with darker points, and a white tip on their bushy tail. Foxes eat small rodents and can be observed mousing like a cat, although their nocturnal tendencies make this a rare sight. These animals do not live in packs, but travel singly – unless they're raising kits, for which the parents remain together and hold a territory of about five kilometres around the den site. Their call is a short, sharp bark.

"The plainsman like myself is likely to find his first plunge into the mountains on the Calgary-Banff run an alarming experience. Not because of the Highway gradients, which are gentle, nor the curves, which are also gentle and well-banked, but because of the sudden feeling of being separated from all familiar things. Before we are aware of what is happening the beautiful but sinister Three Sisters and assorted kinfolk have slipped in behind us and cut off our retreat. But the valley ahead broadens – there is still room to breathe. We are not fenced in. Not quite." [1]

The Early Explorers

One of the first to check out the opening of the Bow Valley into the mountains was David Thompson. Born in London, England, in 1770 and educated in mathematics and navigation, he was expected to enter the navy. Instead, he joined the Hudson's Bay Company and set off adventuring to Canada as a young man. A broken leg required him to spend some time recovering at Cumberland House in what's now Saskatchewan. It was there that he met surveyor Philip Turnor and learned the art of using the chronometer, telescope, and other surveying tools, which turned Thompson's career in the direction of mapping the West.

In 1797, Thompson switched his allegiances to the North West Company, the HBC's rival, in hopes of greater opportunity to travel west. By 1800, he was in what would become Alberta, exploring up the Bow Valley with Duncan McGillivray, looking for beaver and evaluating the trade potential. The two men climbed to a high point – probably Loder Peak, near Exshaw – and were stunned by the surrounding view. Thompson commented in his November 29 journal entry: "Our view from the heights was vast and unbounded; the eye had not the strength to determine its termination. To the westward, hills and rocks rose to our view covered with snow, here rising, there subsiding, but their type nearly of an equal height everywhere. Never before did I behold so just, so perfect a resemblance to the waves of the ocean in the wintering storm. When looking upon them and attentively considering their wild order and appearance, the imagination is apt to say, these must once have been liquid, and that state, when swelled to its greatest agitation, suddenly congealed and made solid by power omnipotent." [2]

Thompson's explorations over the next few years focused on the Columbia River area. In 1812, he left the West after 28 years of mapping the region and settled in Montreal. Sadly, he went blind in the 1840s and died in poverty in 1857.

The next significant explorer was Captain John Palliser, who headed the British North American Exploring Expedition, better known as the Palliser Expedition. From a wealthy Irish family, Palliser was sent to reconnoitre the regions of the West between 1857 and 1861, with the hope of finding a good route to the western ocean. The undertaking was sponsored by the Royal Geographic Society, and covered the region south of the North Saskatchewan River and north of the 49th parallel. This parallel was the border with the United States as far as the mountains – further to the west, it was still undetermined. These yet undetermined delineation helped motivate the expedition. Another factor was that the Hudson's Bay Company's charter (which granted the HBC all the lands draining into the Bay) was up for renewal in 1859, and the Imperial Government desired more information on these lands with that in mind. (Under the Rupert's Land Act of 1868, the HBC sold its vast lands to Canada in 1870 for £300,000 plus one-twentieth of the arable land in the HBC's former holdings.)

There are some suggestions that Captain Palliser was actually acting for the British Secret Service and had been sent west as a spy. The man who had nominated him for membership in the Royal Geographic Society, Lieutenant-Colonel Thomas Jervis, also happened to be the head of the Secret Service. Jervis would have had a great interest in the maps that Palliser created. These maps were, in fact, used by North-West Mounted Police in 1874 when they rode into the "North-West Territories." We will probably never know if there is any truth to this allegation.

As the Expedition approached the Bow Valley entrance to the mountains, Palliser divided the group into three parties, which each headed in a different direction. Palliser headed south down the Kananaskis Valley (as mentioned in Chapter 10), Thomas Blakiston and John Sullivan headed west over a more northerly route. It was left to Dr. James Hector and Eugene Bourgeau to explore up the Bow Valley with their guides, a Metís man named Peter Erasmus and a Stoney Nakoda whose name the others could not pronounce, so they called him Nimrod.

Hector, a young and enthusiastic Scot of 23 years, was the expedition's medical doctor and geologist. Bourgeau, who came from the mountainous Savoy region of Switzerland, was a scientist known for his skills in botany. The pair seem

to have made a good team, and together they worked their way up the valley, examining the plant life and recording the geological features. Bourgeau returned from the expedition with more than 60,000 botanical specimens.

After travelling with Hector over two season, Erasmus recorded his impression of the man in his book *Buffalo Days and Nights:* "Dr Hector alone of all the men of my experience asked no quarter from any man among us, drivers or guides. He could walk, ride or tramp snowshoes with the best of our men, and never fell back on his position to soften his share of the hardships, but in fact gloried in his physical ability after a hard day's run to share in the work of preparing camp for the night, building shelters from the wind, cutting spruce boughs, or even helping gut up wood for an all-night fire. He was admired and talked about by every man that travelled with him, and his fame as a traveller was a wonder and a byword among many a tepee that never saw the man."[3]

The party paused at the foot of what is thought to have been Grotto Mountain, and the explorers climbed the peak. They found a cave full of animal tracks on the slopes and thus bestowed it with an appropriate name. Hector also climbed a peak a little further to the northwest and named it for Palliser's brother-in-law, William Fairholme. We will find locations that still bear the names assigned by Hector and Bourgeau all along the Bow Valley to the west.

At the foot of a mountain with a prominent waterfall, probably Cascade Mountain, Hector left Bourgeau to study plants and continued on his own. Bourgeau was not fond of riding and was happy to avoid it if possible, preferring to explore the local area on foot and work on his collections. Hector climbed Cascade, commented on the sheep, pica, marmots, and even a hummingbird, and continued along

Tree ID: White Spruce

These are the most common trees on the eastern slopes of the Rockies at lower elevations. The white spruce, *Picea glauca,* is often found in mixed stands with other trees – frequently aspen in the lower foothills. The aspen colonize an area first (often after a fire, sprouting from their intact root bundle), creating a moist, shaded environment for the spruce to get started. Often the spruce then go on to dominate the stand. Deeper in the mountains, lodgepole pine offer shade for young spruce.

White spruce prefer north-facing slopes that are not too sunny. At maturity, they reach a height of about 20 m. Their needles are square and sharp (as they are on all spruce) and are about 1.5 cm long. Their 3 cm to 5 cm cones have round scales that are tightly packed when young but relax open with age. These release great clouds of pollen in May.

White spruce are easily confused with the Engelmann spruce (*Picea engelmannii*). And, just to make the situation more confusing, the two hybridize freely. However, the Engelmann spruce tends to prefer higher elevations, and is found more in the subalpine zone. Trees at this lower elevation are white spruce.

White spruce

the Bow. At Castle Mountain, he left the Bow Valley to go over Vermillion Pass, returning later through Kicking Horse Pass. In the section of his trip through this pass, Hector had a frightening accident. While trying to catch his horse, he was kicked in the chest and fell, unconscious. Many stories offer different versions of the event, but the most dramatic is that the rest of the party concluded that Hector was dead, and by the time he regained consciousness they were preparing a grave for him. Hector was only able to alert them to his non-dead condition through eye movements. The pass was named in commemoration of this event.

After rejoining the Bow River east of the Pass, Hector finished his journey of 1858 by proceeding further up the river as far as Bow Lake and then on over Howse Pass back to Rocky Mountain House. In his 57 days of travelling, he

covered the entire Bow Valley, except the section between Castle Mountain and Lake Louise. He was back again the next summer to check out a route using the Fraser and Thompson rivers. This time, he filled in the blanks as he traversed the length of the Bow Valley to the Pipestone River and the North Saskatchewan River. But on that trip he moved quickly and had no time for side explorations.

On October 7, 1858, although Palliser had not personally been in the party that proceeded down the Bow Valley and over Kicking Horse Pass, he wrote to the British Secretary of State: "I have completely succeeded in discovering not only a pass practicable for horse, but one which, with but little expense, could be rendered available for carts also…this pass will connect the prairies of Saskatchewan with Her Majesty's possessions on the west side of the Rocky Mountains."

Rafter Six Ranch

On the south side of the Trans-Canada, next to the Kananaskis River, is the site of the Rafter Six Ranch. An early operation on this site, one that was of interest to the NWMP, was one of the many whiskey-trading posts that had sprung up in what's now Alberta. The traders were seen off by the missionaries and newly arrived police. But their log building remains and now houses the Rafter Six Ranch's museum.

The first established ranch on this site was started by a man named "Soapy" Smith. Herbert A. Smith (not to be confused with the notorious American criminal Jefferson R. "Soapy" Smith) outfitted for hunters and tourists, including the Trail Riders of the Canadian Rockies. He had married a young woman named Eva, and they began to take in guests at the ranch in the 1920s, mostly the families of men who were out with the hunting parties. The operation started with simple tent accommodations, but a few log cabins were built over the years. Soapy died in the 1930s, and his young widow married a cowboy named Alvin Guinn. They developed the concept of the guest ranch much farther. During the time they ran the ranch, Walt Disney Productions made a movie on the site in 1961 called "Nikki, Wild Dog of the North." In 1970, Disney shot "King of the Grizzlies" in the area. Earlier, in 1954, the ranch had been one of the sets used in the filming of "River of No Return" with Marilyn Monroe.

The ranch was purchased by the Cowley family in 1976. Interested in the history of the area, they assembled a collection of memorabilia and artefacts for their small museum. Among the prized items on display is one of the old stagecoaches that ran between Calgary and Edmonton from 1883 until 1891. This stagecoach gained some local fame as the first one to be held up in Alberta. On August 23, 1886, it was being driven north from Calgary when two masked men stopped it and demanded the mail sacks. They found nothing worth stealing in the bags, but relieved the driver and passengers of their valuables. Descriptions submitted in the report on the robbery noted that one of the men was wearing a cut-up Union Jack as his mask, and

indeed a mutilated flag was found during the subsequent search of the area. The pair were immediately dubbed "The Union Jack Gang." The NWMP were informed that two unknown characters were hanging out with Scott Krenger, himself a mysterious character. They checked out this lead, but the men presented reasonable alibis and were released. However, Krenger was found murdered in his home soon after. The culprits never were identified and the case was closed unsolved. The stagecoach, however, is still in operation and is driven regularly in the Calgary Stampede Parade.

When Kananaskis Country was formed, the park's restrictive parameters conflicted with the business activities on the Rafter Six. This problem was finally resolved by transferring the ranch to within the boundaries of the Municipal District (MD) of Bighorn, which encompasses the area around the Trans-Canada from just west of Highway 22 to just west of Canmore. The ranch lands are not contiguous with the MD, so it sits as a "Bighorn island" that's within the park boundaries but not part of it.

The Cowleys have ambitions plans for development at the Rafter Six. They have gained approval for a 40-suite hotel and additional staff accommodations. Beyond that, their vision for the ranch encompasses a bigger resort with a large equestrian centre, conference facility, and health-and-wellness spa.

Rafter Six Ranch, 2008, G. Cowley

The Gap

We enter the mountains where the Bow Valley is squeezed between rising peaks on both sides of the highway, traditionally called The Gap. John Niddrie, a missionary at Morley between 1889 and 1910, described it in poetic style: "I have gazed entranced upon these mighty monarchs with their peaks which seemed to me to pierce the ethereal blue of heaven and their feet thrust into the pines. Again, again, and again have I gazed spellbound upon the different shades of light and shadow as they chased each other across their wrinkled faces upon which the hand of time had written so many different happenings. From my outlook they presented no even chain of serrated peaks, but the eye seemed to rest upon the jagged wall which held the beholder under the spell of its enchantment, this to be broken only by the shrill screeching of the siren as the railroad engine rushed westward toward the gap."[4]

Camp Chief Hector

Just to the west of Rafter Six is the YMCA's Camp Chief Hector. The Y has been running a camp for 80 years, previously on land adjacent to the Stoney Nakoda reserve. When a land settlement added the camp's previous location to the reserve lands, the camp moved its operations to the 1,000 acres it now occupies near The Gap.

The facility caters to youth 7 to 17 years of age, and provides programming through summer and weekend events. It also offers an outdoor school for students in the regional school districts, bringing them in for intensive multi-day experiences. Programs can take advantage of horseback riding, an archery range, ropes course, climbing wall, canoeing (the camp is next to Chilver Lake), craft activities, and environmental studies. The emphasis is on team building, leadership, and environmental responsibility.

Camp Chief Hector is named for Hector Crawler of the Stoney Nakoda.

Looking into the Mountains through The Gap

Widening the road at Gap Hill, Relief Project No. 120, April, 1934, Canada. Dept. of National Defence / Library and Archives Canada / PA-037030

Bottom left:Calypso orchid (Calypso bulbosa)
Bottom right: Columbia lily (Lilium columbianum)

Bow Valley Wildlands Provincial Park

Across the highway from the Rafter Six is Bow Valley Park, one of the designated areas that makes up the mosaic that is Kananaskis Country. This park, established in 1959, covers 329 square kilometres. There are walking trails and it is a particularly fine place to check out wildflowers. The park is at the intersection of three environments – the alpine, subalpine, and montane – so flora from diverse habitats comes together in this area. You can find many species of wild orchids here, as well as the increasingly rare Columbia lily (often called a tiger lily).

The Bow, from Bow Valley Provincial Park

Yanmuska

McConnell Ridge — 1,996 m

In the next section you will learn the source of the name of the small mountain on the south side of the highway just at the edge of the mountains – it is a part of the McConnell Fault system. It is also unofficially known as Barrier Mountain, and as Yates Mountain, after the Yates family, which ranched nearby. The ridge was used by the Stoney Nakoda as a lookout point called *Tokyapebi Îpa*, meaning "lookout point for the enemy." And it is still used as a lookout – but now for fire. The original lookout along the ridge was a relocated guard tower from Prisoner-of-War Camp 130 in the Kananaskis Valley. It was moved to the University of Calgary research station in the valley in 1984, and a modern structure now serves to protect the surrounding area from fire. These structures were built on prominent sites throughout the mountains starting in the 1920s.

New technologies have replaced many of the old fire lookouts, but a number are still staffed with lookout observers. Alberta currently has about 130 active fire lookouts. Lookout personnel usually spend about five or six months on location and are responsible for observing an area of about 5,000 square kilometres. They pass on reports of any "smoke incidents" for further investigation from the ground or by helicopter. About 40% of the fires detected annually are spotted by lookout observers.[4]

Mount John Laurie, Yamnuska, or The Yam — 2,240 m

This mountain, lying to the north as you enter the mountains, is best known locally as Yamnuska, which comes from its Stoney Nakoda name *Îyâ mna thka*, meaning "flat-faced mountain." In 1961, the official name, Mount John Laurie, was assigned in recognition of John Laurie (1899-1959), a local educator and great supporter of the Indians in Southern Alberta. He was Secretary to the Indian Association of Alberta and was adopted in 1940 by Stoney Nakoda chief Enos Hunter and given the name White Cloud.

Yamnuska's impressive 360 metre high cliff, which spans the two kilometres of the mountain's face, makes this probably one of the most-climbed peaks in the Rockies. There are more than 100 climbing routes of varying difficulty along the face, and this is a popular location for climbing schools. Easily accessed, and in good shape early in the season when other locations are still shedding their ice and snow, the cliffs often ring with the shouts of climbers. First climbed in 1952 by Hans Gmoser, Isabelle Spreat and Leo Grillmair (and my father, John Manry – but he was on the second rope that was forced to retreat due to falling rock), the route that they took has become known as the Grillmair Chimney. In addition to the technical climbing routes, there is a great scrambling route that traverses the top of the cliff – mostly an easy hike, although with one slightly more challenging section of down-climbing in the middle. From the top, there is a terrific view out over the foothills to the east.

Geology Notes: Yamnuska

We meet our first significant thrust fault in the middle of a distinctive mountain to the north of where the highway enters The Gap: Mount Yamnuska. Or, to be more official about it, Mount John Laurie – *Yamnuska* is the Stoney name for the mountain (meaning sheer-faced cliff) and the peak is better known by this moniker. If you look at this mountain's exposed southern face, you will see that there are two clear zones: the 350 vertical metres of the cliff region is clearly divided from the broken talus (loose broken rock, often displaced through erosion) that lies below it. Dividing these two zones is the McConnell Thrust fault, named in 1887 for R. G. McConnell, who worked for the Geological Survey of Canada. Here, our thrust-fault organization is plainly displayed… and this is our decisive transition from the weathered-out ridges of the foothills to the Front Ranges.

The cliffs of Yamnuska, so popular with local climbers, are part of the Eldon Formation, which is Middle Cambrian. (See Illustration A in Chapter 8.) The talus below is part of the Belly River formation, which is Cretaceous shale and siltstone, and is younger than the Eldon by some 450 million years – yet lies underneath it!!! So this is an excellent example of the dynamics of thrust faulting discussed in Chapter 8. The rocks that cover the top section of this fault have been moved some 30 kilometres into their present position! If you hike up to the base of the Eldon Formation cliffs (watch for rock knocked loose by climbers overhead), you can actually put your hand into the zone of transition of the fault itself – a pretty impressive moment of time travelling!

The Eldon is a carbonate rock (limestone / dolomite) that resists weathering and is typically a light grey. It will be encountered periodically as we move further west, so keep this first example in mind.

Yamnuska and the McConnell Fault

Wildlife Spotting: The Eagle Highway

Golden Eagle, iStockphoto

In March 1992, a pair of observers were in the Kananaskis Valley doing a survey of bird species in the area. One of the men, Peter Sherrington, noted a Golden Eagle pass overhead. He didn't think much of it because the species is occasionally spotted in the area. A little later he noticed two more, and then a fourth, so he began to pay more attention. By the end of the day, he and Des Allen had counted more than 100 of these great birds passing from south to north. This remarkable observation was repeated a couple of days later, this time tallying a count of about 250 eagles. Something was going on that researchers had been unaware of previously.

Until recently, Golden Eagles were not known to migrate – even in other parts of the world. But this many birds moving purposefully toward the north certainly looked like migration. A study group was assembled to observe the area in the fall, and they counted more than 2,000 birds of this species heading back south. This was definitely migration…

Now alerted to this fact, bird enthusiasts began looking for other locations where the birds could be spotted, and they began to plot a migration route. A regular observation program turned up more and more eagles as understanding of the migration grew. The fall migration in 1994 produced a count of more than 6,000 eagles along the Front Ranges. Further research found that the birds were probably moving between their northern range in Northern Canada and Alaska and their southern range in the Southern U.S. and northern Mexico.

Over a decade of information has now been collected from observation sites that record information such as age, gender, and numbers of eagles, and their movement patterns by date and weather. Analysis of this data has produced some interesting insights about these birds' breeding success in their northern habitat, their survival rates in their southern winter range, and their response to climate change. Because eagles are a key predator at the top of the food chain, they are an important indicator of ecosystem health and of potential concerns for many other species also found in this habitat.

The community has embraced the newly discovered passage of the Golden Eagles, and volunteers man observation sites in both spring and fall. Education programs disperse information about the eagles and their movement patterns, and Canmore now hosts a two-day Festival of Eagles every fall.

At the peak of the migration, from mid-March to mid-April in the spring and during October in the fall, an average of 200 birds pass along the Front Ranges. I vividly remember a hike one fall that ended up on one of the ridges in Kananaskis Valley, and beginning to notice big birds flying overhead. My friend and I spent a couple of hours lying on our backs on the ridge watching more than 100 Golden Eagles pass over us. They would circle in a thermal just to the north side of the ridge, gaining altitude. Then, as we watched, they would change their wing position into a sort of stealth-jet form and shoot forward. (They are said to move at speeds topping 150 km/hr.) The eagles slowly lost altitude as they soared southward until they picked up the next thermal and began to circle upward again. And so they progressed, without a single wing flap, riding the air currents of the mountain ridges.

The Golden Eagle (Aquila chrys*aetos*) is predominantly brown, with golden highlights on its neck and head feathers. It is a big bird – up to a metre from beak to tail, with a wingspan of two metres or more. As in most of the birds of prey, the female is noticeably larger than the male. In addition to the migratory population heading through on its way to the far north, a small population of resident Golden Eagles nest in Southern Alberta. They favour high, open terrain and build their nests on cliff ledges. Returning to the same nest year after year, they commonly lay two eggs but usually only rear one chick successfully.

"I have often thought that the high plain and mountain country of Alberta is no place for an ambitious man. In the city you can build up and tear down skyscrapers and feel yourself a god; but no man can move a mountain or make more than a few scratches, soon to be obliterated, on the limitless surface of the plain." [1]

Power Dams and a Ghost Town

The growing city of Calgary created a tremendous demand for a reliable supply of power. This was initially met, in 1911, by the construction of the hydroelectric project at Horseshoe Falls by Calgary Power. This company had been founded in 1903 by W. Max Aitken (who would become Lord Beaverbrook in 1916), and later joined by R. B. Bennett (who would become Prime Minister in 1930) and other investors. They took over a number of smaller ventures and focussed on becoming the sole provider of power in Southern Alberta.

Even before the Horseshoe Dam project was completed, problems had become apparent. The builders had neglected to do stream-flow studies that would have revealed great seasonal variation. The river practically dried up during winter, then burst the coffer dams and undermined the footings in June. The dam had to be redesigned for greater runoff spill, but that dropped the winter horsepower rating...

So the site for another dam at Kananaskis Falls became desirable. This site consisted of a series of four falls and a 10 metre drop through a canyon. It had great power potential, but the disadvantage of being on Stoney Nakoda land. This factor had presented a considerable obstacle during the construction of Horseshoe Dam. Also, the new dam would flood an area of the Rocky Mountains National Park. The Parks Act had no provision for situations such as this, but Aitken saw it as a surmountable problem, given that a new version of the act was about to go before Parliament, and a revision could certainly be arranged...

Site of Kananaskis Development Project, February, 1910, Glenbow NA-3802-3

At the same parliamentary session, there was also a proposal to "amend the Indian Act to strengthen the right of railroads and other public utilities to expropriate land within Indian reserves. This would ensure that Calgary Power would not be held up to ransom by the Stony (sic) Indians and the Indian Department over Kananaskis Falls in the same way as it had been over Horseshoe Falls."[2]

On the plus side, the site at Kananaskis Falls would tie up the last useable site on the Bow River, and would virtually guarantee Calgary Power's monopoly on hydroelectric power in Southern Alberta. Aitken exerted considerable pressure on the Department of the Interior to lease the site. In the spring of 1912, R. B. Bennett (who had been elected to the House of Commons in 1911) wrote to Aitken that "I have succeeded in getting the Department to agree to give us Kananaskis Falls and will have the lease issued in due course."[3]

Aitken had done well to select as his partner in operations a man who would have considerable sway in corporate-government concerns.

Construction started on the Kananaskis Dam in 1913, even though the builder had not come to any agreement with the Stoney Nakoda. The band had initially demanded payment of $25 for each of its 660 members, for a total of $16,500, plus $1,500 annually for water rights. These demands were refused. Tension mounted, and at one point the Indian agent alerted the NWMP that there was a great risk of an uprising.

By 1914, as construction neared completion, the matter was still dragging on and the Stoney Nakoda were voicing their view that their only alternative would be an attack on the powerhouse. Glen Campbell, the Chief Inspector of Indian Agencies, wrote his assessment: "(the) situation is so dangerous that if there is no immediate prospect of settlement... I advise you most seriously to arrange for immediate police protection of men at Kananaskis Falls. Indians determined to go to extremes to protect rights which they now believe are being sacrificed in favour of rich corporations... Grave danger of trouble."[4]

An agreement was finally reached. However, that did not solve all of Calgary Power's problems on the Bow. The irregular flow of water still caused havoc on power generation. This problem was somewhat alleviated in 1912

with a control dam to store water on the Cascade River, which began the enlargement of Lake Minnewanka. In 1929 Ghost Dam was built (outside the park). No further development was permitted within park boundaries until the 1940s, when Barrier Dam was added on the Kananaskis River (to aleviate problems with silting at the Kananaskis Dam site) and Minnewanka Dam was enlarged. The 1950s saw new dams on the Spray and Kananaskis rivers.

The sign for the town of Seebe is still on the highway, but there is no longer a town there. Named for the Cree word for "river," the town was built in 1911 for employees of Calgary Power, which was busy building dams. Seebe was once the operational hub of a network of hydro-electric projects, including the Spray, Ghost, Kananaskis, Lake Minnewanka, and several other dams. All could be controlled remotely from Seebe to maximize efficiency. But technology made the site obsolete, so TransAlta Utilities Corporation (which Calgary Power had renamed itself in 1981) decided to close shop. The date for the event was set for August 31, 2004. The remaining residents, about 100 people, were told to make plans to move out. They applied for historical status for the town, but were told that the place was unique but not really significant. So Seebe became a ghost town.

Upstream from Kananaskis Dam on the Bow River

The town had a local post office, store, what is said to have been the last one-room schoolhouse in the province (it closed in 1996), and a tiny, single-sheet curling rink. Many of the buildings have since been relocated.

Some of the land has been bought by the Stoney Nakoda and an organization called Moondance Land Company that plans to put in a residential development. The Municipal District of Bighorn maintains that it will permit this only if the developer plans to create local employment opportunities, and that it is not going to allow another bedroom community that involves people only temporarily in residence. Time will tell…

Door Jamb Mountain — 1,996 m; Loder Peak — 2,097 m

To the north, as you pass through The Gap, lies a long ridge that leads back behind Mount Yamnuska. It is unofficially known as Goat Peak. The first prominent bump, Door Jamb, is named for its obvious shape and position. And the next bump, Loder Peak, has an interesting story behind its name.

As early as 1884, a lime kiln was being operated in this part of the Bow Valley by a man with the last name of McCanleish. In 1888, he hired an Englishman named Edwin Loder, who had come to the region as a woodcutter for the railway. Loder had worked at the lime plant for about 15 months when McCanleish disappeared after leaving for a visit to Calgary. No trace was ever found of him, and finally Edwin Loder and his brother gained the rights to the kilns and operated them under the name Loder Brothers. They expanded the business, adding three new kilns in 1914 and hiring a number of people from the Stoney Nakoda reserve to cut wood for the massive amount of fuel needed. The kilns continued to be operated as Loder Lime Company until they were sold in 1952.

Edwin Loder was a popular man in the community, holding annual Christmas dinners for the entire community in his home. He also served as the first postmaster of the Kananaskis District from 1900 to 1935.

Loder Peak was probably the summit that David Thompson and Duncan McGillivray climbed to in 1800

The Cement Plant

The most visible man-made presence in this section of the valley is definitely the Lafarge cement plant. Although its history goes back to the start of the 20th century, it was not the first cement plant in the area. Robert Pim Butchart (founder of the famous Butchart Gardens near Victoria, B.C.) built a small operation west of Exshaw, near Gap Lake, before the turn of the 20th century. This business was bought by the Robinson family in 1907, who kept it going until the major players who would eventually become Lafarge moved into the area.

The predecessor to Lafarge began its existence on this site with a scandal. Joseph Irvin was one of the men behind the very successful Portland Cement Company in Hull, Quebec. In 1905 he saw opportunity in the West and convinced Sir Sandford Fleming, then 78, to invest heavily in his plan for a site along the Bow Valley that combined quality limestone, potential for power production, and proximity to rail transport. Before the plant was even built, Irvin was found to have paid himself a crippling bonus of $500,000 – a vast sum at the time – which put the venture into jeopardy before it had even got off the ground. But the investors were too far along to let the cement plant fail, so they raised more money and the operation got under way.

The town of Exshaw grew up near the plant. There were 36 houses in 1906, and progressive plans were laid for sewers and water. The plant boasted six 80-foot-long kilns and by 1907 was the largest cement plant in Canada. But then financial difficulties hit. The plant had become overextended, there

Door Jamb Mountain (left-most high point), Loder Peak (next high point) and Goat Peak

were transportation problems, competition had increased, and the industrial recession of that year dropped the bottom out of the market. Three kilns were shut down.

In 1910, Max Aitken became involved in an effort to broaden the company base by amalgamating the Exshaw operation with a number of other cement interests to create Canada Cement. But through some dodgy manoeuvres, Aitken managed to come out of the deal with shares that had a suspiciously inflated value, while Fleming was still burdened with a crippling debt. An out-of-court settlement resolved the dispute between these two powerful men, but Aitken's name remained tarnished by the affair and he soon departed for England.

Things improved enough at the cement plant for repairs and upgrades to be undertaken in 1912, and 1920 brought more mechanization and introduction of a steam shovel. Operations continued to grow steadily, and in 1951 a major overhaul and updating was made of the plant, which converted its fuel from coal to natural gas.

Lafarge came into the picture in 1970, after a merger with Canada Cement. More upgrades and expansions followed. Improvements have continued, and it is now the company's only cement plant still operating that dates back to the original amalgamation in 1910. The modern plant is now engaged in efforts to reduce waste, carry out reclamation, reduce water use, and explore the possibility of using alternative fuels.

The contemporary plant has an excellent safety record, but it was not always a safe place. In the early years, the use of fine coal powder in order to achieve high temperatures resulted in a dangerous environment. One witness recounted an incident: "I saw Briggs open the outside door of (the coal grinding) room, and look around for me. Then, while the dust-laden air blew past him through the door, he put his pipe in his mouth and struck a match. There was an immediate explosion. The sheet metal of the building, which was only nailed at the top, moved outwards like the feathers of a frightened hen, with a flash of flame from each opening and from the open door. Briggs was blown about twenty feet into a pile of sand and laid there. We rushed out to see if he had been killed, but he was only knocked unconscious…When Briggs reported for work the next day, he was given the messy job of replacing the sheet steel siding of the building which had been blown off by the explosion."[5]

Other operations

Loder's Lime, near the hamlet of Kananaskis, was bought by Steel Brothers. In 1958, the company realized that the reserve it was working was running out, so it acquired a new deposit 13 kilometres to the west, the site of Butchart's early cement plant. Steel Brothers underwent considerable expansion in the 1970s, as the company also purchased operations in B.C. and Manitoba. The company became Continental Lime in the 1980s, and was purchased by Graymont Limited in 1989, just over a century after McCandlish started the first lime kiln in this area.

Today, Graymont produces a variety of lime and limestone products, including high-calcium quicklime, hydrated lime, pulverized limestone, and screened limestone. It is the third-largest producer of lime in North America.[5]

In the other direction, to the west past Lafarge, is the Baymag magnesium plant. It is the most recent player in the area. This company retrofitted one of the old Lafarge facilities as a refinery for magnesite aand started operations in 1982. A second plant was built in 1989 when the market for magnesium oxide was booming. After further upgrades and expansions at the site, the original plant was closed in 2005.

None of the ore processed on the Baymag site is mined there. It is trucked in from various other mine sites, mostly in B.C. The high-grade calcined magnesium oxide produced is used in pulp and paper, nickel and steel refining, building compounds, fibreglass, animal feeds, soil remediation, and many other products and processes.

Exshaw was named for William Exshaw, son-in-law of Sir Sandford Fleming and managing director at the plant during its early years. About 350 people now live in the town.

Western Canada Cement and Coal Company mill, Exshaw, 1907-1910, Glenbow NA-3357-4

Canada Cement hydraulic mining operation, June 1924, Glenbow ND-32-3

Heart Mountain — 2,149 m

Heart Mountain, on the south side of the Trans-Canada, was named in 1957 for the obvious heart shape of the upper limestone slab. This is a popular easy scramble. A circuit can be made of this route, descending along a ridge to the east of the heart.

Lac des Arcs

This lake was named by Eugene Bougeau of the Palliser Expedition in 1858. The French word *arc* means "bow," and here it refers to a collection of small lakes (as they were then) that formed an enlargement of the Bow River. The many small lakes of Bougeau's day became a single shallow lake with the installation of the Kananaskis Dam. As well as being popular with swans as a resting point in their spring and fall migrations, Lac des Arcs is a choice winter destination for ice boaters, who take advantage of the smooth lake surface and strong winds that blow through this area.

These strong winds created severe dust storms when seasonal water level changes exposed the silty lake bottom. A berm was installed along the southeast edge to aleviate the situation, but the lake is now silting up again, and so the problem is returning. The wildsurfers who once enjoyed the area for these winds now find it too shallow for safe sailing.

Murder in Exshaw

In 1914, a murder took place at the Canada Cement plant. The employees of the plant were paid in cash every two weeks, and Chief Clerk John Wilson and his assistant, James Gordon, had collected more than $2,000 in cash from the train station and were walking back to the plant to distribute it. Wilson walked in front with the cash bag, carrying a pistol for security. On the fatal day, they encountered four men, one of them an employee at the plant named Louis Romeo. One man grabbed the cash bag, while another, Afancy Sokoloff, shot Wilson to death, and the fourth man grabbed Wilson's pistol. The men took off and the Canmore Royal Northwest Mounted Police were called onto the scene. (Canada's national police force wasn't renamed the RCMP until 1920.) All the outlaws except Romeo headed across the Bow River on a raft, with the Mounties in pursuit on another. Two of the three culprits escaped, and one was taken into custody.

Afancy Sokoloff, convicted of the murder of John Wilson, 1914, Glenbow NA-838-22

A reward was set for the missing men, and a huge search posse set out to round them up. Two were found on a freight car in Cochrane. Once their hiding spot was revealed, one of the fugitives tried to shoot the officer who had found him, but his gun jammed. He was found to have the missing cash in his possession.

The remaining man was caught in Calgary when he tried to sell Wilson's gun. All were convicted of murder. Two of them were hanged and the others were given a life sentence.

Mount McGillivray — 2,450 m

Duncan McGillivray came from a powerful family in Scotland's highlands who were stockholders in the North West Company. He travelled into the Bow Valley with David Thompson in 1800. It is believed that they made it as far as Lac des Arcs before the lateness of the season brought harsh conditions that forced them to return to Rocky Mountain House. McGillivray became very ill with rheumatic fever in 1802, forcing him to abandon his explorations in the west. This mountain was named after him in 1957.

There is a secret in the heart of Mount McGillivray. On its slopes you can still see the evidence of what was once part of the general paranoia associated with the Cold War years. An extensive network of vaults and chambers was dug into the north-facing slope of this mountain. Valuable material was to be stored here, safely away from the risk of a nuclear holocaust. It was not, as you would expect, a scheme that spent taxpayer dollars, but instead a pursuit of opportunity by a private enterprise called Rocky Mountain Vaults and Archives. The company offered storage of material deemed vital for picking up the pieces after a nuclear attack. But it's not clear how the owners of the documents were supposed to cope with exposure to the overwhelming destruction of a nuclear war while their documents were nestled securely away underground…

The Development of a National Park

It seems odd to start talking about Banff National Park here because we won't drive through the park entrance for a couple more chapters. But this was once the boundary to Banff Park, and the original gate was just east of Exshaw. So here is a brief summary of the park's early history…

In the late 19th century, the concept of an area protected as a national park was still a new idea. In the U.S., Yellowstone became the first national park in the world in 1872. In Europe, private ownership had been established prior to the designation of areas that were worthy of protection as parks, which presented problems for protecting significant locations. But in North America there was the opportunity to set aside land before ownership became an issue (Native Americans notwithstanding…). The idea of preserving natural areas of significant beauty for the enjoyment of the people began to take root, but the concept could not yet be called visionary in any modern sense of environmental conservation.

Certain individuals saw how the growing idea of protecting areas of sublime scenery would mesh with their own business ambitions, and they became active promoters of the concept. In 1882, William Cornelius Van Horne became General Manager of the Canadian Pacific Railway. He was enthusiastic about tourism in the West (arriving by train was the only option for visitors then), and the concept of a park would support this nicely. The federal government was keen to work with the CPR to ensure that the railway was a successful operation that would help populate the west as it was opened up for settlement. A mutually supportive relationship flourished between these two interests.

Van Horne traversed the Bow Corridor on a tour of the West and commented that the Lac des Arcs area, then a windy mud flat before the dam was built, appeared to offer great potential for tourism. He must have passed through on a particularly good day. Locals, who knew the true character of the locale compared to the more splendid offerings nearby, immediately dubbed Lac des Arcs "Van Horne's Park."

In 1885, baby steps were taken that would eventually play out as a park in progress: 10 square miles around the hot springs at the base of Sulphur Mountain were set aside by a federal Order-in-Council as Banff Hot Springs Reserve. That story shall be told in Chapter 15, but it set the seed that would grow into Banff National Park. Two years later, the Rocky Mountains Park Act was passed to expand this into a 260-square-mile (673-square kilometre) area, to be called Rocky Mountains National Park. The motivation for protecting this area, as described in its documentation, focused on human use and recreation. The emphasis was on the potential for the spiritual renewal that can be found in areas of beauty. The place, as stated in the Rocky Mountains Part Act, was to be a "public park and pleasure ground for the benefit, advantage and enjoyment of the people of Canada." And, of course, it was to encourage visitors to go west and contribute to the budding tourism economy.

In a debate on May 3, 1887 in the House of Commons, Sir John A. Macdonald observed: "I do not suppose in any portion of the world there can be found a spot, taken all together, which combines so many attractions and which promises in as great a degree not only large pecuniary advantage to the Dominion, but much prestige to the whole country by attracting the population, not only on this continent but of Europe, to this place. It has all the qualifications necessary to make it a place of great resort…" Tourism is profitable, and parks promote tourism. That concept was firmly in place from the very beginnings of the national park.

Surveyor George A. Stewart was sent out to establish the boundaries of the new park. His instructions were to "include all points of interest within reasonable bounds" and to include the western end of "Devil's Lake" (Minnewanka) to the Bow and up to the confluence with the Spray. Stewart then went on to become the first Park Superintendent.

In 1897, he was replaced as Superintendent by Howard Douglas, who had a very clear vision of the park as a tourist destination. He believed that an abundance of wildlife was essential for the pleasure of visitors to the park. People came to see animals as much as scenery. The control of poaching and the reduction of predators were therefore on his agenda. Douglas was responsible for hiring the first game wardens to protect wildlife within the park – although he was also responsible for initiating the predator-eradication policy.

In 1902, the boundary of the park was shifted 20 kilometres to the east of where it is now – to the point where we are discussing it in this chapter. This expanded the area of the park dramatically, from 260 to 4,900 square miles (12,690 square kilometres) – from the headwaters of the Bow River to the Kananaskis Valley entrance, and included Exshaw, Canmore, and Seebe within the park boundaries. One of the reasons behind the expansion was the growing awareness of the value of the game population in the area, and the need for the park to encompass a substantial area to ensure the animals' continued viability. But there remained a dual focus on protecting *and* exploiting the park – a balance of concerns that slowly would come to be understood as sometimes incompatible.

The expansion did not last… In 1911, the Rocky Mountain Forest Reserve was established and a chunk of land was transferred from the Rocky Mountains Park into this designation. This reduced the size of Rocky Mountains National Park back to 1,800 square miles (4,660 square kilometres). The federal Minister of the Interior claimed that the park had been too large and cumbersome to administer effectively.

James B. Harkin became the first Commissioner of Dominion Parks in 1911, a position he would hold until 1936. During Harkin's long tenure, we begin to see a change

in emphasis regarding how parks should function. Knowledge of ecological processes was growing, and natural areas were beginning to be seen as functioning systems. Tourism was seen as tolerable, as it did not actively extract anything from the park except enjoyment – but activities such as mining and logging began to be seen as questionable. The approach to park management was gradually becoming more conservation-minded.

In 1917, largely due to Harkin's work, Rocky Mountains Park was extended again, this time to include areas on the upper Red Deer and Panther rivers and a part of Kananaskis Valley. It grew again, slightly, in 1929 with the addition of the area south of the Brazeau River. But another reduction occurred in the 1920s, when the federal government was preparing for the transfer of control over natural resources to the three prairie provinces in 1930. Certain areas that had potential for grazing or hydroelectric development had to be delivered to provincial control. This was when the Spray River lands were taken out of the park.

1930 was an important year for national parks. The National Parks Act was passed, which stated concisely that the main purpose of the parks was not recreation but preservation. This meant that resource extraction would not be permitted within park boundaries. The conflict with operations such as coal mining at Canmore and logging in the Kananaskis was solved by simply removing those areas from the park. The eastern boundary shrank back to west of Canmore, where it remains today. Banff Park now covers 2,586 square miles (6,697 square kilometres). An Act of Parliament would be required to make any future changes.

In 1964, the first Parks Policy Statement was issued, which stated that the park was intended for "the people of Canada for their benefit, education and enjoyment... to be maintained and made use of so as to leave them unimpaired for the enjoyment of future generations." Conservation was becoming more of a public issue in the 1960s and the balance was shifting to a longer focus, toward preservation and sustainability. Tourism, which had been seen as having no impact, was beginning to be understood as a more complex issue. This understanding created a polarization between those who wanted development and tourism opportunities, and those who emphasized the need for ecosystem

RMP - added 1929
removed 1930

·········· Current park boundary

Rocky Mountains Park
extended - 1902

Banff National
Park - 1930

Rocky Mountains Park
added 1917

Rocky Mountains
Park - 1911

Rocky Mountains
Park - 1887

Hot Springs
Reserve - 1885

Park boundaries through the history of the national park

protection and for limitations on what they saw as exploitation of vulnerable environments.

In 1979, there was a new Parks Canada Policy, the "Beaver Book," which again stated clearly that parks are "a national inheritance which should be protected." Park use had increased dramatically, and the impact of this pressure was becoming more evident. At the same time, the concept of ecological integrity had evolved. The importance of managing a natural system in which the diverse components could function to support and sustain each other was a common theme in scientific literature. The 1979 Park Policy made this its primary consideration.

Changes in the decades since then have mostly expanded on the understanding and intent of this 1979 document. In 1984, Banff was declared a UNESCO World Heritage Site, which raised the profile of the park and also raised the bar to protect this status. An amendment to the National Parks Act in 1988 required a management plan with public participation, which led to the Banff-Bow Valley Study in the 1990s. Another amendment in 2001 went even further. It required not only maintenance but *restoration* of the ecological integrity of natural systems. This created more complex management issues.

Thus the concept of the park has developed from simply setting aside a "pleasure ground" of outstanding scenery for the enjoyment of (wealthy) visitors, to an emphasis on the park itself and how it functions as a natural system, separate from any potential use by people. Environmental and ecological issues drive decision-making today. Yet it remains difficult to separate this from the demands of the visiting public, whose tourist dollars still provide the backbone to support the park's existence.

Vehicles in the Park

So – returning to Exshaw (which was the early park boundary) and the development of roads and motor traffic... The first car arrived in Banff even before a road did. In 1904, Charles Glidden and his wife set off from Boston in their chauffeur-driven Napier automobile to motor across the U.S. and Canada to the Pacific Ocean. They entered Canada in Saskatchewan and in Moose Jaw had the vehicle outfitted for travel on rails, then headed for the mountains on the CPR line. They left Calgary well after the scheduled train, but managed to catch up with it and arrive in Banff simultaneously with the train at noon. This audacious act provoked a strong reaction in Ottawa, and an Order-in-Council in 1905

Highway near Exshaw, 1907-1910, Glenbow NA-3357-6

banned all cars from the park and set a three-month jail term for violating the rule.

Despite this, a road was being built between Banff and Calgary. A coach road already linked Canmore and Exshaw, and in 1905 a rough road from Calgary joined this fragment. The remaining stretch to Banff townsite was completed in 1909. The first to drive it was Norman Lougheed – a son of Senator Sir James Lougheed – whose car was impounded as soon as he entered the park boundary. His trip was followed

three days later by two separate travellers – a Mr. Downey of Calgary and a Mr. Gooderham of Toronto. Both were also stopped by the police. There followed six years of argument between the park and the drivers (particularly the Calgary Auto Club acting on behalf of the latter). The auto club's members held a rally in which they drove west in a convoy of cars and entered the park illegally.

The Banff livery operators lobbied against permitting drivers to enter the park. They contended that it would

Eastern Gate, Rocky Mountain National Park, 1924, Glenbow NC-26-196

damage their business, and posed potential danger through increased traffic on the roads. Editorials in the *Banff Crag and Canyon* newspaper commented on the impact of the auto-crazy motorists and the escalating number of accidents on streets in and around the town. However, the powers that be also recognized that tourists entering by vehicle represented economic benefits to the park and that income could be generated through a permit system.

In 1911, cars were allowed to enter the park, although with limitations, and a gate was installed on the Banff Coach Road to control traffic. Motorists were required to sign in as they entered the park, pay a fee, and park their vehicle as soon as they entered Banff townsite.

Objections from the residents of the town were immediately voiced in the *Crag and Canyon*. Alarm was expressed about the crazy driving, and the violation of the 15 mph (24 km/hr) speed limit. Noise issues were a common theme. Most of the traffic was from Calgary, which at the time had a population of less than 50,000, of whom fewer than 10% owned vehicles. So there was hardly a massive surge of cars to Banff…

By 1915, the benefit of automobiles coming into the park was seen as obviously outweighing the disadvantages, so regulations were softened. Auto tourism was increasing across the continent, and the focus turned toward profiting from this trend. All restrictions were soon lifted.

At first, registering for entry to the park was done at the RNWMP office. Then, in 1916, Mrs. Annie Staple of Exshaw was hired as gatekeeper for the park. She set up her office – a table under a tree – and sold the required licences from there. Gateway Lodge was constructed in 1917 and she moved her office indoors. Here she also housed and fed travellers who arrived too late to pass through the park gate before it closed for the night, at which time a chain was stretched across the road with a lantern suspended from it. The first permits were fabricated out of used licence plates, which were strapped onto the car's bumper. They were turned in when exiting the park, and Mrs. Staple washed them and reissued them to another driver. Early park plates were stamped in the shape of a buffalo, and were wired onto the car's front grill.

In 1919, Mrs. Staple's husband died, just months before their fourth child was born, but she remained at her position. When the park boundaries were changed, and the gate was relocated 29 kilometres further west, Mrs. Staple and her family followed. Again she set up shop outdoors in a temporary shack, built for the first season. But this "temporary" accommodation stretched on for six years before she could move into the new permanent gates. Mrs. Staple served as gatekeeper for 32 years, retiring in 1948.

In the 1920s, driving from Calgary to Banff took about four hours. The gate into the park was closed between October and April, although most services were open only in the summer months anyway. Between 1920 and 1922, the road was pushed on from Banff toward Lake Louise. Traffic began to increase and, without improvements in the road conditions, there was demand for services for car and tire repairs along the route. Zeller's garage opened in Exshaw and was responsible for many en-route rescues.

The appalling condition of the roads was a limiting factor for traffic density for a long time. But in 1924 the road to Banff was gravelled, which was a substantial improvement. At about the same time, the opening of the Banff-Windermere road also led to another increase in traffic. The road to Banff was paved in 1932, and its name was changed to Highway 2. Then, in 1941, the name was changed to Highway 1 under the pressure to create a cross-country highway.

The actual Trans-Canada Highway was started in 1957 in this area, routed along the south side of the Bow River and rejoining the old highway near Canmore. It then followed that route into the town of Banff along the south side of Tunnel Mountain. By the time the final routing for the Trans-Canada Highway was completed, this final section had been shifted to skirt Tunnel Mountain to the north.

Birch trees by
Lac Des Arcs

Tree ID: Birch trees

On the western edge of Lac des Arcs, conveniently located by a pull-off, is a fine clump of White or Paper birch trees, *Betula papyrifera*. These are not very common in this area, and are most likely to be sited in moderately damp open locations. It is easy to mistake them for aspen, but a closer look will make the difference clear. They are not found in the massive groves that the aspen create. Birch leaves are similar in size and shape to aspen, but have serrated edges. They frequently have a cluster of trunks, covered with a character-istic white or creamy bark that peels away from the surface. These trees are sometimes called canoe birch, because the bark could be removed in thick slabs, which was historically used to construct canoes as well as sturdy containers. The sap of the paper birch can be collected and processed like maple syrup.

Paper birch easily hybridizes with another birch species, the Water birch, *Betula occidentalis*. This shorter and thicker-growing species prefers wetter areas. The bark of Water birch does not peel like bark does on the paper birch.

More Murders in Exshaw

In October 1935, four Doukhobors – Paul Bogarra, John Kalmakoff, Joseph Posnikoff, and Peter Voiken – were involved in a suspected armed robbery in Manitoba. They were caught, although Bogarra was released on insubstantial evidence. The other three were sent for detainment under the care of constables J. G. Shaw and William Wainwright. But the three men murdered the two constables and fled westward.

Word was sent of the escapees with a description of the vehicle they were driving. A few days later, their car was recognized by Roy Zeller as they stopped for gas at his station in Exshaw. His wife Lucille conveyed the fugitives' whereabouts to the RCMP, and four officers headed east from Banff to intercept the criminals. However, the three had been refused entrance to the Park by Mrs. Staple when they refused to pay the park fee, so by then they were heading back toward Calgary. Mrs. Staple informed the officers of this development, and they continued their pursuit eastward until they found a car by the side of the road that matched the description. As they approached in the dark, shots were fired from the vehicle. More gunfire was exchanged and both Sergeant Thomas Wallace and Constable G. C. Harrison were mortally wounded. The criminals disappeared in the dark.

Magistrate Hawke and Constables J. H. Bonner, G. Coombe, and Grey Campbell set up roadblocks and a search commenced. In the course of rummaging around through the woods in the dark, one of the RCMP shot at some movement in the trees and killed Joseph Posnikoff. The autopsy revealed that he had already been wounded in the earlier exchange.

The search continued through the night, but the remaining two men were not flushed out. A sighting the next day pinpointed a spot about 10 kilometres west of the park gate. Two park wardens, William Neish and Harold Leacock, went to investigate. The tip was confirmed when a volley of shots welcomed their arrival at the site. Another gun battle followed and Neish, who had served in the Canadian Armed Forces, calmly aimed his shots behind a stump in the bushes. Both Kalmakoff and Voiken were wounded and died later that day in the Banff hospital.

The three men involved had been responsible for seven deaths.

Pigeon Mountain — 2,394 m

This is another peak named by Monsieur Bourgeau from the Palliser Expedition. Well, actually it was Pic des Pigeons, for the large flock of these birds that he observed near the mountain. Given that passenger-pigeon bones were among those found in a bonebed inside a cave on Grotto Mountain (see the next chapter), one wonders whether it might have been this now-extinct species that was observed on the wing around these slopes.

In 1962 a ski hill was installed on the lower 250 metres of the west side of Pigeon Mountain. This was an optimistic move given that this area is frequented by Rocky Mountain Sheep precisely because it tends to stay snow-free due to the

Pigeon Mountain from the west

drying chinook winds. The new snow-making equipment helped to solve that problem. A poma lift was installed, and it ran for about three years before going into bankruptcy. A group of investors rescued it and replaced the poma lift with a double chair. This was after a tragic incident in which a young girl was killed by a derailment of the old lift. The operation then limped along until 1974, when the ski hill closed for good. The facilities were reincarnated as Alpine Haven time-share condominiums for a while, and are now Banff Gate Mountain Resort.

To the west of Pigeon Mountain is an open valley that leads up to Skogan Pass, which was a route commonly used by the Indians to access Kananaskis Valley. Don Gardner gave the pass its name in 1972 – a Norwegivan word meaning "a magical forest inhabited by elves and trolls." Mount Collembola rises on the west side of the Pass, unofficially named after the sixteen-eyed snow fleas, also known as springtails. These tiny insects (about two to six millimetres long) hatch in early winter, when they can be seen leaping about on the surface of the snow.

Dead Man's Flats

A name like Dead Man's Flats has got to have an interesting story behind it, and this site has a couple. There is a vague tale about some Stoney Nakoda hunting in the area out of season. In order to avoid being caught when they heard someone approaching, they smeared themselves with blood and played dead. But there is another tale that is more substantial and probably has at least the seeds of truth behind it.

Near the turn of the 20th century, a French immigrant named John Marret had established a small homestead near the base of Pigeon Mountain and started a dairy operation there. His brother, François, came out to join John and help out with delivery and other odd jobs. The dairy was not as profitable as John had hoped, so he took a part-time job in the mines in Canmore.

François had seemed a bit odd, and he occasionally complained about pains and noises in his head. As the days went by, he gradually became convinced that his brother was involved in the creation of some sort of electric machine that was intended to slowly kill him. François surreptitiously searched for the machine, but it was not to be found. On the night of May 10, 1904, the two brothers turned in for the night, but François rose again as soon as John was sound asleep. He went to the home of the Loder brothers, stole a double-headed axe, then returned to the cabin and killed his brother.

After this grisly act, he started hearing other voices in his head telling him that he now had to take his brother's body to the river and revive him. This, obviously, did not work, so he returned the body to John's bed. In the morning, he turned up at the mine in Canmore and offered to work his brother's shift because John was dead. Constable Blyth was sent to investigate… François was eventually found not guilty by reason of insanity and lived out the rest of his life in the mental hospital in Ponoka, Alberta.

Mount Lougheed — 3,105 m

This impressive mountain was called *Ganutha Îpa* by the Stoney Nakoda, which means "windy ridge" for the continuous funnelling of wind through this locale. Eugene Bourgeau recorded its name as Wind Mountain, and noted that it was a spot where he had particularly enjoyed collecting specimens. In 1928, the mountain was renamed Mount Lougheed after Sir James Lougheed, a Calgary lawyer who practised with R. B. Bennett and was later appointed to the senate. His grandson, Peter, was premier of Alberta from 1971 until 1985. Originally, a different peak west of Banff had been selected to receive Lougheed's name, but the family objected to it so this peak was chosen instead. Several members of the Lougheed family, including Peter, have succeeded in making guided climbs to the summit.

Honourable James A Lougheed, 1920, Topley Studio / Library and Archives Canada / PA-026684

Lougheed has four summits, and the name is applied to the highest and most dramatic when seen from the highway. The name Wind Mountain is now assigned to the southernmost summit. To make matters confusing, an impressive cliff-sided summit to the northwest is known as Windtower, and there is another feature slightly to the north known as Wind Ridge…

Mount Allan — 2,810 m

Mount Allen was named in 1948 for Dr. J. Allan, a professor of geology at the University of Alberta. He did the initial mapping of the coal seams in the area. Nakiska Ski area, built for the 1988 Calgary Winter Olympics, is located on the eastern slopes of Mount Allan. There is a superb hiking trail that climbs from the Kananaskis Valley over the summit and down to Dead Man's Flats. Built in 1967 to mark Canada's centennial, it is called… the Centennial Trail. It is closed between April 1 and June 21 because Rocky Mountain sheep use this area for lambing.

Facing Page: Mount Allan, Wind Mountain, unnamed summit, Mount Lougheed and Windtower

Wildlife Spotting: Moose

Wetlands are where one expects to spot these water-loving animals, and they occasionally frequent the marshy ground between the Trans-Canada and the Bow River. The largest of the deer family, moose (*Alces alces*) are the second-largest wild animal in North America after buffalo. They stand about 1.8 metres at the shoulder. The name comes from the Algonquin word *moz* – meaning "twig eater," which seems appropriate as they love to browse the willows and young aspen. Moose are also fond of aquatic plants and will wade out into lakes and rivers to dine. They're even known to dive several metres underwater for delicacies.

Moose are not herd animals and lead quite solitary lives, except during the fall rutting season. They can become quite aggressive then, when hormones seem to deprive them of normal caution, so they should be given a wide berth at that time. Moose live between the valley bottoms and the subalpine, and are diurnal, which means they are active at dawn and dusk.

With their large head and long, rounded nose, moose may not be the winners of any wildlands beauty contest, but they are right on top in terms of antler growing. The male's huge "palmate" (shovel-shaped) rack with tines around the outside edge grows again each year in only about five months. An amazing amount of energy must go into this. As well as the impressive antlers, the male sports a large "bell" under his chin – a pendant of skin and hair into which he works his urine as a communicative scent.

Young moose

Wildlife Management –
Wildlife and Highways

Almost as soon as the Trans-Canada was completed, there was pressure to expand the highway's capacity due to its fast-growing traffic load. It was soon made into a four-lane, divided highway as far as the park boundary.

But continuing this expansion within the park was more complicated. There were concerns that doing so would have a negative impact on the park's natural systems. But the highway is not just a route to provide park access for tourism and recreation – it is the country's primary artery and a busy transportation link. Yet the rising rate of accidents on Highway One within the park was a clear indication that something had to be done. The question was how to make the road larger and safer, but still honour the national parks' mandate that they be "maintained and made use of so as to leave them unimpaired for the enjoyment of future generations." Improvements to make the road safer and alleviate the increasingly frequent traffic jams would inevitably make the situation more deadly for wildlife in the park. Animal mortality on the highway was reaching frightening levels.

Roads – particularly large, busy roads – have impacts on wildlife in a number of ways. They physically decrease the area of land useable as habitat, both through the land covered by the road itself and the impact on land bordering the road affected by noise and human activity. Roads directly cause animal mortality through collisions with cars. And they present a significant barrier for animal movement, which has negative implications resulting from habitat fragmentation. Roads may prevent wildlife that are unable or unwilling to cross them from reaching important resources such as shelter, mineral licks, or escape routes from predators. Roads also divide populations, separating gene-pool groups. We now understand that when the population of a species drops below a certain level, the decreased genetic diversity makes that population much more vulnerable. So the barrier that a road presents for animals is an urgent problem within the park.

When the decision was made in the early 1980s to twin the first section west of the Banff East Gate, a number of criteria were set to mitigate the impact (literally and figuratively) of increased and faster-moving traffic. The obvious way to protect animals would be simply to keep them off the road – with a fence. A wire 2.5 metre fence was installed along both sides of the highway, set back in the woods to minimize the visual impact. One-way gates were installed at regular intervals so that any animal that got onto the road by accident could be sent back to the correct side of the fence.

Because the fence presented a decisively solid barrier to animal movement, a number of wildlife crossings were incorporated into the plan. These had been in use in Europe since the 1950s, and they were also in use in some parks in the United States. There are a number of variations in use – culverts (for smaller animals), creek bridges, underpasses, and overpasses or "green bridges." The crossings on the first phase of the Trans-Canada's twinning were all underpasses. This first phase was monitored carefully by a research team from the University of Calgary so that future phases could be improved from what the team learned.

The use of the underpasses by wildlife was encouraged by seeding them with animal droppings so they "smelled right" and the inclusion of salt licks to lure animals into their vicinity. "Track pads" were laid to provide a record of which animals had passed through the underpass, and motion-triggered cameras recorded animals passing across. Early results seemed to indicate that these might offer a promising solution.

The next phase of twinning of the Trans-Canada advanced the widened highway to the Sunshine intersection west of Banff. When the decision was made to continue the process on to Castle Junction, two overpasses for animals were included (at the controversial price tag of $300,000 each). The underpasses seemed successful for many animals such as sheep, deer, and elk. But large carnivores such as bears, wolves, cougars, and also moose seemed reluctant to use them. It was hoped that the overpasses would prove more suitable for these species. Observations so far indicate that overpasses are indeed successful for moose, which remain reluctant to move through the tunnel-like underpasses. Most of the large carnivores make limited use of overpasses. Still, it appears that some species that were initially reluctant to use the underpasses are adapting to them over time.

Animal fencing

So do the wildlife crossings work? The answer depends on the criteria for evaluating the situation…. They do reduce the number of animals killed on the road. This is particularly true for the ungulates (hoofed animals), with a decrease of highway deaths of 80%.[6a] The figures are lower for the large carnivores, particularly black bears, which sometimes simply climb the fence posts and still end up being killed on the highway. If your criterion for success is whether wildlife crossings increase species viability through allowing population movement and thus preserving genetic diversity, it will probably be a couple more decades before we really know whether this method is working.

On a similar note, the railway presents a similar and frequently lethal hazard to wildlife. To date, the choice has been not to fence the tracks, which would present yet another obstacle to wildlife movement. But animals are frequently killed on the rails. One of the main reasons for this has been spillage from grain cars. Animals are attracted to eat the loose grain and are thus vulnerable. Once an animal has been hit, others may scavenge on the remains, putting them at risk as well.

The CPR has tried to solve this problem by using a vacuum car that sucks up the spilled grain from the rails. This car makes a sweep of the tracks daily and whenever a spill is reported. But the problem continues. Animal deaths on the tracks persist even as prevention efforts on the highway are finding success.

Once you are past the nose of Wind Ridge as it juts toward the Trans-Canada Highway, you will have also rounded the southern corner of Grotto Mountain. The steep face of this mountain stretches to the northeast of the road until you reach the turn-off for the town of Canmore. Grotto is one of a series of peaks along the northeast side of the highway known as the Fairholme Range. This was named by John Palliser after his brother-in-law, William Fairholme. The inspiration for the name came from Palliser's appreciation of a trip he made with Fairholme to Missouri in 1840, which he felt had been the initiation for his later travels farther west.

Grotto Mountain — 2,706 m

Grotto Mountain was explored in 1858 by Eugene Bourgeau and Dr. James Hector from the Palliser Expedition. The pair climbed the southeast slope and there found a cave. Hector described it in his journal: "On one side of this little valley there is a deposit of angular blocks of rock, mixed with calcareous clay, forming the sides to a height of 150 feet. In this deposit we found a large cave, with a high arched roof and narrow mouth, and like Robinson Crusoe's one, with an old goat for a tenant, but in this case he had been long dead. The floor was quite battered hard by the tracks of sheep and goats."[1]

In one of Grotto's canyons that pushes into the flanks of the mountain is a panel of painted pictographs. It has been dated to about 1,000 years ago. Not much is known about the panel (and a few others found in this area). Keyser and Klassen, in "Plains Indian Rock Art", offer a quite complete description of the Grotto panel: "One human with wide 'rabbit ears' and a tapered torso holds a spear and presides over two rows of elk, some with magnificent antlers or bodies filled with a lattice pattern... Another group of three humans is highly abstracted, with tapered lower torsos ending in strange shapes instead of legs and feet... Each wears a detailed headdress and holds rattles or similar objects."[2] The pictographs are painted in vermilion ochre, a pigment that was collected by various tribes at sites farther west (Redearth Creek, the Paint Pots in Vermilion Pass, and others).

The panel is located in a narrow section of the canyon, between the lower approach and the broad alpine meadow that opens above the cleft. Do these images have some symbolic connection to the passage between two realms? Are they a form of communication between groups? Do they tell a story? We will probably never know.

Grotto Mountain

If you should decide to explore up the canyon to find the pictographs, please be diligent about not touching them. They have already suffered much damage from careless contact, and are quite vulnerable to the destructive effect of human skin oils. Look, enjoy, photograph, but don't touch.

Grotto Mountain

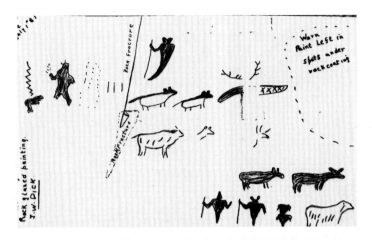

Rat's Nest Cave

It is doubtful that Hector's grotto was what is now known as Rat's Nest Cave. The descriptions just don't fit. There are several cave entrances on Grotto, but Rat's Nest is the most extensive system that has been located on the mountain.

Entrance to Rat's Nest Cave is now restricted to guided trips. With an expert who is familiar with the underground terrain, you can explore and marvel at the range of cave features. A stiff climb of just under an hour takes you to the entrance, which is a low, arched opening that leads to a sloping passage. Inside, the cave maintains a constant year-round temperature of about 5 degrees C. The cave is undeveloped: there are neither artificial lighting nor handrails to help you negotiate the route through the chambers. There is a varied network of passages to explore for about four kilometres back under the mountain.

Rat's Nest Cave is a Karst cave. This means that it was dissolved out along faults in the limestone by water containing carbon dioxide, creating carbonic acid. Water followed the sloping thrust fault and started the process of enlarging the cracks in the rock. Where faults intersected, larger galleries were created. During the glacial periods, melting water flowed through the growing passages – and those who study caves can even tell you which direction it flowed by marks evident on the cave walls. The cave opening now stands well above the present valley bottom. But when it formed, it would have been at the level of the valley floor. The glacial cycles that created the cave also scoured out the valley to the level it has today.

The cave's name is derived from one of the furry residents, the brushy tailed wood rat. These animals form "middens" in crevices in the cave walls – nests filled with bits of food and other treasures that they drag home. Hence their common name: pack rat. Bats and shrews (insectivores) are the other mammals that use the cave, and both little brown and silver-haired bats have been spotted. Other than that, life in the cave is minute: a variety of arachnids (spiders) and insects.

There are records of a huge spectrum of animals preserved in Rat's Nest Cave – animals that lived in the area up to 7,000 years ago. Near the entrance is a shaft that drops 15 metres, and at the bottom of this is a bonebed two metres

Drawing of pictographs on Grotto Mountain, 1959, Glenbow NA-5093-739

Pictographs on Grotto Mountain, C. Schock

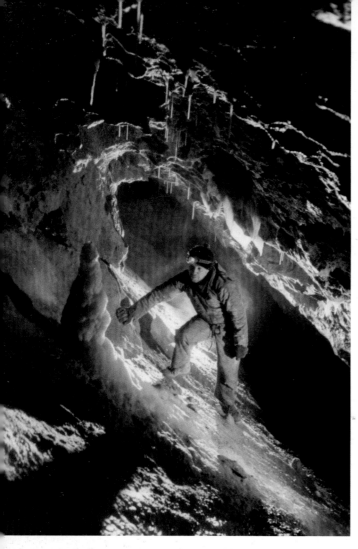

All photos: In Rat's Nest Cave, C. Yonge

Just What is a Speleothem?

The word "speleothem" comes from the Greek words *spelaion* ("cave") and *thema* ("deposit"), so these are cave deposits or formations. The ones we commonly know are called stalagmites and stalactites – those tusks on cave floors and ceilings. They are formed from a mineral called calcite, and their existence depends on a number of conditions not present in all caves.

Water provides the vehicle to carry minerals into the cave. It seeps through the ground and vegetation on the earth's surface, and in the process it picks up carbon dioxide and gains acidity as a weak form of carbonic acid. Next, the water flows through cracks in rock containing calcium carbonate. Calcium is readily dissolved out of the limestone of the Rocky Mountains and is carried in the water. When the water reaches an opening in the cave, it encounters conditions that cause it to release its load as calcite. The drip leaves a minute deposit of mineral on both the roof and floor, thus building a stalactite and a stalagmite. If they grow down and up to the point that they join, they become a pillar.

This all occurs at an average rate of up to a centimetre per century (many deposits grow a lot more slowly, for example taking 2,000 years to grow just one centimetre). It's not exactly a speedy process. So you can image the amazing age of some of the speleothems seen in the underground world.

Speleothems can take an amazing variety of forms, many of which are found in Rat's Nest Cave. Water flowing down walls instead of dripping from ceilings creates flowstone, which looks just like a frozen waterfall. If the drips run along a crack in a sloping ceiling, they can produce shawls or curtains, which are sometimes so translucent that you can see through them. Young stalactites are hollow, and are called straws, which they resemble. Cave pearls form around granules, just like those around sand in an oyster.

In addition to the various shapes, speleothems can take on different colours, though most commonly they are cream- or tan-coloured. Small amounts of organics or trace minerals influence the hue of the formation. If the presence of these elements changes over time, it can produce a striped effect.

These otherworldly sculptures are one of the lures to explore these underground galleries. And their rarity and delicacy makes it imperative that we are mindful of protecting them from damage resulting from our explorations.

thick. It has been carefully excavated and 34 different animals have been identified in the pile. This includes small rodents and mammals that may have been brought in as prey, as well as large animals such as black bear, gray wolf, coyote, swift fox (which are no longer found in this region), lynx, elk, buffalo, and mountain sheep. Remains of some birds have been found, including golden eagle and passenger pigeon (the latter is now extinct). The great value of this bonebed in understanding the history of the region has been recognized, and the cave was made a protected Provincial Historic Site in 1986.

Human use of the cave system seems limited and fairly recent. Only two artefacts have been found: two projectile points, dating back to between 3350 BCE (Before Common Era) and 1000 BCE.

The Three Sisters

To the south side of the highway, there is a line of well-known peaks, starting with one found on many postcards of this area of the Rockies.

The Three Sisters — 2,936 m

This mountain was commented on by Hector, who called it Three Peaks. But it was Major A. B. Rogers of the CPR who gave it the name we know it by now. He viewed these peaks under a fresh blanket of snow, and stated that they looked just like three nuns. They were referred to as The Three Nuns for a while, but were marked as The Three Sisters on surveyor George Dawson's map of 1886 – though we don't know whether he made the change and whether this reflected a preference for a more secular name. The three peaks are referred to as the Little, Middle, and Big Sisters. The Middle Sister is a moderate scramble. The Little Sister is the most challenging ascent and was first climbed in 1925. The highest peak, the Big Sister, was first climbed in 1887 by Dominion Land Surveyor J. J. McArthur.

Lawrence Grassi outside his home in Canmore, 1950, Whyte Museum and Archives NA 66-1457

Mount Lawrence Grassi — 2,685 m

This mountain is named after one of the most unpretentious and well-loved individuals who came to these mountains in the first half of the 20th century. Lawrence Grassi arrived from Italy in 1912 and worked for a few years with the CPR in the Kicking Horse Pass area. A short, strongly built man, he moved to Canmore and worked in the coal mines for many years. He was a very capable climber and became a respected guide in the Banff Rockies (though he would never charge a cent for his services). Grassi made many of the first ascents in these mountains – probably more than will ever be known, as he loved to wander off to summit new peaks solo, never announcing his accomplishments.

After he retired from mining, Grassi worked as a park warden in B.C.'s Yoho National Park. Here on the Alberta side of the continental divide, the evidence of his great enduring contribution to the trails of the Rockies is particularly evident in the Lake O'Hara area. All through the cliffs and slopes are trails that he laid, as well as stone steps finely crafted from the local stone to aid the hiker up tricky sections. His trailwork is found in many parts of Banff National Park and around the Canmore area.

Mount Lawrence Grassi consists of a long ridge with two dramatic outlier summits: Ship's Prow to the southeast and Ha Ling Peak to the northwest.

Ship's Prow — 2,636 m

This steep buttress of 450 metre high cliffs is named (unofficially) for its clear resemblance to the prow of a ship. It is difficult to access and challenging to climb. Only a couple of routes have been put up this portion of Mount Lawrence Grassi, in contrast to the multitude of routes on the high-quality and much more easily accessed rock found at the Ha Ling Peak end. The first ascent of Ship's Prow was by Chic Scott and L. McKay in 1965.

Ha Ling Peak — 2,408 m

This peak on the northwest end was once locally referred to as the Beehive. An event in 1896 changed the name for the next 102 years; it became Chinaman's Peak in honour of a cook of Chinese origin from the town of Canmore. This man was offered a wager of $50 that he could not climb to the top of this peak and return within 10 hours. He promptly went out and did the climb – in just 5½ hours. But Canmore residents refused to believe him, unable to see the small red flag that he had left on the summit. So, the story goes, he promptly went straight back up and planted a 12-foot flagpole with a larger flag visible from the valley.

Chinaman's Peak was made the official name in 1980 – but not long after there were objections to the name for its racist connotations. After a long debate, the name was changed again and the peak was given the name of the man who was believed to have won the double summit. It officially became Ha Ling Peak in 1998.

Ironically, sources have been identified that may indicate that it was not Ha Ling, but a man named Lee Poon who made that trek to the top on a bet[3] – so the name may have been changed to the incorrect one. We will probably never know for sure.

As you come into Canmore, you can see a long ridge with several summits to the northwest of the highway. Like Mount Lawrence Grassi, this mountain has several named (official and unofficial) summits…

Mount Charles Stewart — 2,809 m

The long ridge connecting the mass of the peaks is named after a homesteader in Southern Alberta who went on to become active in politics. A member of the Liberal party (which held power from Alberta's creation in 1905 until 1921, and has been in opposition ever since), Charles Stewart was elected to the provincial legislature in 1909. In 1917, on the resignation of Premier Arthur Sifton, Stewart was appointed Premier. His appointment was made by Lieutenant-Governor Dr. Robert Brett (of Banff). After Stewart lost the 1921 election, he moved on to federal politics, serving as a cabinet minister until 1930.

The mountain was officially named in 1928. The current boundary of Banff National Park runs through its highest point, and along the ridge are several named summits.

Ship's Prow, Mount Grassi and Ha Ling

Mount Lady Macdonald — 2,605 m

To the southeast end of Mount Charles Stewart, rising up from the northern residential communities of Canmore, is the summit officially named for Susan Agnes Macdonald, the second wife of Sir John A. In 1886, after the CPR had finished laying its rail line across the country, Sir John and his wife made the trip across Canada. She seems to have been a spunky sort, and chose to ride a portion of the trip through the mountains on the cowcatcher on the front of the train. The peak was named in her honour in the same year.

On the upper ridge of "Lady Mac" are the remains of some ambitious plans to build a helicopter-access teahouse. The helipad and platform to house the gazebo-style teahouse were built – but that's as far as the project got. The crumbling foundations serve as a picnic site for hikers and a launch pad for hang-gliders.

Lady Susan Agnes Macdonald, 1872, William James Topley / Library and Archives Canada / PA-026416

Princess Margaret Mountain — 2,515 m

To the northwest end of Mount Charles Stewart and across the park boundary (and thus within Banff) is Princess Margaret Mountain. It was officially named in 1958 when the sister of Queen Elizabeth II visited Canada.

Squaw's Tit — 2,514 m

This is a definitely unofficial name for another minor summit to the southwest of Mount Charles Stewart's main ridge. The moniker obviously refers to the shape of a woman's upturned breast. So far this politically incorrect name has not received the ballyhoo of objection that was unleashed on Chinaman's Peak.

Squaw's Tit

Whiteman's Gap

Now here is another name that could raise objections based on ethnic references… though I have heard none… It is not certain which of the early white travellers is responsible for the name attached to this pass above Canmore. To make matters more confusing, there is also a White Man Pass a bit further to the south.

It is unclear which early white traveller is referred to in this name. The first party was a group of Metis, so that is a less likely source. In 1841, HBC trader and explorer James Sinclair was sent west with a group of Red River settlers by Sir George Simpson, Governor-in-Chief of Rupert's Land (the HBC's territories). The Oregon Territory (which comprised the current states of Oregon, Washington, and Idaho, plus parts of Wyoming and Montana) was in dispute between the U.S. and Britain. Occupation being a large part of ownership, there was a push to get settlers onto those lands. It is possible that Sinclair was selected to lead this group partly due to trouble regarding an affair between Simpson and Sinclair's sister. For whatever reason, Sinclair was directed to travel to Oregon via Athabaska Pass. Instead, his Cree guide, Maskepetoon, led Sinclair's party up the Ghost River, down Carrot Creek, and across the Bow River to travel through Whiteman's Gap and then White Man Pass. The 23 families had to abandon their carts and suffered terrible losses on this difficult trip.

Four years later, two parties involving white men passed through the Gap. One was also inspired by the Oregon Territory dispute. Lieutenants Henry Warre and Mervin

Mount Lady Macdonald

Vavasour were sent to review the possibility of sending a military force across the mountains, should the conflict reach that point. They travelled in the guise of gentlemen explorers off on a hunting and botanizing expedition. Warre was an accomplished artist and managed to create a body of sketches and paintings as the two men travelled. Their route took them up the Bow Valley and over Whiteman's Gap and White Man Pass. They had a terrible struggle through the mountains and lost half their horses en route. The pair reported back that crossing the mountains with military troops was a very bad idea. The following year, 1846, the Oregon Treaty was signed, establishing the border along the 49th parallel between the U.S. and what would become Canada.

Amazingly, Warre and Vavasour bumped into the only other white person travelling through the area that year. The Jesuit priest, Father Pierre de Smet, was headed in the opposite direction, from south to north. He had travelled up from Missouri on a mission to visit the Blackfoot. Warre recorded the encounter in one of his sketches.

Whiteman's Gap is a narrow notch between the northwest end of Mount Lawrence Grassi and the southeast end of Mount Rundle. This end of Rundle is affectionately known as EEOR (think Winnie the Pooh) for East End of Rundle. There are several popular climbing routes on the cliffs, as well as a good scrambling route up the south side to the eastern summit. The northern end of the Smith-Dorrian Road (Highway 742) feeds off the Spray Lakes Road above Canmore and eventually connects to Highway 40 via Peter Lougheed Provincial Park. The section that climbs steeply to the Gap from Canmore, built in 1948, is an impressive drive, although it is often closed for periods during the winter due to avalanche hazards.

As you go through the Gap into the valley to the west, you can see the engineering efforts that have been put in place to manage water in this area. The water that now flows down into Canmore through Whiteman's Gap is one of the most heavily altered local drainage systems in Southern Alberta. The Spray River historically flowed out to the Bow River through Spray Canyon, two ranges to the west of the Bow

Whiteman's Gap above Canmore

Valley. It was dammed in 1950 to create the Spray Lakes Reservoir, whose water now flows out through Whiteman's Gap. This is part of a system of dams that generate a limited amount of power, serving principally to store and control water flow for the larger dams on the Bow River.

As the water exits from Spray Lakes Reservoir, it is directed along a canal and then through a tunnel under the base of Ha Ling Peak. It re-emerges briefly on the north side of Whiteman's Pass before being directed into a penstock that drops the water 300 metres down to TransAlta's Spray Plant above Canmore. From there, it passes through another canal, then down another penstock to reach another TransAlta generating station, the Rundle Plant, on the bank of the Bow River.

In the midst of all these water-control features are a pair of lovely clear blue lakes named in honour of Lawrence Grassi. The short (about two kilometres) hike up to the lakes passes over some of the stone trailwork that Grassi was so famous for. The lakes are surrounded by forest on one side and impressive cliffs made up of limestone reefs of the Devonian formation on the other side. Reef formations such as these are of great significance to Alberta, as they contain much of the province's oil and gas reserves.

The cliffs are a popular destination for climbers, and a pair of Great Horned Owls often raises a family in one of the hollows in the rock face. In the pretty canyon above the lakes are some pictographs, thought to be more than 1,000 years old. They are associated with the *Ktunaxa* people, who now live in B.C.'s East Kootenays

meeting with Pere de Smet in the Rocky Mountains

Sketch by Henry J. Warre, meeting Father de Smet, "Sketch of a Return Journey from Oregon to Canada, 1846"; Library and Archives Canada (C-058154)

Development in the Valley

As we near the Town of Canmore, we are in the thick of controversy. Pristine beauty, recreational potential, and lingering environmental integrity come together as a mecca for anyone who values the outdoors. Whether you are a hiker, a wolf, or a developer, this area is among the most desirable real estate in Western Canada. It is an enormous challenge to address the divergent interests of the various stakeholders in an area like this.

Various interests are constantly negotiating for their planning priorities in this part of the Bow Valley. The environmentalists act as constant watchdogs for the interest of wildlife and ecosystem integrity. The developers want to see policies that allow them to maximize profit. Municipalities nned to balance development with quality of community for residents. Recreationalists are concerned about access to places to pursue their various activities. These differing parties will never be in accord onmanaging this fragile area.. The whole mess is strewn with land mines.

The development at Three Sisters is on the south side of the highway, just east of Canmore. It is one of a number of projects that resulted from purchases of land by various developers to take advantage of the enormous growth that the Canmore area was experiencing. Three Sisters Mountain Village is a case in point for most of the issues related to planning for growth and development in the valley. This sprawling complex encompassed over 80% of the available developable land in the region[1], which brought up a plethora of environmental and community issues. After a long series of hearings and objections from environmental groups, permission was granted in 1992 for a $1.5-billion project on the south side of the Trans-Canada between the Wind Valley and Canmore. The approval was given with a number of conditions. The developers must consider input from the residents of Canmore at every stage. Various conditions regarding air and water quality, wildlife management, and other environmental considerations were put in place. In order to facilitate the latter, the recommendations of a group of stakeholders formed for this purpose were to be honoured. This group became the Bow Corridor Ecosystem Advisory Group (BCEAG).

In 2002, an Environmental Impact Assessment was done by Golder Associates, a consultancy whose specialties include environmental services, and specific recommendations were made, particularly regarding wildlife issues.

The Three Sisters project has since gone ahead, but with a number of glitches. There were a number of changes in ownership, and financial problems plagued the project. Further compromises were made regarding wildlife corridors and buffer zones. But a vigilant group of conservationists has been watching the proceedings at Three Sisters diligently and has called the developers to task when guidelines have been contravened. On the other hand, the development has been recognized for progressive environmental considerations such as water conservation and sustainable management practices on the golf courses.

The original plans for the Three Sisters development included 2,600 residential units, 1,600 hotel rooms, three 18-hole golf courses, and 300,000 square feet of commercial development.[4] Only part of this had been completed by 2009, and with the economic downturn the owner went into receivership. So the future of the site remains uncertain.

Another mega-development is in the works for the other side of the Bow Valley, on the lower slopes of Mount Lady Macdonald. Silvertip Resort, a 600-acre residential and golf course development, is planning further expansion as Stone Creek Resorts Club.

The Town of Canmore

The Stoney Nakoda called this area *Chuwap chîmchîyan Kudebi* which means "if I shoot at the bushes I am fooled". This delightful title comes from a trick that warriors would try to play on each other, trying to fool them into shooting their arrows into growths of young spruce trees thinking (in error) that a moose or deer was hiding there.

In the early days of settlement, Canmore was known simply as Siding 27 (because it was the 27th one east of Medicine Hat), Canmore came into existence due to the CPR when it was the divisional point on the eastern side of the mountains. Railways of that time required these points at about 125-mile intervals. There, trains would fill up their stores of fuel and water, and change crews and engines. The divisional points became important centres where crews found residences and provisions were stockpiled for the trains.

The next divisional point was at Field, B.C., after a demandingly steep section known as the Big Hill by Mount Stephen. Extra engines had to be added to the trains to enable them to get up this hill, so these two points were given extra facilities to deal with adding and removing engines. The Roundhouse (which was indeed round) provided both a covered servicing area and a rotating platform where the engine could be spun and redirected in the opposite direction. These elaborate facilities were built in 1883, and the first scheduled train came though in May of the following year.

The naming of the town is credited to Donald Smith, President of the CPR. It came from the Gaelic *Ceann-mor*, which means "Large Headed One," referring to Malcolm III, who became King of Scotland in 1057. Malcolm's uncle, Macbeth, had murdered his father, Duncan I, in 1040, in a play for the throne. Malcolm drove Macbeth from the throne and then claimed it himself. Malcom was killed in battle in 1093. Somebody should write a play about this story…

But back to Canmore. The town began to grow around the CPR station. The first rough settlement was just a row of boxcar houses along Section House Avenue (now Railway Avenue). But as the population became more established, more permanent structures popped up. Some of them were moved here from the dying town of Silver City, to the northwest (see chapter 17). A new Main Street ran south

Top: Canmore, 1886, Glenbow NA-1909-5

Bottom: CPR Roundhouse, Canmore, 1884, Glenbow NA-2622-16

from the station and NWMP barracks were built on the edge of Policeman's Creek. The first restaurant was installed between the roundhouse and the section house by a man named Bill Coffee. Three hotels went up (the Waverly, the Pulman, and the Canmore), as well as a bakery, a furniture store, a general store, a couple of churches.

Community amenities expanded as more families settled in the town. A Presbyterian church was built in 1891, followed by the Roman Catholic Sacred Heart Church two years later. In 1894, the first log school opened for the seven pupils needing an education.

By the end of the 19th century, train technology had progressed so that servicing was being done in Calgary. With the loss of its status as a divisional point, the town's existence came into question. But the change from wood-burning to coal-burning engines gave Canmore a new lease on life.

In 1845, Father de Smet had commented on the visible coal outcroppings he noticed on his journey through Whiteman's Gap. Coal was first "officially" found on the south side of the river near Canmore in 1884, and the Canmore Coal Company started extracting coal at the Canmore No. 1 Mine in 1887. There was no bridge across the Bow River to the railway, so all the coal had to be transported across by ferry in the summer and by sled in the winter. In 1890, an operation around a seam on the north side of the river eliminated this extra step and introduced some competition. Other interests moved in, and by 1891 six seams were being exploited in the area.

By this time, a residential area had sprung up near the mines, on the south side of the Bow, known as Mineside. A store, hotels, and homes clustered not far from the mine. There was a sense of rivalry between the two communities of "townside" (Canmore) and Mineside, until the construction of the bridge in 1892 brought them together. Still more little communities sprang up near other mines in the area. Prospect, just east of the No. 1 Mine, was the first site to install electricity. Another, located to the south of the present park boundary, was called Georgetown. The open pit mine put in at that site is still visible on the slower slopes of Rundle. Both Prospect and Georgetown had a few streets of company-built homes, all painted the same ochre colour. These towns lasted for a few years and then faded away. Many of the residents

moved to Canmore or Drumheller, where mines were still operating. Often they moved their houses with them.

Given the unregulated safety standards of the time, the mines around Canmore did not experience as many disasters as many other mining communities did. But there *were* incidents. An explosion in 1901 in one of the mines killed eight miners, and there were two more fatalities, one in 1902 and the other in 1908. The miners began to agitate for some

Log school built in 1894, no date, Glenbow NA-1909-2

Bird's eye view of Canmore, ca. 1913-19, Glenbow NA-4074-3

No. 1 Mine, Canmore, ca. 1913-19, Glenbow NA-4074-5

No. 2 Mine, Canmore, 1920, Glenbow NA-4074-6

sort of labour organization. Fearing reprisals from the mine owners, they met in secret at first, holding discussions in the bushes by the hoodoos. A branch of the Mine Workers was established in Canmore a few years later.

Things continued to boom until 1911, when the No. 1 Mine was closed due to high production costs. The outbreak of World War I in 1914 gave business a boost for a while by creating huge growth in demand for coal. But once peacetime returned in 1918, the mines became increasingly less viable. Six decades later, in 1978, Mineside was annexed to the town of Canmore. And the following year, the Canmore Mines operation closed down. The age of coal mining in the valley was over and Canmore began to shrink.

Things were looking pretty grim for the community as people moved away to find work and no other prospects seemed to offer themselves. Tourism brought business to a few services, but the vast majority of the traffic simply flowed past Canmore and into Banff National Park. Kananaskis Country was formed in the 1980s, and that gave Canmore a much-needed boost as it became a service centre for aspects of that park. But the real saving factor was the decision to make Canmore the site of the 1988 Olympic Nordic events. The new Canmore Nordic Centre was constructed on the slopes of Mount Rundle above the town, and the world discovered what a magical place Canmore is. Tourists began to flock to the area, and recreational enthusiasts from Calgary came to ski at the Nordic Centre in the winter and to mountain bike in the summer. A segment of these recreational enthusiasts liked Canmore enough that they moved there and made the long commute to Calgary for work. And more and more people began to buy second homes in the town.

Of the original Canmore buildings, only a handful remain. The Canmore Hotel, built in 1890, still stands, largely in its original form. The old NWMP barracks have been restored and are open for visitors, and the Presbyterian Church stands near the barracks. But there is not much evidence of the early mining activity. Most of the mine sites have been reclaimed, largely for safety considerations. The Three Sisters development has integrated a few of the remaining structures in that area as features on its golf course.

"Even the wild animals behave with dignity and decorum in Banff National Park. Banff bears in no way resemble their alleged kinfolk in, say, Yellowstone. Yellowstone bears are overstuffed, revolting, moth-eaten panhandlers who snarl up traffic for miles while pursuing their gluttonous inclinations and make the night hideous by overturning garbage cans in search of snacks to ward off night starvation. Banff bears raid garbage cans too, but they lift the lids off very quietly. And they never hold up traffic. They prefer to walk at twilight along a forest path a few paces behind an unsuspecting tourist who is likely to lose a week's growth if he happens to turn around. Banff bears have a sense of humour." [5]

Wildlife Corridors

One of the principal strategies for maintaining ecological viability for wildlife in this heavily used part of the Bow Valley is the establishment of wildlife corridors. These are designated areas set aside from human activities to act as safe routes for wildlife to move between areas of suitable habitat. Wildlife needs opportunities to move between seasonal ranges, locate mates, and access food, shelter, and other resources. This is particularly important for large carnivores, which have the greatest need for movement and territory. Planning for safe routes set aside for wildlife is also a key element in reducing potentially dangerous human-wildlife encounters.

The initial corridor concept for the Bow Valley was drawn up in the 1980s by Martha McCallum and Dr. Paul Paquet for the Silvertip development on the north side of the Bow Valley. This early planning was based largely on research regarding ungulate movement and did not give much consideration to large carnivores, which have different needs and risks. But it did lay important foundations for subsequent planning work.

Planning for wildlife movement is extremely important in the area around Canmore. This part of the Bow Valley provides an important link between Kananaskis and Banff, and is also part of a system of larger-scale corridors that connect ecoregions across the vast distance between Yellowstone and Yukon. Steep slopes pinch wildlife into a reduced area along the valley bottom – exactly where people want to spend their time and build their structures. There, animals encounter the Trans-Canada, Highway 1A, the railway, the developed areas of Three Sisters, Canmore itself, and Harvie Heights – all

squeezed tightly together. There are projections that more than 16,000 people will be living in this part of the valley by 2015[6] – exerting enormous pressure on an area of significant environmental value.

BCEAG established baselines and criteria for the design and evaluation of corridors, and has designated which activities are acceptable in proximity to corridors. Such things as slope angle, access to protective cover, access to shelter, and other terrain factors were taken into consideration, as well as the human-safety aspect of their location. A map of the corridor network was established, with buffer areas along the routes themselves. But even by 2004, an Action Alert was issued by the Environmental Network to point out that these guidelines were not always being honoured. Some of the golf courses are built right in the corridor area. Trail systems weave through corridors, taking people (and their pets) into areas designated for wildlife presence. It's a thorny issue yet.

"Wildlife corridors are not places wildlife want to be. It's all they have left." (naturalist Mike McIvor)[7]

Bears and People

A sad incident in June of 2005 underlines the challenge in managing wildlife and people in close proximity. Isabelle Dube, a Canmore resident, was out for a run with a couple of friends on the Upper Benchlands trail north of Canmore when the three women encountered a bear. Two of the women managed to retreat to the Silvertip golf course and call for help. Dube climbed a tree to escape the bear – but then either fell or was pulled from the tree by the bear and killed. There had been no bear fatalities anywhere in Alberta since 1998, and Dube's death rocked Canmore. Trail users began to look more closely at wildlife-management policies, which suddenly became a hot topic in Canmore.

Bear encounters were not new to the town. Increasing numbers of bears were entering Canmore, and scares and close calls were becoming all too common. Gardens with fruit trees, bird feeders, garbage that is incorrectly contained, and a multitude of other temptations draw the bruins into areas that create hazards for both bears and people.

It turned out that the four-year-old grizzly that killed Dube, called bear #99, had been relocated to the Carrot Creek area only eight days before, after having approached another person near Canmore. The drop-off point for the bear was only 15 kilometres away from town – and grizzlies are known to cover huge distances in a day. Questions were raised about practices for dealing with problem bears.

Bear management really offers three choices when dealing with an animal that is becoming habituated – that is, too comfortable around humans. The most radical solution is to destroy the bear, and this is often the final outcome after the other options are tried (as ultimately happened to bear #99). Relocation is less final, but often unsuccessful. A third approach, aversive conditioning, is relatively new. It involves subjecting bears to unpleasant noise, physical discomfort (such as beanbag missiles), and other forms of harassment to reprogram them to seek more normal (for bears) habitats with less human presence. Not much research has been completed yet on the outcome of aversive conditioning, but so far it looks promising.

After Dube's death, questions were also raised about the effectiveness of wildlife corridors. The trail that she was on traversed a wildlife corridor. Having overlapping routes designated for human and bear use can actually increase the likelihood of bear-human encounters. Attempts have been made to manage this through trail closures, but this requires a reliable system of reporting bear locations and compliance by trail users. Unfortunately, not only have many trail users failed to comply, but there have even been incidents in which they have removed closure signs.

A number of measures have been undertaken around Canmore to minimize habituation and human-bear encounters. In response to the 2005 fatality, all agencies that manage wildlife, the Canmore community and environmental agencies were brought together to create a strategy to reduce conflict between people and wildlife. A coalition was formed with the goal of generating a proactive conservation strategy that encourages efforts to reduce negative human-wildlife interaction. This group, called Bow Valley WildSmart Community Program, focuses on developing a coordinated approach to education/outreach programs and supports direct management activities that will increase public safety and contribute toward sustainable wildlife populations.

The community of Canmore had already gone bear proof in the 1990s. The municipality has been very proactive in its approach to garbage management – it started one of the earliest garbage-management systems to cope with bears in North America. The garbage issues is currently dealt with by shipping the town's waste out to Calgary. Canmore has enacted a bylaw prohibiting bird feeders in yards during the time of year when bears are active. Composting is also prohibited. Although each of these initiatives is a small measure, collectively they make coming into town a less enticing proposition for bears. There is still need for ongoing public education about natural and non-natural attractants (don't plant berry bushes in your garden!), and about strategies for avoidance of encounters with wildlife such as bears, cougars and elk and what to do in an encounter. WildSmart's involvement has moved from their original three pronged approach addressing education programs on safety, attractant management and assistance with wildlife management such as aversive conditioning to a current focus on programs to teach residents and visitors how to coexist with wildlife. More information is available at www.wildsmart.ca.

Both the provincial and the municipal government have begun attractant management programs on their land to reduce the potential for interaction between humans and bears during the berry season.

What is Bear Shepherding?

Bear shepherding is a practice of aversive bear conditioning in which dogs, usually Karelians, are the aversive element. Originating in Russia, where they were bred for hunting bears, their vicious response to these animals is now being employed to enhance the bears' chance of survival.

The use of the dogs is based on the concept of establishing boundaries that are recognized as territory. The dogs are used on harness (they are never released to chase a bear). When the Karelians are presented to a bear, the dogs' aggressive display is perceived by the bear as territorilaty, which encourages the bear to move on. As soon as the bear moves out of the "no-go zone" and into better habitat, the dogs are stopped, which identifies the perimeter of the territory to be avoided.

The use of the dogs is partly based on scent. It is hard for us olfactory-inhibited humans to understand the degree to which an animal like a bear interprets its environment through smell, but the smell of the dogs is a powerful factor in the program. In fact, when the G8 Summit was held in the Kananaskis in 2002, dogs were used to scent the perimeter of the area as part of the bear management plan for the event.

The dogs may be used in conjunction with other aversive tools such as pepper spray and rubber bullets. There is also some preliminary work being done on using the dogs with cougars.

Canmore's Growing Pains

Overwhelming popularity comes with a price. Canmore has staged a spectacular rebound from its declining days as an ex-mining town, but now it faces a whole new set of challenges. It was one of the fastest-growing communities in Canada until the economic downturn that began in late 2008. However, about 30% of the residences are now owned by absentee landowners. Whole developments are being put in with a lock-it-and-leave-it orientation. This creates a segment of the community who are often not interested in contributing to daily municipal health, whose interest is more in a low tax rate than in schools and arenas.

The pressure is intensified because of the overflow resulting in the "need-to-reside" policy in the town of Banff. There, due to limitations imposed by being a municipality within a national park, residents must have a (generally work related) reason for maintaining residency in the town. Without such a reason, they move down the valley to Canmore.

Worker housing is a difficult issue in both Banff and Canmore. There are simply insufficient affordable units for the number of employees seeking places to live, and little attention is being given to adding low-cost units when building luxury condos is so much more profitable. For a long time, tent towns sprouted up around Canmore as people staked out a spot to hang their hat in the absence of reasonable rental units. Construction workers were sleeping in tents while working on multimillion-dollar houses.

The real estate market was hot to the point of incineration until the recession began in 2008. Properties were being bought on speculation and sometimes changed hands several times before the house or condo was even built. Realtors were bringing charter planes of potential customers over from Europe, and many made a purchase during their stay.[8]

The cost of living in Canmore has skyrocketed, which has made things difficult for many residents. For older residents, it results in high property taxes on limited pensions.

Canmore faces many obstacles to keep the town a desirable place in which to live. Beautiful scenery goes a long way to draw people to the location, but the spirit of the town needs to be given ongoing attention to keep them there.

Karelian bear dog, Northern Lights Wildlife Wolf Centre

Top: Grizzly,
B. Harrison
(SXC Images)

Bottom:
Black Bear,
S. Ditchburn

Wildlife Spotting: Bow Valley Bears

At one time, it could have been fairly safely said that any bear that you spotted from the highway would be a black bear – grizzlies were much more elusive and seldom seen. But they are increasingly losing their reluctance to enter areas frequented by humans, and are occasionally spotted along the road – and even in town. So how do you tell the two species apart?

Black bears (*Ursus americanus*) are the smaller of the two. Despite their name, they are not always black. They can be various shades of brown, or what is colloquially known as cinnamon. Usually less than a metre high at the shoulder, black bears vary considerably in size – a big black bear can be taller than a small grizzly. They exhibit sexual dimorphism – that is, the males and females are substantially different in size. Males typically weigh around 200 kilograms, while females are about 50 kilograms lighter. Their weight varies immensely with the seasons, as they start the spring lean after hibernation and lay on fat to get through the next winter.

Black bears have a distinctive "Roman nosed" profile with a fairly straight line from nose through forehead. They are solitary animals, dispersing themselves with a density of less than 10 bears per 1,000 square kilometres. Grizzlies are seen as a potential threat to black bears, and their territories generally do not overlap – a black bear will make a quick exit if a grizzly appears on the scene.

Preferring wooded areas, black bears have shorter, curved claws and are competent tree-climbers. They are largely herbivorous – about 85% of their diet is plants. They love ants, and they will tear up logs and overturn rocks looking for larvae.

Grizzly bears (*Ursus arctos horribilis*) are a subspecies of the Brown bear (*Ursus arctos*), a term more commonly applied to the coastal bears. They are often slightly taller than black bears, but their greater weight (almost twice that of black bears) indicates how much more robust their physique is. Grizzlies have a large shoulder hump, which is mostly composed of muscle to aid in digging. Watching a griz dig up ground-squirrel burrows is very similar to watching a backhoe at work – wheelbarrow loads of dirt fly out from under the massive paws as the bear excavates the earth. These bears are also predominantly herbiverous (about 80% of their diet), although they will seek more protein in the fall as they fatten up for winter. They particularly love Hedysarum roots and lily bulbs, and alpine meadows sometimes look like they have been worked over by a Rototiller.

Looking at a grizzly's face helps to clarify its species. Instead of the black bear's straight profile, grizzlies have a dished face, with a depression between the eyes and muzzle. Their ears are smaller than those of black bears. Grizzly fur often has a lighter tip, or is "grizzled" – hence their name.

Both bears are false hibernators, rousing and moving about their dens occasionally though winter. The females give birth in the den, usually to two cubs, during the latter part of the winter. They breed every second year, and yearling cubs den with their mother through their first winter before becoming independent over the next year.

Grizzlies are thought to have originally inhabited the Great Plains. Early explorers commented on encountering them as far east as what is now Saskatchewan. With long, straight claws (about 10 centimetres) designed for digging, they are less willing to climb trees, although they are more able to than is commonly believed. Very solitary by nature, each grizzly requires a range about 80 per cent greater than that required by the black bear.

The Park Gate

Driving west from Canmore, you soon pass through the "new" park gates. These were built when the park boundary was moved from near Exshaw to the present location in the 1930s. It was, in part, done as a relief project during those difficult years. Built of local Rundlestone and wood in a blend of mock Tudor and northern "log cabin" architectural references, the style became a hallmark of park construction. The oldest of the three original gates once had gates that closed, and the westerly one served as the attendant's residence.

Travellers passing through Banff National Park without any stops do not need a pass, but those intending to make stops within the park must buy one. Frequent visitors usually acquire an annual pass – those visiting for a day or two get a single- or multi-day pass. Money collected for the entrance passes stays within the park and is used for programs and maintenance. You can also purchase single-day passes back at the Husky Gas Station on Dead Man's Flats or the AMA offices in Calgary if you anticipate a long line.

This is said to be the busiest entrance gate to any national park in Canada. The westbound traffic through Banff National Park's East Gate has exceeded 23,000 vehicles on a busy summer day. Lines can become long and tedious on weekends in July and August.

Mount Rundle — 2,949 m

Mount Rundle
from the
southeast

We met Rev. Robert Rundle in Chapter 9, and for the 14 kilometres after Canmore the Trans-Canada parallels the mountain named after him. It had originally been named Terrace Mountain by James Hector, but John Palliser changed the name to Mount Rundle. There are seven summits along the course of the ridge, the highest being the third from the northwest end of the mountain.

The sport of ice climbing has focussed on the northeastern cliffs of Mount Rundle since its inception in the 1970s. The Rockies are regarded as a mecca for this sport, and Rundle provides it at its best. A series of waterfalls form up that are collectively known as The Trophy Wall, and climbers come from all over the world to test their skills on this ice. It offers a superb selection of routes, the most famous of which is the

150 metre ice pillar known as The Terminator. "It clings to the wall as a series of smears connected to each other and to the ground by pillars. It rarely touches down, but when it does, be sure that there will be line-ups. It is likely the most stared at and watched route, as it sits near the doorway to the Rockies, proud and inspiring. In 1985, after years of being watched and referred to as the 'big drip,' it was finally climbed by Jay Smith and Craig Reason over three days."[1]

The triangular projections along the northeastern cliffs of Rundle are good examples of truncated spurs. These are remnants of long ridges that once extended to the valley floor which were sheared off by the ice sheet during the ice age.

We will consider this mountain again, and examine its geology, when we get a view of it from the north after passing Banff.

The Fairholme Range — North of Carrot Creek

We looked at many of the peaks in the southern section of the Fairholmes as we passed through the Canmore area. The northern part of the range, between Lake Minnewanka and the Bow River, consists of a number of peaks that are hard to see from the highway. However, you get a nice view of them if you look back from the overpass to the western entrance to the town of Banff.

Closest to Carrot Creek is Mount Peechee (2,933 m). It was named after the Metis guide for George Simpson (who was actually called Alexis Piché). Simpson had originally given the name Peechee to Lake Minnewanka, but that had never been officially recorded. So when the lake took the name Minnewanka, the guide's name was instead assigned to a nearby peak by surveyor George Dawson.

The summit to the north of Peechee is Mount Girouard (2,994 m). It is named after Colonel Sir Edward Percy Girouard, a railway builder in Sudan for the British and a hero of the Boer War.

Butting up against the shore of Lake Minnewanka is Mount Inglismaldie (2,963 m). Park Superintendent George Stewart named it after a castle in Scotland that was the home of the Earl of Kintore, who visited the Rockies in 1887.

The Hoodoos

Lining the highway to the northeast is an embankment with some bizarre formations known as hoodoos. The word hoodoo refers to a trans-cultural African-American folk magic that incorporates elements of Native American practices and beliefs. It may have come to be associated with these unusual rock formations because of their otherworldly shapes.

These hoodoos have eroded out of a layer of hardened mud and gravel that is thought to have been the result of a massive flood. About 10,000 to 12,000 years ago, near the end of the most recent ice age, the Bow Valley Glacier filled the valley and created a huge lake in the valley of the Cascade River, around the present-day Lake Minnewanka. As the glacier melted back, it was weakened enough that the water broke through and rushed down this valley, carrying the debris from the softened moraines that had been deposited by the glacier. This layer of moraine material settled in the valley bottom, hardened, and was then eroded as the Bow River found its new channels through the mess. Wind and frost have added their influence to the process, and these interesting natural sculptures are the result.

Along the edge of the escarpment above the hoodoos stand a number of extremely old Douglas fir trees – in fact, they're believed to be the oldest ones in the park. One has been dated at more than 685 years old, which means it would have been a sapling when the Europeans "discovered" the New World.[2] Douglas fir are much more evident around here than in most parts of the park, largely because they have escaped destruction by fire in this area. Look for them along the northern Fairholme range, and the slopes to the north of the Vermilion Lakes after Banff. To pick them out by their shape from the surrounding lodgepole pines, look for tree forms with more open and irregular branches, giving them a less perfect cylindrical silhouette. Older trees often tend to have a more flattened top.

Inglismaldie, Girouard, and Peechee in the northern Fairholme Range

Geology Notes: What is a Mountain Range?

The term "mountain range" is often used in a rather ambiguous manner. At the smaller end of the scale, a range is a group of mountains that are delineated from their surroundings by lowlands or passes. Ranges are not just arbitrary clusters of peaks, but have the same geological structure and are clustered in close proximity. They often take their name from the highest peak in the group. Not all mountains are a part of a range when it is used in this sense.

However, the term "range" is applied to discussion of mountains on a larger scale as well, such as when we talk about the Front Ranges or the Main Ranges. Here the criteria are on a broader dimension, and their commonality is much more general.

The term is even heard on the very broadest level, such as when the Rocky Mountains are spoken of as a North American mountain range. Thus it is important to be aware of the context in which this slippery term is used.

The Banff Legacy Trail

An announcement was made in May 2009 that the federal government was planning to fund, as a part of the ongoing Trans-Canada Trail (which was 80% complete by that year), a multi-use, hard-surfaced trail between Canmore and Banff. It will be 26 kilometres long and will go through the East Gate and follow the south side of the highway to Banff. It is expected to be completed for the 125th anniversary of the Banff Hot Springs Reserve in 2010.

The hoodoos

Fire Management in the Park

The perception of the implications of fire in the park has changed a great deal since the park's inception. Until quite recently, fire was seen only as a dangerous and destructive element, one that was to be prevented at all costs. When prevention was unsuccessful, great efforts were extended to extinguish the fire immediately. There was no conception that fire might play a significant role in a healthy ecosystem.

Fire is now understood to be a normal process – even a necessary one for natural systems to function. Some species of plants, such as the lodgepole pine, are even dependent on a periodic fire cycle to reproduce. As a "fire succession species," these trees require the heat of a fire to open the cones and release the seeds for the next generation. This can be observed along the highway between the Sunshine turnoff and Castle Mountain Junction, where the valley burned during the construction of both the railway and the highway and the lodgepoles have regenerated as a single-species young forest.

The balance of species is greatly affected by fire. Without periodic burns, some species are forced out of the equation, as is happening with the aspen stands in Banff. Aspen are one of the principal food sources for elk, so this species is being forced to seek food from different sources – such as gardens in Banff… Fire also releases nutrients into the soil. The burned material enters the soil in a more water-soluble form that plant life benefits from, encouraging new growth.

The danger with forests that have been fire-suppressed for a long time is that they develop a very high fuel load from mature and dead trees. When fire does occur, it is a very hot, slow-moving, and highly destructive burn. A normal fire cycle would involve burns frequent enough that the fuel load would never accumulate to such a dangerous level. The fire would move quickly through the forest, never developing into a high-intensity blaze. Most trees can withstand this kind of event, and frequent fires are less devastating.

So what about the animals? Again, it is a question of the fire's intensity. Studies have indicated that both vertebrates and invertebrates are fairly successful at surviving low-intensity fires.[3] Further, fire creates a patchwork of habitat areas in various phases of succession (the recolonization of

Tree ID – Douglas Fir

The Douglas fir (*Pseudotsuga menziesii*) has presented scientists with a challenge to classify it. Neither a fir nor a hemlock, its name "*pseudotruga*" means false hemlock – which it really doesn't resemble at all. It has the flat needles of a fir tree. Two varieties grow in Western Canada – a coastal Douglas fir and our interior one, which can also reach heights of 30 to 40 metres if it escapes the effects of fire. These trees are quite resistant to fire and often bear black scars on their trunks.

The cones of the Douglas fir are unusual. Over the round, thumbnail-shaped scales protrude long three-pointed bracts (leaf-like structures below the flowers). Various versions of a Native American story exist that explain them as being mice that the tree allowed to take refuge in its cones to survive a forest fire. And the bracts do, indeed, look like the tail and hind feet of the little rodents.

The tree's name derives from David Douglas, a Scottish botanist who collected samples of the species. The "*menziesii*" part of the Latin name comes from another Scot, Archibald Menzies, a physician and naturalist.

a disturbed area by a sequence of various species of plants). First the faster-growing, light-loving herbaceous plants return, followed by the slower-growing, shade-tolerant woodier plants. Different animals depend on different phases of this cycle, and fire provides for that.

As well as a greater awareness of fire's role in ecosystem function, we have learned more about how it has been managed throughout history by humans. The current theory is that fire has been used by humans to affect their environment for centuries. It created better grazing habitat and brought animals into the mountain valleys at greater density than a heavily forested area would have. This is supported by evidence found of the presence of buffalo in the mountains – which would not have been the case unless some fire management kept the forests open.

So, although fire is damaging, the current understanding is that the absence of fire is perhaps more damaging in the bigger picture. A fire cycle has become a necessary part of park management. In 1979, Banff National Park started to change its fire policies. A plan that involved forest thinning, fuel reduction, and artificial burns was developed.

Artificial burns, "prescribed burns" are intended to mimic the natural fire cycle as closely as possible. The overall goal is to restore 50% of the historic fire cycle as part of ecosystem normalization. The first prescribed burn was undertaken in 1984, and the process continues, becoming more fully understood and better managed with time. All burning is done only under ideal conditions and is carefully monitored. Spring is the preferred season, because of the cooler and wetter weather. Conditions such as weather projections, vegetation, the nature of the terrain, containment considerations, and fuel load are all factors in planning a burn.

A prescribed burn was conducted along the Fairholme Range in 2003. Farther along the highway, the area below Mount Norquay and the Sawbacks was burned in 1993.

"Ecological integrity may only succeed if Banff burns. The trick is to see that it burns properly."[4]

Anthracite

The Cascade Coal Basin was discovered in 1883 at the base of the Fairholmes by the Geological Survey of Canada. In 1884, the Department of the Interior established an area of 36 square miles that would not be put up for general sale at the going price of $10 per acre, but would require a special sale at $20 per acre.[5] In 1885, the Canadian Anthracite Coal Company set up operations, and the demand for coal from the CPR ensured this company a market. A town built up around the mine and the population grew to about 300.

But the story was not as rosy as had been anticipated, and in 1890 the mine closed. The coal turned out to be quite friable (easily crumbled) and difficult to work, and the seam soon became less accessible. Competition from Canmore as mines opened there did not help. An American named W. McNeill came to the rescue and operations recommenced in 1891. Yet the mine remained only marginally viable. The final blow came in the form of floods in 1894 and again in 1897. No human lives were lost, but the town was heavily damaged, and the horses and mules trapped in the shafts were killed. In 1904, the mine was closed and the remaining workers moved to Canmore.

The town of Anthracite had a distinctly different flavour from Canmore. The latter's population included a lot of families, while Anthracite was a town of transient workers and had a much wilder atmosphere. The murderer Ernest Cashel was finally arrested here. The only women in town were there for the work... The best known of these damsels was named Amelia May – or maybe May Buchanan. Her real name is a bit uncertain, and she also went by Trixie Livingstone, Tillie Willis, Violet Decarmin, and Leslie May. Ms May, or Ms Buchanan, or Ms Livingstone, or... had come west from Ottawa. She had married at 16, but found it not to her taste and moved on to Winnipeg. She was kicked out of that city because of her business activities and arrived in Calgary in 1888. She was implicated in the robbery of Jacques Jewellery, although never arrested. She was evicted from Anthracite after six months, and was killed two years later by an admirer in Edmonton.

Tunnel Mountain — 1,690 m

You also get a good view of little Tunnel Mountain from here. Banff nestles against the slope of this lump of rock. There is no tunnel on Tunnel Mountain – but there nearly was…

It now seems amazing that Major Rogers, in his survey of the area, seemed oblivious of the easier route to the north around this small obstacle. Instead, he routed the CPR line through a kilometre-long tunnel through the giant boulder. His boss, William Van Horne, was not convinced of the need for this expense and requested a second opinion from Charles Shaw. Shaw immediately spotted the better route to the north and was quite scathing in his comments about Rogers' selection.

The Stoney Nakoda call Tunnel Mountain *Tatâga îŝîmâ* or "sleeping buffalo" because it is supposed to resemble that form when seen from the northeast.

Top left: The town of Anthracite, ca. 1886-90, Glenbow NA-573-9

Top right: The town of Anthracite, ca. 1886-90, Glenbow NA-573-9

Tunnel Mountain in foreground; the Massive Range with Mount Brett, Massive Mountain, and Pilot Mouvntain in the distance

Kain remarked, "Ye gods, Mr. MacCarthy, just look at that, they never will believe we climbed it".[7]

Mount Louis was named one day in 1886 when Sir John A. Macdonald and his wife Agnes were crossing the country by train. They stopped and made a side trip to a nearby pass in the company of Louis Beaufort Stewart, the son of the park superintendent. Stewart was in the area working as a surveyor, and was pressed into duty to look after the Prime Minister's party. This group included Lady Mac's personal attendant, Edith Orde, and Lady Mac's dog, Fifi. Two other peaks close to Mount Louis are thus officially named Mount Edith and Mount Fifi. I am sure that Fifi is the only peak in the Rockies that can claim a dog as its namesake…

The View of Mount Louis

Mount Louis   If you look ahead just as you pass the Cascade Powerhouse, you'll get a brief glimpse of one of the more dramatically shaped mountains in this area. You are looking right up Forty Mile Creek north of the town of Banff to Mount Louis. This was Lawrence Grassi's favourite mountain and he is said to have climbed it well over 30 times. It is known as a "dogtooth" mountain – a form created when erosion leaves the near-vertical layers standing in a jagged tooth.

The first ascent of Mount Louis in 1917 is one of the classic stories of early climbing in the area. Albert MacCarthy, his wife and nother couple had set out on horseback, in the company of guide Conrad Kain for a gentle day of reconnoitering, with no intention to undertake a climb. However, when they reached the pass between Mount Edith and Mount Norquay they were so impressed by the view of the towering face of Mount Louis that the proceeded to the base... just to check it out. A discussion of potential routes up the cracks and chimneys ensued, and before long MacCarthy and Kain were one the rock face, testing out lines that they thought might work to connect the ledges, chimneys and cracks. Through the day they managed to find their way up the steep face, watched with concern by the remaining party below. They reached the summit, left a cairn with a register in a tobacco tin, and cautiously made their way back to the rest of the group waiting anxiously at the base. Looking back,

Cascade Mountain — 2,998 m

It seems that all the early explorers who passed by the base of this mountain commented on the waterfall that graces its slopes. Father Pierre de Smet wrote of the "crystalline fountain." George Simpson referred to it as "the spout." Henry Warre sketched his party's camp in the meadows at the base of the mountain. James Hector also camped here, and he hiked up onto the mountain and noted the presence of goats, marmots, pika, and even a hummingbird.

The mountain is also known locally as Stoney Chief, but the source of this name is unknown. The small mountain to the west, just east of Mt. Norquay Road, is called Stoney Squaw. The Stoney Nakoda name for this mountain is *Mînî hrpa*, or "mountain where the water falls."

The Stoney Nakoda people have a story of Cascade being the home of the chinook wind. They say that Chinook Wind was the beautiful, blind daughter of South Wind. One day, South Wind was abducted by North Wind, leaving Chinook Wind disconsolate. For the rest of time, she would periodically go out in search of her father.

The frozen falls on Cascade are another popular ice climbing location. The easy approach, sunny exposure, and lower angle make it a popular place for an introduction to the sport. However, as in many locations, the climbing area is below a huge snow funnel and avalanches are a real risk. In 1988, two British climbers were caught in a slide

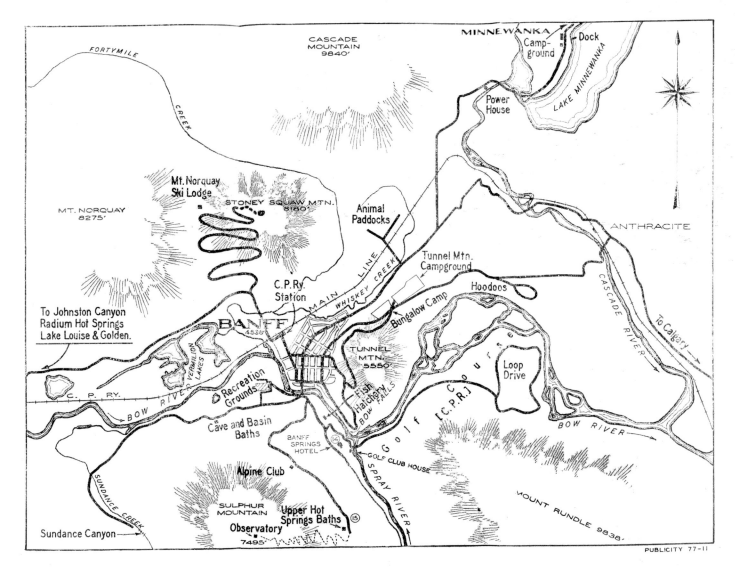

The Old Highway

The first highway into the town of Banff turned west and crossed the Cascade River at this point. It passed the hoodoos by the Bow River and hugged the slopes of Tunnel Mountain on the way in to town. Frank Anderson described the route: "The old road used to cross the railroad at the ghost town and climb Tunnel Mountain to what seemed a dizzying height before plunging down the other side past the dump and into Banff. It was a narrow, slippery, twisting road whose rocky walls glittered with the chrome of a thousand bumpers that kissed it in passing."[6]

Left: Cascade Mountain with layers indicated

Right: Frozen waterfall on Cascade Mountain

while retreating, having decided that the conditions were too dangerous to continue. One man was knocked down by the wall of snow, then swept by his partner, who managed to hold him briefly before the rope broke. Fortunately, they were using a second rope, which stopped the falling man. Even more fortunately for the pair, two wardens were in the area and witnessed the accident. The slide occurred at 1 p.m., and by 2 p.m. they were being taken off the mountain. The fallen climber suffered internal injuries but recovered.

Geology Notes: Cascade Mountain

Observe the shape of this mountain as you approach it. If you understand its structure, you will be able to see the same pattern played out in many other peaks in this area. The top of the mountain is made up of steep cliffs, which have a section of softer, more sloping material below them, then a steeper section again near the base. This is an excellent example of "differential weathering" – or how different types of rock erode to a greater or lesser degree.

The top 900 metre cliff is composed of the limestone Rundle Formation (Mississippian). Below this is 1,000 to 1,200 metres of softer, more erodable, predominantly shale Banff Formation (also Mississippian). This middle of the sandwich forms softer slopes. It, in turn, is underlain by the harder limestone Palliser Formation (Devonian), which again makes steeper cliffs. The resulting sequence of cliff/slope/cliff or limestone/shale/limestone is the classic sandwich combination for all the peaks in this area.

This unit was thrust up repeatedly in side-by-side broken slabs, creating the shingle-like stacked layers of the front ranges. The arrangement of layers and faults (Rundle/Banff/ Palliser) seen here on Cascade is repeated several times in the Front Ranges, which makes sense when you think back to the Trellis Drainage pattern described in Chapter 8. We will see this arrangement again on Mount Rundle. It also makes up Rundle's neighbour, Sulphur, and most of the peaks until we get into the Main Ranges.

At the very base of Cascade is a fault line, the Rundle Thrust, that divides the three-layer sandwich section on the top (known as the Rundle Thrust Sheet) from the rock that it was pushed up and over. And, as we saw with the McConnell Thrust, the rock underneath is younger – in this case Kootenay Formation, which is Mesozoic (again, refer to the first illustration in Chapter 8).

An interesting point is that the carbonate rocks found on Cascade and Rundle are the same formation that contains the natural gas in the Jumping Pound area. Here, exposed as they are, they are not a reservoir for resources – probably a fortunate thing for the future of the park.

Wildlife Spotting: The Corvids
Ravens and Crows

Crows and ravens, the big black birds of the mountains and foothills, are a common sight between Calgary and Banff. They are the most noticeable members of the Corvidae family, which also includes jays and magpies. Many people have a difficult time telling them apart. And they do look very similar, although a closer look will offer clues for differentiation. The Common Raven (*Corvus corax*) is a slightly larger bird than the American Crow (*Corvus brachyrthynchos*; *brachyrthynchos* means raven with a small nose). Ravens are about half a metre long from beak to tail, while crows are 5 to 10 centimetres less. If you look at the raven's beak, you will see that it is large and the upper mandible is more hooked than the crow's. If they are in flight, look at their tail – the crow has a squared-off tail, while the raven's is more wedge-shaped. Also, if you see a big black bird in the winter, you can be sure it is a raven because they do not migrate, whereas crows head south for warmer climates.

Another clue to their identity is their vocalization. Crows can make a variety of sounds, but mostly they stick to their raspy *caah – caah – caah*, often accompanied by a reaching and bobbing posture of the head. They also make a softer cooing sound, although this is less commonly heard. Ravens, on the other hand, produce a tremendous range of vocalizations (one researcher catalogued more than 30 categories of sounds) – from croaks to pronks to toks to a sort of popping noise. These big birds seem to enjoy playing around with sound – and playing around in general. They can be observed sliding down snow slopes like a kid on a toboggan and playing around in updrafts for what certainly looks like the sheer pleasure of it.

Considerable research exists on the intelligence of these birds – particularly ravens, which have impressive abilities to solve complex problems and use tools that they create for specific purposes. Ravens mate for life, forming territorial pairs that defend the area around their nest with zeal. Pitted against these established mature birds are the "floater flocks" of mostly unmated younger birds – sort of the teenaged "gang in the hood" – that are learning the ropes and taking opportunities where they find them.

The raven is found in mythologies all around the world. In Native American stories, they often take the role of trickster or creator – powerful influences on the world and full of potential for both good and evil.

Raven,
D. Ditchburn

Crows,
D. Ditchburn

The Town of Bankhead

As Anthracite was closing its doors, another coal-mining town was coming to life in the Bow Valley. The town of Bankhead was founded when the CPR, under its subsidiary the Pacific Coal Company, licenced to mine coal at the base of Cascade Mountain. The railway was anxious to secure a source of coal for its locomotives, and running its own shop had a certain appeal. There had been rumblings of labour unrest in Canmore, which the railway hoped to avoid in this new mine. Furthermore, a coal mine operated by the largest consumer would exert downward pressure on the price of coal – and the CPR *really* liked that idea.

Operations started in 1903. The coal in Cascade Mountain broke the surface as several distinct seams – part of a folded layer in the Kootenay Formation. The broken and folded nature of the seam meant that it was difficult to work – it tilted at between 40 and 60 degrees, and parts of it would unexpectedly come to a dead end. Rather than working into it from above, as had been done at Anthracite, a different strategy was followed at Bankhead's Black Diamond Mine. The miners worked into the seam from below, digging upward. That avoided problems with flooding and made the material easier to remove, but it was a slow and costly process.

To the CPR's dismay, although this coal was high quality it was also very friable, so it dried and crumbled when exposed to air. And the material's high heat value burned too hot to be used in locomotive engines. So a briquette plant was installed in 1907, which increased the costs of production.

The town of Bankhead was designed to be an appealing community. Named by Lord Strathcona after Bankhead in Scotland (a bankhead is a location in which a coal seam comes to the surface), every effort was made to make it a desirable place to live and work. The residential area was located well away from the mine operations and was serviced with electricity, running water, and sewers long before the town of Banff was. At its peak, it had about 1,000 people, including about 40 Chinese who worked at the tipple and lived in separate quarters behind the slag heaps. There were the usual amenities – a school, a pool hall, stores, a laundry run by Yee Chow, and a Catholic church on the hill. Non-Catholics held services in the Miner's Hall by the post office.

About 100 residences stood on the upper terraces, and a boarding house was provided for unmarried men. Sports facilities included a football field, baseball diamond, tennis courts, and skating and curling rinks. Teams engaged in friendly competition with the towns of Banff and Canmore.

But no matter how pleasant town life was, the work in the mine was pretty grim. At first, 12-hour working days were not uncommon, although an agreement was later reached that limited the workday to eight hours. The mine was a dangerous place. Pockets of methane gas were found throughout it, and explosions were a constant worry. Fifteen men were lost in mining accidents. Worker unrest became more common, and the first of several strikes took place in 1909. Another long one took place in 1911, and again in 1919. Yet another strike, in 1922, started on April 1 – but it was no joke. The workers held firm to their demands for a couple of months while the Pacific Coal Company threatened to close the mine. The workers believed that it was a bluff and stayed away. Then, on June 15, the mine was formally closed. Falling demand in the market coupled with rising costs of production had settled the affair.

Everyone thought the closure would be temporary. The price of coal was sure to rebound after the post-war recession ended and the mine would reopen. But in the meantime, the tolerance that the park's administration had shown for active resource extraction within its boundaries had changed. While the administrators had at one time been willing to turn a blind eye to the mine, they now saw an opportunity to remove an operation they had come to consider contradictory to the mandate of a national park. The administration demanded that all buildings be removed from the site.

Many of the structures were relocated to Banff and Canmore. The church was lifted from its foundations and taken to Calgary, where it remained in use until the 1960s. The old railway station still stands, relocated to Tunnel Mountain Road in Banff.

There is a walking tour with interpretive signs around what remains of Bankhead. You can see the old lamphouse, some mine cars, the steps up to the absent church on the hill, the openings to the mine shafts (now well fenced off), and the slag heaps where the resilient rhubarb from the town gardens still grows.

The Empty Bankhead Cemetery

For many years there was no cemetery in Bankhead. Funeral processions carried the coffins nine kilometres to the cemetery in Banff. A superstitious belief that it was bad luck to be the first person to be buried in a cemetery may have encouraged the resistance to opening one in the mining town. In his book on Bankhead, Ben Gadd explains how another belief forced the town to get its own facilities: it "came about because of [a] strongly held belief: that a fine, drunken wake is the right of the living. It would begin soon after the funeral, often in Banff's Alberta Hotel, and it would continue until the pubs closed – or after. The park superintendent complained formally about these inebriated Bankheaders staggering about the streets of his tidy town… Bankhead must have its own cemetery and thus its own wakes."[8] And so it came about – the cemetery was opened. But it only ever received one body – that of Chee Yow, who was the victim of an unresolved murder or accident. His body was later exhumed and returned to China rather than remain the sole occupant of this unlucky site.

Coal years at Bankhead, c. 1910, Glenbow NA-1363-5

View of street in Bankhead, c. 1904–22, Glenbow NA-1110-3

Lake Minnewanka, Banff National Park

Lake Minnewanka

Lake Minnewanka, c. 1900-25, Albertype Company/ Library and Archives Canada/ PA-032771

At the Trans-Canada's eastern intersection for the town of Banff, you can turn northeast and head between the Fairholmes and the Palliser Range toward Lake Minnewanka. This takes you along another of the main routes into the mountains used by the Indians. Fluted points, stone fireplaces, and the bones of a butchered sheep from a species that is now extinct have been found around Lake Minnewanka, confirming that the area was used by humans 10,000 years ago. Many of the white explorers also entered the mountains by this route, including Rev. Rundle and Sir George Simpson in 1841 and the explorers with the Palliser Expedition in 1858-59.

During the ice ages the Bow Valley flowed out between Ingismaldie and Cascade and out where the Ghost River now flows. This is where the huge lake formed that probably deposited the glacial debris that now forms the hoodoos further east on the highway. Having broken through the ice dam, the Bow found its new route down the valley where we see it today.

Devil's Gap exits from the mountains to the south of Devil's Head, just between Mount Costigan and Orient Point. It is said to have been the site of a terrible battle between the Kootenay and Blackfoot tribes – and the steep cliffs on either side of the Gap would indeed make this a great location for an ambush.

The area is associated with legends about spooky events that are said to have occurred here. One legend tells of how a warrior awoke nightly to the sound of buffalo being herded through the valley by the camp. After many nights of this, he decided to find an explanation for this mystery. He left his mount prepared, and when he heard the sound during the night he quickly climbed on his horse and pursued the noise. He finally caught sight of the buffalo and then spotted a man riding a grey horse. The warrior urged his own mount forward to catch up with the rider, but as soon as he gained on him both the rider and the buffalo simply vanished.

Another story tells of the sound of drums coming up from the water of the lake. Voices, too, could be heard. Then a strange creature rose from the centre of the lake – half fish and half human, and terrible to see. Slowly it disappeared below the water again. The Indians have always been reluctant to go out on this lake because of this spirit that they believe dwells in its depths.

Minnewanka comes from the Stoney word *Mînî wakâ*, which means "lake of the spirits." It is also known as Devil's Lake, and another lake in the valley is called Cannibal Lake. Simpson named it Peechee Lake after his guide (Alexis Piché). That caused some confusion because there is a similar word in Stoney that means "wild cat" – which may be why Rundle referred to it as Lynx Lake. When George Dawson surveyed this area, he named the lake Minnewanka – and the name Peechee was transferred to a nearby peak.

Minnewanka was once one of three lakes along the course of the valley. In 1887, the Minnewanka Loop Road was put in and a tourist lodge called the Beach House was built on the shore of the lake. Cruises were offered on the "Lady of the Lake," "Aylmer," and the "Daughter of the Peaks." Visitors came out by carriage, picnicked, and rented boats to explore along the shore. A wooden dam was built on Devil's Creek by the federal government to make the shore less boggy, and gradually a little village called Minnewanka Landing grew up along the lake's edge.

In 1912, more developments began that would radically alter the lake's configuration over the years. Calgary Power built a dam in Devil's Canyon to control the flow from the Cascade River for its Horseshoe Falls plant on the Bow. This enlarged the area of the lake by about 1,000 acres and raised its level by three and a half metres. Many of the buildings along the shore had to be moved to higher ground. The lodge could not be moved, so it was burned down. In spite of this, another nine blocks were surveyed for the town and 87 lots were put up for sale. More homes were built.

Another government dam was added in 1923, as well as the Cascade Power Plant facility in Devil's Canyon to supply power to the town of Banff. This raised the water level by an additional 30 metres, which submerged both the townsite and the 1912 dam.

Calgary Power made repeated requests for a permit to build a larger dam, but after the National Parks Act was passed in 1930 all requests were turned down. One of the earliest conservation groups formed to rally against the threat of further development on the lake. This became the Canadian National Parks Association, which got support from other groups such as the Alpine Club, the Banff Citizens' Association, and the Calgary Automobile Association.

It looked as if that would be the end of development at the site. But in 1939 the War Measures Act was approved, and it temporarily suspended the National Parks Act that had excluded industrial development in national parks. The following year, Calgary Power lobbied Ottawa for permission to build its dam to provide extra power for the Alberta Nitrogen Company of Calgary, an explosives manufacturer, in support of Canada's war effort. The developments that Calgary Power built in 1941 changed the course of the Cascade River and nearly doubled the size of the lake, which is now 28 kilometres long.

Scuba Diving at Lake Minnewanka

The only ones to visit Minnewanka Landing these days are divers. After moving the buildings from the little town in 1921, they were left in situ for the subsequent dam additions and were submerged. Parts of them remain preserved under the frigid water of the lake. Winter is a popular season for diving because the visibility is better. Divers can explore the foundations of the hotel, several houses, the old wharf and breakwaters, as well as the 1912 dam.

Whiskey Creek Meadows

Whiskey Creek Meadows, below Cascade, were so named because this was where bootleggers conducted their business during prohibition. This area was a favoured camping spot with the Indians when they came into the mountains, and it is believed that Rev. Rundle gave one of his sermons here when he passed through.

The Cascade Corridor

Another wildlife corridor skirts the north side of the road after the Minnewanka turnoff. This section of land was once included a horse stable, an airstrip, a cadet camp, and a wildlife park. Banff and the highway substantially block one side of the road, and these developments took up the other side. As the mobility needs of animals were better understood, this area was seen as an obstacle to connections between the Forty Mile Creek, Cascade, and Bow River valleys. In the late 1970s the area was returned to as natural a habitat as possible in order to provide an avenue for animal movement.

Bringing aviation into Banff in the first place had been a long process. The first person to land a plane in the area was Captain Frank McCall, who we met in the section on Bowness aviation. In January 1929, McCall brought a five-passenger Stinson Detroiter SB-1 owned by Great Western Airways down onto the frozen surface of the Bow River. He hit the pontoon bridge, lifted again for a few feet, and then made an unsteady touchdown on the river. McCall narrowly missed skidding into the boathouse.

Following this, flights from Calgary to Banff were offered by Great Western Airways at a cost of $15. Some Banff residents began to work toward establishing an airport. For a while it looked as if the prairie air-mail system might add Banff to its route from Winnipeg to Calgary, but that did not work out. Finally an airstrip was designated, and in 1937 the first plane landed on the grassy meadow – a family from Oregon had flown up to spend a couple of days exploring Banff. Things looked promising. But then the war intervened and the airstrip was converted into the Cascade Golf Club.

The airstrip finally reopened in 1946. Always a simple facility, it operated for private and unscheduled flights for the next 50 years. When the decision came to close it for the corridor, it simply meant removing the windsock, plane tie-downs, outhouse, and runway pylons. Aviation groups mobilized to fight the decision, but all for naught. Then. in 2008, the airstrip was reopened – but only for emergency use. An Air Safety Risk Assessment had pointed out that the closure had adversely affected aviation safety. So the windsock still flies on the edge of Whisky Creek Meadows.

So has the Cascade Wildlife Corridor been successful for the animals? The outcome has been particularly interesting regarding wolf movement. Radio-collar tracking methods have allowed researchers to plot the activity of wolf packs in the valley. Prior to the establishment of the corridor, there were almost no instances of wolves moving into the valley east of Banff townsite. However, use of the area by wolves has increased significantly since the corridor was established.[9]

The Great Sir Donald

One of the most admired bulls in the Banff herd was known as Sir Donald, named after Sir Donald Smith (a.k.a. Lord Strathcona), who had donated the beasts to Banff. Sir Donald (the buffalo) was captured in Saskatchewan in 1872 when he was still a calf. He was probably among the last few remaining wild-born buffalo. Sir Donald grew to a record size – the largest in the Banff herd – and was the dominant male for most of his life.

But a few years before his death, he lost his leadership to a younger male. His final fate at the age of 38 hardly suited his noble life. After he fell over some logs and was unable to get up, the rest of the herd turned on him and killed him. Sir Donald's enormous head (16 centimetres from horn-tip to horn-tip) was mounted and displayed in the Park museum.

The Buffalo of Banff

In 1800, an estimated 60 million buffalo are thought to have roamed across North America – the vast majority in the plains of what's now the U.S. and the prairies of what's now Canada. Yet by the mid-1880s, there were almost none left. One of the largest of the mammals that had been found along the Bow Corridor was seen no more in this environment.

In 1897, Park Superintendent Howard Douglas decided that something should be done so tourists could still see the great woolly beasts around Banff. He brought in the first three buffalo, donated by Toronto lawyer T. G. Blackstock, and housed them in a pen in Banff's Central Park until a 580-acre paddock was constructed at the base of Cascade Mountain. In 1899, Lord Strathcona donated 13 more from Manitoba, and in 1911, 70 animals came to Banff from the dispersal of the 700-head Pablo-Allard herd in Montana. The number of buffalo rose through natural increase. Then the enclosures were expanded to include other species, such as elk, deer, bighorn sheep, moose, cougar – and even a few non-native species, such as angora goats, Persian sheep, and six yaks (the latter a gift from the Duke of Bedford).

There were occasional escapes from the buffalo paddock. One young bull became particularly adept at jumping the cattle guard. He was allowed to wander, with the wardens keeping an eye on him, until he would turn up back at the gate, waiting to be let in to rejoin the herd. Parks officials considered releasing the entire herd to roam free at one point, but that idea was squelched when some buffalo were released in Jasper National Park and promptly left the park.

Visitors were encouraged to visit the paddock by car rather than on foot. They were warned that "at certain seasons of the year the buffalo, moose and wapiti are very liable to attack persons on foot who venture into the enclosures. It is also advisable to be unaccompanied by dogs, as the cougars are fond of lunching on any dogs that get too near their cage."[10]

All species except the buffalo were gradually weeded out. The last seven buffalo went to Elk Island National Park east of Edmonton in 1998.

Sir Donald, ca. 1903, Byron Harmon, Whyte Museum V263

Wildlife Spotting: Cougars

Well, actually, you are highly unlikely to spot a cougar (*Felis concolor*). They are extremely elusive animals and very seldom seen. They are, however, becoming increasingly active around the Banff area.

Also known as pumas, mountain lions, or panthers, cougars are the largest of the cats that live in the Canadian Rockies. They stand from 60 to 75 centimetres at the shoulder, and the male is noticeably larger than the female. They have a smooth red-brown coat, with a lighter chin, chest and belly, and a black tail-tip.

Cougars are solitary and territorial. Like most cat species, they mark their territory with urine-impregnated scratches in the dirt. Females breed only every other year and usually have two kittens at a time. Their diet is made up almost exclusively of ungulates (hoofed animals), with deer the prey of preference, followed by elk. Cougars are an ambush predator, and they need to take their prey by surprise because they cannot sustain a long chase.

Interestingly, prey preference seems to be learned. Some cougars and their descendants will attack mountain sheep, while other cat families strictly avoid them. This is probably because sheep hunting can be a very risky undertaking. Sheep tend to bolt for safety over the nearest precipice – which they are quite capable of navigating, but that can be highly hazardous to the pursuing cat. Mother cougars that have mastered the tricky art of sheep hunting pass this skill along to their kittens.

Although they are a very efficient predator, cougars seem to avoid contact with humans. However, on January 2, 2001, three incidents took place around Banff, probably with at least two different cats. At 4 a.m., a dog was attacked right in town, but the cougar was successfully scared off. Then, at 7 a.m., a Banff resident was stalked by a cougar while walking her dog, although she escaped into a nearby house. An elk carcass was later found near the site of the incident. But the most sad and alarming event occurred a little further from Banff, on the Cascade Fire Road near Lake Minnewanka. A woman who was cross-country skiing alone was attacked and killed by a male cougar. Wardens shot the cougar when they arrived on the scene and found the big cat still on the woman's body. This was the first known cougar attack in the park.

There are not a lot of cougar attacks in Canada, although the frequency does seem to be increasing slowly, particularly as people move more and more into cougar habitat. But there may be more complex dynamics happening among the cats, wolves, and their prey around townsites. We will look at that more carefully in the section on urban elk in the next chapter.

And yes, cougars do purr.

Cougar,
D. Ditchburn

"Even the most jaded sophisticate must acknowledge that Banff is one of the loveliest spots on earth. Indeed, looking at the town and its environs from the summit of Sulphur Mountain you get the curious impression that in creating Banff, God assumed the role of a far-sighted parks super-intendent and designed the area with a view to future tourism: planting a small, easily accessible mountain or two near the heart of things, a couple of larger ones – Rundle and Cascade – for scenic purposes at opposite ends of the town, directing a river, complete with picturesque falls yet suitable for boating, down a broad valley, studding the valley-floor and lower mountain-sides with magnificent evergreen forests (but leaving enough open space for a golf course), carving out a spectacular canyon or two within easy walking distance of the future town-site, banking the valley at both ends with solid mountain masses, and – the final touch of God-like benevolence – laying on an abundant supply of water, hot and cold." [1]

Before a town grew up where we know it today, a community started along the railway line, at the base of Cascade Mountain. Officially called Siding 29, it was also known as Aylmer Park, after Fred Aylmer, the chief of the railway crew. A few services were installed in the small settlement, including a couple of stores, a butcher shop, and the necessary saloon and hotel.

By the time the name Banff was attributed to the little hamlet, it was already being relocated to its present site along the Bow River. The name was assigned by Lord Strathcona (Donald Smith) after Banffshire, Scotland, where he had been born.

The Woodworth ranch, Aylmer Park, 1886, Glenbow NA-637-9

The Hot Springs and the Early History of the Park

For Banff National Park, it all started with hot water. The Indians who used the area had known about hot springs in the area for years and made use of them as part of various ceremonies. Walking Buffalo recalled that sounds were often heard around the springs, like those made by whistles or singing. "We would wait around, trying to see who it was and what was making the sounds... but we could never see anything in the waters." [2]

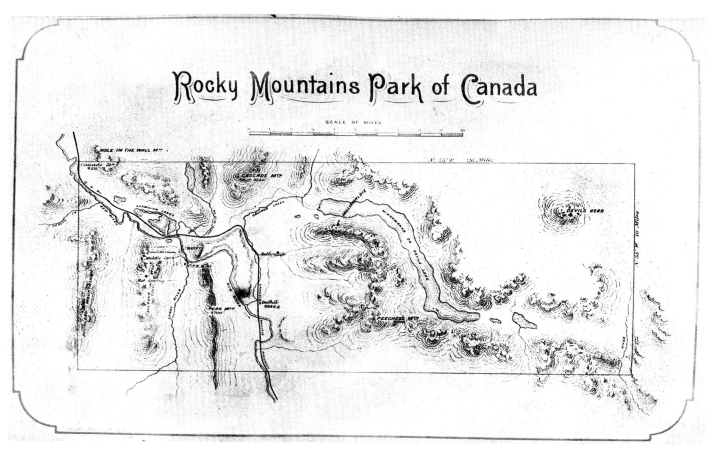

Rocky Mountains Park of Canada

James Hector commented on the presence of hot springs when he passed through in 1859. Joe Healy claimed to have "discovered" a hot spring that flowed out of a cave on the flanks of Sulphur Mountain when he was prospecting in the area in 1884. Frank McCabe and brothers William and Thomas McCardell described "their" discovery of the hot spring in a cave, when they noticed steam rising from a hole in the ground and descended into the gloom by climbing down a notched tree. The enterprising group built a fence around the area and a cabin on the site. Understanding its potential, they hoped to be able to claim squatters' rights. Another interested party, David Keefe, built a raft from "borrowed" CPR ties and telegraph wire and rigged up a line across the river to ferry people over to the springs.

Controversy erupted as different parties laid claim to the wonderful springs. In 1885, William Pearce, Superintendent of Mines, reviewed the situation and recommended settling with none of the claimants but instead creating a park at the site. A conversation in 1883 with Van Horne of the CPR had put the suggestion of the park on the table, and Pearce was interested in this possibility. He had visited the Rockies in 1884 and 1885, and returned convinced that steps should be taken to protect the area for the future. To convince the federal government of the value of such a plan, he suggested developments modelled after the European spas. "This would bring people to Banff, and money to the government's coffers."[3] The government like the idea and sent out surveyor George Stewart to review the boundaries. He was told to include "all points of interest within reasonable bounds," including the western end of Devil's Lake (Minnewanka) and down the Bow to the confluence with the Spray River. Stewart went on to become the first park superintendent.

On November 25, 1885, an Order-in-Council was passed to remove 10 square miles around the hot springs from the lands available for settlement and create the Banff Hot Springs Reserve. If you recall the discussion about the formation of Banff National park in Chapter 12, this was the seed that would soon grow into Rocky Mountain National Park. The boudaries of this new park are shown in a map from 1887 on page 187.

The McCardells immediately hired James Lougheed to fight for their case. An assortment of other individuals came out of the woodwork to claim ownership to the hot springs site, including D. Woodworth, a Member of Parliament who had talked McCabe into selling him his rights. Most of the claims were dismissed. But Woodworth received $1,000 in settlement (even though he had not even paid the agreed $1,500 for his purchase of the site), and McCabe and the McCardells each received $675 to compensate for their "developments" at the site.[4]

The pools at the springs were deepened in 1887 – the Cave to four feet and the Basin to five – and given a concrete lining. A few simple log buildings were erected near the hot springs. These were replaced in 1914 by the structure that is now found at the Cave and Basin site. (The current one is a replica.) In addition to the natural hot pool itself, a swimming pool in the aquacourt was heated by the hot springs water. The developments were encouraged by the growth of tourism as an expanding middle class found the resources to travel. The development of a facility in a beautiful setting that would provide recreational and restorative opportunities for visitors was a timely notion. The healing properties of mineral water were taken very seriously, and the paths to both the Cave and Basin and the Upper Hot Springs were embellished by crutches nailed to trees, discarded once the users had benefitted from the miraculous waters.

Bathing has been prohibited in the Cave and Basin natural pool since 1971 because the water could not be properly chlorinated. In 1993, the aquacourt was closed. There is now a historical exhibit at the site.

Cave and Basin hot springs pool, ca. 1900-39, Samuel J. Jarvis / Library and Archives Canada / PA-02505

Cave and Basin swimming pool, no date, Library and Archives Canada / PA-179859

The Upper Hot
Springs, 2009

receive that dubious honour. This creature is highly sensitive to human intrusion into its habitat. In fact, an incident occurred a few years ago that confirmed this, when a group of partiers broke into the Cave and Basin for an illegal swim. A snail count after the event determined that the population had dropped as a result of this intrusion.

Why is a snail important? The researcher who is examining the snail population explains: "I don't have any doubt that they are as important as the grizzly. Just as grizzly bears are used to measure the ecological integrity of large areas of wilderness extending, for example, from Yellowstone to the Yukon, snails can be used to measure the health of smaller, perhaps more unique environments, like these hot springs."[5]

The site of the Cave and Basin is just one of the about seven hot springs that flow from the slopes of Sulphur Mountain. The only other one to be developed is the Upper Hot Springs, farther to the southeast. In 1885, George Whitman erected a tent there and provided meals. He soon built a cabin on the site, which became the first restaurant in the Banff area. In 1886, Dr. R. G. Brett got a permit to build a sanitorium by the Upper Springs. It started as a log structure cobbled together from material salvaged from Silver City. (See the next chapter.) Brett soon expanded this into the Grand View Villa, a three-story hotel with room for 50 guests and 40 patients.

The buildings at the Upper Hot Springs today were built in 1932. They are a good example of what has come to be known as "Banff Style" – which was based on a rustic interpretation of what was referred to as "Swiss Style," with a crossed-log decorative element on the walls and rock walls built from the typical stone quarried from Mount Rundle.

Wildlife Spotting??? The Banff Springs Snail

Even though this critter is held captive a few feet from where you stand, you are still no more likely to see it than to see a bear. The snails that live in some of the Banff hot springs (look for them in the Cave and Basin) may be small – just 5 to 9 centimetres long – but they are rare and protected.

The snail, *Physella johnsoni*, is found in only one location in the world – in hot springs around Banff. It was first identified in the 1920s, and is one of only two species of snail known to use this type of steamy habitat. As well as having had to adapt to a steady heat treatment, they have adapted to low oxygen levels and a high level of hydrogen sulphide.

This snail may actually be a refugee – it may have moved into the hot pools as a way to survive the glacial periods. It was listed as endangered in the 1970s – the first mollusc to

Geological Notes: Hot Springs

The water in the springs on Sulphur Mountain is heated as it circulates deep down beneath the earth's crust. The temperature of the earth increases by about 25 degrees Celsius for each kilometre below the surface, which is known as the thermal gradient. Water travelling along faults gains access to deeper layers of the earth, where it is heated. While it is underground, it comes into contact with various minerals (commonly calcium, sulphur, and magnesium) and, since hot water is a good solvent, it picks up traces of these substances. Pressure finally forces the heated and mineralized water to exit through openings in the limestone formation along thrust faults. The water at the Cave and Basin is about 30 degrees Celsius when it reaches the surface. The Upper Hot Springs water is significantly warmer, at 38 degrees.

The Town of Banff

A settlement grew quickly on the north bank of the Bow River near the hot springs, now some distance from the community at the railway station. This settlement lay outside the newly reserved land, so the reserve was extended to include it and plans were made to lay out a town. Banff was set out in a grid along the edge of the river, and it was decided that 42-year leases would be granted, renewable into perpetuity. In 1887, leases for 180 lots had been applied for, and there were six hotels, nine stores, two churches, a school, and a post office. In 1888, the facilities that had remained at the hamlet below Cascade Mountain were moved and integrated into the town's new location. The old railway depot at Siding 29 became a tree nursery, irrigated by water from the falls. The plan was to replant trees in areas that had been burned during the building of the railway, but this early experiment in silviculture proved a flop.

By this time, although development had taken place on both sides of the Bow River, there was still no bridge, so a pontoon bridge was installed as a temporary solution. A road was built from the station to town, then on to the Cave and Basin. Another road went out to the new hotel development by the CPR on the southwest side of town by Bow

Falls. The first steel bridge was put across the Bow River in 1887. William Mather opened the Bow River Boathouse on the south bank of the river and rented canoes to the public. A steamboat took tourists on day trips from Homestead Landing on the north bank of the Bow upstream to a spot called North Landing near the outflow of Healy Creek. The town could offer plenty of recreational opportunities for visitors.

Accommodation was needed for the tourists who were beginning to find their way to Banff. Moulton Park Hotel went up where the park is now situated on the north bank of the Bow. Like Brett's first Sanitorium, it was built from logs from Silver City that were floated down the Bow to the new site. The National Park Hotel was built in the 1880s, later to become the Alberta Hotel, run by Frank Ricks and William Potts. Norman Luxton put up the King Edward Hotel in 1904. The Mount Royal was added by David McDougall in 1908 and taken over by Jim Brewster in 1912. Visitors were beginning to find a range of places with rooms that offered an alternative to the costly accommodation in the fancy CPR digs across the bridge. The Mount Royal and King Edward are both still in operation on Banff Avenue.

Dr. Robert Brett, the company doctor for the CPR, had arrived in Banff in 1883 and immediately started capitalizing on the many entrepreneurial opportunities he saw there. By 1886, he had built a sanatorium on the grounds southwest of the river (the current site of the Park Administration buildings). Brett's development consisted of a hotel with beds for 50 guests, a healing spa, and a separate hospital. The facility was renamed Rundle Hall, but became better known as Bretton Hall. The hospital facilities were removed from it when Brett built Brett Hospital on the other side of Spray Avenue (where the YMCA now stands). Bretton Hall burned down in 1933.

Brett also built Grand View Villa Hotel, as mentioned, as well as a hospital on Spray Avenue. When the Villa burned down in 1901, Brett's lease was not renewed, and the federal government then built the Upper Hot Springs bathing facility at that site. The enterprising Brett also set up a bottling plant and sold the local spring water as Banff's Lithiated Mineral Water, using water from Kidney Springs near the Upper Hot Springs. Brett later moved on from his entrepreneurial activ-

Bretton Hall Hotel, Banff, 1926, Glenbow NA-554-5

Main street of Banff, ca. 1890s, Glenbow NA-529-16

ities to politics, and served as Alberta's lieutenant-governor from 1915 to 1925.

In 1903, a landmark building was built in Banff that still stands on the edge of the park. The Banff Park Museum was built in what was called "Railroad Pagoda Style." Early architecture in the park tried to develop a style that reflected the mountain environment by using local materials such as logs and Rundlestone. Shingle ornamentation was typically used, as was the crossed-log motif. The Banff Park Museum, now a National Historic Site, houses the park's natural-history collection. The core of the displays came from the specimens collected by Professor John Macoun, who had been sent west in 1891 by the Geological Survey of Canada to assemble a collection from the flora and fauna of the Rocky Mountains Park.

Banff's zoo was located on the grounds behind the museum. It was started in 1904 when William Whyte, Vice President of the CPR, presented the town with 10 pheasants. An aviary grew from this, and then larger mammals were gradually added. At one point, the zoo even had a polar bear. It closed in 1937.

After Brett's sanatorium burned down, the federal government put up the Administration Building in 1935 as one of the relief projects during the Depression. This building still retains its original appearance, as designed by Harold Beckett.

The Town of Banff offers an interesting self-guided historical walking tour. The brochure "Walking Through Banff's History" is available at the information centre.

Banff Park Museum, National Historic Site

Banff Main Street, 2010

The Banff Springs Hotel

The CPR's presence dominated the development of the town, as the railway had received significant land and resource rights through its contract with the federal government. It put those rights to good use on an array of various projects. Who else but the CPR would have been allowed to open a coal mine at Bankhead within the park? The company moved fast to exploit the tourism potential by building grand facilities for the well-heeled guests arriving on its trains.

As tourists began to come west to explore the Rockies, the first challenge was to provide basic facilities for housing and feeding them. Dining cars on the trains were impractical at first, because the trains could not pull any additional weight up the steep grades through the mountains. Facilities

for meals were provided at the stations while the trains stopped for servicing. But people wanted to spend time in the mountains and needed places to stay. Simple hotels had sprung up in Banff, but the CPR knew there was a market for a sumptuous hotel that would appeal to the travelling upper class.

The original version of the Banff Springs Hotel was begun in 1886, designed by New York architect Bruce Price. While it was in the early stages of construction, Van Horne visited the site and found to his alarm that the whole plan had been turned around 180 degrees so the kitchens had the best view of the Bow River Valley. He quickly dashed off a new design for a rotunda pavilion to be added on to the back side (now the front) to return this vista to the guests. The hotel opened in 1888 and charged $3.50 for a room.

In 1903, a second wing was added. But the number of guests arriving to see the Rockies far exceeded the hotel's capacity in those years. So, in 1912, the hotel underwent redevelopment, replacing the wooden structure with a stone-and-concrete one designed by Walter Painter. This is when the CPR began to articulate its concept of a grand hotel in the style of a French chateau. Painter was even sent on a tour of France's Loire region to do research. The result was a sort of 11-story hybrid combining what he saw in France with a Scottish manorial house. The new Banff Springs was open for business in 1914. However, it burned down in 1926. (Fires

The Fairmont Banff Springs Hotel, R. Lai (SXC Images)

Some Colourful Characters

No discussion of Banff would be complete without introducing some of the interesting individuals who helped make the place what it has become. Many of the local outfitters were men who came from a comfortable, often even privileged, background in "the old country." But they were deeply attracted to the raw, engaging existence in the lands opening in the Canadian West, and the mountains drew them into their heart. These men quickly found their place in the emerging mountain culture, and their names will forever ring in our ears in association with the exciting early days of Banff.

Tom Wilson

One of the first to arrive in Banff, and among those who were born in Canada, was Tom Wilson. After working for the North-West Mounted Police for a while, he sought greater opportunities and independence by heading west with the CPR in 1882. He worked as a packer for Major Rogers for a while – which was not a happy relationship at first, but they seemed to have worked out a respectful arrangement. Wilson got his start in guiding when he was asked by the manager of the Banff Springs to take out a group of hunters in 1887. The trip was a great success, and Tom established himself as a capable and trustworthy guide. His business grew as demand increased to guide visitors on longer, more complex trips. Wilson needed more help, and hired some of the other men who would go on to make a name for themselves in the local culture – men such as Bill Peyto and Jimmy Simpson. By the early 1900s, Banff had become too developed for Wilson, so he switched the focus of his outfitting activities to Laggan (Lake Louise) and Field, B.C.

Wilson married Minnie McDougall (no relation to the McDougalls of Morley) and in 1904 left guiding to pursue other interests. He maintained a home in Banff for his wife and five children, and also operated a horse ranch on the Kootenay Plains to the north of the park. A story is told of his trip, on foot, returning from that ranch to Banff to be with his family for Christmas in 1908. He took the route

were common in Banff's early days…) The hotel was rebuilt in 1928, with new wings added, and has the same general layout today.

The Banff Springs opened only during the summer months until the late 1960s, when it was winterized to operate year-round. In 1987, the Manor Wing was added in anticipation of the crowds that would arrive with the Calgary Olympic Winter Games in 1988, and a conference centre was added in 1991. In 1992, the Banff Springs was declared a National Historic Site – which, together with today's tougher park regulations, will make any further expansion a challenge.

through the Pipestone – a well-known connection that was familiar to Wilson. But the weather was grim that year, and to make matters worse, he broke through a snow bridge over a creek and got soaked to the waist. Unable to get a fire going to dry himself, Wilson simply kept moving – for three days. By the time he stumbled, barely functioning, into Laggan (Lake Louise), he was suffering badly from exposure. He was taken directly to the hospital in Banff and ended up losing part of both feet to frostbite. But Wilson, true to form, made a joke of the affair and commended the doctors for removing equal parts of both feet so he was still in balance. The partial loss of his limbs didn't seem to slow him down much.

Wilson moved to Vancouver in 1920, but he missed the mountain life and by 1927 was back in Banff. He saw out his days until his death in 1933 spinning yarns for guests at the CPR hotels. A storyteller par excellence, he was able to draw on his many years of experiences to entertain guests with tales of mountain life – although frequently with quite a few embellishments.

In 1894, he is said to have instigated what would grow into Indian Days in Banff. Wilson is also the individual who "discovered" Lake Louise and brought that gem to the public eye. (See Chapter 18.)

There is a photo of Tom Wilson with Hector Crawler on page 105.

Bill Peyto

Ebeneezer William Peyto was born in Kent, England. Seeking adventure, he left for Canada at the age of 18. He did a stint working for the CPR, then tried his hand at homesteading, and eventually found work with Tom Wilson's outfitting business. Peyto stayed with Wilson for seven seasons before heading off to fight in the Boer War.

Back in Banff after the war, Peyto set up his own outfitting business. He gained a reputation as a reliable, if a bit cantankerous, guide. He had fully adapted to the wild western life and cultivated an appearance to suit. Walter Wilcox described Peyto's attire: "A sombrero, with a rakish tilt to one side, a blue shirt set off by a white kerchief (which may serve in civilization for a napkin), and a buckskin coat with a fringed border, add to his cowboy appearance. A heavy belt containing two rows of cartridges, hunting-knife and six-shooter, as well as the restless activity of his wicked blue eyes, give him an air of bravado. He usually wears two pairs of trousers, one over the other, the outer pair about six months older. This is shown by their dilapidated and faded state, hanging, after a week of rough work in burnt timber, in a tattered fringe knee-high."[6]

When not working for clients, Peyto tended toward the wild life, drinking and playing hard. In the off-season, he did some prospecting and staked a number of claims in the Simpson Pass area. At one point, Peyto was having trouble with break-ins at his cabin near his claims. So he booby-trapped it with a bear trap whenever he left the cabin. On his return, Peyto would trigger the trap with a rifle shot before entering himself. But he never managed to catch the intruder.

In 1901, Peyto met Emily Wood, and they married and had a son. Sadly, Emily died suddenly in 1906, and Peyto decided to send his son to live with relatives in B.C. He sold his outfitting business and concentrated on trapping and prospecting. He was rarely seen in Banff, but one of his visits made a memorable impression with some of the locals. One of Peyto's pursuits was live-trapping animals for the Banff zoo. He had managed to trap a lynx and had trussed the animal up and stuffed it into a sack. Back in Banff, he developed a powerful thirst and stopped by the Alberta Bar for a drink before delivering his load. Peyto swung the sack off his shoulder and sat down at the bar. Pretty soon it became apparent to the other patrons just what he had carried in, and the barroom emptied in a flash. Peyto calmly finished his drink and headed on his way.

In 1915, he joined the armed forces and headed for Germany. Peyto was wounded during the war and discharged back to Canada. On his return, he was hired as a game warden by the park, and he remained in that service until 1936. The park probably thought that having the suspect characters work within the fold was preferable to leaving them to operate on their own.

Peyto died of cancer in 1943 at the age of 74.

Jimmy Simpson

Another individual who got his start with Tom Wilson, Simpson, like Peyto, came out from England at the age of 18. He arrived in Laggan (Lake Louise) in the late 1890s after being dumped off a train between there and Banff following his discovery as a stowaway. After learning the ropes at Wilson's operation, Simpson used some inheritance money to set up his own outfitting business. He bought horses from Wilson and Frank Ricks, and soon acquired a number of rich and influential clients.

Hunters liked hiring Simpson for his abilities as a tracker – particularly for bears. On one occasion, he ended up rather too close to a grizzly. He got in one shot at the bear before it forced him up a tree. But the beast gave him a good slash along his leg before Simpson scrambled out of reach, and he bore the scar for the rest of his life. Like many of the

Jimmy Simpson and his dog, Dooley, ca. 1910, Glenbow NA-3466-20

outfitters who catered to hunters, Simpson had a hard time adjusting to the restrictions on his activities imposed by park regulations. He was caught poaching sheep within park boundaries in 1909 and lost his licence for a year as a result. Simpson trapped and logged, like most of the men, to make ends meet, but his life really gained focus when he established his first camp on the edge of Bow Lake.

Simpson had been powerfully attracted to this lake since first laying eyes on it. In 1920, at the age of 43, he was finally given permission to build a permanent structure on the site, and Num-Ti-Jah Lodge had its beginnings. Because the timber in the area was small, he was forced to use an innovative eight-sided design to make a log structure of a reasonable size. After the road to Jasper came through in the 1930s, the popularity of his lodge grew. The place has had a number of expansions over the years, but remains in the Simpson family.

Jim Brewster

In 1887, the entire Brewster family moved from Kingston, Ontario, to Banff, where Jim's father set up a dairy to serve the little community. The Brewster family became close friends with William Twin (see Chapter 9) of the Stoney Nakoda, and Jim and his brother Bill spent many happy days exploring in Twin's company and learning the ways of the mountains. When the management at the Banff Springs needed someone to guide some clients on a fishing excursion, the young brothers, then 10 and 12, were pressed into service, and the rest unfolded from there. Not too many years later, they set up their own guiding business and soon became busy as Banff drew more visitors. In 1902, the CPR sent the pair to New York for the Sportsman's Show. They brought a display of hides and big-game heads, and came home with a lot of new business from American hunters. In 1904, the Brewsters received an exclusive licence as guides

Brewster Tally-Ho at Lake Louise Chateau, 1912, Glenbow NA-1263-3

for the CPR in Banff, and this was soon extended to Laggan (Lake Louise).

In 1908, Bill left Banff, but Jim stayed on and extended his business involvements. Jim had operated a livery service in both Banff and Laggan for some time, and in 1911, after fighting to gain permission from the regulatory powers, he launched the area's first motorized transit and sightseeing services. He provided car transport from Laggan Station to the Chateau on the lake, until the tram line was built as a connector. When cars were allowed outside the towns, Brewster mounted the frame from a number of horse-drawn "tally-hos" onto the chassis of some Kissel trucks and offered tours out to nearby scenic spots. He later added a Baby Overland, then a few other vehicles – until he had a fleet, and Brewster Transport Company aggressively entered the motoring age. The company grew into a major bus-transport company serving the Banff and later the Jasper areas.

Jim Brewster died of a stroke in 1947.

Banff Indian Days

The story goes that Tom Wilson initiated what was to become Indian Days when the railway was washed out in 1889. The stranded guests needed some entertainment and Wilson was asked to drum up something. He and Dave White approached the Stoney Nakoda, who agreed to go to Banff to put on a show for the guests.

About 250 Indians arrived on horseback, dragging travois. They set up their tepees and for a week showed visitors to Banff a bit about native culture. Events included a grand parade, horse races, a tug-of-war, dancing, and singing. There was also an opportunity for the tourists to look into the tepee homes of the Indians camped on the site. The guests were delighted, and the decision was made to make it an annual event. Banff Indian Days later grew to include rodeo events, and bleachers and an infield were built for the show.

The event was first held in an area by Bow Falls, but it soon outgrew this spot and was moved to the base of Cascade Mountain. For a week, the Whiskey Creek meadows were transformed into a native encampment. In the years that followed, other tribes were invited, but it was always the

Stoney Nakoda people who primarily carried the show. Each family received a stipend for attending and a bonus for putting up a tepee.

By the 1930s, the event had become so popular that the park tried to impose a restriction on how many Indians could attend, limiting it to 150. The Stoney Nakoda responded that all of them should be allowed to attend – or none of them would. Their threat to stay away convinced the park to drop the restriction. By the 1960s, the participating Indians were mostly coming by car and there were no longer many horses around during Indian Days. Many of the participants decided that they preferred to stick to the rodeo circuit instead of what was becoming a rather outdated event. It started to fade away and finally ended in 1978.

The Banff School of Fine Arts

The art school in Banff started as an offshoot of the Department of Extension at the University of Alberta. Dr. E. Corbett saw Banff as a good fit for the department's mandate to bring educational opportunities to rural areas. He started a school of theatre arts in 1933 using borrowed facilities. Donald Cameron, from the University of Alberta, took over in 1935, and worked hard to expand the school. Music and painting classes were added in 1936.

At about this time, the watercolourist A. C. Leighton had been invited to head up an art school at the Provincial Institute of Technology and Art in Edmonton. This involved summer sketching trips into the mountains, and these were amalgamated into the Banff School.

Many renowned painters have resided in Banff or visited frequently on painting excursions. Belmore Brown was one of the first, and Peter and Catherine Whyte are among the best known. Carl Runguis came out at the invitation of Jimmy Simpson, returning frequently to paint his wildlife images. Several members of the Group of Seven painted in the area. A.Y. Jackson and Lawren Harris were particularly taken with what Banff had to offer. A creative community blossomed in the town and gave support to the growing school.

In 1940, a theatre was built on Banff Avenue and for a time became the home of the Banff School of Fine Arts. Then the

Banff Indian Days, 1927. Dept. of Interior / Library and Archives Canada / PA-040770

Banff Indian Days, 1937, Lloyd harmon, V108-584

federal government granted a lease to a large piece of land on the slopes of Tunnel Mountain to allow the school to expand there. The theatre on Banff Avenue is now a tourism-information office.

The Banff Centre, as it has been called since 1972, is now affiliated with the University of Calgary. Its focus has changed over the years. Although the centre defines its mandate as "inspiring creativity," its activities have moved away from the traditional arts, such as painting, and toward new media. As well as art, programming now includes management and leadership development. A conference centre has been a big part of the Banff Centre's activity since the 1950s.

The Banff Centre is also home to Mountain Culture, a locus for sharing ideas and experiences that grow from mountain environments. Mountain Culture is behind the Mountain Film and Book Fesivals, photography competitions, seminars for outdoor enthusiasts, opportunities for writiers and many other initiatives.

Wildlife Spotting: Urban Elk

Elk (*Cervus elaphus*) or Wapati are the largest of the red deer species. The males stand about one and a half metres at the shoulder and weigh up to 500 kilograms. Cows are smaller and lighter. They have a smooth, light brown coat, with darker, coarser hair over their neck and shoulders and a white rump (wapiti means "white rump" in Shawnee). They have a prominent canine tooth in their upper dental work, sometimes called elk ivory. This tooth was used by the Indians for jewellery and was prized by the Elks Club (a social and philanthropic group originating in New York) for its badges. Bull elk develop very impressive racks of antlers that may reach over a metre across and weigh around 20 kilograms.

Historically, elk were primarily a plains animal. They were rarely seen in the newly created Rocky Mountains Park in the 1880s and were almost gone by the early 1900s. In 1919, an agreement with the U.S. Park Service resulted in a herd of 235 elk that were facing starvation in Yellowstone National Park in Wyoming being relocated to Banff. Their numbers have grown steadily ever since, and there are now about 500 elk in the park.

Bull elk, D. Ditchburn

Elk are mainly grazers, but they will also eat bushes and tree bark, particularly aspen, which has a nutritious layer rich in chlorophyll. As a result, these trees often show black scars on the bottom two to three metres of their trunks. This marking is also used by males to identify their territories. Elk live in herds of 20 to 30 animals, with each one made up of a dominant male and his harem. Non-dominant males form bachelor herds for much of the year. These herds tend to amalgamate into larger herds in the winter months, when they move down to lower valleys. In the fall, you can hear the thrilling sound of the males bugling their presence to receptive females – and rival males. Elks' other vocalizations include an assortment of grunts and squeals.

The success of the elk in Banff National Park has created problems. They have had an ecological impact by overgrazing and destroying stands of aspen and willow, and there are concerns regarding the predator-prey balance. Furthermore, the elk population has concentrated in the town of Banff, causing havoc for residents, visitors, and park management. Their urban inclination has been due to a number of factors, including predator avoidance, access to desirable food sources (people's gardens!), and habitat degradation in other places. The number of human-elk conflicts has risen sharply.

There are other concerns about how the elks' concentration in the town affects other species. The wolves are making kills closer and closer to the townsite, taking elk that wander just slightly away from the developed areas. There are even thoughts that the 2001 incident in which the woman

was killed by the cougar may be related to this change in wildlife dynamics. It has been shown that, since the elk are avoiding the wolves by staying in town, the wolves have taken to driving cougars away from their kills. A hungry cat may resort to unnatural behaviour, such as targeting humans.

So, the question, then, was how to manage this issue. For a time the elk were culled each fall and the meat was donated to the Stoney Nakoda at Morley. That is now not a popular solution. An Elk Advisory Committee was formed in 1992 to examine alternatives, which led to Parks Canada's adoption of the Banff National Park Elk Management Strategy. More than 200 elk were trapped and relocated, and the remaining animals were given an "aversive conditioning program" to make them less habituated to humans and keep them out of town.

This story is an excellent illustration of how complex park management has become. A functioning ecosystem can depend on the balance between species as seemingly distant as aspen trees and wolves via an intermediate factor, such as elk population levels.

A Town Within a Park

Municipal organization started, in part, as a response to the CPR's influence. In 1912, there was talk of relocating the railway line so it would cross the river close to Bow Falls and pass by the Banff Springs. This would have bypassed the town centre, so local businesses saw it as a threat to their survival and established the Banff Board of Trade to lobby against it. The idea of moving the rail line eventually died a natural death, but the town decided to keep the board around.

All decisions regarding the town of Banff had to go through the federal government, which could be a slow and highly frustrating affair. The topic of allowing vehicles into the park and onto town streets generated particularly heated exchanges among Banff residents – which were largely ignored by the feds. The sense of disenfranchisement grew until, in 1920, the residents convinced Sir James Lougheed, then federal Minister of the Interior, that they needed an advisory board that would have a voice in the management of park affairs. This became the Banff Citizens' Association. This new body started working on ways to levy taxes on residents to support such programs as local firefighting and health care. The Banff Citizens' Association had much greater influence than the

Elk on edge of Banff, K. Manry

idea of true representative government. But the genie of self-government had been let out of the bottle as a result of these discussions, and it would never be fully put back in. This issue would thereafter dominate the subsequent relationship between the town and federal authorities responsible for park administration, ultimately providing a battleground for the struggle between development and preservation that would become the hallmark of its subsequent history."[7]

And so the battle continued... The larger issues of growth, development, and revenue – which were increasingly at loggerheads with issues of conservation, cultural preservation, and ecosystem sustainability – were played out within the town's affairs. Banff, which has remained limited within the 745 acres surveyed in 1885 (slightly less now due to wildlife corridor and habitat patch allowances), was bulging at the seams. The pressure to provide residential services to all those who wished to live in this mountain paradise resulted in the introduction of a "need-to-reside" regulation in the 1960s. Since that time, in order to live in Banff, one must be employed or operate a business there, be retired after having lived for at least five years there, or be married to someone who meets these criteria. This ensures that the limited residential spaces are available for those who most need them. But it is also seen as a one-sided regulation imposed by the federal government – always a sore point. It also means increased pressure on Canmore, which does not have equivalent legislation to limit its growth.

In 1990, Banff gained status as an independent municipality within the park, giving it the right to tax citizens and set its own regulations under the "guidance" of the park's vision. The town now makes its own decisions about how to manage growth and how to harmonize municipal management with environmentally sustainable practices.

The town has adopted a "no net negative environmental impact" policy that will guide infrastructure decisions in years to come. As is pointed out in the vision statement of the Banff Community Plan, "We will cultivate Banff's uniqueness while embracing opportunities to enhance our economic health, diversity of lifestyles and ecosystem. And above all, we will continue to build on our town's rich heritage as a source of enchantment and renewal for others... always."[8]

Board of Trade ever had, and it gained support from the community and helped shape government decisions.

In the mid-1920s, Banff (inside the park) and Canmore (outside the park) opened discussions about municipal planning. The difference in their autonomy and ability to make decisions was becoming a sore point. Letters were sent to the Minister of the Interior regarding issues such as the powers to tax and make local decisions regarding civic affairs. E. J. Hart describes the situation that followed very concisely: "Stewart and R. B. Bennett... quickly responded that no such powers could be granted, attempting to nip in the bud any

The road that continues west from Banff was built in 1911. This was the same year that cars were allowed to enter the park, but they were required to go straight to the town and park there – no exploring on the new roads being built. Visitors were to make use of the local livery services for any movement within the park. So, for a short time, the track was left to slower-moving horse carts and wagons. For a long time, the road remained just a rough dirt track. But soon the park gave in to pressure to allow cars to move freely throughout Rocky Mountains Park, and vehicles started to make their way westward past the town of Banff.

Mount Norquay and Early Skiing History

The first pair of skis in Banff were sent to Banff resident George Paris in 1894 by a Norwegian guest who had stayed at Bretton Hall. Paris promptly broke one on his first experimental run – and swore off skiing forever.

In 1910, Conrad Kain, an Austrian climbing guide, arrived in the area with his skis and taught a few of the locals. Skis were not easily available, and those who were sufficiently motivated made themselves a pair from wooden cheese boxes with leather straps attached. Then Dave White and Company finally started to bring in real skis and the sport took off.

Ski jumping was popular before what we would refer to as downhill skiing came into vogue. Three ski jumpers came through town and gave a display at the winter carnival one year, and that prompted many of the local lads to take up the sport. A practice jump was built on Tunnel Mountain during the winter of 1919. By the early 1920s, sliding – or "ski running," as it was called – was gathering momentum, and people were learning to make turns in the open glades.

The Swiss guides gave occasional lessons, and more and more people started heading for the slopes.

Before there were any runs on the local hills, the keeners climbed up the slopes of Stoney Squaw below Mount Norquay and schussed down. A ski club was organized, and in the late 1920s the club's members were given permission to cut some runs on the slopes of Norquay. Gus Johnson explained that, "When they asked for permission from Superintendent Major Jennings to do this, he agreed, but asked them not to cut every tree. Obediently, they left one beautiful pine. Hence, 'The Lone Pine' run."[1]

In 1928, Cliff and Jack White and Cyril Paris formed the Norquay Ski Club and built the first ski lodge at the base

Banff – Lake Louise highway, ca. 1928. Dept. of Interior / Library and Archives Canada / PA-040731

of the new runs. It burned in 1938 and was later rebuilt by a private developer. That lodge burned in 1994, and after a couple of years when Atco trailers were used as temporary quarters, the present lodge was built in 1996.

Mount Norquay (2,522 m) was named after Sir John Norquay, premier of Manitoba from 1878 to 1887. He was reputed to have been the first one up the mountain – although this fact is disputed. Norquay rose from humble beginnings as a Metis orphan to play a major role in prairie politics.

It is worth a quick side trip up Mt. Norquay Road to get a view over the Bow Valley. At the "green spot" (the result of a local fire) on the way up, you can see some huge old Douglas fir trees – as well as an established colony of Columbian ground squirrels. This is also a good spot to see sheep. There is an excellent view from here over Vermilion Lakes and across to Mount Rundle.

Sulphur Mountain — 2,451 m

Looking across the valley, you can see Banff snuggled into the slopes of the mountain that provided the springs that gave birth to the park. Originally called Terrace Mountain, the source of this peak's official name is obvious if you have ever visited the hot springs. A trail was put up to the summit in 1903, and the hardier tourists hiked up to enjoy the view. But many others chose to rent the horses available for hire at the trailhead. In 1940, a teahouse was built on the summit, run by the Swiss immigrant John Jaeggi. He later added a halfway house to re-energize visitors for the second half of the climb. For a while he even offered a B&B at the top, but that was short-lived.

Next, Jaeggi installed a tractor that powered a sled that people could ride for the first section, although they still had to get off and walk the second, steeper section. He dreamed of making access even easier. In 1951 and again in 1953,

he travelled to Switzerland to check out new developments in mechanized lifts. In 1957, he got the federal government's permission to install one.

The gondola opened in 1959. It rose 700 metres in its 1,500 metre stretch of cable, and was the first bi-cable gondola in North America. Jaeggi's gondola was a great success and traffic to the top of Sulphur Mountain heated up. In 1997, the original gondola underwent updates and improvements.

On the summit of Sulphur Mountain is the Banff Meteorological Observatory, installed in 1903. Norman Sanson, curator at the Banff Park Museum, made a weekly trip up the mountain to take weather readings. In 1931, he climbed it for the 1,000th time, an event that was celebrated with much fanfare by the community with a sunrise breakfast at the top. In 1945, Sanson made his last climb to the top, at the age of 83, to observe a solar eclipse. The summit upon which the Meteorological Observatory is located was named Sanson Peak the year before Norman Sanson died and the observatory is now a National Historic Site. The epitaph on his gravestone in the Banff Cemetery reads "Gone Higher."

A cosmic ray station was installed on Sanson Peak by the National Research Council of Canada in 1956, and was run by the University of Calgary until 1978. The road up the western side of Sulphur Mountain accesses this site.

The gondola terminal at the top of Sulphur Mountain, J. Eber (SXC Images)

Vermilion Lakes, Wetland Ecology, and Archaeological Finds

The flats below Sulphur Mountain are the marshy remains of Glacial Lake Vermilion. There was once a deeper lake here, but it is gradually filling with vegetative matter and silt, thus becoming more of a marsh and less of a lake. This is the natural process of succession as marsh plants (grasses, rushes, and horsetail) invade and generate more of a soil base for shrubs such as willow. Beaver have contributed to the process through their dams, which raised the water level during the 1970s and killed the spruce trees, whose corpses still stand on the western shore. Most of the beaver have moved on, but a few muskrat still work along the shores.

In the 1880s, the parks department seeded the area with wild rice to encourage waterfowl for the pleasure of park visitors. The rice has not survived, but the area is still a great bird habitat. There are a variety of ducks, osprey, and bald eagles, and swans often take a break at the western end during their migration. The water is kept open by cool springs that run year-round.

The south-facing slopes that look out over Vermilion Lakes are the site of one of the most important archaeological finds in the park. In 1983, as the highway through this section was about to be twinned, an archaeological survey was conducted in the area. Evidence was found of seven campsites estimated to be 10,700 years old. They had a central hearth surrounded by a circle of postholes and rock debris from toolmaking scattered in a broad circle within that. One of the theories is that these were circular dwellings, and that as the debris from work on making stone tools flew up, it hit the walls and settled in this distinct round pattern within the walls. The site's location on these south-facing slopes would have made a fine encampment. A warm exposure and good access to water were combined with a fine view to watch for game.

The Vermilion site was unusually well preserved, probably because of subsequent mud flows that buried the artefacts in situ, protecting them from disturbances. The artefacts indicate that the site was used continuously for thousands of years. The deepest layers contain charcoal chips, which allowed carbon dating to verify the great age of the remains. There are also bones from caribou, sheep, moose, and rabbits.

The next layer contained two points, which gave a definitive date to the Plains-Mountains and Agate Basin Complex – 8,000 to 10,500 years ago. The highest layer of artefacts were those of the Tobacco Plains People, who were associated with a particular type of atlatl (spear thrower) and who lived here 7,000 years ago.

The sites where the digs were conducted were reburied when the study was finished in order to preserve them.

Rundle from the Vermillion wetlands

Wildlife Spotting: Beaver and Muskrat

Vermilion Lakes are one of the spots where you might be able to see a couple of the wetlands animals. Our national symbol, the beaver (*Castor Canadensis*) is one of the largest of the rodents – about 30 kilograms and more than a metre long (one third of that is tail). Its pre-Ice Age ancestors were even larger. Remains of giant beavers have been found in the North that were more than three metres long and probably weighed more than 300 kilograms!

If these animals find the existing water level insufficient for their requirements, they build elaborate dams to create ponds to accommodate their lodge. These structures can be huge – up to five metres in diameter – and have an underwater entry and exit. The pond that surrounds them must be deep enough that it does not freeze to the bottom, allowing movement and access to the food stored on the bottom throughout the winter.

Beavers eat aspen, poplar, and willow, as well as the roots of water plants. They are very well adapted for their underwater lifestyle, with a thick double layer of fur that they keep well oiled from a gland near their tail. Their flat, leathery tail serves as a rudder underwater and as a balance aid on land.

When alarmed, they slap the water with this paddle-shaped appendage to warn of perceived danger.

Beavers are diurnal, so you are most likely to see them going about their business at dawn and dusk. Their numbers were drastically reduced through the fur trade across the country, which exported 200,000 pelts a year at its peak. But the beaver population has since rebounded, and in some areas they are even regarded as pests because of their destructive effect on trees near wetlands.

Muskrats (*Ondatra zibethicus*) are also a rodent and are commonly mistaken for beavers, even though they are only about half the size. Unlike beavers' flat, paddle-shaped tail, muskrats have a skinny, hairless tail like that of a rat – which is indeed the family they belong to. Muskrats do not cut down trees to access tender shoots and leaves, as beavers do. Instead, muskrats dine on shore plants such as sedges and cattails, and will also eat frogs and invertebrates when they find them.

More solitary than the beavers, which live in family groups in their large lodges, the muskrats build smaller structures and burrows along banks for their dwellings. They do not create dams to control water levels.

Left: Beaver, iStockphoto

Right: Muskrat, iStockphoto

Mount Rundle from the North

The view of Mount Rundle from the slopes of Mount Norquay and the Vermilion Lakes area is probably the scene most frequently depicted by artists of any location in the park. Artist Walter Phillips expressed this sentiment in his comment: "Mount Rundle is my bread and butter mountain. I never tire of painting it, for it is never the same. In deep shadow in the morning, it borrows a warm glow from the setting sun at the end of the day. Its colour runs the gamut from orange to cold blue-grey, with overtones of violet and intervals of green."[2]

Rev. Rundle passed by the base of "his" mountain twice – in 1844 and again in 1847. On his first trip, he recorded a climb up a peak in the area, although we do not know which one. But his attempt is charmingly described in his journal, and the description gives some insight into the nature of this gentle missionary. Saturday, 1844: "Am now climbing a mountain. Here are two veins, perhaps of spar, in the bed of rock where I am now sitting (*illegible*) I became quite ill thro' fatigue &c. but was in good spirits when climbing, until I was very high up. I made two attempts to get up an elevation but could not succeed. Rocks very steep – felt very weak, that at last I was near fainting whilst passing over a projecting ledge or rock. What a moment of anxiety. I have some recollection of calling to the Almighty to assist me & praised be His name, my prayer was heard. I descended to the next stage. It was presumptuous of me I know, but I began again to see if I could not find a way to scale higher, but I could not succeed so I now abandoned my design & commenced descending. I was not careful about the road & had great difficulty in descending. I was very weak from want of food, having left without breakfast, & began to feel afraid ever & anon too I heard the moving of stones which terrified me. How hard, too, to pass along the steep sloping sides away to fearful descent. At length, however, I reached the bottom, but how was I to get to the encampment? I had lost the road. Very tired, weak, & unwell. Heard a gun fired!! & so guided!! Reached at last, thanks to Providence. Took some medicine & had *breakfast* abt sunset."[3]

Geology Notes: Mount Rundle

Along this section of the Trans-Canada, there is unfortunately very little opportunity to stop and have a good look at the view. The only option for westbound travellers is to drive up to the turnoff for the Banff Parkway and loop back to take advantage of the eastbound pullouts.

We have now had a good look at Mount Rundle from two very different perspectives. This more northerly view is geologically more informative regarding mountain formation in the region. The eastern face exposes the layers of strata that resulted from thrust dynamics, while the western slope is a smooth, more gently inclined sheet that follows the angle of the top-most layer. We again see the three clear layers that make up the Rundle Thrust Sheet: another expression of the Rundle/Banff/Palliser sequence we met on Cascade Mountain.

Rundle offers the archetypal view of a desktop-shaped mountain. The angled northwest face is the "back," so to speak, of the resistant Rundle layer that it follows on the angle of the "dip," which is forced upon that layer through thrust faulting. This is the up-dip side. Erosion by glaciers at the base of this slope would have resulted in the entire layer

Geological diagram of Mount Rundle

sloughing off, and the angle would be maintained at the same degree. The southeast face, on the other hand, exposes all the layers to erosional forces, but is less subject to the undermining effect of glaciers tearing off a whole layer at a time. The face maintains a steeper, more severe slope, and is known as the down-slope side. Hence the name "dip-slope" for this type of mountain structure.

The Sundance Range — 2,902 m

The next range to the west of Sulphur Mountain is the Sundance Range. It is believed to have been so named because of the native ceremonies held above the canyon along Sundance Creek.

Vermilion Lakes and the Sundance Range from Mt. Norquay Road

Wildlife Spotting: Bighorn Sheep

Prior to the installation of animal fencing, this stretch of road presented a hazard to drivers because sheep used to be found all over the road, attracted by the salt licks in the area. Today, sheep are less likely to be spotted, but may hang out on the slopes above the road where they have escape routes from predators. It is thought that about half a million years ago a primitive sheep similar to the present-day Marco Polo sheep of central Asia migrated the Bering land bridge that connected what is now Russia and Alaska. From there, they were isolated by subsequent ice ages and evolved into the northern Dall sheep (*Ovis dalli*) and the more southern Rocky Mountain Bighorn (*Ovis Canadensis*).

Bighorn are not huge animals – they stand about a metre at the shoulder – but they are chunky, strong specimens. The rams are muscular, tough animals, well designed for the aggressive "ramming" contests they indulge in during the rut. These animals have extra bone in their skulls to protect them from concussions as they challenge each other in head-on duels in the fall.

Sheep move up into the high country for the summer, where the ewes raise their lambs in close proximity to the safety of steep cliffs for escape when necessary. It is amazing to watch the confidence and agility of these days-old youngsters as they negotiate terrain that seems suicidal to the two-legged spectator.

Bighorn sheep, ewes above and rams below

Healy Creek and Sunshine Ski Area

Directly to the west from the broad section of the Bow Valley that includes Vermilion Lakes is another open valley. Down this valley runs Healy Creek, named by George Dawson after Joe Healy. Healy was in the Union Army during the U.S. Civil War, then came north into Canada, where he helped to establish the whiskey trading post at Fort Whoop-Up. We encountered him in the "discovery" of the Banff Sulphur Springs, and will again in the section on Silver City, just a bit farther down the highway…

One of the earliest white travellers through this area used Healy Creek as part of his route. Sir George Simpson became governor of the Hudson's Bay Company in 1826. In 1841, he set off on a tour of inspection of the HBC's mammoth holdings as part of a round-the-world tour. An arrogant and uncompromising man, he was nicknamed "the Little Emperor." Simpson travelled across Canada in a canoe paddled by voyageurs. He was accompanied by his official assistant and bagpipe player, who would "pipe him in" with great fanfare whenever they approached an HBC post.

Simpson was led by the Metis guide Alexis Piché, who Simpson called Peechee. The party had intended to travel farther north using Athabaska Pass. But they learned that the Columbia River was in flood and their planned route would be too dangerous. So Piché instead took them through Devil's Gap from the Ghost River to Lake Minnewanka and along the Bow River to where the Sunshine turnoff is now located. Here they travelled up Healy Creek, over what is now called Simpson Pass (where Simpson commented that the heather reminded him of Scotland), and on into the Windermere area by way of the Simpson and Vermilion rivers.

Simpson and his companion, Chief Factor John Rowand, carved a blaze into a tree in the area of the pass. In 1904, Jim

Looking up Healy Creek (valley to the right); Mount Howard Douglas and Eagle Mountain

Brewster found this blaze, which bears the initials of the two men and the date, and carved the section out of the tree. This artefact now resides in the Banff Museum.

Two sad incidents are associated with Healy Creek. The first, in August 1986, involved a plane crash in the narrow valley. In spite of poor flying conditions, a family from California had taken off from the Banff airstrip in their Cessna 172 to head home. They became disoriented and instead of continuing along the Bow Valley ended up following the Healy Creek valley. Their plane crashed, killing both parents. However, their six-year-old daughter, Tammy, was able to pull her injured older sister, Corinna, from the plane, then head off down the creek to find help. The little girl followed the creek until it dropped into an impassable canyon, where she became stuck. Fortunately, that section of the creek is not far from the Healy Creek trail, and Tammy's cries were heard by hikers, who reported the situation to the wardens. A rescue was organized and both sisters, and even the family dog, were saved.

The second incident occurred in the winter of 1990. A group of four skiers had headed up the trail and stopped for lunch near one of the avalanche paths that crosses the trail. Although they wisely chosen to remain in the treed area untouched by previous slides, a slide occurred that was on a scale much larger than those before. A massive volume of snow roared down, taking in even the area surrounding the path made by previous slides. The force of the wave of air pressure created by the moving snow even snapped the branches of trees well away from where the snow itself swept through.

When the scene was discovered, a rescue was called immediately. The huge amount of snow presented a large and difficult search area, and the severe cold and strong pine scent from the downed trees made it difficult for the search dogs to be very effective. It took four days to finally locate all four bodies – a sad outcome.

On the south side of Healy Creek is Mount Howard Douglas (2,820 m), named after the second superintendent of Rocky Mountains Park. Douglas was appointed by the Liberal federal government to replace Charles Stewart after the Conservative government that had appointed him fell in 1896. During Douglas' tenure, he moved park management forward toward a more conservationist style of management. He laid the groundwork for the warden service in the park (which was initiated in 1909) and worked hard to have the park boundaries expanded.

Eagle Mountain (2,820 m) is a northern outlier from Mount Howard Douglas. Remember the section about the Golden Eagles in Chapter 11?

Awareness of the beautiful area that would become Sunshine Village was given a boost in the 1920s when an Alpine Club of Canada summer tent camp was established there. This provided accommodation on a leg of the popular "Banff to Mount Assiniboine Walking and Riding Tour." In 1928, the first small log cabin was built at the base of the meadows by the CPR for use by the Trail Riders of the Canadian Rockies (a CPR-supported summer horseback trip that was hugely popular).

In 1933, the CPR building was leased by the Brewster family, who started taking guests for all-inclusive ski weeks at a cost of $30. The guests were brought in by a Ford Model T, then rode on horseback before covering the final leg on snowshoes. There werev no ski lifts – all the elevation to access the ski runs was gained by climbing with slip-resistant skins attached to the skis.

In 1936, Jim and Pat Brewster bought the lodge, expanded it, and hired Cyril and Herb Paris and Bruno Engler as guides. Access to the runs was provided by Bombardier snow vehicles, and in 1941 the first rope tow was installed. Access to the lodge was improved.

Mount Bourgeau

By 1960, when the Trans-Canada Highway came through the valley, Sunshine was owned by Cliff White and more lifts were being added. Cliff sold the resort to Power Corporation in order to finance ambitious developments, but stayed on as manager. Modern, fast-moving chairlifts were added, and in 1980 the shuttle by bus to Sunshine Village was replaced by a speedy ride in a gondola. Ralph Scurfield bought Sunshine in 1981. He updated the gondola and undertook further improvements and updates. But, happily, the original log cabin remains – now descriptively called Old Sunshine Lodge.

The Massive Range and Mount Bourgeau — 2,930 m

The beautiful peak straight ahead of you as you drive west from the Vermilion Lakes toward the Sunshine turnoff was named by Hector for his travelling companion on the Palliser Expedition. Bourgeau spoke no English and hated riding, but he revelled in being in the mountains and in the abundance of plants he found there. During his time in the Bow Valley, Bourgeau collected more than 60,000 specimens. He never got as far as the mountain that is named for him, though, since he stopped at the base of Cascade Mountain to focus on botanizing there.

Bourgeau is the south-ernmost mountain in the Massive Range. The next mountains you see in that range are Mount Brett, which is up a valley in the distance, and Massive Mountain (2,434 m), which juts toward

the highway. Massive Mountain is a bit of a misnomer – it is not, in fact, particularly massive.

Just after the Sunshine turnoff, you can look up a pretty, terraced valley toward the summit of Mount Brett (2,983 m), the highest peak in the range. It was named in 1916 after Dr. Robert Brett, the Banff physician, entrepreneur, and politician. Brett was such an integral part of Banff that when he died in 1929, schools and services in the town were closed for a day of mourning.

Pilot Mountain (2,935 m) was named by Dawson in 1884. It is highly visible where the Bow Valley curves, not far from where several other valleys join it. Pilot was used as a navigational marker by early travellers, and can even be seen from places near the towns of Banff and Lake Louise. Brett, Massive, and Pilot Mountain are visible in the distance in the photo of Tunnel Mountain in Chapter 14.

Pilot Mountain

Wildlife overpass with Mount Brett and Massive Mountain behind

mostly during the day; cougars, hares, and martens at night; and coyotes whenever they feel like it…). Grizzly bears, wolves, and the ungulates seem to prefer overpasses to underpasses. Use of the crossing structures seems to have increased over the years, indicating that the animals are becoming accustomed to them.[4]

The Sawback Range

The Sawbacks are a 15 kilometre long range composed of tilted strata that has eroded such that it has a distinct sawtooth configuration. This is a sort of hybrid between the dogtooth form (Mount Louis) and the dip-slope form (Mount Rundle). The range was named by Hector.

The southern tip of the Sawbacks is Mount Cory (2,802 m), named for William Wallace Cory, who was Deputy Minister of the Interior from 1905 to 1930. Its claim to fame is a cave called Hole in the Wall that is visible on its west-facing cliffs. The cave, like Rat's Nest on Grotto, is evidence

Wildlife Crossing Structures

Just after the Sunshine turnoff, you encounter the first of the wildlife overpasses that we discussed in Chapter 12. The use of these structures by animals has been heavily studied. Even the time of day that animals tend to cross has been documented (moose, elk, deer, wolves, and bears use them

The Sawbacks

of the effect of glaciers that filled the valley 70,000 years ago. Actually, the term "cave" is a bit grandiose for this erosional feature, because it doesn't go back very far into the mountain. Hector commented on it in his journals.

Cockscomb Mountain and The Finger are the next named peaks along the Sawback Range. Cockscomb (2,776 m) is the second-highest point along the range, and is named for its shape. The Finger (2,545 m) protrudes dramatically from the northwest side of Cockscomb. It was named by Lawrence Grassi in 1935 and became the official name in 1967. This spire-like feature is most clearly seen just after the Sunshine turnoff and after the first wildlife overpass. It is referred to in Earle Birney's poignant poem "David," which ponders a difficult ethical decision resulting from a climbing tragedy. This poem is well worth tracking down in order to read it.

Next is Mount Ishbel (2,908 m), the highest point in the range and the last significant peak visible before the Sawbacks are hidden behind Castle Mountain. The name Ishbel is attributed both to the daughter of Prime Minister Ramsay MacDonald of Britain and to Ishbel Maria Marjoribanks, daughter of the first Lord Tweedsmuir, whose husband, the Earl of Aberdeen, became a Governor General.

Facing Page:
Larch trees in the fall

The Finger and Cockscomb (under cloud)

Redearth Creek

This creek to the west of the highway was formerly known as Vermilion Creek. It was renamed by George Dawson in order to avoid confusion with the Vermilion River, which is in the next valley to the north. Both were named for the pigment that the Indians extracted from the sites. The *Ktunaxa* were particularly associated with the extraction of ochre, which they processed by heating it to create iron oxide, a strong red pigment. They traded this pigment with other tribes.

In interviews with George McLean, Maurice Barbeau recorded some of the beliefs that the Stoney Nakoda held about the site along the Vermilion River where they collected the ochre: "The old people thought that mud, red paint, was medicine. We still use it as a medicine. I heard it myself that they know when there are some spirits around there, at Vermilion Springs. We have been told, if ever we go to this place and get some of this mud, to drop some gifts into this spring… If we take this red earth, it will appear to have life. When we want to decorate someone, or to give a sign of peace, it will seem to give life to it. We don't know what kind of spirit is in there. Some saw things or could hear singing. It sounded like a flute, an Indian flute, a whistle, and singing. And it talks, but we can never see anything."[5] The Stoney name for Redearth Creek is *Wîsna eyagubi* or "ochre creek".

This is also the route Bill Petyo took to the site where he found talc deposits just over the provincial boundary in BC. He filed for the right to mine but was told that no access road would be permitted under the new National Park Act. Peyto sold his claim to the National Talc Company, (Natalco) but the latter's managers were likewise told that they could not do any development within the park for access. However, during the Second World War the demand for talc soared (it was used as insulation in electrical equipment) and the company was allowed to built a road along Redearth Creek to do a limited amount of mining in this valley. A bridge was constructed over the Bow River to the CPR siding at Massive. It was removed when the Trans-Canada Highway was put through the area. The mines were near the appropriately named Talc Lake, now in Kootenay Park. It is still marked as Natalco Lake on some maps.

Tree ID — Alpine Larch

One of the delights of fall in the Rockies is when the Alpine Larch trees (*Larix lyalli*) turn gold and the high slopes are swathed with their gleaming hues. Although they are a conifer (they have cones), these trees shed their needles for the winter. In the spring, the soft, pale green of the new needles is almost as delightful as their flashier fall wardrobe.

Larch seldom exceed 15 metres in height, and their branches are covered with bulbous needle bases. From 10 to 40 needles of about 2.5 centimetres spring from each base. The trees have a scaly grey bark.

There are two species of larch in Alberta (the Tamarack or American Larch is found farther north), but this is the only one that thrives in the high subalpine zone, above 1,800 metres.

Larix lyalli was named after the Scottish surgeon and naturalist David Lyall.

Castle Mountain, the cirque, Stuart Knob, and Helena Ridge

The Cirque on Castle Mountain and Television Peak

If you look ahead in the section of the Trans-Canada after Redearth Creek, you will find yourself looking right into the cirque on the back of Castle Mountain. A cirque is a valley high on a side of a mountain that has been scooped out by a glacier. It usually has a round, basin-like shape and may contain a little lake called a tarn. The tarn in the cirque on Castle is descriptively called Rockbound Lake, and it is a lovely spot located in the open valley. To the northeast is Helena Ridge (2,862 m). It is named after the wife of Charles Walcott, a geologist who worked in the area in the early part of the last century. Stuart, whose name is bestowed on Stuart Knob (2,849 m) on the ridge to the north, was the Walcotts' son.

Copper Mountain — 2,795 m and Silver City

A couple of years before the railway was built through this section of the Rocky Mountains, a Stoney Indian named Gold Seeker is said to have shown a piece of ore to Joe Healy and explained that it had come from the area around Castle Mountain. Healy reputedly took a sample to Fort Benton, Montana, for assay, then returned to stake a claim. Other prospectors soon followed, and by the time the railway came through in 1883 a town was growing rapidly in the valley. The CPR may have encouraged the rumours of riches to be had in order to encourage men to travel west on the new railway. There was a lot of talk about great deposits of copper and even silver. (The latter turned out to be lead sulphite.) By December 1883, there were 175 buildings at the site and about 350 men living there. Hotels, a pool hall, stores, and boarding houses were built. Mail service came from Banff by horse.

As the town grew rapidly, the NWMP decided it would be wise to station some men there. These were prohibition days, but miners will always find a source of something to drink. A party at the shack owned by Jack Currie was informed that the place was about to be raided. "Jack tried to persuade his guests to leave but met with little success. Seeing stronger

Silver City, 1887, Glenbow NA 1753-28

means of persuasion were needed, Jack placed a carton of dynamite he just happened to have on top of a hot kitchen stove. Needless to say, his guests beat a hasty retreat. Jack then hid the whiskey and, when the police showed up, they found him fast asleep, his snores practically shaking the walls of his flimsy shack."[6]

Healy established the first mine, called the "Homestake," and started selling shares to eager investors. He would display his rock samples and talk of the great potential of the area. "Healy…was not at all particular, it was said, in making sure that the specimens he showed interested parties were

from Montana or Castle Mountain, which was at Silver City. Many old-time settlers still hold, uncherished and unsaleable, those shares they purchased during that mining fever that raged in Calgary and the small towns of the West during the next year or two."[7] Two other shafts were tunnelled into the mountains – "Queen of the Hill" on the slopes of Castle Mountain and the "Alberta Mine" on Copper Mountain, but neither proved very productive. Rumours spread that the site had probably been salted. Men started to cut their losses and leave town.

By 1886, the town had shrunk back to almost nothing and many of the buildings had been moved to Banff. But one old-timer stayed on. Joe Smith had come out from Montreal with the CPR, arriving in Silver City in 1883 with the railway crew. He had run a rooming house and various services for miners during the peak of the craze.

Everyone loved old Joe, and lots of folk made a point of keeping an eye on how he was doing on his own in the deserted town. The parks management turned a blind eye to his activities, and Joe managed to continue hunting and trapping for many years. But eventually his vision failed and he could no longer cope with his solitary life. His friends talked him into "paying a short visit" to the Lacombe Home in Calgary, and he stayed on there until he died in 1937. He had lived for more than 50 years in Silver City below Copper Mountain.

The Internment Camp at Castle Mountain

Over the years there were a few developments around the base of Castle Mountain. The CPR put up a construction camp in the area, and in the early 1900s there was a ranch operating in the vicinity. But the saddest bit of the history of this area involves an internment camp that was set up here. During the First World War, there was a growing sense of concern about "enemy aliens" within Canada's borders. People of German or Austro-Hungarian descent – many of whom had been recruited to come to Canada as homesteaders and labourers – were now seen as a danger to the nation. Many of them were incarcerated. In the tense atmosphere of the time, they often found themselves unemployed, and

Joe Smith, ca. 1930s, Glenbow NA-163-1

many gathered in cities as they looked for jobs. The danger perceived in their congregating together and their often poor language skills all contributed to a feeling of potential threat.

This situation meshed rather nicely with the need for cheap labour to help put a road through to Lake Louise, which was definitely on the national park agenda at the time. This road had been mandated for completion, but the funding for the project had dried up. J. B. Harkin began to wonder if these two problems could be put together for a beneficial outcome. He proposed to Ottawa that a camp be set up to employ (involuntarily, of course) these people and keep work on the road moving forward.

Most of the men who ended up in the camp between Castle Mountain and Pilot Mountain were of Ukrainian origin. The first group arrived in June 1915, and within a month there were 200 men in an enclosed and guarded tent town. At its peak, 600 men were put to work here. They were given pickaxes and shovels and sent to work under guard. The expectation was that they would complete at least 12 miles (19 kilometres) of road over the summer.

The Hague Conventions signed before the First World War – which were among the first international agreements on war and war crimes – were quite clear in distinguishing between enemy combatants and non-combatants in terms of incarceration. The conventions provided for prisoners to work, but only toward their own upkeep. According to international law, it was allowable to demand labour of this nature from those who were interned as long as the work was not related to the war effort, was of a reasonable level of demand, and fair compensation was paid to the internees. The men at the Castle were paid 25 cents a day and worked six days a week.

The plan was to complete the stretch of road from Castle Mountain to Laggan (Lake Louise). By the end of the first summer, the internees had cleared four

Castle Mountain Internment Camp, 1915, Glenbow NA-1870-18

miles (8 kilometres) and gravelled only one. They were moved out of their tent facilities to Banff for the winter, where they were housed in rough dormitories that had been built for construction workers near the Cave and Basin. There they worked on clearing the recreation grounds on the southwest side of the river, building a bridge over the Spray River, and other local tasks.

The work on the road west from Castle Mountain resumed the next summer, but only another four miles was completed. Complaints about inadequate food and poor treatment escalated over the two years and a number of internees managed to escape. In August 1916, a man was shot during an escape attempt.

Gradually, those men who were determined to be of lower risk were released and others were transferred to other camps. The Castle Mountain Camp was discontinued by the following summer and the remaining 47 men sent elsewhere. The mountains, which inspire feelings of liberation and national pride for so many Canadians, had represented just the opposite to a group of the country's early immigrants. In 1994, a monument was erected in recognition of this unfortunate piece of Canadian history.

A road was finally completed from this point to Lake Louise in 1920. This was an additional four years after the internees at the Castle Mountain Camp completed their stretch of eight miles.

As of 2010, the push is on to finish twinning this section, with a completion date expected in 2011. After careful evaluation of the success of the wildlife overpass structures that were built in the Banff to Castle Junction section, larger overpasses are being installed in this 82 kilometre section of highway to provide for animal movement.

The Windermere Highway

This point is the junction with another significant route. The highway that connects southward into the Columbia Valley, Highway 93, intersects with the Trans-Canada Highway below Castle Mountain. Hector followed this route on his first trip through the Rockies.

The idea for a road that would go through Vermilion Pass and connect to the Columbia Valley was originally proposed in 1911 by Randolf Bruce, a resident of Invermere who had worked for the CPR. He was aware of the tourism opportunities that would derive from a connection from Rocky Mountains National Park to the Windermere area. The CPR also saw benefits in linking its line to the new railway line through the Crow's Nest Pass.

At first, no agreement could be reached between the dominion and provincial governments regarding such a road. However, in 1916 Bruce came up with an idea for relieving the province of the financial burden of building the road. He proposed that a strip of land adjoining the highway be transferred to the dominion for a national park in exchange for the feds taking on the responsibility for the highway's construction costs. An agreement was reached in 1919, and Kootenay National Park came into being in 1920. It covered a 10 mile-wide swath spanning the area around the highway.

The Mountains to the West at Castle Junction

Storm Mountain (3,161 m) is located on the south side of the Windermere Highway. It is well named – as those who drive this highway with any frequency know. The weather may be quite fair in the Bow Valley, but as the highway climbs up around this mountain's shoulders it often deteriorates. And it may be snowing at Vermilion Pass, only about another 150 metres higher up.

George Dawson is said to have named this peak. Confusingly, another peak about 100 kilometres away in the Kananaskis has the same name. It is frowned upon to have two mountains in such proximity with the same title, as I am sure you recall from Chapter 5…

Castle Mountain from the Banff – Windermere highway, 1923-24, W.J. Bolton/Canada. Dept. of Manpower and Immigration/ Library and Archives Canada / PA-031345

Top left: Mount Ball and Storm Mountain

Top right: Mount Whymper

Middle: right: Boom Mountain, Chimney Peak to its right

Bottom right: Mount Bell (the ridge right of centre, not the bell-shaped ridge left of centre)

To the north of the Windermere Highway is Boom Mountain (2,760 m). There are two theories as to the origin of this name. One suggestion comes from the driftwood that collects in Boom Lake, which looks like a lumberman's log boom. Others claim that the boom of the avalanches that bring the logs down off the slopes is the inspiration.

Mount Whymper (2,845 m), farther to the south along the Windermere Highway, is named after Edmund Whymper, who in 1865 made the famous first ascent of the Matterhorn in the Swiss Alps. He visited Canada in 1901 and – at the age of 61 – made the first ascent of the peak now named after him. Hector had originally named this peak Mount Lefroy, after an astronomer. But now the name Lefroy has somehow been applied to a peak behind Lake Louise, so this peak retained the name of the first man on its summit.

Directly west of both Whymper and Boom is Chimney Peak (3,001 m). The glacier on its slopes is the source of the Vermilion River. The name comes from the rock crack, or "chimney," that is part of the route first used to attain its summit.

Mount Bell (2,910 m) was named after one of the founders of the Alpine Club of Canada. It is part of a high ridge that goes behind Taylor Lake and connects to Panorama Ridge.

Panorama Ridge (2,824 m) is separated from Mount Bell by Taylor Pass. On the western side, it has a splendid view over Consolation Valley and the Valley of the Ten Peaks - likely the reason for its name.

Wildlife Spotting: Nesting Ospreys

For many years, a pair of ospreys (*Pandion haliaetus*) have raised a family in their huge nest on the bridge over the Bow River, between the Trans-Canada Highway and the Bow Valley Parkway. These birds pair up for life and return year after year to the same nest site. They favour high platforms (often power poles) near water – so the bridge is regarded as prime real estate for these fish hawks. They prey almost exclusively on fish, and watching them dive toward the water, swinging their taloned feet forward to grasp the fish, is a spectacular site. Their feet are covered with sharp scales that help them to grasp their slippery catch. Once back in the air, they will manoeuvre the fish around so that it travels head-forward in order to improve the aerodynamics as the bird carries its catch back to the nest.

Ospreys have very distinctive markings that make them easy to identify. They are dark on top (although immature birds less so) and have white underparts and a white head with a dramatic black eye stripe. The underwing has a distinctive dark spot at the wrist. The female may be identified by the soft mottled brown "bib" around her neck. Ospreys are about a metre long from beak to tail, with a wingspan of 130 to 180 centimetres.

The osprey population experienced an alarming decline in the mid-1900s, due to shooting, habitat loss, and the effect of pesticides. The prohibition since the early 1970s on the use of DDT has helped the species recover, and osprey numbers have stabilized in Alberta. These birds are in their northern breeding habitats from about March to September, then head south to the coasts of California, Florida, and on down as far as Central America.

Osprey are quite vocal birds, and you can hear their *kyew kyew kyew* call around the nest. They are also quite sensitive to disturbance, so if you stop to have a look, stay well back from the nest area (you can't see much up close and below, anyway). A pair of binoculars is a great help.

Ospreys on nest

Tree ID: Lodgepole Pine

Lodgepole Pine

Mountain Pine Beetle infestation, Dion Manastyrski

Facing page: Storm approaching Castle Mountain

The Lodgepole Pine (*Pinus contorta*) gets its name from the traditional Native American use of these strong, slender trees as the structural support for their lodges or tepees. The Latin name suggests a contorted form, which may be true of coastal varieties, but this tree grows tall (about 20 metres) and straight. They make tall, dense stands (sometimes descriptively called "dog-hair stands"), with branches restricted to the upper area of the trunk because the shade these stands create allows no growth lower down. These trees favour the lower elevations of the subalpine.

Lodgepole have hard cones with tight, flat scales. In order to release their seeds, these cones require the intense heat of a fire to open the resin that seals them closed. Thus, the practice of fire suppression in the park has resulted in stands of over-mature trees that can be vulnerable to disease and pests. Like all pines, Lodgepoles have both male and female cones on the same tree. The male cones are small and less noticeable, and generally fall off after the pollen has been released in late June or early July. You can see clouds of this thick, yellow pollen on the wind at times, and floating on the surface of bodies of water. The long needles grow in pairs about five to six centimetres in length.

The Lodgepole Pine is the provincial tree of Alberta.

Pine Beetle Problems

Since 2001, the Mountain Pine Beetle (*Dendroctonus ponderosae Hopkins*) has been invading the forests in British Columbia and Alberta. An insect about the size of a grain of rice, it can wipe out whole stands of mature pine forest within a month of infestation. Needless to say, the park, the forestry industry, and conservationists have responded with alarm. A number of management systems have been put in place, with limited success, to hold back the destruction.

The beetle kills trees by damaging their conductive tissue. Its presence infests the tree with a blue-stain fungi, and then the larvae of the beetle feed on the phloem (the innermost bark layer) of the tree. This impairs the transfer of nutrients.

The potential of a park, forested predominantly in pine, becoming a vista of dead stands of trees is a horrifying prospect to park management. What to do? Management policies specify that natural systems, such as disease or parasites, should be permitted to work their normal cycles. So should the beetle simply be left to do its dirty work?

At the same time, though, park management also has an obligation to consider the impact of its policy on adjacent land – and Alberta's Sustainable Resource Development ministry elected several years ago to make an active attempt to control the spread of the pine beetle. Pine beetles prefer mature and over-mature stands of pine – which is precisely what exists in the parks after more than 80 years of fire suppression. Thus, one of the options to control the beetle's spread was to meld it with the ongoing policy of burning as a part of the restoration of a normal ecosystem. Interestingly, there may also be a link with climate change, as prolonged cold spells were considered to have been a factor in preventing the beetle's eruption. A cold snap of -40° C for 10 days is required to kill beetle populations. So park management may be hoping for long, cold winters to assist in their beetle battle.

Active management of the Mountain Pine Beetle started in 2003, and the situation is currently described as "static."

Castle Mountain — 2,785 m

Castle Mountain was named, obviously, for its resemblance to the crenulated walls of a medieval castle, with its small, rounded teeth. Hector commented on the remarkable form of this mountain when he recorded the name in his journal. The vertical walls of reddish rock make it a very impressive presence in the valley. Indeed, it dominates the Bow Valley for a distance of more than 15 kilometres. James Hector and Robert Sutherland went around to the back of this mountain, where they hiked up to the cirque that was pointed out in Chapter 16. They marvelled at beautiful Rockbound Lake in its amphitheatre setting. Hector and Sutherland did not make it on to the summit, although there is a reasonably easy scrambling route up to it. The highest point is at the northwest end of the long ridge. But the most impressive element of the mountain is the tower on its southern end.

Amazingly, despite the obvious suitability of its present name, this mountain was renamed in 1946 to honour an American general. In a move to mark the occasion of the visit to Canada of Dwight D. Eisenhower, who had been the Supreme Commander of Allied Forces in the Second World War, this mountain was picked to bear his name. Prime Minister Mackenzie King announced the decision just as Eisenhower – who six years later was elected President of the U.S. – was to arrive in Canada. King did so without any prior discussion with Alberta. The province was horrified and responded by forming a geographical names board to review the decision – and any made in the future. It took three decades of lobbying, but the name was finally changed back in 1979. The prominent tower on the south end is still called Eisenhower Peak.

There is a second Castle Mountain farther to the south in the Rocky Mountains near Pincher Creek. Another infraction of the geographic names rule…

Geological Notes: Castle Mountain and Main Range Geology

Castle Mountain marks the transition into the Main Ranges. These mountains, in the heart of the Rockies, still have a southeast-to-northwest orientation, although it is much less regular and thus less evident than in the Front Ranges. The organized Trellis Drainage pattern no longer applies. Both the summits and the dividing valleys are higher, so it is cooler and wetter, and thus there are more glaciers.

The shape of this mountain is different from the steeply slanted Front Range structures we have been observing. Castle Mountain is an example of a form known as a "castellated mountain," which is characterized by horizontal layers with more vertical, towering sides. The layers of rock have remained more intact, even though they have still been pushed a distance of about 40 kilometres toward the northeast (more than 100 million years ago). The older rock was thrust up and over the younger rock by the Castle Mountain Thrust (which lies at the base of the cliffs on Castle).

Geological diagram of Castle Mountain

Here, instead of being stacked up in sequential inclined sections side by side, as the Front Ranges were, these layer sandwiches (in this case Pika/Eldon/Stephen/Cathedral) came to rest nearly horizontally over one another. The top of the sandwich is a weathered remnant of the Pika layer, a shaley limestone, and dolomite. Below this is the very hard Eldon limestone – which. as you can see, remains a tough, vertical cliff as long it is supported below. However, it is supported by a thin, softer shale layer of the Stephen Formation, which weathers more readily and has resulted in the step back above the lower cliffs. These bottom cliffs are again a harder limestone and dolomite – more resistant to erosion and thus steeper. Then the sequence is repeated as the Castle Thrust Fault is crossed and the Pika formation turns up again below.

Protection Mountain — 2,970 m

Another long ridge that parallels the Trans-Canada to the northeast, Protection Mountain was named by James Porter in 1911. The highest point, at the southeast end, is unofficially known as Television Peak because of the communications towers were once installed there.

Moraine Lake and The Valley of the Ten Peaks

Moraine Lake is a jewel of a lake – but it is sadly misnamed. The pile of rock rubble that borders the lake to the northeast is not a moraine at all (that is, a rock dam pushed up by a glacier). It is simply a pile of rock rubble from a landslide off Mount Babel. This rubble was first sighted by Walter Wilcox in 1893 while he and Samuel Allen were waging their campaign to climb Mount Temple. (See the next item.) Wilcox was not impressed by his first view of the valley, however, and dubbed it Desolation Valley. Happily, that name did not stick.

The western end of the valley is enclosed by the Valley of the Ten Peaks. Wilcox and his companions named all of them by using the Stoney words for the numbers 1 through 10: Mount Heejee *(Îyâ Wazi)*, Mount Norn *(Îyâ Num)*, Mount Ymanee *(Îyâ Yamnî)*, Mount Tonsa *(Îyâ Ktûtha)*, Mount Sapta *(Îyâ Thaptâ)*, Mount Shappee *(Îyâ Sakpe)*, Mount Sagowa *(Îyâ Sagûwî)*, Mount Saknowa *(Îyâ Sahrnorh)*, Mount Neptuak *(Îyâ Nâmchirhîk)*, and Mount Wenkchemna *(Îyâ Wîkchemnâ)*. All have since been renamed, except Sapta, Neptuak, and Wenkchemna.

A trail was cut to the lake by Tom Wilson in 1900. This was expanded by the CPR in 1902, which boosted traffic to the lake. A lodge was built by the CPR at Moraine Lake in 1912, and the road was improved for cars in the early 1920s. The original building was replaced in 1923, and the facility was sold into private hands in 1958. The old buildings were replaced again in 1993. The lodge is open only during the summer.

Protection Mountain

Mount Temple
from Highway 93

Mount Temple — 3,543 m

This peak is thought to have originally been called Mount Lefroy by George Dawson in the 1880s, but it was corrected to Temple in 1884. (The name Lefroy really got bounced around – remember Mount Whymper?) Temple is the highest peak in the Lake Louise area, and it dominates the valley to the south of the lake. You can see it from a great distance as you approach along the Bow Valley. Walter Wilcox observed that: "One who travels west from Banff up the valley of the Bow will see in front of him, shortly after leaving Cascade Siding, a tall helmet-shaped peak rising in a series of inaccessible cliffs to a snow tipped summit. But it is not until Laggan [Lake Louise] is reached, and the western face of the peak is seen – now to the southeast – that its height or beauty is adequately realized, although from all points it dominates the landscape."[2]

Temple was not named in reference to a religious edifice, but after Sir Richard Temple, who led the first British Association trip to the Rockies in 1884.

This massive peak offers quite a different appearance from various locations. It is probably most impressive seen from Lake Louise, where its great north face looms above the lake. It was first climbed in 1894 by Walter Wilcox, Samuel Allen, and L. F. Frissel – the first ascent of a peak in the Canadian Rockies higher than 11,000 feet. Wilcox recalled the moment by writing: "Many a hearty cheer rent the thin air as our little party of three reached the summit, for we were standing where no man had ever stood before, and, if I mistake not, at the highest altitude yet reached in North America north of the United States boundary."[3]

The first ascent was via the southeast ridge, now a popular and not too difficult route that some even refer to as "the tourist route." But Temple offers plenty of highly challenging routes as well. The north face was not climbed until 1969, and the route up the east ridge is considered one of the 50 classic climbs in North America.[4]

Mount Temple was the site of one of the Rockies' saddest climbing tragedies. In 1955, a group of 18 boys from the Wilderness Club of Philadelphia came to the area for an adventurous holiday. They set off to climb Temple by the southeast ridge, led by their trip organizer, William Oeser. He was not familiar with the route, and the party was ill-prepared, with only light clothing and poor footwear. At about 2,600 metres, Oeser and five of the boys fell behind. The rest of the party continued ahead, crossing snow slopes in spite of the sound of avalanches booming down nearby. By the time they reached 2,900 metres, it had become clear to them that they would not make the summit and that they must turn back. So they began their retreat.

The boys tied themselves together with a series of manila ropes that they chained together, and they started to work their way down. But as they descended, the party was hit by an avalanche. The rope broke and 10 of the boys were swept down the mountain, leaving the other boys perched precariously on the snow slope. One of these lads carried one of the few ice axes in the party, and he was able to dig it in and secure them.

The avalanche stopped about 100 metres down the slope – just above a large cliff. Amazingly, one 13-year-old boy was unhurt. Another boy was not buried, but had a serious head wound. Another had a broken leg. The remaining boys were hidden under the snow.

The uninjured boy headed down to get help while the boys clinging to the slope above carefully made their way down the mountain. Another boy was located and dug out.

Park officials finally learned of the disaster at about 5 p.m. The wardens set off for the site immediately and a larger rescue party was assembled and sent in, arriving in the dark. On their way in, they met Warden Gilstrof struggling out with one of the boys on his back. He turned over his injured charge and immediately turned around to lead the rescuers back to the accident scene. They arrived there at midnight. All the still missing boys were located – but, sadly, all of them had died. Seven young men lost their lives in this terrible event.

Paradise Valley

The valley next in line to the west, to the north of Mount Temple, is known as Paradise Valley. Wilcox and crew discovered it as well, when they were making an attempt to climb Mount Aberdeen in 1894. They originally called it *Wathte*, which is Stoney for "beautiful."

Wildlife Spotting: More Furry Little Critters – The Squirrel Family

We met our first ground squirrels not far out of Calgary – remember the discussion about gophers/Richardson's ground squirrels? There are a lot more of this family – *Sciuridae* – in the mountains. The Columbian ground squirrel (*Spermophilus columbianus*) looks much like the Richardson's, and is about the same size, with a tawny coat and reddish undersides. But it lives only at higher elevations than the Richardson's does. Columbian ground squirrels live in small colonies, but hibernate singly in separate chambers .

Mount Temple from the north

The Golden-mantled ground squirrel (*Spermophilus lateralis*) is slightly smaller, but has a fancier coat. Over their grey-brown pelt, two white stripes run down their back from the neck to the hips, with black edges. Their belly is cream coloured, which results in these animals frequently being called chipmunks. But they have some distinct differences. The most obvious is their size – these guys are 30 centimetres long, while the diminutive chipmunk is only 22 centimetres. Golden-mantled ground squirrels have two white stripes, while true chipmunks have five, with a distinct central line that extends forward over their head.

Ground squirrels live in groups. But the chipmunk (genus Tamias, meaning "storer" in Greek) is solitary, with a smaller burrow surrounded by a territory where it is the dominant animal. Chipmunks hold their tails straight up, like a flagpole, while ground squirrels tend to hold theirs in a low position. If you want to get really specific about your chipmunks, there are three distinct types in the Rockies: the Least (*Eutamias minimus*), which likes drier, lower terrain; the Yellow pine (*Eutamius amoenus*); and the Red-tailed (*Eutamius ruficaudus*).

Finally, the Red squirrel (*Tamiasciurus hudsonicus*) is hard to miss, as they scold intruders from the safety of nearby trees. The ones that live in the Rockies are really more brown than red. They are about 31 centimetres long,

including their ever-active bushy tail. Red squirrels remain active all winter – unlike their cousins, which sleep through the cold months.

Although Red squirrels are most frequently seen in trees, they nest in burrows in the ground and accumulate piles of cones near their tunnel, which they emerge to eat on milder days. You may observe their middens – mounds of discarded cone scales around the burrow. They also dine on berries, mushrooms, insects, and even birds' eggs.

Bubonic Plague in Alberta

We usually think of bubonic plague as something only in history books. But the bacterium that causes the plague, *Yersinia pestis*, is still around. We also associate the disease with rats, and they are indeed the most common vector,. Infections of plague from rats have not occurred in North America for almost a century. But other rodents can carry the infected fleas that bring about this disease, and this has been found to be the case with some ground squirrels. Scientists observed high death rates in ground squirrels in parts of the United States and confirmed that there were a few human cases of plague resulting from contact, mainly with California ground squirrels. Plague bacterium have been found on some ground squirrels in Alberta, although this remains rare and is certainly not a serious threat. But you might want to think about this before letting that cute critter begging for peanuts climb up your pant leg.

Top left: Columbian ground squirrel, D. Ditchburn

Middle left: Golden-mantled ground squirrel

Lower left: Chipmunk, D. Ditchburn

Top right: Red squirrel, D. Ditchburn

Chapter 18 - The Lake Louise Area

"Lake Louise, forty miles west of Banff, is a place familiar to all Canadians and most Americans even though they have never visited it, for it is surely the most photographed beauty-spot on the continent and it looks exactly like its photographs." [1]

An area of 55 square miles (142 square kilometres) around Lake Louise was made into Lake Louise Forzest Park in 1892. Only in 1902 did it become part of Rocky Mountains Park. The CPR had arrived at this point in 1883, and the first track that would become a wagon road and later a highway was laid in 1887. For a long time, there was little traffic coming this far down the Bow Valley. But once the beauty of the area became appreciated by the public, people started flocking to the Lake Louise area to take in the natural wonders and climb the peaks.

The Mountains to the West of the Trans-Canada Highway

As you approach the intersection for Lake Louise, the cluster of mountains to the southwest of the Trans-Canada changes rapidly, according to your viewpoint. The view shown here is from the overpass. Some of the peaks are quite easy to identify. Saddle Peak (2,437 m) looks exactly like the back of a saddle. It was named by Samuel Allen (more on him below) in 1894. Here again, the "no duplicate names" rule of the Geographical Names Board is broken – there are three Saddle Peaks in Alberta (another one was mentioned in Chapter 5). So much for rules...

The pass that connects Saddle Mountain to its neighbour, Fairview, is known as The Saddleback. A teahouse was built there in the 1920s, but the lack of water made it short-lived. It is an easy hike up and offers a terrific view of Mount Temple.

Fairview Mountain (2,744 m) was first called Goat Peak by Walter Wilcox and Samuel Allen, who named it when

Mount Victoria from the Trans-Canada

they explored this region in 1894. Fairview is now its official name. This rather unprepossessing peak was viewed as a real point of beauty by some of the early travellers. Dr. Charles Walcott, a geologist who was in this area in the early 1900s, went so far as to say that this peak is "worth a journey across the continent to see"![2] But Fairview does hold a valuable position as a landmark in the Bow Valley.

In his classic book, Monroe Thorington speaks fondly of his hikes up the mountain: "A small peak as a rule is the best viewpoint because there is still something left to look up to… And so it is with Fairview. Year after year we have come back to it; perhaps as a convenient training walk, but more likely on account of the sheer beauty with which it is surrounded."[3] From the Saddleback, it is indeed pleasant to continue to Fairview's summit for the splendid vista.

Just peeking (peaking?) over Saddle Mountain is Mount Sheol (2,779 m). Sheol is the Hebraic name for hell, and this peak was so dubbed by Samuel Allen for its brooding demeanour. I find it rather delightful that Sheol looks down over Paradise (Valley).

Haddo Peak (3,070 m) is high enough that it also makes an appearance between Saddle Mountain and Fairview. It was named for Lord Haddo, eighth Earl of Aberdeen. For the first half of summer, Haddo holds a snow field on its shoulder, known as the "Haddo Spot." Sheol and Haddo are along a ridge system that connects to Mount Aberdeen, which is not visible from this vantage.

Mount Victoria, which lies behind Lake Louise, is just visible from the Trans-Canada, but we won't get distracted by that beautiful peak just yet. Farther to the northwest, two peaks are visible that border Lake Louise on the other shore. Mount St. Piran (2,649 m) was named for the patron saint of Cornwall, England. This was the birthplace of the first manager of the chalet at Lake Louise. Behind it is Mount Niblock (2,976 m), named after John Niblock, a superintendent for the CPR. Just to the left is Mount Whyte, named for a Vice-President of the CPR.

Lake Louise

One day, when Tom Wilson was camped in the Bow Valley just northwest of Mount Temple, he was puzzled by a booming sound he kept hearing. He mentioned it to Edwin Hunter, the Stoney Indian accompanying him. (Hunter, a.k.a. Gold Seeker, had shown Bill Peyto the ore sample.) Hunter explained that the noise came from avalanches crashing down in a valley nearby. He called the place *Ho run num nay*, meaning "lake of little fishes." Wilson convinced Hunter to show him this place, so they hiked up through the forest and came out of the trees to see the green water of the lake spread out in front of them. Wilson was awestruck. He named this breathtaking body of water Emerald Lake.

Some time later, Wilson returned to the lake and was amazed to see that it was no longer green – it had turned a beautiful blue. He is said to have then renamed the lake after the young lady who accompanied him that day, whose name was Louise. She is variously said to have been the daughter of Sir Richard Temple, Pollock, Markham, Edwards… In other words, we don't know. Officially, the lake is said to have been named after Princess Louise Caroline Alberta, the sixth child of Queen Victoria and Prince Albert and the wife of the Marquis of Lorne. Wilson later wrote to park Superintendent J. Harkin to object to the association: "What did Princess Louise ever do for Canada, to have her name on the most beautiful spot in Canada…? Marquis Forlorn!"[4] Wilson later named a lovely lake farther to the west Emerald Lake.

Mount Victoria and Mount Lefroy

The southwest end of Lake Louise is beautifully framed by Mount Victoria (3,464 m), with its cap of ice sparkling in the sun. Yes, it is named for the monarch. But it had previously been named Mount Green after Rev. William Spotswood Green, a member of the British Alpine Club who visited the Rockies in 1888. After visiting the lake, Green is said to have had an enthusiastic discussion with Van Horne of the CPR about the great tourism potential that the location offered.

Victoria is made up of a long ridge with three summits, the centre one the highest. The glacier probably filled the entire valley and carved out the basin that is now the lake about 25,000 years ago. Evidence of its passing is left in the form of striations marked in the rock, and in the moraines around the edges and at the end of the valley. The Chateau Lake Louise sits on the terminal moraine of this great glacier.

A high pass, now named Abbot Pass, separates Mount Victoria from the other peak that frames the end of the lake. There is considerable confusion about the naming of Mount Lefroy (3,234 m), and this name was applied to various other peaks (including Victoria) before it was determined that this is the peak that would officially bear the name. General Sir John Henry Lefroy was an astronomer who worked all across Canada in the 1840s making observations used for mapping. His focus was particularly on magnetic declination, and his work was instrumental in locating the magnetic north pole.

Lefroy had long been the target for mountaineers keen to do first ascents around Lake Louise. In 1884, it was almost conquered by Walter Wilcox, Louis Frissel, and Wandell Henderson, but they came very close to disaster in their failed attempt. Frissel, nearing the top of the mountain, took a hold on a loose rock that gave way, sending him tumbling off the wall. Although he was caught by the rope, he sustained a head injury. Dangling from the rope, Frissel was unable to help himself, and the remaining pair had to lower him to a secure place. Once they got Frissel to a safe spot, Wilcox went down for help, and they all lived to climb again.

Then, in 1896, Lefroy became the site of the first climbing fatality in the Canadian Rockies. Philip Stanley Abbot of Boston, a member of the Appalachian Mountain Club and an experienced climber, had earlier made two unsuccessful attempts on this peak together with Charles Fay and Charles Thompson. They returned in 1896, determined to reach the summit that year. They ascended the pass between Victoria and Lefroy – a treacherous narrow gulley named the Death Trap because of the constant rockfall that careens down it. The party safely made the pass and, figuring that they were past the area of greatest risk, climbed upward and reached a steep and difficult section that offered no view ahead. Abbot went ahead and let the others know that he was making his way along a cleft that looked like it would take him through.

Falling rock forced the remaining party to unrope and move to a more sheltered position. There, they asked Abbot whether they should try another route, but he assured them that he had a good lead and could proceed. And with that, they were startled by Abbot's form hurtling past them down the cliff face. He fell and rolled about 300 metres onto a narrow ledge. It took three hours for the remaining party to make their way down to where he lay. To their horror, they found that Abbot was still alive, despite a terrible head wound. He died as Fay and Thompson attempted to carry him down.

The pass between Lefroy and Victoria was named for Abbot, and a mountaineering hut of the same name was built there.

The year after the accident, a memorial climb was organized on Mount Lefroy. Professor Charles Fay (who had been on the fateful climb the previous year), together with J. Norman Collie, H. B. Dixon, and Swiss guide Peter Sarbach, summited Lefroy and went on to do a first ascent of Mount Victoria the next day.

Why is Lake Louise so Green – or Blue – or...?

In her book "Indian Legends of Canada," E. Clark recounts a story told to her about Lake Louise. She does not specify which tribe the story comes from:

"Long, long ago, when the world was very young, giants lived in this country. A chief of the giants was a famous hunter. Many large game animals he killed with his bow and arrows. Many birds and small game animals he caught in his traps. But he was never satisfied; always he wanted more.

"One day, as he stood watching a rainbow, he had an idea: he would get the rainbow and from it he would make a giant bow for hunting. The more he watched, the more he wanted the rainbow. With it he could be a truly great hunter.

"So he climbed the tallest tree on the highest mountain, reached up to the sky with his long arms, and tore the rainbow from its place. But when he seized it, the colours disappeared. The bow in his hands was colourless.

"Angrily the giant threw the rainbow against the nearest mountain-top, a peak overlooking the lake. There the bow broke into pieces and the pieces rolled on down into the water. At the bottom of the lake the fragments regained their colours, and the colours spread through the water.

"After a while the spirit-power in the sky made the smaller bow which we still see after a rain. Sometimes, even today, the colours of the rainbow which was shattered by the giant-chief may be seen at sunrise in the water of the lake we now call Lake Louise."[5]

Rupert Brooke, an English poet, visited Lake Louise in 1916 and described the water as only a poet could: "In the lake, ever-changing, is Beauty herself, as nearly visible to mortal eyes as she may ever be. The water, beyond the flowers, is green, always a different green. Sometimes it is tranquil, glassy, shot with blue, of a peacock tint. Then a little wind awakes in the distance, and ruffles the surface, yard by yard, covering it with a myriad tiny wrinkles, till half the lake is milky emerald, while the rest still sleeps. And, at length, the whole is astir, and the sun catches it, and Lake Louise is a web of laughter, the opal distillation of all the buds of all the spring."[6]

That is the creative response to the colour – now for the science… The colour we see any object to be is the result of which part of the colour spectrum of light the object absorbs, and which it reflects. A red apple absorbs all but the longer wavelength part of the spectrum – the red light – and that is reflected back to our eyes. Thus we see the apple as red.

Pure, clear water is transparent, and thus absorbs the full range of the light spectrum and reflects nothing back to the viewer. So we see clear water as colourless. But the water in the glacially fed mountain lakes is not pure. It carries a load of tiny particles, or silt, which are tiny bits of rock ground up by the glacier. These particles are extremely minute – hence their name "rock flour." Smaller particles reflect the shorter wavelengths of light – that is, the blue and green end of the spectrum. And that is why we see the glacial water as blue or green.

The colour of Lake Louise varies with the season. This depends on how charged the water is with these particles. In the heat of the summer, when the glaciers are melting and streaming down into the lake, there are more particles in the water, and that alters the hue. In fact, viewed from above, one can even see variations in the lak colour at one time, as the particles settle and are affected by currents.

Facing page: Lake Louise and Mount Victoria (highest summit in the centre); to the right, Mount Collie, Pope's Peak and Mount Whyte (with no snow)

Lake Louise Chalet before 1893, Glenbow NA-1804-1

The Chalet at Lake Louise, no date, William James Topley/
Library and Archives Canada / PA-009452

Chateau Lake Louise

The CPR was quick to see the potential of this beauty spot. The first accommodation was built in 1890 – merely a simple log building on the edge of the lake.

The first log structure burned down in 1893 and was rebuilt on a larger scale. In 1900, two wings were added, designed by B.C. architect Francis Mawson Rattenbury. A concrete wing was added in 1912, the work of Walter Painter, which enclosed a grand dining room that looked out over the lake. Then, in 1924, fire struck again, burning down Rattenbury's work and leaving only the concrete wing standing.

Like a phoenix from the ashes, the hotel rose again. In 1925, a second wing was added to the surviving one – a grand eight-story structure that cultivated the baronial or chateau style. There were further expansions in the 1970s, and in 1983 the Chateau Lake Louise remained open through the winter for the first time. A conference centre was added in 2003.

In the early days, transport up the hill from the train station presented a problem. It was a long and demanding trip by carriage, and the horses could take only light loads. In 1912, a narrow-gauge tram was built that ran until 1930. The first road was constructed in 1917, as the pressure of growing auto tourism generated more access roads in the mountains. The old tram line is now a popular cross-country ski trail.

Wartime Experiments at Lake Louise

The Chateau Lake Louise was closed down for a number of years during the Second World War due to rationing and a steep decline in tourism. But the site was put to work on highly secret experiments for the war effort.

A man named Geoffrey Pyke developed a material made of 14% sawdust and 86% ice that he proposed as a construction material for a gigantic, unsinkable aircraft carrier. The substance – called Pykrete in his honour – had a degree of strength similar to concrete, but with greater resilience and, of course, the ability to float. It had a slow melting rate because of the way the sawdust affected thermal conductivity.

The story goes that Lord Montbatten learned of the material and rushed over to tell Prime Minister Winston Churchill about it. After being told that the PM was unavailable because he was in the bath, Mountbatten exclaimed, "Perfect!" and dashed into the bathroom to drop his sample of the material into the Prime Minister's bathwater.[7]

Tests were done, under the name Project Habbakuk, at Lake Louise and Patricia Lake (near the town of Jasper). But as the war neared its end, improvements in the flying range of aircraft and the high cost of Pykrete kept this material from ever being put to use. No application has been found for it since.

Above: The Fairmont Chateau Lake Louise, 2009

Right: Canadian Pacific Railway Chateau Lake Louise, ca. 1900-25, Albertype Company/Library and Archives Canada / PA-031852

Mountaineering

The first summits to surrender to climbing boots were those scaled in the name of surveying. Some of the early surveyors became excellent mountaineers out of necessity as they worked over a span of 20 miles on either side of the CPR line through the mountains. They covered the area of what is now Banff National Park between 1886 and 1892, and many of their names have remained associated with locations in the mountains.

One of the earliest groups of recreational-climbing enthusiasts to explore the area around Lake Louise was what became known as the Lake Louise Club. In the summer of 1893, Walter Wilcox, a student at Yale University, came out to this area and ended up exploring it with Samuel Allen, who he had met in Banff. The next year the two men returned, staying in the log cabin on the shore of Lake Louise and trying to get to the top of as many peaks as possible. They were determined to climb Mount Victoria and Mount Temple, but failed to do so that summer. So they returned in 1895, when they made the failed attempt on Lefroy that ended up with Frissel being injured. But they did summit Mount Temple that year.

Even though this group of enthusiasts did not achieve all its summit dreams, they did thoroughly explore the area of Lake Louise and its surrounding valleys. They made detailed maps and are responsible for the names of a great many features. Wilcox wrote a popular book called "Camping in the Canadian Rockies" that brought the region to the attention of many eastern climbers. He returned to the Rockies many times over the years. His last trip was in 1940 at the age of 71.

As climbing became increasingly popular, and with more near-disasters in the mountains, the CPR began to consider the advantages of offering a guide service for guests. This would encourage more climbers to come to the area, and would make the sport safer once they arrived. A climbing party that had come to the area in 1897 had brought Swiss guide Peter Sarbach with it, and his presence made the possibility of reaching summits in the area seem more realistic.

The CPR invited a number of prominent climbing guides to come over from Switzerland. The first to arrive were Edouard Feuz and Christian Häsler, in 1899. These men were joined over the years by other guides — well-known names within the climbing culture, such as Rudolf Aemmer and Ernest and Walter Feuz. For the first year, they worked farther west out of Glacier House, but by 1920 a guides' centre had been built for them at Lake Louise. Their presence became a locus of mountaineering activity in the years that followed.

In his history of mountaineering in the Rockies, Bob Sanford pointed out that the presence of these experienced mountain men meant much more than safer climbing conditions: "Perhaps more importantly, they brought an attitude about mountains and a disposition towards climbing that would gradually change the way many Canadians would think about their own summits. The Swiss had a reverence for the alpine that would gradually permeate the fabric of Canadian culture. Through the Swiss guides, Canadians gradually learned the real value of the overwhelming heritage of peaks that nature left behind for hikers and climbers to enjoy."[8]

The presence of an established guiding service did not prevent a very tragic accident on Mount Victoria in 1957. A party of seven female climbers arrived from Mexico. They had heard of the fine climbing in the Canadian Rockies and brought their own guide, Eduardo Sanvicente, to lead them to the top of this spectacular peak. Sanvicente consulted with Edward Feuz, who advised him to take more guides who knew the route. But Sanvicente set off in the early morning guiding the women on his own.

The climbing party made it up through the Death Trap to Abbot Pass and stayed overnight at the hut there. In the early morning, they set off up the mountain on two ropes. But they did not take the known successful route up the ridge. Instead, they went straight up the steep snow-covered east face. Guides watching through binoculars from the Chateau were horrified to see what the group was doing. And they were even more worried when they saw that the group, after successfully summiting, was descending the same way — a choice that would prove lethal for the party.

The observers were further alarmed when they saw that the climbers had made another grave error: all them were moving at once, without any of the party providing a safe anchor to protect the others. Then the inevitable happened.

One of the climbers on the first rope fell and dragged the others with her. All three women and their guide slid down and over the cliff into the Death Trap far below. The three women on the second rope froze to the spot in terror.

Since the event had been witnessed, a rescue party was sent out immediately. But it was a long way to the end of the lake before the rescue party could even start climbing toward the Mexicans. Then there was the Death Trap to negotiate, and then far more elevation before the rescuers could reach the three terrified women. Ernest Feuz, then about 65, made it in an amazingly short time, and together with another rescuer got to the women in the late afternoon. They then took them up to the safe route on the ridge and on down to Abbot Hut. Knowing that the route below would take them directly past the crumpled bodies of their fallen companions, they did not stay at the hut to rest. Instead, the rescuers hustled the women on down the mountain in the dark so they would not see the wreckage that had been their friends. It was a terrible accident, and an amazing rescue.

Mary Schäffer Warren

After giving considerable text to the male characters that are part of the early Banff Park story, it is time to balance that out by introducing a woman who spent many years exploring the Rockies – not for any personal ambition, but because of a driving love for the wild places she found there and an intense curiosity to explore new terrain.

Born Mary Townsend Sharpies into a Quaker household in Pennsylvania in 1861, Mary grew up with the comforts of a well-off family and an education that allowed her to pursue her interests in art, literature, and natural sciences. These interests led to travels, and her travels eventually brought her to the Canadian Rockies. In 1889, she visited Glacier House in the Selkirk Mountains with the Philadelphia Academy of Natural Sciences. There she fell in love with the mountains – and met the man she would marry.

Charles Schäffer was 25 years Mary's senior, but they shared a passion for mountains and botany, and they travelled into the mountains yearly, collecting samples and doing botanical illustrations. On a trip to Lake Louise, they were provisioned

Mary Schaffer Warren, V527-NG-17

by Tom Wilson, who set them up with Joshua and William Twin as guides. These men brought their families, and they set up a camp on the shore of the lake from which the Schäffers collected flowers, Mary painted, and she and her husband enjoyed the outdoor life. After Charles' death in 1903, Mary continued their work, which resulted in her publication of "Alpine Flora of the Canadian Rockies."

That project completed, the pure love of exploration brought Mary back to the mountains year after year. Together with her friend Mollie Adams, a professor of geology at Columbia University in New York, she organized summer-

long trips guided by Tom Wilson and Billy Warren. Travelling with Charles, who had suffered from a heart condition, had meant being restricted to gentle walks. Now, Mary was free to stretch her wings, so she set out to explore further afield. Much of her and Mollie Adams' exploration took them out of Banff National Park and up into the Jasper area. They visited the Columbia Ice Fields (remember that there was no highway between Banff and Jasper until the 1930s – this was wild country) and located a lake that Mary called Chaba Imne, now known as Maligne Lake.

Mary lost her travelling companion in 1908, when Mollie died while they were in Japan. In 1913, Mary moved to Banff permanently, purchasing a home she called "Tarry-a-while." Two years later, at the age of 54, she married Billy Warren. Although she no longer made the more adventurous expeditions, Mary enjoyed sharing her experiences with interested visitors. She had, over the years, written articles about her travels and given slide shows, and in 1911 she had published a book called "Old Indian Trails of the Canadian Rockies."

Encouraging others in the joy of exploration was a pleasure to Mary, but she had no time for those who approached it as a form of competition or a way to achieve personal glory. She saw her journeys as having value only because she undertook them in the pure sense of pleasure and peace of mind. For Mary, the point was to "delve into the heart of an untouched land, to turn the unthumbed pages of an unread book, and to learn daily those secrets which dear Mother Nature is so willing to tell to those who seek."[9]

Mary Schäffer took on both the challenges of the wilderness and the tight social parameters imposed on women of that period. She pursued her passion, shared what she found pleasure in, and contributed where she felt it would help to protect the places she so loved. Her courage and sense of adventure were a catalyst for a life richly lived and an inspiration to those around her.

Mount Schäffer and Schäffer Lake in Yoho Park were named after this intrepid woman.

Laggan — More than a Bakery...

Most of us who frequent the services in Lake Louise have a Pavlovian response to the word Laggan that involves visions of baked goodies and fresh coffee. But Laggan goes back further than the modern destination for hungry hikers.

When the CPR came through this area in 1884, the station was called Holt City, in the tradition of naming the sites after the local rail foreman. Lord Strathcona named it Laggan in 1901, after a spot in the Great Glen in Scotland where Clan Fraser was defeated in a bloody battle by Clan Macdonald. The original log Laggan Station now resides in Heritage Park in Calgary. It was renamed Lake Louise in 1914.

The hamlet of Lake Louise has not grown into more than a local centre for tourism services. Park planning now limits the area to accommodation for a maximum of 2,700 visitors.[10] The focus is on providing services for day users, so the hamlet will not become a community such as Banff. The local residents number about 1,500 people.

Wildlife management in the Lake Louise area faces the same issues as the other mountain communities. The Fairview and Whitehorn wildlife corridors run along either side of the Bow Valley. The area sees higher use by grizzly bears than either Banff or Canmore. There has been talk of fencing off the entire hamlet, but so far, the proposal has been rejected, except for the campground which has an electricied fence enclosing it. Bear activity in the area is closely monitored.

Wildlife Spotting: Those Cheeky Birds

If you spend any time in the mountains, you will encounter two bird species that are known locally as "camp robbers." Like their larger cousins, crows and ravens, these birds are members of the *Corvidae* family and have the brash attitude that runs in that family. They are not shy about raiding a picnic . I have even had them land on my sandwich as I was putting it in my mouth!

The Gray Jay (*Perisoreus Canadensis*), formerly called Canada Jay, and sometimes labelled Whiskey-jack, is the smaller and less raucous of the two – but don't be fooled, these are bold little beggars. These birds spend the summer storing food away for the winter. They use their sticky saliva to ball up nuts and berries, then glue this stored food to tree branches and in crevasses for later retrieval.

These birds start laying their eggs at the end of February, which seems alarmingly early to anyone who has spent time in the mountains at that time of year. They build super-insulated nests, and by March are using their stored supplies to feed their chicks. Once out of the nest, the young birds have a jump-start on the rich early-summer food supply compared to species that start their families later in the

Clark's nutcracker

warmer temperatures. Gray jays usually lay three eggs, but the strongest one usually forces the other two out of the nest. The survival rate of the evicted pair is poor – about 50%.

The Clark's Nutcracker (*Nucifraga columbiana*) looks quite similar to the Gray Jay, so these two are often confused. Both are about 30 centimetres long, but the nutcracker is more robust than its fluffier cousin. Nutcrackers have a much larger beak. In fact, Captain William Clark of Lewis and Clark fame, named it, misidentified it for a woodpecker. Clark's Nutcrackers are the noisier of the two, especially when there are young around. Nutcrackers are black over their wings and tail, where Jays are dark grey, and Nutcrackers have white tail feathers on the sides of their tail. Jays have a black "cap" on the back of their head, which Nutcrackers lack.

The Clark's Nutcracker also stores food, but it stashes its collection in the ground, in caches of 5 to 10 seeds each, over an area of about 20 square kilometres. Although studies have shown that these birds have an amazing memory for where they have stored their seeds, they do miss some. However, those that go unretrieved help generate new forest growth.

These birds do not really migrate in the conventional sense, but move down to lower elevations for the winter. They return to the high country to nest in April.

Gray jay, D. Ditchburn

The Slate Range

As you near Lake Louise, the Trans-Canada Highway crosses the Bow River for the first time since just after Vermilion Lakes. To the northeast of the highway lies the Slate Range – and it is, indeed, composed largely of slate. George Dawson made this observation and assigned the name.

The southernmost peak in the Slate Range is Lipalian Mountain (2,714 m). It is named for a geological interface between the Precambrian (800 million YBP) and the Cambrian (550 million YBP), when life forms began to multiply and diversify. Lipalian Mountain has the youngest Precambrian rocks in North America.

Next in line to the northwest is Mount Whitehorn. It was once named Mount O'Brien – probably after the artist Lucius O'Brien, who painted in the area in 1887. But by 1912, it was called Whitehorn, the name given to it by A. O. Wheeler when he climbed in the area. The Lake Louise Ski Area is on the slopes of this mountain.

Skoki Lodge

Here I am going to digress a bit far off the Trans-Canada – and I admit that it is partly for reasons of personal sentiment. But to consider the history of skiing in this area, you really must start several valleys back from the present Lake Louise Ski Area, at a backcountry lodge called Skoki.

To the north of the Bow Valley, between the Slate Range and the Sawbacks and east of the Pipestone Valley, is a very pretty area filled with lakes, meadows, and glaciers. Early skiing enthusiasts recognized its value and in 1930 the first simple backcountry ski lodge was built in this area. It was put up by the Norquay Ski Club, which grew into the Ski Club of the Canadian Rockies, and for its first few years it was run by Cliff White and then Peter and Catherine Whyte, well-known names in local Banff culture. In the early days, visitors had to ski almost 20 kilometres in from the train station to Skoki Lodge. A simple hut was erected partway, suitably named Halfway Hut, which allowed guests to break up the journey if they got a late start.

Once at Skoki, there was a wealth of ski-touring potential. Merlin Ridge beckoned, with great views into the Pipestone Valley. A number of glaciers in the area offered challenging day trips from the lodge. Or if skiers wanted to spend their time making turns closer to Skoki, the slopes on Fossil Mountain, Pika Peak, and Ptarmigan Peak were popular.

Skoki did not open for the summer hiking season until 1934, and the winter season was always the most popular during the 1930s and 1940s. Many loyal visitors returned year after year. There is a wealth of stories associated with this one location in the park. I grew up with them because my

mother, Jeannette Farman, ran the lodge in the late 1940s… If you are interested in more of the stories of this area, my 2001 book "Skoki: Beyond the Passes" is an account of the lodge and the people associated with it.

During the 1940s, an eccentric Englishman named Sir Norman Watson became involved in Skoki and had grand dreams of turning the area into a Switzerland of the Canadian Rockies. His intentions for the area included a network of six chalets accommodating about 30 guests each. Watson had visions of importing Swiss brown cows that would graze peacefully in the meadows and bringing in Swiss families who would live in high meadows, making cheese and cutting hay. His grand vision never came to pass (parks administrators were horrified by his proposal), and Skoki continued to attract skiers who liked it just as it was, a simple backcountry ski lodge. Still, one part of Sir Norman's dream did come to fruition with the construction of Temple Ski Chalet in 1938. It was nestled in the valley between Lipalian Mountain and Mount Whitehorn, a much more accessible destination than Skoki.

Lake Louise Ski Area

Temple Lodge became the seed for further development in the Lake Louise Ski Area. For many years it remained a ski destination that ski touring enthusiasts used as a base for self-propelled exploration of the surrounding slopes. Years of financial preparation and of negotiation with the Parks Department were required prior to every stage of development. In 1952 the first ski lift went in on Larch Slope. It climbed 150 metres from Temple Lodge up the northwest face of Lipalian Mountain. In 1959 the first aerial lift was installed – a sedan lift that went from beside the highway on the valley floor up the lower face of Whitehorn. This was the first lift of its type in the world and there were only two of this type ever made - the other was for the Matterhorn attraction at Disneyland. The lift remained open all year, giving summer visitors easy access to the high country. But ski traffic remained low, partly because the lift's lower portion crossed over rather uninspiring, low-angled terrain. Skiers needed to be able to access the more challenging upper

slopes before the numbers would increase to a viable level. Finally, in 1960 the addition of a platter-style lift to the top ridge of Whitehorn solved this problem, allowing skiers to link runs with those on Larch Slope. The ski business at Lake Louise began to take off.

However, the resort was still not attracting the numbers of skiers that were needed to make it viable. Blame was

Lake Louise Ski Area,
Chris Moseley

View from Lake Louise Ski Area, Chris Moseley

Temple from Lake Louise Ski Area, Chris Moseley

placed on the Parks Department, which was firm in not allowing overnight accommodation would be allowed on the hill. Weekend skiers were not enough – Lake Louise needed to tap the larger ski tourism market. The management finally hit on the idea of making a bid for the Winter Olympics to raise international awareness of the facility, and a bid was put forward for the 1964 Winter Games. They were turned down. But new runs were cut and named the Men's and Women's Olympic Downhill and another bid was put forward for the 1968 Games. That effort was turned down by a narrow margin. A third attempt was made for the 1972 Games, but by then the conservation movement was gathering momentum, and presented a formidable opposition to the proposal. Those Games went to Sapporo, Japan.

The bids for the Olympics did bring in some new business for Lake Louise, and it managed to add more lifts and expand operations. But the influence of a successful Olympic Games was finally felt when Calgary was awarded the 1988 Winter Games. Although the skiing events were held in the Kananaskis and Canada Olympic Park instead of Lake Louise, all of the ski areas of the Canadian Rockies were placed firmly on the map as a ski destination. A large portion of visitors to Lake Louise Ski Area are now here from abroad – the largest group coming to ski from the United Kingdom. Lake Louise has undergone considerable expansion in the last few decades. The ski runs now cover an area of over 4,000 acres – only 20 per cent of this is visible from the Trans-Canada.

The original sdan lift has been replaced by the Glacier Express Quad chairlift, which runs all year. During the summer gondolas are interspersed with the chairs on the lift.

One of the great attractions in the summer is the fact that Lake Louise area has been identified as one of the key habitat areas for grizzly bears. The Rock Garden in the Larch area on Lipalian Mountain is a popular winter denning area for grizzlies. This has resulted in some concern about summer use of the ski area. Out of their period of hibernation, bears are likely to be impacted by activity around the resort. It appears that bears, and grizzlies in particular, are attracted to the lush growth that occurs on the open slopes where ski runs have been cut. It is prime foraging terrain for them. In order to minimize impact on these bears and to avoid possible bear-human confrontations, the lodge area is surrounded by

Park planning has recently engaged in more discussion about the appropriateness of a large commercial ski development within Banff National Park. So what is the likely future for Lake Louise, as well as Sunshine and Norquay?

In 2000, Parks Canada determined that existing facilities such as golf courses and ski hills within the park were "non-conforming uses." This means they are to be managed into the future without expanding their footprint within the park, and that efforts must be made to minimize and mitigate any negative impact on ecological integrity. Ski-resort managers in the park have objected fiercely to what they see as discriminatory restrictions that put them at a disadvantage compared to expansion options available to resorts outside the park. But if the vision of the park involves a mandate for maintaining functioning ecosystems, then the avoidance of further negative impact from development must be a part of that. Ski resorts are working on accommodating this factor in their operations. Lake Louise now recycles its grey water, and seeks methods of minimizing water consumption for snow making. The struggle to find an appropriate balance that fits within the context of a national park will be an ongoing endeavour.

Grizzly sow and cubs on the Lake Louise Ski Area slopes in summer (note both chairs and summer gondolas on lift in background), Chris Moseley

Lake Louise Ski Area in the summer, Chris Moseley

an electric fence and the lower slopes are closed during the summer. Visitors glide by overhead on the gondola to explore the higher open meadows above timberline, which the bears do not frequent, and to visit the excellent interpretive centre at Whitehorn Lodge.

Accommodations for wildlife are essential for a resort such as Lake Louise. Efforts are being made to maximize a situation of successful human/wildlife co-use wherever possible. For example, when the downhill race course is being used, which requires fencing both sides of the run for its length down the mountain, all of the fencing is removed and stored each night to allow free movement for wildlife during the early and late hours of the day when they are most active.

The Pipestone River

The northwest side of the Slate Range is bounded by the Pipestone River. It takes its name from the blue-grey argillite rock found here, which was valued by the Indians for carving pipes. The Stoney name for the river is *Pahuto eya gubi wapta*, which refers to this highly valued stone. This route over the Pipestone Pass offers the most direct connection between the Bow Valley and the North Saskatchewan River to the north, and it had long been an important route for the Indians.

James Hector made use of this connection when he travelled through the area in 1859. James Carnegie, the Earl of Southesk, went through later that year and found a tree that had been freshly blazed with the words "Exploring Expedition, Aug 23, 1859, Dr. Hector."[11] One of the first tourists to travel through the Rocky Mountains, Carnegie is said to have travelled with copies of his preferred works of Shakespeare to read. Amazingly, when climbers Hugh Stutfield and Norman Collie travelled the Pipestone in 1898, they found "an old weather-beaten copy of Hamlet," probably dropped by the Earl.[12] You may also recall the story from Chapter 15 of Tom Wilson's horrendous trip through Pipestone Pass on his way home for Christmas.

Peter Wesley, the Stoney Nakoda chief who we met in Chapter 9, travelled regularly through the Pipestone Valley from the Stoney land near Kootenay Plains to the north. It was his responsibility to collect and distribute the treaty money to his people. This arrived in the form of a bag of cash, delivered to Lake Louise. However, the trains did not make a stop in Lake Louise for most of the year, and so Wesley would walk (he disliked riding horses) up the valley of the Siffleur and over Pipestone Pass, (a journey of about 70 kilometres) to be standing by the side of the tracks when the train passed. The sack was thrown from the train for him to catch, and he then had to make the rather nerve wracking journey home with this bag of money on his person.

On one of his return trips, Wesley passed by Tom Wilson's ranch and was approached by Wilson's two children. He had not met the pair and when he found two strangers running toward him he carefully levelled his rifle for what looked like a threatening encounter. The children quickly retreated to find their father, who laughed and explained to them who this man was, and why he was so defensive!

Pipestone Pass also represents the end of our exploration along the Trans-Canada Highway. We have travelled over many historical trails, and this old connecting route that has been used for centuries seems a suitable point to call our destination. From here, the Trans-Canada continues through the Kicking Horse Pass and then the Rogers Pass. Or you may wish to branch off and take the Icefields Parkway toward Jasper – a spectacular highway with continuous views of magnificent peaks. But a lot of people make Lake Louise their final destination, and a very fine one it is.

Between Calgary and Lake Louise, we have covered millenia of history and met many interesting individuals. It is fun to try to imagine how this country must have looked to the earliest visitors as they passed through – from the first native people arriving thousands of years ago to the very early white explorers to the first tourists to arrive on the CPR. The issues and struggles that people grapple with as they participate in the growth and management of this region have changed over the years – and will continue to do so. But the magnificence of this vast country remains, and will continue to bring a sense of awe and appreciation to those who travel the Trans-Canada Highway for years to come.

"The mountains surrounding Lake Louise are splendid to look at and uncomfortable to live with. Mountains, I feel, are unsuitable companions for the daily round. For they have nothing in common with temporal things – they belong among the most awesome symbols of eternity." [1]

Visitors at Lake Louise

The road was first put through to Field, B.C., in 1926. Twinning of thie section of the Trans-Canada as far as the BC border is expected to be completed in 2012. There are so many stories that have taken place here in those intervening years – but let's limit ourselves to looking ahead to what we can see from our end point in this book.

Mount Hector 3394 m

It seems fitting that surveyor George Dawson chose to name one of the three great peaks in the Lake Louise area that rises above 8,000 feet (2,438 m) after Sir James Hector. His accomplishments during two years of exploration certainly merit at least this much recognition. He traversed the full length of the Bow Valley within the mountains and left a detailed account of many aspects of what he found. His work resulted in a much clearer understanding of the geology of the Rocky Mountains, and laid the

Mount Hector from the Lake Louise intersection

Mount Bosworth and Mount Daly, Bath Glacier, and Waputik Peak to the right

foundation for establishing a workable route through this mountain barrier.

Those who travelled with Hector consistently commented on his agreeable nature and his willingness to pitch in and carry his weight on difficult journeys. He was universally regarded with respect and the men hired as his guides and assistants particularly appreciated his humble and positive disposition.

Hector was honoured with a knighthood after his work in Canada. He moved to New Zealand, where he became the head of the Geological Survey. In 1903 Hector made a return trip to Canada with his son Douglas. He had longed to show his son the places where he had travelled almost 50 years before. But tragically, Douglas died suddenly from appendicitis while they were making their way through the mountains.

Mount Hector is seen in the distance as an impressive steep faced peak. It marks the point where Highway 93 diverges from the Trans-Canada Highway and heads on to Jasper. The mountain was first climbed in 1895 by P. S. Abbot (who died the next year on Mount Lefroy), C. E. Fay and C. S. Thompson.

The Waputik Icefield

From the Lake Louise overpass, you can just see the edge of one of the great glacial icefields of the Rocky Mountains. The Wapta and Waputik icefields are at the southern end of a series of these massive blankets of ice that link the mountain ranges between Lake Louise and Jasper. The Wapta and Waputik icefields span the Continental Divide, and drain into the Bow, Mistaya, Blaeberry, and Kicking Horse rivers. Together, their ice mass covers more than 120 square kilometres. The name Wapta is the Stoney Nakoda word for "water".

These icefields are a popular destination for backcountry skiers and mountaineers. There is a system of four huts spread across the Wapta Icefield, making a traverse of the high glaciers a popular route.

The bits that we can see from this point are Mount Bosworth (2,771 m) and the long ridge that leads back from

it to Mount Daly (3,152 m). Just below the ridge is the slender white stripe of the Bath Glacier – which leads into the main part of the icefield to the north. This glacier takes its name from Bath Creek, which drains it, and is the place where Major Rogers was thrown from his horse and took an involuntary bath.

The Big Hill

From here, the Trans-Canada Highway winds through Yoho National Park in B.C. and makes its descent down the Big Hill into Field, another CPR town. Much of this section of the highway makes use of the old CPR roadbed, which fell into disuse when the CPR decided to reroute the railroad.

When the CPR line was put through this section in 1884, there had been talk of building a tunnel in Mount Stephen to soften the grade. But in the end, this idea was abandoned. The CPR instead built over the top, which resulted in a 4.5% grade – far greater than the 2.2% grade the tunnel would have allowed. This represented a horrifyingly steep grade for the trains of the time, requiring elaborate safety switches and brake-test procedures from the trains going through. Even so, there were too many disasters. So a tunnel was eventually built for the rail line after all – between 1906 and 1909 – into the bowels of Cathedral Mountain. Even once the tunnel had reduced the grade dramatically, for many years the hill remained a serious challenge for trains coming through.

There are a multitude of stories associated with this short section of road and rail – but we are getting far beyond the scope of this book. But do explore on. Follow the highway and find the stories, and enjoy the way the past and the present come together in this land.

Looking Back

In the course of our route along the ribbon of highway that is the Trans-Canada, we have met ranchers and outfitters, examined homesteading regulations and national park policies, seen the effect of fire on the prairie and in mountain forests, and touched on the varied forms of resource extraction that this thin strip of land supports. We have learned about the ancient presence of humans throughout this region, and about the animal and bird life that populates it now. This is such an amazing stretch of terrain – and the changing beauty that is a constant inspiration along the route west from the big city is available as a constant source of renewal for travellers. For Canadians, this is a part of our collective identity.

It is easy to be judgemental about how our parks are managed, to despair about how well they will be preserved for future generations, or, on the other hand, to struggle with the lost opportunities for economic growth imposed by the limits on development. But whatever our view, we can all derive peace and pleasure from the way this area touches us at a deep level, and we can allow it to reconnect us with a sense of greater perspective in our lives. Nature and history both have a way of reminding us of that which is true and real – and we can drink deeply from both those cups as we make our way through this land.

For some final thoughts, consider the words of James Harkin, the visionary park superintendent between 1911 and 1936, who struggled with the early definition of what this place was to become: *"National Parks are maintained for all the people – for the ill that they may be restored; for the well that they may be fortified and inspired by the sunshine, the fresh air, the beauty, and all the other healing, ennobling agencies of Nature. They exist in order that every citizen of Canada may satisfy his craving for Nature and Nature's Beauty; that he may absorb the poise and restfulness of the forests; that he may fill his soul with the brilliance of the wild flowers and the sublimity of the mountain peaks; that he may develop the buoyancy, the joy, and the activity that he sees in the wild animals; that he may stock his brain and mind with great thoughts, noble ideals; that he be made better, be healthier, and happier."*

And then temper that, gently, with the insights injected by the National Parks Act of 2000, which states that:

"Parks are hereby dedicated to the people of Canada for their benefit, education, and enjoyment, subject to the provisions of this Act and Regulations, and such Parks shall be maintained and made use of so as to leave them unimpaired for the enjoyment of future generations."

Those quotes are quite a distance apart in their poetic quality – but are they so far apart in their intent? I feel certain that Harkin would have added the "unimpaired for the enjoyment of future generations" aspect had he the benefit of hindsight from our modern-day perspective. In the efforts to protect what is whole and functioning, what is real and inspiring, we are engaging in hope for the future. Even if we now have to manage the natural systems in our parks, even if we have to artificially reintroduce elements such as fire, we are engaging in a system governed by rules that are much bigger than we are. This task forces us to shed our cultural hubris and work with forces that are greater than what we can ever bring into the equation.

Harkin touched the core of why we need these wild places. And we now need them more than ever. In a world of virtual friends, of artificial intelligence, of distance this and engineered that, we need to be able to retreat to natural places. There we come face to face with raw beauty, with the thread of real people creating real history. And there we connect with parts of ourselves that find solace in the enduring landscape, and sustenance in mountains and rivers and unalterable truths in the eternal forces of weather and time.

Peace and pleasure on your future journeys.

> "Rolling down that ribbon of highway
> I've gone another mile, another day
> Going places I ain't never been
> Seeing things I'll never see again"
>
> Scooter Lee, "Ribbon of Highway"

These are brief notes, only to serve to remind you of who is who in this book. There are many aspects of these people's biographies that I don't mention, but cover only their part in this book.

Aitken, W. Max (Lord Beaverbrook) – founded Calgary Power (with R. B. Bennett) and was also behind the formation of Canada Cement.

Allen, Samuel – came to Banff in 1893, met Walter Wilcox, and climbed and explored around the Lake Louise area for several years.

Barbeau, Marius – a Canadian ethnographer who, in the first part of the 19th century, studied the Indians of Canada and recorded their stories.

Bateman, John – postmaster at Jumping Pound after 1905.

Beaverbrook, Lord (see W. Max Aitken)

Bennett, R. B. – lawyer and politician. Bennett was the first leader of the Conservative party in Alberta, serving as an MLA before moving on to federal politics. He was Prime Minister of Canada from 1930 to 1935.

Blakiston, Thomas – a member of the Palliser Expedition in 1858 (did not take route along the Bow River).

Bourgeau, Eugene – a botanist from France, explored the Bow Valley with Dr. James Hector as part of the Palliser Expedition in 1858.

Brett, Dr. Robert G. – physician, entrepreneur, and politician. Brett developed a number of hotels, hospitals, and businesses in Banff in the 1880s. He later became Alberta's lieutenant-governor.

Brewster, Jim – came to Banff with his family in 1887 and worked as an outfitter before becoming occupied with Brewster Transport Company.

Butchart, Robert – ran a cement plant near Exshaw in the early 1900s. He later developed a famous garden in a quarry near Victoria.

Bull Head, Chief – leader of the Tsuu T'ina, he fought to get a separate reserve for his people after they were placed on a reserve with the Siksika.

Calf Child, Chief (Hector Crawler) – chief of the Chiniki band, Stoney Nakoda, a medicine man, and one of the first to adopt Christianity.

Cashel, Ernest – an outlaw who progressed from petty crimes to murder near Calgary. He was captured near Canmore and hanged in 1904.

Chiniki, Chief – leader of the Chiniki band, Stoney Nakoda, and a signatory to Treaty No. 7.

Cochrane, Senator Matthew – took advantage of the grazing leases available to start the Cochrane Ranche west of Calgary in 1881. Copithorne family – brothers John, Richard, and Samuel came to Canada from Ireland and homesteaded in the Jumping Pound area. Their families have grown to become one of the largest ranching families in the region.

Coulliard, Joe – manager at Paskapoo (predecessor to Canada Olympic Park).

Crawler, Hector (see Chief Calf Child)

Crowfoot, Chief – leader of the Siksika at the time of Treaty No. 7. CHe is often seen as the spokesperson for the Indians during these negotiations.

Cummer, Fred – one of the men who started Paskapoo Ski Hill, predecessor to Canada Olympic Park, in 1906.

Douglas Sutherland Campbell (Marquis of Lorne/Duke of Argyll) – Governor General of Canada, visited the West in 1881.

Dawson, George – surveyor who worked in the Rocky Mountains in 1883 and 1884.

Diefenbaker, Prime Minister John – Prime Minister of Canada from 1957 to 1963.

De Smet, Father Pierre – a Jesuit priest, he came through Whiteman's Pass on his way north from Missouri to minister to the Blackfoot in 1845.

Douglas, Howard – first commissioner for national parks in Canada.

Duke of Argyll (see Douglas Sutherland Campbell/Marquis of Lorne)

Edwards, Michael – British ski jumping competitor in the 1988 Calgary Winter Olympics, who became affectionately known as "Eddie the Eagle."

Elias, Bob – one of the men who started Paskapoo Ski Hill, predecessor to Canada Olympic Park, in 1906.

Erasmus, Peter – Metis guide and interpreter, worked for Dr. James Hector on his trips into the mountains.

Fidler, Peter – travelled to the West for the Hudson's Bay Company and saw, but did not enter, the mountains in 1792.

Fleming, Sir Sandford – engineer in charge of the construction of the CPR.

Gardner, Captain Meopham – homesteader in Springbank, a hunting and polo enthusiast.

Glidden, Charles – in 1905, he became the first person to take a car into Banff. But it travelled on rails, as there was no road at the time.

Gold Seeker (Edwin Hunter) – Stoney Nakoda guide who took Tom Wilson to Lake Louise for the first time, and who showed the ore sample from Copper Mountain to Joe Healy.

Goodstoney, Jacob – a leader of the Wesley band, Stoney Nakoda.

Grassi, Lawrence – Italian immigrant who settled in Canmore, worked in the mine, guided, and built trails throughout the mountains.

Ha Ling – a Chinese cook working in Canmore, said to have won a bet to ascend a nearby mountain (now named after him).

Haakenstad, Clarence - one of the men who started Paskapoo Ski Hill, predecessor to Canada Olympic Park, in 1906.

Harken, James B. – first commissioner of the Dominion Parks Branch.

Healy, Ebenezer – dairyman and cheesemaker in the Springbank area.

Healy, Joe – prospector and explorer, involved in the excitement at Silver City in the 1880s.

Hector, Dr. James – a member of the Palliser Expedition, Hector explored up the Bow Valley with Eugene Bourgeau in 1858 and again on his own in 1859. Between those two trips, he covered the Bow River from its source to where it leaves the mountains.

Henday, Anthony – explorer with the Hudson's Bay Company, may have seen the mountains from near Innisfail in 1754.

Hexall, John – early land speculator in Bowness.. He donated the land to the City of Calgary that became Bowness Park.

Hunter, William and Joshua (William and Joshua Twin) – Stoney Nakoda who worked with Banff outfitters. Hunter, Edwin (see Gold Seeker)

Irvin, Joseph – promoter of the cement-plant development at Exshaw that became Canada Cement.

Jaeggi, John – operator of the early tea house on Sulphur Mountain.

Kelsey, Henry – explorer for the Hudson's Bay Company, travelled west in 1690 and 1692. We are unsure whether he saw the mountains.

Laurie, John – teacher and advocate of native rights, he made extensive records of Indian stories and traditions.

Livingstone, Sam – early prospector and trader, lived for a period west of Calgary near the location of the Our Lady of Peace mission.

Loder, Edwin – ran Loder Brothers cement plant near Exshaw.

Lougheed, Senator James – businessman, senator, MP, and grandfather of Alberta Premier Peter Lougheed.

Lougheed, Norman – one of Senator James' sons, he was the first person to drive a car into Banff (illegally).

Macdonald, Sir John A. – Prime Minister of Canada from 1867 to 1873 and from 1878 to 1891. Macdonald travelled across Canada on the CPR in 1886, soon after the line was completed late the previous year.

Macoun, John – naturalist who explored into the west with CPR expeditions between 1872 and 1881.

Marquis of Lorne (see Douglas Sutherland Campbell / Duke of Argyll)

Marrett, John and François – brothers who lived in the area of Dead Man's Flats. François murdered his brother, hence the name of the locale.

McArthur, J. J. – Dominion surveyor and climber, did many first ascents in the Rockies.

McCabe, Frank – one of the individuals who claimed that they had discovered the hot springs near the town of Banff.

McCall, Captain Frank – World War I flying ace, active in promoting flying from Bowness Airfield, and the first to land a plane in Banff.

McCanleish – operated a lime kiln near Exshaw from 1884, but disappeared and his operation was taken over by Edwin Loder.

McCardell, William and Thomas – brothers who claimed that they had discovered the hot springs near the town of Banff.

McCourt, Edward – Canadian writer and professor of English, he travelled across the country and wrote about it in "The Road Across Canada."

McDougall, John, David, and George – John (father) and George (son) were missionaries to the Stoney Nakoda at Morley, and David (son) operated a trading post there.

McGillivray, Duncan – travelled with David Thompson to the Bow Valley area in 1800, exploring for the North West Company.

McLean, George (Walking Buffalo) – a Stoney Nakoda who was raised by John McLean, Methodist missionary, involved in the Moral Rearmament movement, medicine man, and chief.

Nevitt, Richard Barrington – came to Southern Alberta as assistant surgeon with the NWMP. Nevitt was an amateur artist and left a collection of sketches of people and places from his time in the west.

Pearce, William – Dominion Land Surveyor, did the initial survey around the Banff Hot Springs Reserve.

Pepper, William and Harriett – early homesteaders in the Springbank area.

Peyto, Bill – originally from England, Peyto was a Banff outfitter and adventurer. He did some prospecting and later worked as a Banff park warden.

Piché, Alexis – Metis man who guided for George Simpson, who called him Peechee.

Ricks, Frank – cowboy and rancher who had a ranch called The Hermitage west of Calgary. Ricks also ran Alberta Hotel in Banff.

Rogers, Major A. B. – hired by the CPR in 1881 to find a route for the railway through the passes to the west of the Bow Valley.

Robinson, Cliff – an Alberta artist, primarily a printmaker, who taught at the Banff School of Art. Robinson lived at Morley in the early 1940s and recorded his experience there in a collection of prints and drawings.

Rundle, Rev. Robert Terrill – Methodist missionary who travelled around Western Canada from 1840 to 1848, working with various Indian tribes.

Sanson, Norman – curator of the Banff Park Museum and keeper of the weather station on Sulphur Mountain.

Scollen, Father Constantine – Jesuit missionary, assisted the Blackfoot through the Treaty No. 7 negotiations, established the Our Lady of Peace Mission west of Springbank.

Scott, Tom – homesteader west of Calgary near what is now called Scott Lake Hill.

Sibbald, Andrew – teacher at the Morley mission school.

Sibbald, Howard – son of Andrew Sibbald, Howard became the first park warden in Banff.

Simpson, Sir George – governor of the Hudson's Bay Company, travelled through the Rockies in 1841.

Simpson, Jimmy – came to Banff from England in the late 1890s and worked as an outfitter. He later developed Num-ti-jah Lodge on Bow Lake.

Sinclair, James – led two expeditions of Red River Settlers through the Rocky Mountains on their way to Oregon.

Smith, Sir Donald (Lord Strathcona) – chief commissioner for the Hudson's Bay Company, politician, and one of the key organizers of the CPR.

Snow, Chief John – minister and leader of the Stoney Chiniki band.

Stewart, George A. – surveyor, laid out the town of Banff in 1886.

Strathcona, Lord (see Sir Donald Smith)

Stuart, William – postmaster at Jumping Pound from 1892 to 1905.

Sullivan, John – a member of the Palliser Expedition, but did not take route along the Bow River.

Sykes, Taylor – homesteader in the Brushy Ridge area.

Thompson, David – explorer for the North West Company, travelled up the Bow Valley in 1800 with Duncan McGillivray.

Twin, William and Joshua (see William and Joshua Hunter)

Van Horne, William Cornelius – general manager, then vice-president, then president of the Canadian Pacific Railway. He oversaw the CPR's construction through the Bow Valley.

Vavasour, Lieutenant Mervin – sent west in 1845 to scout out a route for military movement, should the Oregon dispute require such action.

Walker, Colonel James – came west with the NWMP and then worked for Senator Matthew Cochrane on the Cochrane Ranche for two years before leaving to pursue lumbering and ranching on his own.

Walking Buffalo (see McLean, George)

Warre, Lieutenant Henry – sent west in 1845 to scout out a route for military movement, should the Oregon dispute require such action.

Warren, Mary Schäffer – an adventuress from Philadelphia who regularly travelled in the Rockies, first with her husband and then, after he died, with a friend. She was interested in botany and published and illustrated a book on Rocky Mountain flowers. Schäffer later married William Warren, a Banff outfitter.

Wesley, Peter – leader of the Wesley/Goodstoney band who led a group of that band back to their traditional lands near Kootenay Plains, which later became their reserve.

White, Dave – store owner in the early days of Banff.

Wilcox, Walter – a student at Yale when he first came to the Rockies in 1893, and who returned over following years. Wilcox climbed and explored with Samuel Allen. Made the first ascent of Mount Temple. Published "The Rockies of Canada."

Wilson, Tom – worked for the NWMP and then moved to Banff, where he worked as an outfitter and guide. Wilson eventually started ranching north of Banff National Park.

Young, James and Lily, William and Mary – homesteaders in the Springbank area, this family was instrumental in developing services within the growing community.

Timeline

10,000+ years ago – Humans known to have inhabited area

1754 – Anthony Henday may have been first white man to see e Rockies

1779 – North West Company officially formed

1780 – Smallpox epidemic affects native population

1792-93 – Peter Fidler visited the Rockies

1798 – David Thompson's first trip into what is now Alberta

1800 – David Thompson and Duncan McGillivray travel up Bow Valley as far as White Man's Gap

1803 – 1806 – Lewis and Clark travel to the west coast

1818 – 49th parallel established as far as the mountains (Treaty of Ghent)

1822- 23 Peigan Post established and abandonned

1837 – Smallpox epidemic – particularly decimated the Blackfoot

1841 – James Sinclair first person over White Man Pass on way to Oregon

1841 – Sir George Simpson, Governor of the Hudson Bay Company, makes trip around the world and travels through the Rockies

1844 – Rev Rundle travels up Bow Valley

1845 – Warre and Vavasour sent to scout route for troops across mountains to defend Oregon Territory

1845 – Father de Smet in area

1846 – Oregon Treaty establishes boundary at the 49th parallel through the mountains to the coast

1847 – Rev Rundle holds service near site of Banff for Stoneys

1850 – James Sinclair – through White Man's Pass to check on HBC forts

1854 – James Sinclair travels up Kananskis to Kananaskis Pass

1858 & 59 – James Hector and Eugène Bourgeau enter mountains through Bow Corridor

1859 – Earl of Southesk travelled east through Bow Corridor

1859 – Hector up Bow Valley over Pipestone Pass

1850s and 60s – Peak of whiskey trade

1861 – Caribou Gold Rush

1867 – Formation of the Dominion of Canada

1869 – North West Territories proclaimed

1869 – Dominion Land Survey commenced

1869-70 – Smallpox epidemic

1869-70 – Northwest Rebellion

1870 – Hudson's Bay Company turns over Rupert's Land to Dominion of Canada

1871 – British Columbia became part of Canada

1872 – Dominion Lands Act

1873 – Our Lady of Peace Mission

1873 – NWMP formed by Order in Council

1873 – Sam Livingstone opens trading post in Jumping Pound

1874 – Hot springs on Sulphur "discovered"

1875 – North West Territories Act

1877 – Treaty No. 7

1879 – Buffalo are virtually gone from Alberta

1881 – Grazing leases commence

1881 – Major Rogers surveys Bow Valley and Kicking Horse for CPR

1881 – Gov Gen Marquis of Lorne visits area of Bow Valley

1882 – Tom Wilson "finds" Lake Louise

1883-85 – Silver City springs up

1883 – Hot springs "discovered" on Sulphur Mountain

1883 – Padmore (now Canmore) established

1883 – railway reaches Banff and Lake Louise (Siding 29 and Laggan)

1883 – Kicking Horse Pass route chosen by CPR and railway pushed through to Lake Louise

1884 – 85 – George Dawson in area for GSC

1885 – (Nov) – Last spike on the CPR

1885 – Riel Rebellion

1885 – "Hot Springs Reserve" established near Banff – first steps toward a park

1886-1893 – James McArthur, with Dominion Land Survey, maps mountains along CPR

1886 – George Stewart appointed to organize infrastructure for Hot Springs Reserve

1886 – Sir John A. and Lady Macdonald ride across the country on the new rail line

1887 – Tom Wilson establishes route from Bow Valley to Lake Louise

1887 – Establishment of Rocky Mountains Park

1888 – Original Banff Springs opens

1889 – Mary Sharples (later Mary Schäffer Warren) visits the Rockies for the first time

1890 – First chalet at Lake Louise

1890 – No hunting permitted in the park (except predators)

1892 – Lake Louise Forest Park established – added to the Rocky Mountains Park

1893 – Walter Wilcox and Samuel Allen make their first visit to Lake Louise

1896 – Grazing leases cancelled

1896 – Phillip Abbot is killed on Mount Lefroy, the first mountaineering fatality in the Canadian Rockies

1897 – Jimmy Simpson arrives in the Rockies

1899 – Swiss guides brought over by the CPR

1902 – Formation of Rocky Mountain Park ??

1905 – Formation of the province of Alberta

1907 – Jasper Forest Park created (boundaries changed until 1930)

1910 – Foundation of Alpine Club of Canada

1911 – Cars allowed in Banff Park

1911 – Power arrives in communities west of Calgary

1911 – Kananaskis taken out of Park

1911 – Dominion Forest Reserve and Parks Act passed

1912 – First dam at Lake Minnewanka, CPR builds a teahouse there

1913-1930 – tram from Lake Louise town to chateau

1915 – POW camp near Castle Mountain

1917 – Kananaskis returned to Park

1917 – Bowness street car service starts

1920 – Kootenay Park established (since reduced in size)

1921 – Road from Banff to Lake Louise opened (much constructed by POWs)

1923 – Radium highway opens

1923 – CPR builds lodge at Moraine Lake

1924 – Fire destroys one wing of the Chalet at lake Louise

1925 – Reconstruction of the CPR Hotel at lake Louise as Chateau Lake Louise

1926 – Road pushed on from Lake Louise to Field

1926 – Fire destroys north wing of Banff Springs Hotel

1928 – Finish of reconstruction of Banff Springs Hotel

1930 – National Park Act – Banff Park boundaries established (and Jasper, Kootenay and Jasper)

1930 – Control of crown lands and resourced passed to the provinces by Natural Resources Transfer Act

1931 – Start of construction of Jasper highway – Icefields Parkway – opened 1940

1934 – Road built between Seebe and the current location of the Kananaskis Forest Experimental Station

1936 – First forestry trunk road was built

1936 – First lodge established at Sunshine Ski Area

1936 – Brushy Ridge fire

1936 – Old Canmore Trail widened to allow wagons (Dead Man's Flats over Skogan Pass to Boundary Cabin in Kananaskis)

1945 – First ski lift at Sunshine

1948 – Alberta government improved the Forestry Trunk Road – opened in 1952

1948 – First lift at Norquay

1951 – Jumping Pound Gas Plant opens

1952 – Trans-Canada built between Banff and Lake Louise

1962 – Official completion of the Trans-Canada highway

1967 – Indians given the right to vote

1968 – Indians given right to self-government

1973 – Construction of Highway 40 begins

1975 – Formation of Kananaskis Country which became Peter Lougheed Park

1977 – Kananaskis Country (larger area) formed

1990 – Banff Town becomes self governing as a municipality

Acknowledgements

So many people have helped me in the course of putting this book together. I am appreciative of their enthusiasm and assistance beyond what I can express here.

For assistance with material for the book I would like to express my gratitude to the following people: Sandy Best (Lake Louise Ski Area), Andrina Butler (Lake Louise Ski Friends), Steve Byford (forestry issues), Dene Cooper (MD of Bighorn), Stan and Gloria Cowley (Rafter Six Ranch), Derrick Ditchburn (photographer), Edmond Duggan (kayaking), Canadian Rockies Rafting, Ian Getty (Stoney Tribal Research Director), Jay Honeyman (bear management), Tom Jacklin (kayaking), Chuck Lee (Alberta Whitewater Association), Lindsey MacDougall (Vehicle Inspection Station), Lorraine Maclauchlan (pine beetle issues), Stewart McDonough (Winsport Canada), Chris Moseley (Lake Louise Ski Area), Northern Lights Wildlife Wolf Centre, Gladys Serafino (Winsport Canada), Larry Stock (Springbank Airport), Craig Taube-Schock (pictographs), Kim Titchner (WildSmart), Ernest Waterchief (Siksika Nation), Brian Vivian (Archeologist), Buddy Wesley (Stoney Nakoda Administration) and Chas Yonge (Canmore Caverns).

I am sure that there are other names that I should have included here – I have talked to so many people in the course of research… thank you to all!

The staff at the Stockmen's Memorial Foundation Archives and Library, The Glenbow Archives, The Whyte Museum Archives and the National Library and Archives have all been a great help to me – thank you to all these folks.

A special thank you to Jim McElgunn for his technical assistance with editing, and also for his insight and support.

Special thanks also to Peter Spear, who has driven the Trans-Canada Highway over a thousand times on his way to hiking, climbing, backpacking, ski patrolling and as a tour guide, for offering his assistance to the project. The book is stronger for benefiting from his input.

To Stephen Ditchburn for his technical support to the project, a huge thank you (again…).

Thanks to friends who gave me feedback on drafts-in-progress – Carrie Stenvig and Joanne Wyvill.

And, as always, very special appreciation to Mark Zimmerman for his patience throughout the project – especially those times with approaching deadlines and high panic levels! Mark, you brought a sense of calm and perspective that I needed at times!

Finally, I would like to thank the Alberta Historical Resources Foundation for their support in making this project possible.

Chapter 1

1. David Monaghan, Canada's "New Main Street": The Trans-Canada Highway as Idea and Reality. (Ottawa: Canada Science and Technology Museum, 2002), 8.
2. Ibid., 11.
3. Ibid., 29.
4. Centre for Spatial Economics. Roads and Highways: Critical to Canada's Competitiveness. Report prepared for the Canadian Automobile Association. November 2006

Chapter 2

1. Judith Barge, "John Hexall and Bowness Estates," Bowness: Our Village in the Valley, ed. unknown (Calgary: Bowness Historical Society, 2005), 28.
2. Valentine Urie, "The Bowness Streetcar," Bowness: Our Village in the Valley, ed. unknown (Calgary: Bowness Historical Society, 2005), 59.
3. City of Calgary. Planning Department. East Paskapoo Slopes Area Structure Plan. Calgary: Planning Policy, Land Use and Mobility, November 2006.
4. Gail Helgason, The First Albertans: An Archeological Search. (Edmonton: Lone Pine Publications, 1987), 76.
5. J. Thomas West, "More Than a Ski Hill: From Paskapoo to Canada Olympic Park," Journal of Olympic History, Vol. II, No. 3, September 2003, 27.
6. Ibid., 28.

Chapter 3

1. Frank Anderson, A Frontier Guide to Calgary, 1968, 16.
2. Helen Hutchison quoted by James Gray (ed.), Chaps and Chinooks: A History West of Calgary. (Calgary: Foothills Historical Society, 1976), 87.
3. No author, in a short report on the Cashel case, Canadian Cattlemen, Vol. 4, No. 2 (Sept. 1941), 51.
4. Glenbow Archives, Ernest Cashel fonds, M196.
5. From notes in the Neil Nicholson fonds, Glenbow Museum.

6. Ian Bailey, "The Link between Private Grief and Public Safety," The Globe and Mail (Toronto), November 8, 2008, A3.

Chapter 4

1. Marius Barbeau, "Indian Days on the Western Prairies" in No. 163, Anthropological Series No. 46 (Ottawa: Dept of Northern Affairs and National Resources – National Museum of Canada, 1959), 12.
2. Scollen fonds, Glenbow Museum.
3. Ibid.
4. Jon Whyte, Indians in the Rockies. (Banff: Altitude Publishing Inc., 1985), 58.
5. Alexander Morris, The Treaties of Canada with the Indians of Manitoba and the North-West Territories (Saskatoon: Fifth House, 1991; reprint from 1880), 272.
6. Scollen fonds.
7. Evelyn Buckley, ed., Chaps and Chinooks (Calgary: Foothills Historical Society, 1976), 302.

Chapter 5

1. Edward McCourt, The Road Across Canada. (Toronto: Macmillan of Canada, 1965), 167.
2. James G. MacGregor, Behold the Shining Mountains: Being an Account of the Travels of Anthony Henday, 1754-55. (Edmonton: Applied Arts Products, 1954), 196.
3. Lorne E. Render. The Mountains and the Sky. (McClelland and Stewart West, 1974), 10.
4. Heritage Community Foundation, "Place Names of Alberta: The Land, The People, Their Stories," Alberta Online Encyclopedia 2005. Available from
hhtp://www.albertasource.ca/placenames/regions/mountains.html. Internet: Accessed 13 March 2009.
5. David Birrell and Ron Ellis. Calgary's Mountain Panorama. (Calgary: Rocky Mountain Books, 1990), 17.
6. Ibid., 49.

Chapter 6

1. L. V. Kelly, <u>The Range Men: The Story of the Ranchers and Indians of Alberta</u> (Toronto: William Briggs, 1913), 147.
2. Ibid., 152.
3. Ibid., 153.
4. Evelyn Buckley, <u>Chaps and Chinooks</u> (Calgary: Foothills Historical Society, 1976), 25-26.

Chapter 7

1. Evelyn Buckley ed. <u>Chaps and Chinooks</u> (Calgary: Foothills Historical Society, 1976), 124-135.
2. Judy and Roy Copithorne eds. <u>Copithorne History</u>. (Published privately, 1982), 56.
3. Buckley, 262.
4. Buckley, 44.
5. Buckley, 45.
6. Buckley, 141.
7. Buckley, 148.
8. Graham Chandler, "Sour Gas University: Pioneer Jumping Pound Gas Plant Turns 50," Oilweek Magazine, November 5, 2001, 64.
9. Ibid.
10. Ibid.
11. L.V. Kelly. <u>The Range Men: The Story of the Ranchers and Indians of Alberta.</u> (Toronto: William Briggs, 1913), 170.
12. Michael C. Grant, "The Trembling Giant," <u>Discover</u>, October (1993); Available from <u>discovermagazine.com/1993/oct/thetrem-blinggiant285</u>; Internet; accessed March 2009.

Chapter 9

1. Jon Whyte. <u>Indians in the Rockies</u>. (Banff: Altitude Publishing, 1985), 28.
2. E. J. Hart. <u>The Place of Bows</u>. (Banff: EJH Literary Enterprises, 1999), 33.
3. Thompson, David. <u>Travels in Western North America 1784-1812</u>. Toronto: Macmillan, 1971.
4. Ibid., 44-45.
5. Hugh Dempsey, ed. <u>The Rundle Journals</u>. (Calgary: The Glenbow Institute and the Historical Society of Alberta, 1977), xv.
6. Ian Getty (Research Director, Stoney Nakoda Reserve). <u>A Brief Overview of Stoney Land Claims and Specific Claims</u> (pamphlet).
7. F. W. Wilkins, D.L.S. <u>Field Notes of Wesleyan Methodist Mission Surveys N.W.T.</u> Report addressed to the Minister of the Interior, November 27, 1887.
8. A. Brabazon, D.L.S. <u>Field Notes</u>, 1888.

9. Jon Whyte. <u>Indians in the Rockies</u>. (Banff: Altitude Publishing, 1985), 69.
10. Glenbow Archives, John Laurie Fonds, "The Stoney Indians of Alberta" manuscript, M-4390.
11. John Snow. <u>These Mountains Are Our Sacred Places</u>. (Toronto: Samuel Stevens, 1977), 19.
12. Marius Barbeau. "Indian Days on the Western Prairies." <u>Bulletin No. 163 Anthropological Series No. 46</u>. (Ottawa: Department of Northern Affairs and National Resources – National Museum of Canada, 1959), 69-70.
13. John Snow, 19.
14. John Snow, 61.
15. John Snow, 169.
16. Marius Barbeau, 96-97.
17. Marius Barbeau, 95-96.
18. Jon Whyte, 66.

Chapter 10

1. Walter Hildebrand. <u>An Historical Analysis of Parks Canada and Banff National Park, 1968 – 1995</u>. Prepared for the Banff-Bow Valley Study Task Force. (December 1995), 9.
2. Doug Hogg, <u>The Memory Project Digital Archive</u>; Available from <u>www.thememoryproject.com/digital-archive/profile.cfm?cnf=cf&collectionid=763</u>; Internet; Accessed December 16, 2008.

Chapter 11

1. Edward McCourt. <u>The Road Across Canada</u>. (Toronto: Macmillan of Canada, 1965), 168.
2. Victor G. Hopwood. David Thompson: Travels in Western North America, 1784 – 1812. (Toronto: Macmillan, 1971), 225.
3. Peter Erasmus. <u>Buffalo Days and Nights</u>. (Calgary, Fifth House, 1999), 75.
4. John Niddrie. <u>Niddrie of the North-West: Memoirs of a Pioneer Canadian Missionary</u>. (Edmonton, University of Alberta Press, 2000), 49.
5. "Wildfire Detection," <u>Government of Alberta, Sustainable Resource Development</u>; June 11, 2009; Available from <u>www.srd.alberta.ca/ManagingPrograms/PreventingFightingWildfire/WildfireDetection.aspx</u>; Internet; Accessed November 20, 2009.

Chapter 12

1. Edward McCourt. <u>The Road Across Canada</u>. (Toronto: Macmillan of Canada, 1965), 173.

2. Christopher Armstrong and H.V. Nelles. Competition vs. Convenience: Federal Administration of Bow River Waterpowers, 1906-1913.

3. Ibid.

4. Rob Alexander and Lutz, Jenn. The Exshaw Cement Plant – 100 Years. (Lafarge, 2006), 20.

6. Graymont. Available from www.graymont.com/locations_exs5aw.shtm; Internet; accessed January 11, 2010.

6. Shelley Alexander and Jeff Gailus, "GIS-Based Approach to Restoring Connectivity Across Banff's Trans-Canada Highway, Technical Report #4," Miistakis Institute for the Rockies (April 2005); Available from www.rockies.ca/downloads/COMPLETE%20TCH%20Report.pdf; Internet; accessed November 14, 2009.

Chapter 13

1. Charles Yonge. Under Grotto Mountain: Rat's Nest Cave. (Calgary: Rocky Mountain Books, 2001), 101.

2. James Keyser and Michael Klassen. Plains Indian Rock Art. (Seattle: University of Washington Press, 2001), p. 105.

3. Brian Birrell, "Ha Ling Peak," Peakfinder; Available from www.peakfinder.com/peakfinder.asp?Peakname=Ha+Ling+Peak; Internet; Accessed January 7, 2010.

4. "Canmore and Kananaskis," Visitor's Choice pamphlet (Banff: I G Publications, 2008/09), 22.

5. Edward McCourt. The Road Across Canada. (Toronto: Macmillan of Canada, 1965) 171-172.

6. Robert Remmington, "Canmore megaproject developer in receivership," Calgary Herald (March 3, 2009).

7. Jacob Herrero Environmental Consulting, Scott Jevons/GeoWORKS Environmental Consulting & GIS and KH Communications, "Wildlife Corridors in the Southern Canmore Region," Stratalink (September 2000); Available from www.stratalink.com/corridors/default.htm; Internet; Accessed January 2010.

8. Ursula Tillman, "Moving the Town Into the Country – Canmore," NowPublic (January 8, 2008); Available from www.nowpublic.com/environment/moving-town-country-canmore; Internet; Accessed January 6, 2010.

Chapter 14

1. Brandon Pullan, "Six Rockies Ice Classics." Gripped (October 20, 2009); Available from gripped.com/2009/10/sections/articles/six-rockies-ice-classics; Internet; Accessed January 14, 2010.

2. Brian Patton. Parkways of the Canadian Rockies: A Road Guide. (Banff: Summerthought Press, 1995), 34.

3. K. Jeffery Danter. "Fire Dependent Ecosystems of the United States." National Interagency Fire Centre. Available at www.nifc.gov/preved/comm_guide/wildfire/fire_6.html. Internet. Accessed January 13, 2010.

4. Stephen Pyne, "Burning Banff." Western Institute for Study of the Environment Colloquium (December 11, 2007). Available from westinstenv.org/ffsci/2007/12/11/burning-banff; Internet. Accessed January 13, 2010.

5. E. J. Hart. The Place of Bows. (Banff: EJH Literary Enterprises Ltd., 1999), 99-100.

6. Frank Anderson. A Frontier Guide to Calgary – Banff Highway. (1968), 54-55.

7. Albert MacCarthy, "The First Ascent of Mount Louis," in Canadian Alpine Journal, Vol. 8 (1917) 86.

8. Ben Gadd. Bankhead: The Twenty Year Town. (Calgary, The Coal Association of Canada, 1989), 47.

9. Shepherd, Brenda and Jesse Whittington, "Response of Wolves to Corridor Restoration and Human Use Management," Ecology and Society Vol. 11, no. 2, Art. 1 (2006); Available from www.ecologyandsociety.org/vol11/iss2/art1; Internet; Accessed January 7, 2010.

10. "The Animal Corrals," Crag and Canyon (June 2, 1906)

Chapter 15

1. Edward McCourt. The Road Across Canada. (Toronto: Macmillan of Canada), 170.

2. Hugh Dempsey. Indians of the Rocky Mountain Parks. (Calgary, Fifth House Publishing, 1998).

3. Eleanor Luxton. Banff. (Banff: Summerthough Press, 1975), 54.

4. Ernie Lakusta. Banff and Lake Louise History Explorer. (Canmore: Altitude Publishing, 2004), 23.

5. Ed Struzik, "Rare Banff snail [Physella johnsoni] an ecological barometer for hot springs," Edmonton Journal, November 27, 1999. Available from raysweb.net/specialplaces/pages-species-ej/banffsnail-ej.html; Internet; Accessed October 27, 2009.

6. Walter Wilcox, "Bill Peyto," in Tales from the Canadian Rockies, ed. Brian Patton (Edmonton: Hurtig Publishers, 1984), 151.

7. E. J. Hart, The Place of Bows, (Banff: EJH Literary Enterprises Ltd., 1999), 326.

8. "Banff Community Plan," The Town of Banff (February 2009); Available from www.banff.ca/Assets/PDFs/Business+PDF/communityplan-2007-signed.pdf ; Internet; Accessed January 11, 2010.

Chapter 16

1. Eleanor Luxton. Banff. (Banff: Summerthought Press, 1975), 112.

2. Lisa Christensen. <u>A Hiker's Guide to the Art of the Canadian Rockies</u> (Calgary: Glenbow Museum, 1996), 14.

3. Hugh Dempsey, ed. <u>Rundle's Journals 1840-1848</u>. (Calgary: The Glenbow Institute and the Historical Society of Alberta, 1977), 164-165.

4. Tony Clevenger. "Monitoring of the Wildlife Crossing Structures," <u>Banff Wildlife Crossings Project Report, 2002</u>. Available from <u>www.pc.gc.ca/pn-np/ab/banff/docs/routes/chap3/sec1/routes3b_E.asp</u>; Internet; Accessed January 18, 2010.

5. Marius Barbeau. "Indian Days on the Western Prairies." <u>Bulletin No. 163 Anthropological Series No. 46</u>. (Ottawa: Department of Northern Affairs and National Resources – National Museum of Canada, 1959), 211.

6. Harold Fryer. <u>Ghost Towns of Alberta</u>. (Langley: Stagecoach Publishing Company, 1981), 10.

7. L. V. Kelly. <u>The Range Men: the story of the ranchers and Indians of Alberta</u>. (Toronto: William Briggs, 1913), 160.

Chapter 17

1. Emerson Sanford and Janice Sanford Beck. <u>Life of the Trail 1: Historic Hikes in Eastern Banff National Park</u>. (Calgary: Rocky Mountain Books, 2008), 109.

2. Brian Patton, ed. <u>Tales from the Canadian Rockies</u>. (Edmonton: Hurtig Publishers, 1984), 142 – 143.

3. Dave Birrell, "Mount Temple" <u>Peakfinder</u>. Available from peakfinder.com. Internet. Accessed March, 2009.

Chapter 18

1. Edward McCourt. The Road Across Canada. (Toronto: Macmillan of Canada, 1965), 172.

2. Dave Birrell. <u>Peakfinder</u>. Available from peakfinder.com. Internet. Accessed March, 2009.

3. J. Monroe Thorington. <u>The Glittering Mountains of Canada</u>. (Philadelphia, John W. Lea, 1923). 4.

4. Don Beers. <u>The World of Lake Louise</u>. (Calgary: Highline Publishing, 1991), 27.

5. Ella Elizabeth Clark. <u>Indian Legends of Canada</u>. (Toronto: McClelland and Stewart Limited, 1960), 97.

6. Rupert Brooke, "The Rockies," in <u>Tales from the Canadian Rockies</u>, ed. Brian Patton (Edmonton: Hurtig Publishers, 1984), 204.

7. Paul Collins, "The Floating Island," <u>Cabinet Magazine</u>. Issue 7 (Summer 2002); Available from <u>www.cabinetmagazine.org/issues/7/floatingisland.php</u>; Internet; Accessed January 19, 2010.

8. R. Sanford. <u>The Canadian Alps: A History of Mountaineering in Canada, Vol. I</u>. (Canmore: Altitude Publishing, 1990), 164.

9. M. Deborah Bialeschki. "Mary Schaffer Warren: A Seeker of Untrodden Paths." <u>Leisure Challenges: Bringing People, Resources and Policy into Play</u>. (Ontario Research Council on Leisure, 1990).

10. "Banff National Park Management Plan," <u>Parks Canada</u>, November 15, 2009; Available from <u>www.pc.gc.ca/pn-np/ab/banff/docs/plan1/chap7/plan1f_e.asp</u>; Internet; Accessed January 12, 2010.

11. Emerson Sanford and Janice Sanford Beck. <u>Life of the Trail 1: Historic Hikes in Eastern Banff National Park</u>. (Calgary: Rocky Mountain Books, 2008), 77.

12. Don Beers. <u>The World of Lake Louise</u>. (Calgary: Highline Publishing, 1991), 102.

Chapter 19

1. Edward McCourt. The Road Across Canada. (Toronto: Macmillan of Canada, 1965), 172.

Abasalom Clark fonds, Glenbow Archives, Calgary, Alberta

"Alberta's First Stagecoach Holdup." In Outlaws and Lawmen of Western Canada, Volume II, 98-103. Surrey: Heritage House, 1983.

Alexander, Rob. "A Dark Secret: Your Friendly Neighbourhood Fall-out Shelter." Highline Magazine (Winter 2009).

Alexander, Rob and Dene Cooper. Exshaw: Heart of the Valley. Exshaw: Exshaw Historical Society, 2005.

Alexander, Rob and Jenn Lutz. The Exshaw Cement Plant – 100 Years. Lafarge, 2006.

Alexander, Shelley and Jeff Gailus. "GIS-Based Approach to Restoring Connectivity Across Banff's Trans-Canada Highway, Technical Report #4." Miistakis Institute for the Rockies (April 2005). Available from www.rockies.ca/downloads/COMPLETE%20TCH%20Report.pdf; Internet. Accessed November 14, 2009.

Anderson, Frank. A Frontier Guide to Calgary – Banff Highway. 1968.

Anderson, Raoul. "Alberta Stoney (Assiniboin) Origins and Adaptations: A Case for Reappraisal." Ethnohistory Vol. 17, No. 1-2 Winter-Spring (1970) 49-60.

Appleby, Edna. Canmore: The Story of an Era. Calgary: Edna Appleby, 1975.

Armstrong, Christopher and H. V. Nelles. Competition vs. Convenience: Federal Administration of Bow River Waterpowers, 1906 – 1913.

Bailey, Ian. "The Link Between Private Grief and Public Safety." The Globe and Mail. 8 November, 2008 A3.

Barbeau, Marius. "Indian Days on the Western Prairies." Bulletin No. 163 Anthropological Series No. 46. Ottawa: Department of Northern Affairs and National Resources – National Museum of Canada, 1959.

Beck, Janice Sanford. No Ordinary Woman: The Story of Mary Schäffer Warren. Calgary: Rocky Mountain Books, 2001.

Beers, Don. The World of Lake Louise. Calgary: Highline Publishing, 1991.

Best, Sandy (Lake Louise Ski Area). Personal interview. March 2010.

Bialeschki, M. Deborah. "Mary Schaffer Warren: A Seeker of Untrodden Paths." Leisure Challenges: Bringing People, Resources and Policy into Play. Ontario Research Council on Leisure, 1990.

Big Hill Country. Calgary: Privately printed by the Cochrane and Area Historical Society, 1977.

Birrell, Dave and Ron Ellis. Calgary's Mountain Panorama. Calgary: Rocky Mountain Books, 1990.

Birrell, Dave. Fifty Roadside Panoramas in the Canadian Rockies. Calgary: Rocky Mountain Books, 2000.

Birrell, Dave. Peakfinder. Available from peakfinder.com. Internet. Accessed March, 2009.

Bohdan, S. Kordan. Enemy Aliens; Prisoners of War. Kingston: McGill – Queen's University Press, 2002.

Boles, Glen, Roger Lauilla and William Putnam. Place Names of the Canadian Alps. Revelstoke: Footprint Publishing, 1990.

Bowness Historical Society. <u>Bowness: Our Village in the Valley</u>. Altona: Friesens Corporation, 2005.

Bradford, Tolly. "A Useful Institution: William Twin, "Indianness," and Banff National Park, c. 1860 – 1940." Native Studies Review Vol. 16, No. 2 (2005) 77 – 98.

Brennan, Brian. <u>Scoundrels and Scallywags</u>. Calgary: Fifth House, 2002.

Buckley, Evelyn. <u>Chaps and Chinooks</u>. Calgary: Foothills Historical Society, 1976.

Burns, Robert J. and Michael J. Schintz. <u>Guardians of the Wild: a history of the warden service of Canada's national parks</u>. Calgary: University of Calgary Press, 2000.

Butts, Ed. <u>The Desperate Ones: Forgotten Canadian Outlaws</u>. Toronto: Dundurn Press, 2006. 64-65

"Canada Unveils New Training Centre." <u>The Globe and Mail</u>. January 23, 2009. Available from www.theglobeandmail.com/servlet/story/RTGAM.20090123.wspt-can-olympic-park-23/BNStory/VideoLineup Internet. Accessed March 15, 2009.

<u>Canadian Cattlemen</u> Vol. 4, No. 2 (Sept. 1941) 51, 75-79, 85.

Chandler, Graham. "Sour Gas University: Pioneer Jumping Pound Gas Plant Turns 50." <u>Oilweek Magazine.</u> November 5, 2001.

Clark, Ella Elizabeth. <u>Indian Legends of Canada</u>. Toronto: McClelland and Stewart Limited, 1960.

Collins, Paul. "The Floating Island," Cabinet Magazine Issue 7 (Summer 2002); Available from www.cabinetmagazine.org/issues/7/floatingisland.php; Internet; Accessed January 19, 2010.

Copithorne, Judy and Roy, ed. <u>Copithorne History</u>. Published privately, 1982.

Cowley, Stan. Personal interview. December 10, 2009.

Danter, K. Jeffery. "Fire Dependent Ecosystems of the United States." National Interagency Fire Centre. Available at www.nifc.gov/preved/comm_guide/wildfire/fire_6.html; Internet. Accessed January 13, 2010.

Dempsey, Hugh. <u>Indian Tribes of Alberta</u>. Calgary: Glenbow-Alberta Institute, 1979.

Dempsey, Hugh. <u>Indians of the Rocky Mountain Parks</u>. Calgary: Glenbow-Alberta Institute, 1986.

Dempsey, Hugh ed. <u>Rundle's Journals 1840-1848</u>. Calgary: The Glenbow Institute and the Historical Society of Alberta, 1977.

Duke, D., M. Hebblewhite, P. Paquet, C. Callaghan, and M. Percy, "Restoration of a Large Carnivore Corridor in Banff National Park, Alberta." <u>University of Montana College of Forestry and Conservation</u>. Available from www.cfc.umt.edu/HebLab/PDFS/Duke%20et%20al.%20Cascade%20Chapter_2001.pdf; Internet. Accessed January 6, 2010.

Erasmus, Peter. <u>Buffalo Days and Nights</u>. Calgary: Fifth House, 1999.

Ernest Cashel fonds, Glenbow Archives, Calgary, Alberta

"Find Mountains and Rocks." <u>SummitPost</u>. Available from summitpost.org. Internet. Accessed March 2009.

Fluker, Shaun. "Ecological Integrity and the Law: The View from Canada's National Parks." Social Science Research Network (January 16, 2009). Available from papers.ssrn.com/sol3/papers.cfm?abstract_id=1329094. Internet; Accessed December 5, 2009.

Follett, Amanda. "Rocky Mountain Low." <u>Kootenay Mountain Culture</u> (Summer, 2009) 39-43. Available from www.kmcmag.com/features/KMC15_dispatch.pdf; Internet. Accessed January 6, 2010.

Fraser, Esther. <u>The Canadian Rockies: Early Travels and Explorations</u>. Edmonton: M. G. Hurtig Ltd., 1969.

Gadd, Ben. <u>Bankhead: The Twenty Year Town</u>. Calgary: The Coal Association of Canada, 1989.

Gadd, Ben. Handbook of the Canadian Rockies. Jasper: Corax Press, 1995.

"Geographical Names of Canada." Natural Resources Canada. Available from geonames.nrcan.gc.ca. Internet. Accessed March, 2009.

Getty, Ian (Researcher, Stoney Nakoda). Personal interview. October, 2008.

Getty, Ian (Research Director, Stoney Nakoda Reserve). "A Brief Overview of Stoney Land Claims and Specific Claims" (pamphlet).

Getty, Ian A. L. and Erik D. Gooding. "Plains Indians." In Handbook of North American Indians, Vol. 13. ed. Raymond DeMallie, 596 – 603.

Gow, Sandy and Bonar Alexander Gow. Roughnecks, Rock Bits and Rigs. Calgary: University of Calgary Press, 2005.

Gowans, Bruce. Wings Over Calgary, 1906 – 1940. Calgary: Chinook Country Chapter: Historical Society of Alberta, 1990.

Gryba, Eugene M. "Sibbald Creek: 11,000 Years of Human Use of the Alberta Foothills." Archeological Survey of Alberta. Occasional Paper No. 22 (1983). Alberta Culture, Historical Resources Division.

Hamblin, Jennifer and David Finch. The Diva and the Rancher. Calgary: Rocky Mountain Books, 2006.

Hart, E. J. The Place of Bows. Banff: EJH Literary Enterprises Ltd., 1999.

Helgason, Gail. The First Albertans: An Archeological Search. Edmonton: Lone Pine Publications, 1987.

Hildebrandt, Walter. An Historical Analysis of Parks Canada and Banff National Park, 1968 – 1995. Prepared for the Banff-Bow Valley Study Task Force. December 1995.

Hogg, Doug. The Memory Project Digital Archive. Available from www. thememoryproject.com/digital-archive/profile.cfm?cnf=cf&collectionid =763; Internet; Accessed December 12, 2008.

Honeyman, Jay. "Bow Valley Bear Hazard Assessment" (April 2007). Available from www.bearconflict.org/site_assets/www. bearconflict.org/images/dynamic/BVBHA%20FINAL%20Sept_2007_ reduced%20version%206.pdf; Internet. Accessed January 6, 2010.

Honeyman, Jay (Karelian Bear Shepherding Institute of Canada). Personal interview. January 7, 2010.

Hopwood, Victor G. ed. David Thompson: Travels in Western North America, 1784 – 1812. Toronto: Macmillan, 1971.

Jackson, Lionel and Michael Wilson. "The Ice-Free Corridor Revisited." GeoTimes February 2004. Available from geotimes.org/feb04/feature_ Revisited.html. Internet. Accessed November 2008.

Jacob Herrero Environmental Consulting, Scott Jevons/GeoWORKS Environmental Consulting & GIS and KH Communications. "Wildlife Corridors in the Southern Canmore Region." Stratalink (September 2000). Available from www.stratalink.com/corridors/default.htm; Internet.Accessed January 2010.

John Laurie fonds, Glenbow Archives, Calgary, Alberta

Jonker, Peter. Stoney History Notes. Morley: Chiniki Band 1983 (booklet)

Kelly, L.V. The Range Men: The story of the ranchers and Indians of Alberta. Toronto: William Briggs, 1913.

Keyser, James and Michael Klassen. Plains Indian Rock Art. Seattle: University of Washington Press, 2001. 105-106.

Kirkby, Bob. "Banff's Field of Dreams." Skywalker (March 2002). Available from www.stratalink.com/corridors/default.htm; Internet. Accessed January 2010; Internet; Accessed October 12, 2009.

Kordan, Bohdan and Pete J. Melnycky. In the Shadow of the Rockies: Diary of the Castle Mountain Internment Camp. Edmonton: Canadian Institute of Canadian Studies, 1991.

Lakusta, Ernie. Banff and Lake Louise History Explorer. Canmore: Altitude Publishing, 2004.

Lakusta, Ernie. <u>Canmore and Kananaskis History Explorer</u>. Canmore: Altitude Publishing, 2002.

Langshaw, Rick. <u>Geology of the Canadian Rockies</u>. Banff: Summerthought Press, 1989.

Larin, Amy. "A Rough Ride: Automobiles in Banff National Park, 1905 – 1918." In <u>Alberta History,</u> January 1, 2008.

Lee, Chuck (Alberta Whitewater Association). Personal interview. November, 2009.

Lombard North Group (1980) Ltd. With Western Oilfields Environmental Services Ltd. <u>Ozada Camp 133 – Reclamation Report</u>. Calgary, August 30, 1992.

Luxton, Eleanor. <u>Banff</u>. Banff: Summerthought Press, 1975.

MacCarthy, Albert. "The First Ascent of Mount Louis". <u>Canadian Alpine Journal</u> Vol. 8 (1917) 79-86.

MacDougall, Lindsey. Personal interview. June, 2009.

Manry, Kathryn. <u>Skoki: Beyond the Passes</u>. Calgary: Rocky Mountain Books, 2001.

Marchildon, Gregory. <u>Profits and Politics</u>. Toronto: University of Toronto Press, 1996.

McCourt, Edward. <u>The Road Across Canada</u>. Toronto: Macmillan of Canada, 1965.

Monaghan, David. <u>Canada's "New Main Street": The Trans-Canada Highway as Idea and Reality</u>; 1912 – 1956. Ottawa: Canada Science and Technology Museum, 2002.

"Mountains, Mountain Parks, and Foothills Region." <u>Place Names of Alberta</u>. Available from www.albertasource.ca/placenames/regions/<u>mountains.html; Internet. Accessed March 18,</u> 2009

Mussieux, Ron and Marilyn Nelson. <u>A Traveller's Guide to Geological Wonders in Alberta</u>. Edmonton: Provincial Museum of Alberta, 1998.

Neil Nicholson fonds, Glenbow Archives, Calgary, Alberta

Niddrie, John W. <u>Niddrie of the North-West: Memoirs of a Pioneer Canadian Missionary</u>. Edmonton: University of Alberta Press, 2000.

"Ozada." <u>Ghosttownpix</u>. Availble from www.ghosttownpix.com/alberta/<u>ozada.html;</u> Internet; Accessed December 16, 2008.

Patton, Brian. <u>Parkways of the Canadian Rockies: A Road Guide</u>. Banff: Summerthought Press, 1995.

Patton, Brian, ed. <u>Tales from the Canadian Rockies</u>. Edmonton: Hurtig Publishers, 1984.

Pullan, Brandon. "Six Rockies Ice Classics." <u>Gripped</u> (October 20, 2009). Available from <u>gripped.com/2009/10/sections/articles/six-rockies-ice-classics;</u> Internet. Accessed January 14, 2010.

Pyne, Stephen. "Burning Banff." <u>Western Institute for Study of the Environment Colloquium</u> (December 11, 2007). Available from <u>westin-stenv.org/ffsci/2007/12/11/burning-banff;</u> Internet. Accessed January 13, 2010.

Quan, Holly. Early Guides and Outfitters in the Canadian Rockies. Canmore: Altitude Publishing, 2003.

Read, Tracey. <u>Acres and Empires: A History of the Municipal District of Rocky View No. 44</u>. Irricana: AB Tall-Taylor Publishing Ltd., no date.

Rev. Scollen fonds, Glenbow Archives, Calgary, Alberta

Rocky Mountain Eagle Research Foundation (2009). Available from www.eaglewatch.ca; Internet. Accessed November 22, 2009.

Rosenvall, L. A. and S. M. Evans, eds. <u>Essays on the Historical Geography of the Canadian West</u>. Calgary: University of Calgary Press, 1987.

Sanford, Emerson and Janice Sanford Beck. <u>Life of the Trail 1: Historic Hikes in Eastern Banff National Park</u>. Calgary: Rocky Mountain Books, 2008.

Sanford, R., The Canadian Alps: A History of Mountaineering in Canada, Vol. I. Canmore: Altitude Publishing, 1990.

Smith, Cyndi. Off the Beaten Track. Lake Louise: Coyote Books, 1989.

Snow, Chief John. These Mountains are our Sacred Places. Toronto: Samuel Stevens, 1977.

Stock, Larry (Springbank Airport). Personal interview. March, 2009.

Taylor, Colin F. and Hugh Dempsey. With Eagle Tail. Toronto: Key Porter Books, 1990.

The City of Calgary. Planning Department. East Paskapoo Slopes Area Structure Plan. Calgary, Planning Policy, Land Use and Mobility, 2006.

"Three Sisters Mountain Village Adventure Centre SSR." The Town of Canmore (May 28, 2008). Available from www.canmore.ca/index.php?option=com_docman&task=doc_download&gid=606&ItemId=187; Internet. Accessed January 6, 2010.

Touche, Rodney. Brown Cows, Sacred Cows. Hanna: Gorman Publishers, 1990.

Vivian, Brian (archaeologist). Personal interview. October, 2008

West, J. Thomas. "More Than a Ski Hill: From Paskapoo to Canada Olympic Park." Journal of Olympic History, Vol. II, No. 3 (September, 2003) 26 – 34.

White, Cliff and E. J. Hart. The Lens of Time: A Repeat Photograph of Landscape Change in the Canadian Rockies. Calgary: University of Calgary Press, 2007.

Whyte, Jon. Indians in the Rockies. Banff: Altitude Publishing Inc., 1985.

Woodsworth, Glenn. Hot Springs of Western Canada. Vancouver: Gordon Soules Book Publishers Ltd., 1999.

Yeo, Bill. "Gateway to the Rocky Mountains." Remembering Chinook Country. The Chinook Country Historical Society. Calgary: Detselig Enterprises Ltd., 2005, 217-223.

Yonge, Charles. Under Grotto Mountain: Rat's Nest Cave. Calgary: Rocky Mountain Books, 2001.

Yorath, C. J. How Old is That Mountain? Victoria: Orca Book Publishers, 1997.

Yorath, C. J. Where Terrains Collide. Victoria: Orca Book Publishers, 1990.

Index

Comments, corrections and other communications regarding the content of this book are welcomed, and may be addressed to the author care of:

pipestonepress@gmail.com

Additional copies of this book may be ordered online from Pipestone Press:

www.pipestonepress.ca/westonone